To Louise,
Best wishes & good luck with the research,
Tony

The persistence of prejudice

To Mag

Tony Kushner

The persistence of prejudice

Antisemitism in British society during the Second World War

Manchester University Press
Manchester and New York

Distributed exclusively in the USA and Canada by St. Martin's Press

Published by Manchester University Press
Oxford Road, Manchester M13 9PL, UK
and Room 400, 175 Fifth Avenue,
New York, NY 10010, USA

Distributed exclusively in the USA and Canada
by St. Martin's Press, Inc.,
175 Fifth Avenue, New York, NY 10010, USA

British Library cataloguing in publication data
Kushner, Tony
The persistence of prejudice:
antisemitism in British society during
the Second World War.
1. Great Britain. Jews. Racial
discrimination, 1939–1945 by society
305.8'924'041

Library of Congress cataloging in publication data
Kushner, Tony (Antony Robin Jeremy)
The persistence of prejudice:
antisemitism in British society during
the Second World War / Tony Kushner.
p.cm.
Bibliography: p.244.
Includes index.
ISBN 0-7190-2896-5
1. Antisemitism—Great Britain—History—20th century. 2. Jews—Public opinion—History—20th century. 3. Public opinion—Great Britain—History—20th century. 4. Great Britain—Politics and government—1936–1945. 5. Great Britain—Ethnic relations.
I. Title.
DS146.G7K87 1989 88-16842
941'.004924—dc19

ISBN 0 7190 2896 5 *hardback*

Typeset in Great Britain
by Megaron, Cardiff

Printed in Great Britain
by Biddles Ltd, Guildford and King's Lynn

Contents

Page

Preface vi
List of abbreviations viii
Introduction 1
1 Organised British antisemitism and fascism in the Second World War 14
2 The East End and evacuation experiences 48
3 Jews in British society
(1) The Jewish question in Britain 1939–45 78
4 Jews in British society
(2) The Jewish image in Britain in the war 106
5 The British government and the Jews 134
6 The response to antisemitism 163
Conclusion 188

Notes 203

Bibliography 244

Index 249

Preface

Myths of Britain's essential tolerance and decency die hard. It is thus often assumed – regardless of any evidence to the contrary – that antisemitism is simply alien to the British experience. The historiography of the subject is therefore still relatively undeveloped. It is also warped to the most easily identifiable forms of hostility – fascist or other organised manifestations of antisemitism. This book will go further, investigating the almost uncharted waters of British culture's relationship to antisemitism, and the exciting, but equally unexplored, area of Jewish–Gentile relations in this country. More such studies are needed, not just for Anglo-Jewry, but for all ethnic and minority groups in Britain. If the strength of antisemitism, or any other form of racism, is to be evaluated, it must be contextualised in terms of much wider relationships. After all, purely negative reactions form only a part of the minority experience in Britain. Ambivalence is the norm.

This book then attempts to cover and analyse reactions to Jews from all sections of British society, the state as well as the populace, and to place these responses in terms of the Anglo-Jewish experience. The chapters that follow are firmly rooted in the domestic history of Britain in the Second World War. It is important to stress that developments in Palestine, which have been well covered elsewhere, are only mentioned when they had a direct impact on Jewish–Gentile relations in Britain, as was the case with the assassination of Lord Moyne in 1944.[1]

The Persistence of Prejudice will hopefully stimulate new areas of research, but it would not have been possible itself without the pioneering study of British antisemitism by Colin Holmes. I am deeply thankful for his guidance and encouragement whilst I was undertaking my doctoral research. I have also benefited from discussions and comments from Richard Thurlow, Alan Booth, Tony Sutcliffe, David Martin, Bryan

Cheyette, David Cesarani, Bill Williams, Charles Esdaile, Paul Smith and Greg Walker.

I wish to express my gratitude to the various libraries and institutions which have allowed me to examine their collections, in particular the Wiener Library, the Board of Deputies of British Jews and the Parkes Library at Southampton University. My appreciation is due to those who were willing to be interviewed, and to the people who made available their private collections (too many to be named here, but all listed in the bibliography). I am indebted to friends and relatives who provided accommodation and refreshment on my research visits across the country, and to Peggy Ahlquist, Liz Brock and Rosemary Morris for typing this work at its various stages. Lastly to my family with love and deep appreciation of your support. Maybe one day I will get a *real* job!

List of abbreviations

The following abbreviations have been used either in the text or in the notes.

AIR	Air Ministry
AJ	Anglo-Jewish Archive
BBCWAC	British Broadcasting Corporation Written Archive Centre
BCCSE	British Council for Christian Settlement in Europe
BD	Board of Deputies of British Jews archive
BIPO	British Institute of Public Opinion
BNP	British National Party
BPP	British People's Party
BT	Board of Trade
BUF	British Union of Fascists
CAB	Cabinet Office
CCJ	Council of Christians and Jews
CPGB	Communist Party of Great Britain
ENA	English National Association
FO	Foreign Office
HC	House of Commons

HL	House of Lords
HO	Home Office
IFL	Imperial Fascist League
ILP	Independent Labour Party
INF	Ministry of Information
IWM	Imperial War Museum
JDC	Jewish Defence Committee
JC	Jewish Chronicle
JPC	Jewish People's Council
MAF	Ministry of Food
MCP	Militant Christian Patriots
MEPOL	Metropolitan Police files
M-OA	Mass-Observation Archive (D: Diarist; DR: Directive Respondent; FR: File Report; TC: Topic Collection)
MPA	Medical Policy Association
NCCL	National Council for Civil Liberties
NJC	National Jewish Committee of the Communist Party
PCLP	People's Common Law Parliament
PCOM	Police Commission files
PEP	Political and Economic Planning
PPU	Peace Pledge Union
PREM	Prime Minister's Office
PWE	Political Warfare Executive
STDL	Stepney Tenants' Defence League
TAC	Trades Advisory Council

Introduction

The horror of the attempted extermination of European Jewry in the Second World War remains a unique experience, not only in Jewish, but in world history. It is hard if not impossible to find a parallel, and as far as our understanding of it is concerned, the Holocaust is 'the unconquered Everest of our time'.[1] Thus to compare British antisemitism in the years 1939–45 directly with the Nazi experience is quite meaningless; if studies of British antisemitism are to be valuable, not only in analysing the security of the Jewish minority but also in throwing light on the nature of British society, they must be strongly rooted in the economic, social and political context of that country.

Since the readmission in 1656, opposition to Jews has never reached the same level of violence as that across the Channel. The state, though not necessarily sympathetic, has refused to condone attacks on the Jewish community, a factor of great significance elsewhere. As Todd Endelman suggests, Anglo-Jewish history 'cannot be subsumed under the general category of Western European Jewish history'. In Britain, Jewish emancipation never became a major political issue, and when the final legal disabilities were removed in 1858, it was achieved without any loss of blood or indeed any great interest on the part of the British or even the Jewish population.[2]

Does this suggest that Anglo-Jewish history must be studied in strict isolation from events elsewhere? The answer must be no, for although British Jewish development followed a different path from that of Continental and East European Jewry, there were features that were common to both experiences, and the impact of events abroad were to have their effects at home. With the issue of antisemitism, there is little to compare in Britain with the Russian pogrom or Nazi brutality, or indeed with the showcase trials in France (the Dreyfus case), Russia (the Beiliss case) or indeed America (the Leo Frank trial). However, this lack of violence, or prominence in national politics, does not mean that British antisemitism should be dismissed as unimportant. Gisela Lebzelter in her *Political Antisemitism in England 1918–1939* has justified her research by suggesting that 'one cannot reduce the subject of antisemitism to its German variant alone if one wants to assess its rank with modern history in general', yet it must be suggested that there are wider benefits from such studies; analysing antisemitism – which tends to cut across lines of class, intelligence, sex and age – can reveal much about the receiving society.[3]

The term antisemitism must be defined before going any further. The disreputable nature of being labelled an antisemite is well illustrated by the refusal of any of the leading anti-Jewish campaigners to accept the tag. The word is of recent origin and has been credited to Wilhelm Marr who in a pamphlet in 1879 attacked what he saw as the Jewish domination of Germany. Marr differentiated antisemitism from previous attacks on the Jewish religion which he dismissed as idiotic. Marr was concerned with the effects that Jewish emancipation was having upon German society and he defined antisemitism as being opposed to Jewish power. Marr's definition presupposes the existence of a Jewish influence but his attack on Jews as Jews will be the starting point in defining the term. James Robb has suggested that hostility towards Jews, to be categorised as antisemitism 'must be associated definitely with the quality of being a Jew', and this study will follow Robb's definition.[4]

There are many serious problems with this definition and they must be examined before it can become functional. Firstly, it covers possibilities ranging from polite tearoom type attacks to advocating and embarking upon genocidal policies. There is no room within this definition to solve the contradiction of those like Harold Nicolson who could write: 'Although I loathe antisemitism I do dislike Jews.' Nicolson's attack on antisemitism was not confined to his diary – he was active in trying to put pressure on the British government to do more for the Jews of Europe during the war. However, Nicolson's remarks, in suggesting that there is something in someone being Jewish that he objected to, must be defined as antisemitic. It is clear, therefore, that there are many types of antisemitism and as Geoffrey Field suggests: 'The qualitative differences between this [social dislike for Jews] and political antisemitism should not be minimised.' The term 'antisemitism' readily conjures up images of Nazi concentration camps, yet despite this, it must be used for many other forms of hostility to Jews.[5]

A second difficulty with defining antisemitism as hostility to Jews as Jews is that historical events do not always fit so clearly within an antisemitic/non-antisemitic pattern. A good case in point, illustrating the complexity of the subject, was the dismissal in January 1940 of the only Jewish member of the Cabinet, Leslie Hore-Belisha, Secretary of State for War. Few have gone as far as the champion of Jewish refugees, Colonel Wedgwood, who suggested that Hore-Belisha was removed from office simply because of his Jewish origins, yet the fact that the Minister of War was a Jew cannot be dismissed as irrelevant to the question.[6]

Hore-Belisha had joined the War Office in 1937 and had recorded in his diary that Duff Cooper, of the Treasury Department, had told him 'that the military element might be very unyielding and they might try to make it hard for me as a Jew'. Hore-Belisha's background, apart from being Jewish, was middle-class and there was much opposition to his appointment from Conservative die-hards, as well as from the Army, where colonial privilege had managed to remain undisturbed until his appointment. Hore-Belisha immediately set about democratising the Army and as if this was not bad enough, he carried out his reforms without going through the 'proper' channels, further alienating the military elite.[7]

By the time of the outbreak of war, the opposition to the Minister of War from the military and high social castes had become near-conspiratorial. On 24 November 1939, Hore-Belisha summonsed Major-General Pakenham-Walsh, the chief engineer of Lord Gort (Commander-in-Chief in France), concerning weaknesses in the British sector. Hore-Belisha was eventually to be proved correct on the BEF Defences, but his criticism lost him any remaining support he had in the War Office. After this incident Gort, Ironside (CIGS) and the king's brother worked to get Hore-Belisha removed and on 4 January 1940 the Prime Minister, Neville Chamberlain, told the Minister of War to resign. When asked for an explanation, the Prime Minister told Hore-Belisha that 'there was a prejudice against him', and the latter interpreted this as being antisemitic.[8]

Hore-Belisha's fears cannot be dismissed as those of an egocentric politician suffering from paranoia. After his dismissal, he was to have been offered the Ministry of Information, a position he would have suited perfectly. However, Lord Halifax, the Foreign Secretary, vetoed the idea because he felt it wrong for a Jew to become Minister of Information, and his Under-Secretary, Sir Alexander Cadogan, summarised the view of the Foreign Office: 'Jew control of our propaganda would be a major disaster'. A week after Hore-Belisha's resignation, Captain Ramsay, the antisemitic MP of Peebles, distributed copies of the 12 January 1940 issue of *Truth* to all MPs in the Commons, in which there were allegations about Hore-Belisha's financial activities.[9]

Despite the efforts of Ramsay and *Truth* to give the issue a definitely antisemitic flavour, it is difficult to analyse how important the Jewish factor was in Hore-Belisha's dismissal. Had Hore-Belisha not been Jewish and he followed the same policies, the opposition to him would still have been strong; the fact that he was Jewish made the situation even less tolerable. An examination of the diaries and letters of Hore-Belisha's political allies and foes shows an acute awareness of his Jewish origins, and while it is wrong to suggest that he was dismissed because he was a Jew, it would be naive to believe his Jewishness was irrelevant to his removal.[10]

The Hore-Belisha case poses several other questions about the defining of antisemitism. Captain Ramsay and *Truth* were not the only ones who welcomed the removal of the Jewish Cabinet Minister; the BUF's *Action* celebrated the resignation of Hore-Belisha, 'this little Jew who was inflated to become Minister of War in a time of grave national emergency'. However, it was only a small, distinct minority who attacked Hore-Belisha's Jewishness so clearly. As John Higham has perceptively pointed out, referring to the terms antisemitism and philosemitism: 'most people waver between conflicting attitudes and seldom enjoy an undivided state of mind'. Attitudes to Leslie Hore-Belisha illustrate this point clearly. Neville Chamberlain admired his abilities: 'his courage, imagination and drive' and felt that he 'appeared to have special qualifications' for the job as Minister of Information, yet the Prime Minister also believed Hore-Belisha was 'so impatient, ebullient – so Jewish . . .' Sir Henry 'Chips' Channon MP was a great friend of Hore-Belisha through the 1930s and 1940s, a frequent dinner guest, who could nonetheless be described by Channon as 'an oily man, half a Jew, an opportunist, with a semitic flare for publicity' or as ' "the Jew boy" bundling and self-important . . . [yet] I am fond of him'.[11]

The ambivalence in attitudes towards Jews, where many are 'both pro and anti-Jewish at the same time', shows the complexity of the area, and the danger of relying too heavily on concepts such as philo- and anti-semitism. It is indeed revealing that the image of the Jew in extreme antisemitism is only matched in its unreality by that of 'the Jew' in extreme philosemitism. Todd Endelman has suggested that to seventeenth century English philosemites ' "the Jews" were little more than the personification of some abstract religious idea or feeling, like the negatively charged symbols of the Beast and the Antichrist'. Stephen Spender remembers that in the Second World War he regarded the Jewish people in the concentration camps collectively as 'sacred' and in 1943 Ada Jackson, in an award winning poem, could describe the Jews as 'manna-bringers, prophets, seers'. It must be suggested that the vast majority of the British population in the Second World War neither viewed the Jews as 'timid mice' nor as a 'dirty, stinking, lot of swine: nothing but a lot of parasites battening on decent people'. Most people are much more irresolute, capable of complex and often contradictory views on Jewish matters, as this study will reveal.[12]

Another issue that the defining of antisemitism as a hostility against Jews as Jews does not take into account, is the highly controversial question of the Jewish role in the occurrence of antisemitism. Colin Holmes has suggested that to understand antisemitism, one 'needs to take account of the interests and activities of both sides in the conflict equation' and to attempt to achieve objectivity in the subject; this is important advice. In the example of the Hore-Belisha case, it is impossible to understand the tension that arose without including the impact of the Minister of War's personality. Hore-Belisha was at times brilliant and could be charming, but he was also arrogant and 'aggressively tactless'. His democratisation of the Army and his social origins had alienated the Military elite, but it was his tactless handling of a difficult problem that was the catalyst in his removal from office. Had Hore-Belisha been a member of the Anglo-Jewish aristocracy and had he been merely a mouthpiece of the military caste (as was expected of him), it is possible that opposition to him as a Jew would not have been so prominent. To understand why the antisemitism towards Hore-Belisha became so intense one has to take account of the deeply held social prejudices in the War Office, but also Hore-Belisha's personality as well as his policies.[13]

Since the publication of Oswald Mosley's autobiography in 1968 and, more importantly, Robert Skidelsky's study of the BUF leader in 1975, there has been a heated debate on the scapegoat versus interactionist, or convergence explanation of antisemitism. Memories of the street fights involving fascists in the 1930s still provoke strong emotions and it must be suggested that the passion that the topic arouses has hindered a clear understanding of the problems of both interactionist and scapegoat models. At its worst, the interactionist explanation can degenerate into a simple well-earned theory of antisemitism such as Mosley's own contention: 'There is not the slightest doubt that some Jews began it [the 'quarrel' with the BUF] in Britain', or Skidelsky's explanation of why the BUF became increasingly antisemitic: 'the attitude of Jews themselves'. Equally, with the scapegoat model there is a danger in Yinger's and

Simpson's words that 'it does not explain the direction that prejudice takes'. A study such as Geoffrey Alderman's on the riots against Jews in South Wales in 1911 shows the strength and weakness of a 'scapegoat' explanation. Alderman locates the tension that existed in the South Wales Valleys in 1911 and suggests that the problems created by the coal and railway srikes led on to the antisemitism: 'As has so often happened, the Jews became scapegoats for economic distress.' This contextualising of the riots is vital in understanding the hostility, but Alderman suggests the limitations of the scapegoat model when he examines why the tension was channelled towards the Jews; as he points out: 'The true nature of that [antisemitic] cause is difficult to discern.'[14]

Colin Holmes, using an interactionist approach, has also stressed the economic and social pressures operating in South Wales at that time, but additionally points out that 'Jews [in this area] had special characteristics which made them visible.' The Jews' role as economic middlemen, as landlords and shopowners, must be taken into account if the disturbances are to be understood, suggests Holmes. In re-examining the case in the light of the recently released Home Office papers, he puts further stress on the Jewish role in creating the conflict. There is a danger in going too far in this approach and overemphasising the role of individual Jews in producing the causes of antisemitism. The Home Office papers pay particular attention to the activities of a Mr Joseph Cohen, a Jewish landlord in Tredegar. In these papers the Superintendent of Police in the area is reported as saying 'that this Mr Cohen is the man who . . . is, more than any other Jew, the cause of the anti Jewish feeling'.[15]

Cohen's role in creating the conflict needs to be severely qualified in regard to this statement. He was probably the only Jew involved in blatant rack-renting and although some Jewish shopowners exploited the problems of the local residents, they were no worse than their Christian counterparts. Despite this, 'stories of financial dishonesty on the part of Jews were widely believed in the riot areas'. Cohen was one of the few Jews who was outstanding in abusing the local population, but the economic and social tension was so great, and the image of the Jew as exploiter strong enough that all Jews in Tredegar were attacked as Mr Cohens. What is being suggested here is that the Jewish role does not need to be great for it to be taken into account. In a tense situation, the tiniest of half-truths, when combined with a powerful prevalent image of Jews, can become significant. In the South Wales example, there is a strong need to examine what the images of the Jew were in Wales prior to the riots before a more complete explanation can be reached.[16]

What does this suggest about the scapegoat/interactionist debate? It will be suggested here that the discussion has suffered from ill-defined terms. The 'scapegoat' school suggests that the interactionists pay too much attention to the Jewish role, and the latter suggests that the scapegoat theory is one that implies 'that Jews themselves play no part in creating antisemitism'. Neither side really does the other justice. On the one hand, the Jewish role does not have to be very great to become important, and on the other, as Gordon Allport has pointed out: 'Scapegoats need not be lily-white in their innocence.' What is important is that the historian of British antisemitism (as well as other countries) needs to study not only the groups who attack Jews, but the Jews themselves, the economic and social background of the conflict and the image of the Jew in society. The continuous nature of antisemitism does not justify an ahistorical approach to the subject; studies need to be firmly rooted in the economic and social conditions of their time. However, it needs to be remembered that although there is a danger of under-contextualising antisemitism, there is also a risk of over-contextualising. One can explain how individuals or groups became antisemitic to an extent, but as J. M. Roberts reminds us, 'something remains'. One has to also take account of the irrational, the unexplainable. How else does one understand the contention, made throughout the war, that Hitler, Arnold Leese and other leading antisemites were controlled by the Jews?[17]

With all these difficulties associated with defining antisemitism as a hostility to Jews as Jews, should the term not be dropped and replaced by examining attitudes to the 'Jewish question'? The answer, I would suggest, must be no. Firstly, referring to the Jewish question gives the subject an element of legitimacy. It has been pointed out that many leading British antisemites rejected the word antisemitism, claiming they were impartially interested in the Jewish problem or question. Secondly, and linked to the last point, by using the term the 'Jewish question', one is refusing to categorise attitudes to Jews. It is true that only a tiny percentage of the population can be regarded as having totally negative views on Jews, and that most people show ambivalence on the subject, but it does not mean that one should be afraid to use the term antisemitism, even with those who can simultaneously attack and praise Jews as Jews. It is vital to differentiate between different forms of antisemitism; they will vary in their importance and implications. However, one must not totally lose sight of the connections of the various attacks on Jews. Ideas do not exist in social and economic vacuums, and in the Second World War, many, such as Orwell, re-examined their own antisemitism in the light of

Germany's policies. The late E. H. Carr pointed out the need for historians to generalise, and as a generic term, antisemitism – defined as a hostility to Jews as Jews – will be a useful tool in analysing the various forms of reactions to Jews in the 1939–45 era in Britain.[18]

The six years of the Second World War are a distinct period in British domestic history. In the analysis that follows, the hostility that occurred against Jews will be closely contextualised in a British society undergoing profound social, economic and political change. Nevertheless it is important to be aware that 'the history of antisemitism bears the signs of being a seamless garment'. Thus before the precise period of the war is examined, a brief overview of the nature and trends of modern British antisemitism previous to 1939 will be necessary.[19]

The continuous nature of antisemitism must not disguise the fact that times of relative toleration of Jews have followed years of brutal persecution. In Britain, whilst examples of the latter have been comparatively few, it is still possible to locate episodes or periods of severe dislocation in society that have led on to particularly intense antisemitism. Sometimes this has come in written form – such as the anti-Jewish tracts produced at the time of the readmission of the Jews in the seventeenth-century, the Jewish emancipation debate in the nineteenth-century, the hostility generated by the Marconi scandal before 1914 and the accusations linked to *The Protocols of the Elders of Zion* in the 1920s. On other occasions it has taken the form of physical violence – most notably in the Jew Bill controversy in the 1750s, the antisemitic riots of 1911 in South Wales (part of the social dislocation of late Edwardian Britain), the disturbances against Jews in Leeds and London during the First World War, and the fascist activities in the 1930s when Britain was suffering the misery of the Great Depression.

Of particular relevance to this study are the antisemitic riots of 1917. The reasons for these riots are complex and have been covered in detail elsewhere. Nevertheless it will be valuable to examine some of their causes for they bring into focus the often vulnerable position of minorities during wartime. External conflict *can* create internal solidarity as a society unites to confront a common enemy. However, unification of the majority under patriotism can make the minority group even more vulnerable to attacks on nationalistic grounds. The 1917 riots occurred at a time of great war-weariness when there was no sight of an end to the conflict, a general shortage of goods and despair at home due to the losses at the front. The marginality of Jews, especially foreign Jews, was exposed, and there is little doubt that a scapegoat factor was in operation. This explains the scale of the violence in the riots, although the immediate cause was the issue of alien Jews and military service.[20]

The relationship between the minority and the enemy is another important factor in the former's treatment in war. Jews of German origin or birth were particularly at risk in the Great War, facing either deportation or internment. It was a factor that was also to come into play in the Second World War. However, wars can also have a positive impact on minorities. As catalysts of economic and social change, wars can often create opportunities previously denied to minority groups. Whilst this might lead to jealousy it can also help to remove friction in the longer term. It has been suggested that in the East End during the First World War, although 'war had emphasised the difference between the East London Jewish community and the surrounding population', it had also 'contributed to the gradual process of integration of the foreign Jews into East London society'. The anti-alien campaign against the 100,000 East European Jews who came to Britain before 1914 was at its most intense level in the East End, and it was the same area that was to be the focus of Mosley's antisemitic campaign in the 1930s. Nevertheless it must not be forgotten that the integration created by the war led to a marked improvement in Jewish/non-Jewish relations in the 1920s. As one inhabitant recalled: ' "frontiers" got very blurred and in some instances did not exist. Jews and "Yoks" mixed quite freely in several kind of activities.' Antisemitism is thus not an unvarying force and its dynamic character needs to be kept in mind. Furthermore British antisemitism was not monolithic. This last point requires further elucidation for it is vital to analyse on what grounds the Jews were attacked.[21]

The two clearest features of modern British antisemitism are that Jews are perceived firstly as a foreign group and secondly as a malevolent power in society. Both have their roots in the medieval view of Jewry, although such images were fundamentally readjusted to suit the modern world. The first charge, of being 'un-British', was aimed particularly at foreign Jews – East European Jews around the turn of the twentieth-century and Central European refugees in the 1930s. However even anglicised Jewry, including the aristocracy, 'the Cousinhood', could not escape the alien tag.[22]

It is possible to trace an organised tradition, from the 'Chesterbelloc' circle in the Edwardian period to the Mosleyites in the 1930s, which demanded the reversal of the emancipatory rights of Jews. This school of thought believed that whether a British Jew was of the first or twenty-first generation was irrelevant, for he would always remain an alien. Neither the Chesterbelloc's National League for Clean Government or Mosley's BUF had a mass membership. Yet, although few of the public actively wanted to remove the Jew's rights of citizenship, the less rigid view that Jews were somehow not fully English was a popular one.[23]

This is not simply a theoretical concern. What might be termed the 'antisemitism of exclusion' operated against all sections of Anglo-Jewry. To the elite it could be found in public schools, clubs and universities. To the new immigrants, discrimination – either at work or in the housing market – was common. The impact of such exclusion was powerful. Firstly, it shaped the economic and social make-up of the Jewish community. Jewish residential and employment patterns reflected both the reality and fear of non-Jewish hostility, as well as Jewish ethnic and religious solidarity. Hence in the East End and other immigrant areas, certain districts and occupations were almost totally Jewish. Whilst discrimination was not absolute, it was prevalent enough to create understandable fear among Anglo-Jewry. This introduces the second feature of the antisemitism of exclusion – its profound psychological effect. Its existence – whether in the form of street riots, personal hooliganism, blatant discrimination or simply the threat of such hostility – indicated to the Jewish population its marginality in society. The psychological impact was greater because it was part of a dual pressure on Anglo-Jewry.[24]

The other feature of this Anglo-Jewish dilemma was the pressure put on the Anglo-Jewish community to conform. The basis of this objection to Jewry was the same as that of the exclusionists – Jews were seen as a foreign body. It differed in that it believed Jews could cease to be a separate group in society and that if they did so their persecution would end. There was thus a force acting upon Anglo-Jewry which insisted that the price of toleration was to abandon any distinctiveness. The Anglo-Jewish elite were most aware of this emancipation contract, and through their activities in providing schools and accommodation for the mass of Jewry at the turn of the century much of the East European culture, such as language and religious habits, were removed.[25]

The power of British antisemitism in the period from the late nineteenth-century until 1939 was thus felt most directly by Anglo-Jewry in the form of hostility to Jews as foreigners. Jews were urged to assimilate but were effectively excluded from many areas of British society. Through immigration legislation, the State added another dimension to this insecurity.

It is often assumed that the British state has been immune from antisemitism. Whilst it is true that no blatant discrimination has been passed in the modern period, this does not exclude the possibility of governmental hostility to Jews. This is well illustrated with the example of the Aliens Act of 1905. The Act itself cannot be described as antisemitic. It did not include the term 'Jew' and even included a clause preserving the right of asylum for those fleeing religious persecution. Nevertheless, it is clear that the major purpose of the Act was to stop the flow of East European Jews into Britain. Moreover the pressure for the Aliens Act, both at a parliamentary and public level, contained a significant antisemitic element – the aliens were attacked as Jews and not just as foreigners. Moreover, an individual such as Arnold White, a believer in the Jewish conspiracy could operate as an antisemitic street orator for the British Brothers' League, and at the same time as a respectable advisor to the government on alien matters. By implementing this Act, the state, rather than removing potential for antisemitism in Britain, actually increased its legitimacy. The years 1905–14 saw an intensification of hostility to Jewish aliens, and in World War One the government's powers in this area increased dramatically. Twenty thousand aliens were deported and 32,000 were interned, both totals including many Jews.[26] In 1919 the Aliens Act confirmed this new power of the government. As a representative from the Board of Deputies of British Jews was forced to acknowledge in the 1920s, 'the fear of deportation hangs over the whole alien [Jewish] community'. Thus whilst the aliens legislation was not *per se* antisemitic, in practice it was used specifically against Jews in Britain. As Colin Holmes has suggested 'antisemitism can shelter behind a different facade'. The Aliens Acts are an indication of the need to be flexible in the use of the term antisemitism. In the 1930s the Aliens legislation would be used against Jewish refugees from Nazi oppression. Here the British government was wary of letting in too many Jews; partly because they were seen as a security risk, partly because they might *create* antisemitism.[27]

It is therefore being suggested that antisemitism is not alien to the British experience, or simply unrespectable. The widespread nature of the second major objection to Jews, that they are a dangerous power in society, confirms this analysis. Since the emancipation of the Jews in Britain, the major influxes of Jewish immigrants in the period 1870–1914 and in the 1930s have reinforced the image of the Jew as alien. Similarly the involvement, or alleged involvement, of Jews in international activities, either as financiers or socialists, helped those already suspicious of Jews to justify their fear of Jewish influence. To significant sections of the socialist and radical world, international Jewish finance was responsible for the

Boer War. The Jews involved in South Africa were seen not as individuals acting in self-interest, but as a cohort manipulating international events. In the Marconi Scandal before the First World War, it was the radical right – the Chesterbelloc school and Leo Maxse's *National Review* – that believed a Jewish conspiracy was at work in the British political financial scandal. Thus concern over Jewish power was neither a monopoly of left or right, but was in fact part of a wider cultural tradition in Britain. The career of *The Protocols of the Elders of Zion* illustrates the strength of this concern.[28]

Before the exposure of this document as a forgery in 1921, the high-Tory *Times, Morning Post, Spectator, Blackwood's Magazine, Plain English* as well as many members of the establishment and the security forces believed that *The Protocols* were an accurate description of recent world events, or at least that Jews were responsible for the Bolshevik revolution. After *The Times* discredited the document, only the remnants of the Tory diehard world – including *The Patriot* – and more extremist antisemitic groups such as The Britons and sections of the social credit movement kept the document in circulation.[29]

Yet fear of Jewish power continued. In the 1930s it was not only Mosley and the fascist movement that warned of the impending 'Jews' War'. Lord Beaverbrook represented the concern of many that somehow the Jews were dragging Britain into war. He wrote in 1938: 'They do not mean to do it. But unconsciously they are drawing us into war. Their political influence is moving us in that direction.' This from a man whose biographer claims he 'had no sympathy with antisemitism'.[30] Whilst Jews in the pre-1914 period were relatively prominent in international finance, this cannot be said of the 1930s when the essential feebleness of world Jewry was exposed. Nevertheless the belief that Jews were a sinister world power was still widespread in Britain.

By 1939 in Britain as Malcolm Muggeridge suggested, 'antisemitism was in the air', and Britain was becoming increasingly 'Jew-conscious'. Nazi antisemitism abroad, and the arrival of 60,000 refugees increased this awareness of Jews. Yet there were also domestic roots to this hostility. It was most blatant in fascist antisemitism from the BUF and other much smaller groups such as the Imperial Fascist League, the Nordic League, the Right Club, the British People's Party, the pro-Nazi Link and National Socialist League. However it was also more widespread across society. 'Jews' as the saying went, 'were news' and antisemitism was common in daily discourse, literature and the press. In 1938 Gordon Liverman, a member of the Board of Deputies Defence Committee, warned that 'within three years we may be faced with anti-Jewish legislation in this country'. Liverman's fears are an indication of the insecurity that Anglo-Jewry felt before the Second World War. If the years 1914–18 were to act as a model, the Second World War was not going to be a comfortable period for Jews in Britain. The following chapters will analyse the complex responses that emerged in Britain to the Jewish minority in the war against fascism.[31]

1

Organised British antisemitism and fascism in the Second World War

The *Encyclopedia Judaica* has discriminated between groups that have temporarily adopted antisemitism and those that are founded with the sole purpose of fighting Jewish influences.[1] However, in the case of the former, this wise differentiation could be extended further to include those organisations which have an element of antisemitism in their ideology, but to whom it is not all-embracing. Such antisemitism can be as persistent as the 'total' form. In Britain before the end of 1945, only the IFL and The Britons (as well as a few other minor organisations) can be said to have been totally devoted to the 'Jewish Question'. To devote this section on extremist organisations to these groups would be highly limiting. Instead it will concentrate on those which can be said to operate *outside* the mainstream of Britain's political and social life. Fascist and quasi-fascist groups will be included, as will social credit and distributist circles. Such a classification will not necessarily indicate the intensity of antisemitism. For example, the *Weekly Review*, *The Patriot* and *Truth* all had common contributors and were capable of profound attacks on Jews, yet the latter, given its respectability and popularity, will be studied in the section on British society and antisemitism. Equally, few matched the level of antisemitism in Douglas Reed's war novels, but again Reed's work was mainstream and not limited (at least up to 1945) to the lunatic fringe.

It has been suggested that war can have two (often simultaneous) effects on ethnic or racial minorities – it can push them together under a common unity, or apart due to the tensions of the conflict. Much the same can be said of fascist and radical right wing groups in Britain in the Second World War. At one level these extremist organisations entered the war in a highly fragmented state; at another, their common vulnerability (given their previous support of Nazi Germany) was a stimulus towards co-operation. Those on the radical right, who had made so much play of their patriotism, were now faced with a most serious crisis. They saw their country plunged into war against a country whose ideology had been their source of inspiration. The immediate impact of the war on these groups will now be examined.

Throughout the 1930s, the BUF, the IFL and the whole host of other fringe groups had been united on one issue – the importance of avoiding what they saw as a 'Jews' War' of vengeance against Nazi Germany. As war approached, increasing attention was placed on this issue. The BUF's peace campaign culminated at Earl's Court in July 1939 where up to 20,000 people heard Mosley fulminating against the threat of war, where he stated: 'We fight for Britain, yes, but a million Britons shall never die in your Jews' quarrel.' The imminence of war certainly helped to stop the decline of the BUF, but claims that it had recovered by the start of the conflict to its peak level of support of 1934, are much exaggerated.[2] Other claims that peace meetings in East and North London were 'larger and more enthusiastic than any in the British Union's history' do not seem to be borne out by the facts. Indeed, Special Branch reports in November 1938 and September 1939 indicate that East End support for Mosley had declined considerably in the year before war.[3]

Elsewhere in London, recruiting was brisk for the BUF immediately after Earl's Court, but August was quiet again. Some increase in membership occurred in Manchester and East Lancashire, and in Yorkshire a recovery was made, but this was from a miniscule base, the same being true in Birmingham. Altogether, the figure of 9,000, quoted by Home Secretary Sir John Anderson, which represented those BUF members who had paid their last subscription, would represent fairly the total BUF support in the country.[4] This low figure, and the fact that the BUF was the only mass fascist organisation in Britain in the 1930s, puts the importance of its rival extremists in perspective.

The most notorious, the Imperial Fascist League, had an active membership of fifty in 1936. Other splinter groups from the BUF such as the British People's Party and the National Socialist League had equally limited support. By 1939 secret, or semi-secret groups such as the Nordic League and the Right Club had come into existence, propounding extreme antisemitism and demanding an agreement with Hitler. Linkages were made between these groups, the *New Pioneer* being one forum through which communication was made. Yet even taken together, this group of fascist appeasers appears unimpressive, their general impotence strengthened by their political isolation. Only 'The Link', Admiral Barry Domvile's pro-Nazi German friendship group could claim a mass membership. From March 1938 to June 1939 The Link's support grew from 1,800 to 4,300. Unlike other pacifist groups, The Link did not so much avoid the subject of Nazi antisemitism as support it. However, it is probably the case that most of the extremists were at the top of The Link, and that most of the rank and file were well-meaning pacifists. One suburban member was genuinely shocked when she heard of The Link's Nazi sentiments, a reaction which shows a peculiar naivety, given the nature of the organisation's propaganda.[5]

How then were these various organisations and individuals to react when war was declared? Predicting a pattern on past behaviour proves difficult. The head of MI5, Sir Vernon Kell, commenting at the end of 1936 on William Joyce, stated that nothing would 'shake his basic patriotism'. A few days before the outbreak, he was to slip out of Britain to become, as Lord Haw-Haw, the most famous German broadcaster to Britain. Before then the Nazis had approached A. K. Chesterton to be such a propagandist. However, their assumptions were proved to be wrong, as Chesterton refused and volunteered in the British army immediately at the declaration of war. Others were more torn in their loyalty. Unity Mitford, member of the BUF and devotee of Hitler, could not bear the thought of an Anglo-German conflict, and made an unsuccessful suicide attempt.[6]

The official BUF instructions to its members were not so severe. Mosley in a message of 1 September 1939 claimed, as neither Britain nor her Empire were threatened, that the British Union would have nothing to do with 'an alien quarrel' brought about by 'the dope machine of Jewish finance'. Even so, Mosley added 'I ask you to do nothing to injure our country, or to help any other Power.' Unofficially, members were urged to join the various civil defence units and carry on the peace message there. The impact of the war on BUF membership is difficult to assess. John Beckett claimed that in the first couple of months, numbers doubled from 5,000 to 10,000. Such an estimate is difficult to sustain, for although (as a Special Branch report suggested), there was 'a steady stream of new recruits', there were also many resignations, and perhaps more importantly 'many more just ceased'. Special Branch in the second week of the war estimated sales of *Action* (the BUF's populist paper) to be 14,000, the same as that in February 1938 when the movement was in a general trough.[7]

Perhaps a better indication of the negative effect of the declaration of war on BUF fortunes is supplied by their activities on a street level. In September 1939 only twenty-one BUF meetings took place in the capital compared to 313 the month before. The leadership was clearly aware of the danger of total disintegration of the BUF, sending out orders to tighten discipline and to ensure that no propaganda be used without the organisers' consent. Meetings in Ridley Road, the BUF stronghold in North East London, attracted 'fair crowds', in one case 300, but these were fewer than was usual, and in any case, the meetings were attended only by 'stalwarts'.[8]

According to a Special Branch report Mosley's war line was to abandon pro-Nazism and to concentrate on opposition to the war waged 'on behalf of Jewish financiers'. However, as this explicit attack on Jewish power had fallen foul of the censors for the first war issue of *Action*, the BUF also avoided attacking Jews by name in its meetings in September 1939. This did not stop veiled attacks exemplified by 'Mick' Clarke, the BUF's East End leader, who warned that the last war did not benefit workers, who again would 'be sacrificed in the interests of profiteers'. The BUF did turn the problems created by war to one beneficial end – exploiting the black out to create a rash of slogans and stickers in public places, including the antisemitic disfigurement of government propaganda posters. Little imagination was required to produce the net result of 'Your Courage; Your Cheerfulness; Your Resolution; Will Bring JEW Victory.'[9]

The BUF had not been the only fascist organisation to have street meetings. The war was, however, to have a dramatic impact on its extremist rivals. The National Socialist League, which although small had had violently antisemitic meetings, closed down immediately with its leader Joyce having left the country. The Imperial Fascist League closed down its headquarters in the West End, as well as its branch in Dalston. The view of Special Branch that the League had 'ceased to exist' proved to be premature, but certainly no public meetings took place for the first few months of the war. Instead activities were centred on distributing antisemitica and spreading anti-Jewish rumours. Its main publication *The Fascist* ceased production but its in-house organ, *Weekly Angles* continued, helping to keep the IFL alive, if not kicking. Similarly the Nordic League tranformed from a public antisemitic front to a secret coterie whose activities will be examined later.[10]

The only organisation of an extreme antisemitic type to expand in the first weeks of the war was the Nationalist Association. Its leader was 'Jock' Houston, who had been a leading speaker for the BUF in the East End and had indeed been credited with the initial success of Mosley's group in Bethnal Green and Shoreditch. However, the inability to control his antisemitism, and his subsequent frequent arrests led him to be demoted to the provinces and eventually out of the BUF. By the summer of 1939, the Nationalist Association was formed and Houston once again had a platform for his violent antisemitism. Active in Finsbury Square in North East London, Houston had attracted, by the outbreak of war, 'a good number' of 'tough' followers. For the first months of the war, Houston managed to control his antisemitism like his BUF rivals – not referring to Jews but to 'Eskimos' or 'Mongolians'. By December 1939, the strain of this was too much for Houston who once again reverted to inciting language, suggesting that as far as Jews were concerned: 'pogroms do not go far enough'. Houston also translated his words into action and was arrested for violence against an old Jewish couple.[11]

This lapse back to open antisemitism was a pattern that the BUF was also to follow as 1939 came to a close. Sir Philip Game, head of New Scotland Yard, suggested as late as 20 October 1939 that the BUF was 'not now concentrating on antisemitism', but by then Game's case was becoming increasingly dubious. In October both the size and frequency of BUF meetings increased. Explicit attacks were made on the International Jewish Financiers' responsibility for the war by both Mosley and Raven Thomson in North East London. At the Stoll Theatre on 15 October 1939 up to 2,700 people heard Mosley repeat the theme and demand a referendum on the war.[12]

In November this pattern generally continued, with more meetings, more antisemitism, but apart from Mosley's own meetings, there was a general decline in attendance. At Bethnal Green, Mosley proved his own personal popularity, bringing in 2,000 supporters, though as one report suggested, all but a few hundred were BUF diehards. Mosley claimed that war had not been declared on Russia because 'Russian communism had long been controlled by the same force that controlled British capitalism – namely International Jewish Finance.' This language is not far removed from that of a total conspiracy theory, a development in Mosley's character further emphasised by a new element in BUF propaganda – attacks on Federal Union. Mosley was to launch this campaign at Bethnal Green and elaborate it shortly after in his only war publication – *The British Peace – How to Get It*, first issued in January 1940. In it he claimed that 'Federal Union' was 'the biggest racket which Jewish Finance has yet attempted.' He continued that Federal Union attacked the organised nation, 'the last remaining in their path to world dominion'. Mosley, who according to his son 'often had a conspiracy theory of history', was thus close at the start of the war to accepting the message of *The Protocols*.[13]

The war antisemitism of the BUF was not limited to international matters. For the nine months that it operated in the war, much attention was spent on attacking the 'refujews'. *Action* in November 1939 revived an accusation of the First World War, claiming that Britain would 'shortly have British Tommies at the front while alien Jews take their jobs at home'. Later the domestic issue of jobs and international matters were combined, as *Action* urged the conscription of 'refujews to fight in their own war'. The BUF was also quick to accuse the Jews of profiteering, claiming that 'in this war as in every other war the Jews are playing their old game of cornering commodities and profiteering at the National Expense'.[14]

According to one BUF member this antisemitic campaign was successful and there appears to be some truth in this belief, despite the general unpopularity of the fascists in Britain at this stage. A government Home Intelligence memo of March 1940 commented that fascist propaganda was generally unsuccessful, even less so than the Communist Party, but that 'Their only popular appeal is . . . antisemitism.' As late as May 1940, when the public had largely turned against the fascist movement, a BUF meeting in Brighton managed to change the initial hostile feelings of the audience to ones of warmth, via the use of antisemitism.[15]

However, despite this populist appeal, the winter months were lean for the BUF as far as public support was concerned. In December 1939 attendances were 'very meagre', and in January 1940 only twenty-nine public meetings took place. A minor revival took place in February, but generally the cold weather, and Mosley's absence from the public stage, left the BUF with fewer than a hundred regulars at their meetings. Mosley did appear at a private BUF conference at the end of January, where future policy was worked out. One official, Donovan, summarised this in the two short phrases: 'Mosley and Peace' and 'Jewry and War'. The aim was to connect in the public's mind the former with peace, and the latter with 'war and suffering'. It is doubtful whether the first aim was achieved, though the BUF undoubtedly had some success with the second. A Mass-Observation poll in November 1939 found that 17% of the population gave a cynical reason for Britain's war aims, including many statements that it was 'for the Jews'.[16]

In the first few months of 1940, the Nationalist Association appeared to enjoy more street success than the BUF. Its leader, 'Jock' Houston's message is interesting for the deep-rooted antisemitic tradition that he played upon. In January 1940 he suggested that the war was prophesised in *The Protocols* and that the Jews who had planned it would not fight in it. The next month he praised Edward I's treatment of the Jews, and his associate, John Webster, revived accusations of Jewish White Slave trafficking. The alarming feature about these meetings is the degree of success they achieved, with crowds of up to 900 at Finsbury Square. Moreover, Houston's antisemitic jibes were not only popular with the audience, but with the supervising police. Some co-operation seems to have been achieved at this extreme level of organised street antisemitism. Both Houston and P. J. Ridout, the principal public speaker for the IFL, swapped platforms, and indeed the former recommended and sold the latter's organ *Angles*. Apart from Ridout's speeches, the IFL's public activities in the early part of 1940 were confined to circulating *Angles*, which was transformed from a 'house organ' to one sold at a variety of peace meetings.[17]

The flagging fortunes of the BUF seem to have been recognised by the leadership and three remedies were put forward to attempt to revive the movement. Firstly, it was decided to contest several by-elections, not because a heavy poll was expected, but because of the publicity that this would receive. Secondly, an attempt was made to involve women in the BUF's peace campaign. Finally, the BUF was to concentrate its efforts in the area where it had received its only mass support – the East End of London.[18]

The first by-election the BUF was to contest was at Silvertown, a Labour stronghold in the docks of the East End. Although the BUF had seven branches in the dockland, there was no local organisation in Silvertown. Tommy Moran, the BUF South Wales organiser, was brought in as the candidate and faced a hostile electorate with no local support whatsoever. The BUF's strategy was on the one hand to stress the socialist element of the organisation's ideology, rather than attack socialism completely. *Action* pointed out the need to preserve its radical British past, or 'real socialism'. On the other hand, it stated that both the Communist and Labour candidates were controlled by the world power of international Jewry.[19]

The whole of the BUF campaign was brought together with a strong antisemitic basis. Forty thousand copies of Moran's election address were circulated, including a BUF sheet called 'The Silvertown Dawn'. In it, the BUF warned of the war bringing destruction to the West with the 'barbaric hordes of Judaic Communism' overthrowing civilisation. On a less fanciful level, it cautioned against foreign refugees stealing local jobs. The impact of Moran's campaign was negligible; he received 151 votes, or just 1% of the total. A Mass-Observation poll found that no one could remember anything of Moran's 200,000 leaflets, whereas 4% recalled the

Communist Party's literature. Despite the emphasis on 'British peace' and British 'socialism', 18% of the electorate believed the fascists had links to Germany, and anti-German feelings thus contributed to Moran's unpopularity. The BUF failed to exploit any antisemitism in the area, and it would seem that those wanting to register an anti-war protest vote looked to Pollitt (the Communist candidate) rather than Moran.[20]

The BUF had to admit it was 'a very poor vote', yet compared it favourably with the electoral fights of the early Labour leaders. Two weeks later, the BUF achieved its most successful result at Leeds North-East, where 722, or just less than 3% of the vote, was gained by Sydney Allen. Allen made his appeal specifically to ex-servicemen, and indeed received support from the 'League of Ex-Servicemen'. Again stress was put on antisemitism, in literature and wall-writings. Whether antisemitism explained the higher BUF vote is debatable. The local Labour Party agent clearly believed that this was the case, claiming that 'The Fascist . . . got most of his votes on antisemitic lines.' In support of this analysis, surveys at both Leeds and Silvertown found antisemitism generally higher in the latter, although intense antipathy was stronger in the former. Those strongly prejudiced could well have voted for the BUF. Other factors need to be taken into account as well though – there was no other anti-war rival; the BUF had better roots than in Silvertown; and linked to this, a fuller campaign was launched with a well attended speech by Mosley.[21]

The second aspect of the attempt to resuscitate the BUF was the campaign to introduce women into the fascist peace movement. The new policy was not without impact, especially due to the activities of Commander Mary Allen, a formidable woman who had joined the BUF in December 1939. Allen combined her moralistic campaign to the negotiated peace movement and helped to attract some female support to the BUF. This new addition did little to moderate the BUF. Indeed in March 1940, it was female fascists who helped disrupt a peace meeting in Caxton Hall, and at a BUF meeting in Holborn Hall in the same month, a *Jewish Chronicle* reporter was struck by the fact that the women 'adopted a more hysterical anti-Jewish attitude than did their men-folk'.[22]

The third prong of the BUF revival plan, to strengthen the East End support, is harder to assess. The war brought a decline to BUF activities in the area, and meetings, as has been pointed out, tended to be supported by only the loyal diehards. In March 1940, with the improved weather, more meetings took place in the metropolis and *Action* claimed that 1,000 were present at a meeting in Bethnal Green. The press generally ignored such activities, and despite a continued recovery in April, the *New Statesman*'s comments at the end of that month, that 'we hear little today of British fascism' reflected the general obscurity of the BUF in British society.[23]

In the East End meetings, there was an increased tendency towards antisemitism. The editor of *Action*, Ravon Thomson, was arrested at a Finsbury Square meeting for attacking 'the filthy and corrupt practices of the alien Jew', and another BUF speaker at Bethnal Green for collecting money for a Jewish pogrom. Mosley also showed such tendencies in London and Leeds, but this desperate attempt at popularity could not match the increasing hostility towards the movement as a whole, as Germany progressed across Europe. However, there were signs of advance for the BUF – their British Traders' Bureau was attracting lower middle class support, especially from North East London, and in early May 1940 Special Branch reported that the BUF activities had 'increased considerably'.[24]

The climax of this intensely antisemitic campaign came at the May Day meeting of the BUF at Victoria Park. Much preparation went into the event and 'an anti-Jewish demonstration' was expected by members. Morning and afternoon rallies culminated in a speech by Mosley attended by up to 4,000 followers. The audience responded warmly to Mosley's antisemitic outburst, including a statement that the purpose of the war was to create 'a land fit for Hebrews to live in', but any antisemitic disturbances failed to materialise. Mosley's claim that it was 'the greatest day that British Union has yet witnessed', was an exaggeration, but the turnout clearly indicated a revival for the movement. Other large meetings in North East London took place in the first weeks of May, but as events in Europe reached a crisis point with the fall of the Low Countries, the BUF faced a totally hostile public. In the last few weeks of May, the police were required to close four BUF meetings, owing to anti-fascist disturbances, and at Dalston, usually the stronghold of the BUF, a meeting was cancelled owing to the extreme anger of the crowd.[25]

This antipathy was clearly shown in the last by-election the BUF was to contest at Middleton, North Manchester, on 22nd May 1940. F. Haslam, the BUF candidate, fought a campaign nearly identical to that in Leeds, but whereas in the latter city there was some active support for the Mosleyites, the Middleton by-election was totally dominated by anti-fascism. Mosley was physically attacked and in these circumstances the BUF did well to poll 418 votes. On the day of the election, the Cabinet decided to amend the Defence Regulation 18B, and Mosley and other leading BUF members were detained – much to the public delight. With further arrests of up to roughly 750 BUF members, the organisation was effectively crippled and on 20 June 1940, via Regulation 18AA, the BUF was made illegal. No other far right group received such a ban, but the internment of prominent members of such groups as the Imperial Fascist League, the Nationalist Association, the British People's Party, the Nordic League and the Right Club, destroyed any chance of them continuing.[26]

The issue of fascist internment, and the controversial questions it raises, such as the ultimate loyalty of Mosley and his followers, is still an emotional subject. To understand why the government acted as it did, and to evaluate the evidence on the loyalty question, it is necessary to turn to another side of BUF and fringe group activity, from the outbreak of war to May 1940. The radical right in this phoney war period cannot be judged on its public meetings and proclamations alone; for it also operated on another, secret level and it is to this that attention must now be turned.

The day after war was declared Admiral Domvile's Nazi friendship group, The Link, was officially closed down. However, as the security forces were soon to find out, fascist appeasement groups were soon to reappear, both publicly and privately. Two main groups were to develop – those centred around The Link and the British People's Party (whose main forces were Domvile and the Duke of Bedford), and the Nordic League/Right Club coterie centering around Captain Ramsay. Both had common supporters and both were eager to enlist the co-operation of Mosley.

Out of the first group emerged a semi-public organisation, the British Council for Christian Settlement in Europe (BCCSE). Its leading members had some fascist connections, although some naive pacifists were also drawn into the group. Certainly its leaders aimed at a mass peace group, although John Beckett's (the secretary's) claim that it had 14,000 to 18,000 members would seem to be a two figure exaggeration. The BCCSE's line that there was no reason for fighting a war that was 'not due to one country, or one man', did not convince the public which quickly identified the movement with the discredited Link. However, by mid October contact had been established between this group and the BUF's leader.[27]

The Nordic League was numerically smaller than the latter group, but was still, according to MI5 'deserving of close attention'. Some of its leaders would 'go to almost any lengths to further their subversive and revolutionary aims'. With the war, two of its prominent organisers were interned and some confusion emerged as to whether the League would continue. Members were instructed to spread antisemitic rumours and defeatism and urged to join the BUF and the Peace Pledge Union. Similar instructions were given to Right Club Members. However, the latter were not so keen to co-operate with Mosley. Despite this reluctance amongst the rank and file, their leader, Captain Ramsey MP, had (according to Special Branch) agreed to co-operate with the BUF as early as 16 September 1939.[28]

By late October 1939, in what Domvile called 'a historic event', the major personalities in the fascist pacifist movement met. The group, organised by Domvile, included Mosley, Tavistock, Ramsay, Laurie, Lymington and Lawton and Hay. What was discussed is not clear, Domvile loosely commenting that 'We talked all round', and regular meetings of the group were arranged. Throughout November and December 1939 the meetings continued with the added presence of extremists such as H. T. Mills and A. T. O. Lees of the Nordic League. The gatherings would appear to have been informal social gatherings where issues such as 'the menace to freedom' and 'the struggle for Peace' were discussed.

In January and February 1940 these meetings continued, with a tendency amongst the whole of the British fascist movement to assume a private, or at least a semi-private character. The most important development of these gatherings occurred in early February, when Tavistock announced his intention to travel to Ireland to discuss peace terms with the German legation in Dublin. Permission was received from Lord Halifax, the Foreign Secretary, and a wide range of individuals, from Mosley to John McGovern of the ILP, and Lord Beaverbrook, took a great interest in the success of the mission, which turned out to be fruitless.[29]

The secret sessions continued during March, April and May 1940, while Tavistock and the BCCSE were having public peace meetings – several times sharing a platform with the ILP. The content of these secret meetings could well explain some of the reasons why Mosley and other leading fascists were interned in May 1940. In his last meeting with the 18B Advisory Committee on 22 July 1940, Mosley was told by the Chairman, Norman Birkett, that there was no evidence that he was a traitor or had been contemplating any act of treachery. Mosley was relieved by this statement and it was used in his defence by Richard Stokes in Parliament in December 1940. However, doubt still remained in the Advisory Committee's mind, some of it stirred up by Mosley's relationship with Captain Ramsay.[30]

In an earlier interview, Mosley had claimed that before internment he only knew Ramsay 'slightly' and had met him just three or four times. There was, according to Mosley, no thought of joint action and that in fact they only 'loosely discussed questions of common interest', such as their 'mutual dislike of certain aspects of Jewish activities'. The Committee were unimpressed. They were unable 'to accept at face value many of Mosley's professions' and believed his answers over Ramsay were 'lacking in frankness and candour'. The basis of the Committee's complaint was the statement that Ramsay had made in his 18B interview – that he had been 'invited by Mosley to take over Scotland in certain circumstances'.[31]

Mosley's connections with Ramsay were indeed stronger, as has been shown, and the two knew each other as early as July 1939. When A. T. O. Lees, ex-civil servant and prominent member of the Nordic League and British People's Party was arrested, he had in his possession letters relating to secret meetings that took place in London in March, April and May 1940. These letters indicated that Mosley and Ramsay had convened the meetings which pro-Nazis and antisemites attended. The object of these meetings, according to the Special Branch report, 'was to secure the greatest possible collaboration and make preparation for a fascist coup d'etat'.

There is little doubt that there were extremists within the Right Club, the Nordic League, the Imperial Fascist League and possibly even the BUF who would have welcomed a Nazi invasion and who contemplated actions which might have helped to bring this about.[32] It is not too difficult to label such individuals as potential traitors. However, there is another category which is harder to define. Some members of these organisations were not willing to actively assist the enemy, but were prepared to consider an overthrow of the British government and to immediately arrange peace terms with the Nazis. Groups or individuals proposing such actions cannot be regarded as treacherous, but their activities would have justified strong government intervention. It will be suggested here that Captain Ramsay of the Right Club falls into this category, and that a similar case can be made against Sir Oswald Mosley.

In the last month before internment, the BUF did its utmost to prove its loyalty. In *Action* for 9 May 1940, Mosley called upon his members to resist the foreign invader if he came, however rotten the British government. The British Union was 'at the nation's disposal'. A day later instructions were issued to all districts repeating Mosley's message of 1 September 1939: 'I ask you to do nothing to injure our country, or to help any other power.' With the fall of Belgium and Holland, the BUF message was 'peace but Britain undefeated'. To emphasise their own loyalty, BUF policy in late April 1940 was to attack the extremists of the Nordic League as Nazi traitors.[33]

As late as 18 May, the Cabinet were impressed with these declarations; the Home Secretary, John Anderson, pointing out that no action should be taken against the BUF as there was no evidence 'that the organisation as such was engaged in disloyal activities'. Four days later, Anderson reversed this decision and Mosley and other leading fascists were arrested. Why did this turnabout happen? The most obvious development between the two Cabinet meetings that could explain the change in policy was the arrests of two associates of Captain Ramsay – Tyler Kent and Anna Wolkoff. Several recent commentators have gone as far as to suggest that these arrests were actually part of a plot so that Mosley could be interned.[34] Such an analysis simplifies what was a multi-causal complex event, but first of all it is necessary to outline briefly the Kent-Wolkoff-Ramsay affair.

The Right Club, which according to Ramsay had met only once or twice, was officially closed at the start of the war. However, the organisation did not totally disappear; members met informally to discuss the war and to distribute leaflets such as 'Land of Dope and Jewry' and 'Do you know the real causes of this war?' In this way the coterie survived, enabling some of its members to involve themselves in more substantial activities. One of these was Anna Wolkoff, the daughter of an aristocratic Russian emigre. Coming from an intensely antisemitic background, she acted as Ramsay's political secretary on matters relating to the Right Club. In the war, in connection with her antisemitic whispering and leaflet campaigns, she met up with Tyler Kent, an American cypher clerk in the US Embassy, who had transferred from Russia in October 1939.[35]

Through his employment, Kent had access to secret documents, and he abused his position to photocopy up to 1,500 items. Some of these were of a highly sensitive nature, involving correspondence between Roosevelt and Churchill. By March 1940, Kent had been in touch with Ramsay via Wolkoff, and the MP had seen some of the illicit files. However, at this stage a new MI5 infiltrator, Joan Miller, had discovered Kent's activities and the security forces were biding their time before acting to bring in the conspirators. There seems little doubt that Kent desired to bring down both the British and American governments and, hopefully, to replace them with administrations sympathetic to a negotiated peace with the Nazis. The Churchill-Roosevelt correspondence certainly gave him the opportunity to create a major political scandal, some of it relating to US aid for the Allied cause. On the surface, Ramsay with access to the House of Commons, was the ideal man to communicate it.[36]

Ramsay was definitely interested in the correspondence, but there is no evidence of what he intended doing with it. In early May, rather than break the scandal to the House, Ramsay preferred to ask the Home Secretary whether the government distinguished between antisemitism and pro-Nazism in its defence regulations, indicating his concern about his own personal liberty. Ramsay aimed to re-examine Kent's files after a break in Scotland, but in fact he never had the opportunity to do so as he was arrested on his return to London on 23 May 1940. By then, Kent and Wolkoff (who had attempted to communicate with William Joyce) had been hauled in by MI5. In a Confidential Annex, the Lord President of the Council presented a report on the Right Club to the Cabinet suggesting that Ramsay had been 'engaged in treasonable practices in conjunction with [Kent]'. The Home Secretary continued that Ramsay had been in relations with Mosley, but not over the Kent-Wolkoff affair. The same day, 22 May 1940, the Cabinet agreed to intern Mosley and other BUF leaders.[37]

Was the timing of the Kent-Wolkoff arrests simply an MI5 plot to find an excuse to intern Mosley? Anthony Masters, the biographer of Maxwell Knight (who master-minded the MI5 Right Club campaign), believes that this was the case. What is more, Masters believes that 'Knight stated quite erroneously, that Ramsay was an associate of Mosley's . . . [and] that Mosley was "in relations with Captain Ramsay", and without any concrete evidence, poured in the right ingredients to believe that a major right-wing coup was at a far more developed and coherent stage than it could ever have been with such different . . . personalities.' However, as we have seen, Mosley was an associate of Ramsay throughout the war, and there is evidence that Mosley and Ramsay were co-operating and planning a fascist coup d'etat. Ramsay and the Right Club had been considering such an action since the start of the war, when members had been contacting sympathisers in the Armed Forces. The Home Office also felt that, at a meeting of BUF London Officials on 30 January 1940, speeches by Mosley and Donovan suggested that the organisation 'may abandon constitutional methods and try to gain power by force'. Given Ramsay's claim that he had been appointed by Mosley to take over Scotland (under circumstances which remain unclear), and the material in the possession of Aubrey Lees which suggests that the March–May 1940 meetings of Ramsay and Mosley were intended to secure collaboration and prepare for a fascist coup d'etat, it is more than possible that Knight was in fact correct. Where Knight was probably wrong, was in his belief that the coup was in a developed stage. Whilst Mosley and Ramsay may have talked about the need for a replacement of the government, there is no evidence that they received any support for it outside their own coteries.[38]

Ultimately, Ramsay and Mosley were interned because of the military crisis in Europe. With the invasion of the Low Countries on 10 May 1940 and the disintegration of France, fascist liberty was a luxury the British government could no longer afford. Churchill, who claimed he was responsible for Mosley's internment, believed there was a danger that if the Germans broke through, and Mosley had become Prime Minister, such a pro-German government might obtain easier terms from Germany by surrendering the fleet. It was thus the threat of an alternative Mosley government, combined with the dire crisis in Europe, that explains why the fascist internments took place. There was no evidence that Mosley, or indeed Ramsay, intended any treacherous activities (that is actively helping a German invasion). There was evidence, however, that the two intended to reach a negotiated settlement by means that were unacceptable to a country on the verge of being invaded.[39]

The final, more hypothetical question remains. Would Mosley, Ramsay and other fascists and pro-Nazis have collaborated with the Nazis had they invaded Britain? Mosley claimed to the 18B Advisory Committee that if the Germans invaded 'then I am finished'. In such circumstances, Mosley believed that the Nazis would rule through a military dictatorship, or failing that a weak local leader like Petain in France. They would not want 'a movement of renaissance'. There is some strength in Mosley's argument and it could be backed up by the fact that the Nazis had spent more attention on groups like The Link than the BUF. A puppet leader like Ramsay or Domvile would have seemed a more manageable proposition to the Nazis, rather than the more formidable Mosley. Indeed, whereas Ramsay was on the German 'White List' of possible collaborators, Mosley was not. However, the case against Mosley being part of a Nazi-ruled Europe is not totally secure. In a wartime prison meeting with his solicitor, according to an officer present, 'Mosley admitted that Hitler had, in fact, appointed him to be a sort of co-leader in England.'[40]

Ramsay also denied that he would help the Germans after an invasion. He claimed that he was not prepared to sit under the Nazis at any price and that like the Jews, the Nazis were Britain's enemies. He also violently attacked the idea suggested by Lord Marley that Ramsay had been nominated 'Gauleiter of Scotland'. Ramsay in his perverse way was a patriot, and how he would have behaved under a German government is open to doubt. Of Ramsay's Right Club associates a similar ambivalent pattern can be found. Anna Wolkoff was no foreign agent, despite her attempt to contact Joyce. Her extreme antisemitism and desire for peace may have led her into the Nazi camp, however, and one of the MI5 Right Club infiltrators claimed that Wolkoff boasted that she would be Britain's Julius Streicher when the Germans occupied the country. Kent again was, in his own mind, an American patriot, although he had requested a transfer to Germany in February 1940. Whether he would have helped the Nazi cause directly is again open to debate.[41]

For such extremists, the war forced a balancing act between their patriotism and their virulent antisemitism. An element within the extreme were, in Arnold Leese's words, 'more German than the Germans'. Two friends of Wolkoff were distraught when the German ship, Graf von Spee, was sunk, calling it a 'day of black despair'. In the IFL, whereas Leese disapproved of the German invasion of Scandinavia, others such as Elizabeth Berger and H. T. Mills were in full support of it. Many more were torn in between the two camps, typified by John Hooper Harvey, who wrote to Leese in April 1940: 'I would not give away secret information to the Germans unless affairs reached the stage they did in Spain, where foreign assistance was our only hope of cleaning out the pig-sty, but only in [the] very last resort.' He added: 'I don't want to be ruled by Germany or any other foreigner, but at a pinch even that is preferable to being ground to pulp under the heel of the Jew financier, and his pimps and proselytes.'[42]

Of the BUF membership, Mosley claimed that fewer than 5% would welcome a Nazi victory, and that in Liverpool only three out of 600 supporters were in that category. MI5 were less generous, suggesting that 25–30% 'would be willing, if ordered, to go to any lengths'. Throughout the war some individuals belonging to the BUF were arrested for passing information to the Germans, but these seem to be exceptional cases. More common according to Herbert Morrison, reviewing the situation in 1943, were those 18B internees who said they would join up if released, and then did not. Again 'patriotism' did not imply a desire to help the British war effort.[43]

Organised fascism and antisemitism after 18B

Two years after the major implementation of Regulation 18B, which saw a maximum of 1,428 people interned at the end of August 1940, a Jewish observer could write that 'antisemitism in Britain today is dead'. As far as the organised variety is concerned, the statement is accurate enough, but it must not be assumed that the regulation totally destroyed British fascism. Lacking a deep rooted historical tradition in Britain, the British fascists were acutely aware of the need to preserve their continuity. The story of their activities from June 1940 until the end of the war is not one of a robust rebirth but of a fragile shadowy existence, with the stress on keeping alive their movement.[44]

As if to emphasise the need for continuity, *Action* at the end of May 1940 carried the headline 'We carry on.' An appeal fund for internees' dependents was launched and the BUF in early June even managed a few street meetings. However, at this point the majority of the arrests were made and the BUF was reduced to chaos. Replacements for those who wrote for *Action* and were subsequently detained, found themselves arrested in turn. The last issue came out on 6 June 1940 with the defiant message 'We can take it.' Outside London the confusion was greater, with no central instructions and the continuous arrest of leaders. The movement was reduced to a voluntary organisation, depending on local initiatives to survive.[45]

The BUF headquarters were moved and manned by volunteers ostensibly for administrative purposes, although some propaganda was still circulating. After 25 June 1940, such activities had been made illegal and the production of leaflets from the Bethnal Green branch in early July was soon stopped by the police. Thereafter, activities were confined to the odd wall chalking and the sending of anonymous cyclostyled letters. In the blitz in September 1940, most non-interned BUF sympathisers kept a low profile, especially in areas of the East End where the fascists had made the least impact. Elsewhere, BUF supporters were more daring, trying to create antisemitism in certain North and North West London tube shelters. Such activities were not tolerated for long by the authorities.[46]

As late as November 1940, when Mosley was using his cell in Brixton for meetings of the 'Fascist Grand Council', the *Daily Telegraph* was reporting on secret meetings of BUF members aimed at forming the nucleus of an organisation to keep the party going. As will be shown, this was one of the main reasons for the existence of the 18B groups which emerged in 1942, but until then no national BUF supporting group was created. In October 1941, a small clique calling itself the British Union of Freemen was caught by Scotland Yard after a long investigation. Its members had been producing antisemitic leaflets advertising the New British Broadcasting Station, a Nazi propaganda network. In the Christmas of the following year, a publication called *The Flame* appeared. Of its four pages, the first was a reprint of *Action* of 20 May 1940, the second was in support of Mosley and an attack on Jews and the war. According to the *Daily Worker*, it was being distributed freely. In 1943

Herbert Morrison reported that there had been several attempts to revive the BUF, chiefly in London, but apart from local and isolated groups they were unsuccessful.[47]

In the other antisemitic and fascist worlds, the impact of 18B was more devastating. Of the Nazi appeasement groups, the British Council for Christian Settlement in Europe, Information Policy and the Right Club, the internment of such prominent leaders as John Beckett, Ben Greene, Norman Hey and Captain Ramsay assured their destruction. The eventual arrest of Arnold Leese had the same effect on the IFL. Despite the closure of these organisations, the extreme antisemite still had many outlets to satisfy his hatred. Antisemitic publications such as *The Patriot, The Vanguard, The Social Crediter* and others, as well as the Britons Publishing Company, were still allowed to continue by the authorities. However, by 1942 to some ex-internees and other fascists, this was not enough, and new organisations were demanded.

The first to fill the vacuum was Edward Godfrey, who set up his British National Party (BNP) in August 1942. Godfrey, who claimed earlier naval connections to Domvile, was an ex-BUF member who refused to recognise Mosley as his leader. A man of little talent, he collected a group of malcontents to his party which numbered about one hundred members according to the Home Secretary, or between twenty to thirty to the less generous Jewish Defence Committee. Despite these feeble statistics, the BNP created an enormous reaction, with protest marches and petitions for its banning involving thousands of people.[48]

The degree of animosity that the BNP produced cannot be totally explained by the nature of its programme. Although Godfrey denied being a fascist, preferring the title 'English nationalist', his organisation's policies were reminiscent of the BUF's. It was for 'the national traditions of the British people against alien influence and infiltration', against the parliamentary system, international finance and planning, and for the small trader and the revival of the guilds and apprenticeship system. Godfrey regarded the Jews as unassimilated foreigners and praised Edward I's expulsion policy, and claimed that he would pursue a similar policy if given the chance. Finally, like the BUF, the BNP demanded a negotiated settlement with Hitler.[49]

The BNP became useful for both ex-18B internees and for the extreme left. For the former it gave the chance to be politically active again, and for the latter it was a convenient group to attack as fascists. When the emotional reaction to the BNP is taken into account, it is surprising how little the group actually achieved. Activities were confined to distributing a mere handful of their own publications, as well as perhaps more importantly, that of other antisemites such as Count Potocki and Alexander Ratcliffe. As for public meetings, the popular outcry stopped any of these taking place. This antagonism forced the organisation to close down, although it reappeared in April 1943 in the guise of the English National Association (ENA). Apart from Herbert Morrison's refusal to ban the organisation, its only other major publicity came in December 1943 when Godfrey fought the Acton by-election.[50]

Standing as an English nationalist, Godfrey's election address was an attack on 'the enemy within'. It was not explicitly antisemitic, unlike the rest of his campaign, though Godfrey did attack 'the hidden forces' which were attempting to destroy the English heritage. Godfrey managed to poll 258 votes, despite having been 'roundly abused as a Fascist'. Generally he does not seem to have been taken seriously, according to Mass-Observation 'he provided most of the comic relief of the election'. However, as a *News Chronicle* reporter suggested, there was reason to examine Godfrey with 'a straight face'. The BNP/ENA acted as 'a clearing house' for those interested in continuing the fascist movement. In his election campaign, Godfrey received the support of Captain Bernard Acworth of *Truth* and *The Patriot*, and of the League of Ex-Servicemen – a group that had supported the BUF candidate at Leeds in 1940 and was shortly to be at the forefront of the attempted fascist revival. Finally, Godfrey had close links with the Duke of Bedford, who had continued a one-man campaign against Regulation 18B since the demise of the British People's Party.[51]

After Acton, Godfrey disappeared into relative obscurity, forming a more explicitly antisemitic group, the English Legion. It and the ENA were involved in the immediate post-war fascist resurrection, though Godfrey was never to achieve such notoriety again. Godfrey may have been the first to attempt a fascist or quasi-fascist revival, but by 1943 he was not alone in the field. In the middle of that year there were only 429 detainees left under 18B, and many of those freed were anxious for political activity. In this type of atmosphere an obscure group, the People's Common Law Parliament (PCLP), came into prominence as 'a stalking horse for fascists'.[52]

Formed in 1940 by R. J. Scrutton, the PCLP's outlook was an amalgam of its leader's cranky world outlook – pacifism, social credit and 'Christianity'. That former members of the BUF and other antisemites should be attracted to this group is not totally surprising. At the start of the war, Scrutton's earlier group, the United Christian Petition Movement, had also been popular with BUF members. The PCLP's first two years were unimpressive, limited to near-empty public meetings and attacks in its organ, *Parliament Christian* on international usury. By late 1942 this changed with larger audiences many of whom shouted support for the BUF and Mosley. Although the PCLP was tinged with the antisemitism associated with social credit circles, its leaders did not encourage fascist support. Scrutton barred Godfrey from speaking to the organisation, and by the middle of 1943 its use by ex-Mosleyites seems to have stopped.[53] That such a feeble group should be chosen by ex-18B detainees shows the desperation of these men and women to return to politics and to resuscitate British fascism. Via two other organisations explicitly geared to the 18B cause, the revival of the BUF took a step nearer completion.

Throughout 1942, Mosley received a series of visits in Brixton by ex-18B detainees and sympathisers with the aim of setting up an 18B organisation. Mosley was adamant that such an organisation should be non-political, but many others on the outside wanted to collect funds to use to fight by-elections on a negotiated peace line. Mosley's will largely prevailed and by September 1942 the 18B (British) Aid Fund was registered as a war charity. At the same time a sister organisation, the 18B Publicity Council, was launched. However, if the groups were not explicitly 'political', they were also not as widely based as Mosley had hoped. Prominent authors such as Osbert Sitwell, Henry Williamson and Hugh Ross Williamson refused to take an active part, and apart from Francis Yeats-Brown, the group was limited to support from ex-18Bs and *The Patriot*.[54]

Not surprisingly, its first public meeting in December 1942 was widely perceived as an attempt to revive the BUF. Fascist and antisemitic remarks were heard throughout the meeting and, in general, the 18B groups gave the impression that the regulation was imposed on British citizens for their anti-Jewish activities. The groups operated to fulfil two functions simultaneously. At one level, to protest against 18B and to collect funds for the dependants of detainees, at another to maintain political contacts, and as Herbert Morrison suggested to 'serve as a nucleus for a political party until the ban on the BUF is raised'. Francis Yeats-Brown confirmed Morrison's analysis in a letter to Henry Williamson before the first meeting: 'So we aren't all sheep, and we still want to hear of British Union!' As a result, the groups became a reunion club for ex-detainees, partly social with concerts and house meetings, and partly political with the emergence of new leaders to pave the way for Mosley's return.[55]

Meetings continued into 1944 and 1945, but by this time the 18B groups had spawned their own successors, as yet again the British fascist movement was to splinter. By 1943 the more explicitly pro-Mosley 18B groups were rivalling Godfrey's English National Association, but the demands for a purely political Mosleyite group were still growing. On the street level, fascist activities were reviving; slogans and defacements reappearing especially in London. In February 1943 the most notorious incident happened, with the discovery of the painting of the slogan 'P.J.' (Perish Judah) on the Lenin memorial. In August of that year, the ex-18Bs showed their renewed confidence and attempted to break up a left-wing meeting in their old territory of Ridley Road. With the release of Mosley and his wife in November 1943, tensions between fascists and anti-fascists grew stronger. Although left-wing groups were at the forefront of the campaign against the BUF leader's release, there is little doubt, as Mass-Observation suggested, that 'the indignation . . . was spontaneous, deeply felt and felt by an overwhelming majority'. Even Conservative groups joined in the chorus of disapproval.[56] After this, any attempt which could be vaguely seen as a revival of fascism would face violent opposition.

Despite this atmosphere, fascists were willing to risk public meetings. In June 1944 the Jewish Defence Committee reported on the first open-air antisemitic street meetings since the fascist internments three years earlier. Later that summer, both the 18B Detainees Group and the League of Ex-Servicemen attempted meetings in Hyde Park – a hostile crowd faced both organisations. The latter group had been active in the Leeds and Acton by-elections supporting the fascist candidates, but in 1944 it was to come into its own at the forefront of the attempted fascist revival. Even as late as October 1944, it was not particularly active, concentrating its attack on aliens and on the policy of the British Legion.[57] A month later it was to be transformed as its platform saw scenes of conflict not seen since the 1930s.

Leading its transformation was Jeffrey Hamm, an ex-BUF member and 18B detainee. Hamm's internment in the Falklands appears to have strengthened his commitment to Mosley, and after a spell in the army he was determined to revive the BUF. In November 1944, the first meetings of the new style League of Ex-Servicemen were held in Hyde Park. Only three meetings took place, with up to 200 people in the opposition. Due to police protection, Hamm was to get his message across of 'Britain for the British' as well as his attacks on 'international finance' and the 'House of Rothschild'. His partner Victor Burgess announced that those not '100 per cent British by race' would be disqualified from voting and confirmed that the League was a fascist body. Dunlop, the main force behind the 18B groups, was upset at this, as he had carried out Mosley's instructions regarding the non-political status of the 18B groups since 1942. Out of this disagreement came the first split in the post-18B world of British fascism. Hamm was to continue as leader of the League of Ex-Servicemen, being heavily involved in an anti-alien campaign at the close of the war. Burgess was to run an antisemitic publishing company, Corporate Utilities, and his own political group, the Union for British Freedom. Finally Dunlop, who had laid the basis for the Mosleyite revival, disappeared into obscurity.[58]

The pattern for post-war British fascism was clearly set by the close of hostilities. On a 'street level', Jeffrey Hamm's League of Ex-Servicemen would come to represent the dangers of a fascist revival with its violent public meetings in London. Yet by 1945 another level of fascist/antisemitic activity had been firmly established. In June of that year a group calling itself the National Front After Victory held its first secret meeting. As Lord Vansittart was to suggest a year later, what was remarkable about this group was its interesting membership. Its Chairman was A. K. Chesterton, by now deputy editor of *Truth*, and other individuals involved included Collin Brooks, also of *Truth*, G. F. Green, Cuthbert Reavely and H. T. Mills of *The Patriot*, Pepler of the *Weekly Review*, Henry Williamson, J. F. C. Fuller, Ben Greene and Lord Portsmouth. Taken together, the group represented a fair cross-section of the antisemitic radical right-wing world (excluding Mosleyites).[59]

In fact, the National Front had been formed twelve months earlier, but it was only with the end of hostilities in Europe that this group, which aimed to co-ordinate the various anti-Jewish organisations, started to operate. Although the Front's main aim was to protect national sovereignty from 'the further extension of Jewish power and influence in Britain', members were wary of adopting an openly anti-Jewish policy. Instead a more guarded statement on 'the real Jewish problem' was produced. Co-operation was the key word for the Front and contact was made with the whole spectrum of groups in Britain's antisemitic network. Closest links were achieved with the newly reformed British People's Party which included moderates such as Bedford, and extremists such as A. T. O. Lees. Indeed, the National Front nearly became a branch of the latter organisation. At the other end of the fascist spectrum, contact was made with ex-members of the Imperial Fascist League, who were supposedly considering an armed uprising. However, such activities as well as sympathy towards William Joyce were frowned upon by the Front. Support was also given to Hamm and the Hampstead petition movement.[60]

The National Front was like its later namesake, an unstable coalition bringing together moderate antisemites and Nazi supporters. All were united in a profound anti-communism, but such a bond was not sufficient to keep the Front together. Instead, it managed a separate existence for only a year or so before being swallowed up into the British People's Party. This in turn contributed members to A. K. Chesterton's League of Empire Loyalists which in 1967 was one of the two major components of the second National Front. Over the first twenty post-war years, the radical right in Britain had turned full circle.[61]

In considering in 1947 why the fascist revival had happened so quickly and thoroughly, Douglas Hyde perceptively pointed out that 'the answer is that [in the war] the Fascist organisations never went out of existence'. Some of the groups covered here were feeble enterprises with limited funds and only a few dozen members. However, as they self-consciously realised, they filled a function of keeping a fascist and antisemitic tradition in Britain alive. To do so in a total war against the Nazi enemy was in its way a major achievement, showing perhaps the strengths and weaknesses of liberal democracy. Civil libertarian feeling was strong enough for the government to tolerate the revival of fascism. Fortunately for parliamentary democracy in Britain, the post-war world did not offer the opportunities for fascism to expand outside the fringes of society.

If there is a paradox in the continuity of organised British fascism during the Hitler war, then it is strengthened when the parallel existence of a strong British antisemitic ideological movement is also taken into account. If the British antisemite had to hunt around for a suitable organisation to join in the war, this was not true of the printed word. At least four weekly antisemitic journals continued throughout the war, supplemented by five or more publishing companies devoted to antisemitica.[62] In the course of the war against the genocidally antisemitic Nazis, some 'classic' and virulent printed antisemitism was produced in Britain. The purpose of this last section will be to examine how the Second World War affected contemporary British antisemitic ideology, and to see what impact this had on society.

No man likes to be an island, and this includes those in the antisemitic world in Britain. Antisemitic propagandists have made constant reference to what has been said or written before. Yet this must not disguise the fact that even at its low intellectual level, antisemitic ideology (including its most extreme form), has developed and responded to economic and social change. It has been suggested that the fast changing world of post-1918 Britain could be viewed by some in terms of a crisis, and that this needs to be taken into account when explaining the growth of conspiratorial antisemitism in the 1920s and 30s.[63] In the Second World War, with radical internal developments and the external battle against an antisemitic enemy, this sense of crisis intensified in the extreme world of British Jew-hating. How then did antisemitic ideology adapt to the war?

Whatever their differences, fascists and antisemites of all shades and hues could agree in the 1930s, that the Jews were planning a World War. To some it was all written in *The Protocols*, to others a slightly less conspiratorial but vaguer concept of Jewish power was responsible for war. However when war came, such general ideological agreement disappeared. By then the Nazi-Soviet Pact had been signed, and the antisemitic groups, which had viewed Hitler as the saviour of the world against international Jewry, and Russia as the home of the latter, were thrown into a state of confusion.

The Patriot showed these tensions most clearly. A strong supporter of Hitler since 1936, it reverted back to its original anti-German policy with the pact. Nesta Webster defended *The Patriot*, saying it would support the war 'now that Hitler by his base betrayal of the anti-Soviet cause . . . and reversion to the old Prussian system of broken pledges . . . has forfeited the sympathy that many of us felt for him'. Others in the extreme antisemitic world followed *The Patriot* in reversing their policy with the war. The Militant Christian Patriots, the group that had attempted to co-ordinate antisemitic activities in Britain, and which had also supported Hitler in the late 1930s, claimed it was closing its offices and paper, attacking the Nazi regime as 'Prussianism in a new guise'.[64]

Yet to some groups such a turnabout was unnecessary. The advantage of a conspiracy theory is its total flexibility. It could be said that elements within the Social Credit movement brought the conspiracy theory to its ultimate absurdity. One section, the Social Credit Secretariat, based in Liverpool and controlled by the movement's founder, Major Douglas, believed that not only was international socialism and finance controlled by Jews, but the Nazi movement itself. The antisemitism of Hitler had not impressed this group which was convinced that the Pan-German-Jewish threat continued, and that the war was inevitable given the power of this secret force. Douglas himself wrote in November 1939 that 'not only is antisemitism (anti-Judaism) not Nazi-ism (sic), but Nazi-ism is pro-Judaic'. Belief in the theory that 'Hitler's Policy is a Jewish Policy', would seem to be asking too much even of the conspiratorially-minded extreme antisemitic world in Britain, yet it is perhaps surprising how successful it was amongst the fringe. *The Patriot* of 21 September 1939 referred to 'the sinister significance of [the] Moscow-Berlin Pact' and reported shortly after that Hitler has 'sold his soul to the devil'. Nesta Webster commented that she had always pointed out the Pan-German as well as the Pan-Jewish danger, and James Dell of The Britons and *Free Press* concurred, suggesting that Hitler was 'doing what the Jewish leaders desire'.[65] These arguments were also to be used by the popular publicist, Douglas Reed.

However, whilst the Douglas Social Credit movement opposed the war, as it would only lead to the Judaising of Europe 'via Hitler or via Mr Greenwood', both *The Patriot* and the Militant Christian Patriots reluctantly supported it, if only for the sake of the British Empire. The distributist *Weekly Review* also offered lukewarm support of the war effort, largely because Catholic Poland was being threatened by 'Jewish Bolshevism-Nazism'. Angus Calder has commented on the paradox of 'antisemitic right-wing patriots' fighting against Hitler, but this was not, of course, true of all the extremists. Whilst Arnold Leese was shocked by the Soviet-German pact and remarked that 'Hitler has been a marvel, but is no longer one,' he did not lose all faith in Hitler and could not bring himself to support the war effort. Although others in the IFL supported Hitler in all his actions, Leese's criticism of Hitler stopped short of suggesting that he was under Jewish control. Leese could not support the Social Credit theory being propagated by his one time ally, the Britons; as he wrote to the leader of the latter: 'No, Dell, I think it's all Bunk with a big B'. Alexander Ratcliffe, leader of the Scottish Protestant League, lost even less faith in Hitler than Leese, opposing a war fought for 'World Jewry and the Papacy'.[66]

If there were bitter ideological disagreements in the antisemitic world on the nature of the war and the position to be adopted towards Hitler, then on internal war developments there was much more consensus. Even those supporting the war stressed the need to keep an eye on Jewish activities at home. *Free Press* summarised this viewpoint. Whilst supporting 'the Government in the War against our open enemies', it warned that 'the subtle forces which are working ceaselessly to destroy our religion and country is (sic) as great as ever'. These extreme right wing groups, which had seen any attempt at planning the British economy in the 1930s as evidence of the Jewish conspiracy, continued to view any such activities in the war in a paranoid manner.

The greatest bugbear of the radical antisemitic right had been PEP, a non-party group that represented a growing interest in the planning movement in the 1930s. Any antisemitic reference to this group was inevitably linked up to the involvement of Israel Moses Sieff in PEP, and from there a direct link was made to *The Protocols*. With the war even more was blamed on the organisation. Miscellaneous statements made by PEP throughout the 1930s, claiming that war would bring good opportunities for planners, were constantly churned out by the antisemitic groups as explanations for the imposition of Jewish control over society. It has to be said that the Second World War gave good opportunities for those worried by planning to have their worst fears confirmed. If, essentially, the planning movement of the 1930s had caused concern only to the radical right, the Second World War developments created shudders across the majority of the Conservative Party.[67]

In the fringe world of the radical right, the explanation for government interference was automatic – Jewish power. At the start of the war, ARP and evacuation were seen as alien-Bolshevik plots, the former to introduce local socialism, and the latter to destroy the English countryside by the introduction of 'verminous Jews'. However, such minor plots paled into insignificance compared to the new development in the supposed Jewish World Conspiracy – Federal Union. This 'Utopian Project' originated in America and was popular amongst liberal and left wing circles as a way of solving international problems by creating a European federal state. In Britain, interest was shown by the publication of a Penguin Special advocating Federal Union in November 1939. At the same time, fascist and antisemitic groups began attacking the movement. The *Social Crediter*, always quick to spot a conspiracy, was the first to identify Federal Union as part of Israel Moses Sieff's world plan. The MCP's *Free Press* soon followed claiming it was all outlined in *The Protocols of the Elders of Zion*'.[68]

It has already been pointed out that at this same point, Mosley was also attacking the Jewish plot of Federal Union. This shows not only the tendency of the BUF leader to move towards a conspiracy theory, but also the wide degree of ideological agreement of British antisemites on this matter. Indeed, it is hard to find any such extremist group or individual who did not attack 'Jewish' Federal Union at some point in the war. Why the Jewish connection was made is not immediately obvious. Few Jews were prominent in the movement, nor did it say much about Jewish matters. However, Federal Union could be viewed as a typical PEP stunt if one so wished, even if the latter or kindred bodies had no official connections to it. As the *Social Crediter* succinctly put it, 'the Jew must be adjudged guilty until he is proved innocent'.[69]

By the end of 1940 both the left and the antisemitic right had lost interest in Federal Union. However, the latter did not take long to find other evidence of the Jewish conspiracy. From the start of the war, some antisemitic groups had warned about the government powers under Regulation 18B. After the mass arrests in 1940, these fears enlarged and the regulation came to be seen as yet more evidence of the Jewish conspiracy in Britain. Jews were using the regulation to prevent any criticism of their behaviour and at the same time removing long held civil liberties, enabling their stranglehold on Britain to tighten. The identification of 18B as a Jewish regulation, either as racial revenge, or more sinisterly, as part of *The Protocols*, was a constant feature of the propaganda of the revived fascist movement in the war.[70] However, the regulation was seen as only part of the conspiracy in antisemitic circles. Government actions in social policy were viewed with even greater alarm.

In late 1942, the long awaited Beveridge Report was published; the huge queues for it revealing the public's deep concern over the Welfare State. The report, which examined the three areas of family benefits, employment and the national health service, gained nation-wide support except, according to the government's Home Intelligence, from 'a hostile minority'. This latter opposition, as will be later shown, came from large sections of the Conservative Party, but it also included fringe groups on the extreme right who saw the 'Beveridge Plot' as more proof of the increasing Jewish domination of Britain.[71]

By the start of 1943, most in the extreme antisemitic world were despairing of Britain's future. They had warned that 'Jewish' planning groups would exploit the opportunities of war to enslave Britain; the Beveridge Report confirmed their worst fears. Beveridge's linkages to the 'London School of (Judaic) Economics' and to Israel Moses Sieff 's PEP were stressed and his report was viewed as a culmination of plots all stemming from *The Protocols*. Out of this concern came a group specifically created to oppose one aspect of the Beveridge Report – the proposals on the Health Service. The Medical Policy Association (MPA) was formed in March 1943 and it was soon to achieve both notoriety and some success.[72]

The background of the MPA's leadership shows the importance of the antisemitic tradition in Britain in providing an ideological structure for its later adherents. Of the four men who controlled the organisation, two had been weaned on the conspiracy theories of *The Patriot* since the 1920s, another was a leading Douglas Social Crediter, and the final one's world view owed much to the British volkisch-mystical tradition and British-Israelitism. Such a collection does not appear impressive, and given that the first bulletin of the organisation directly linked medical planners to

The Protocols (via PEP and the LSE), it could be expected that the MPA would have been limited to an obscure fringe of the medical world. Its relative success as a pressure group needs a convincing explanation.[73]

It has been suggested that part of the MPA's appeal came from its antisemitism. This argument suggests that the MPA played upon a strong tradition of antipathy to Jews in the British medical world, born out of insecurity, the threat from refugees and money lenders. However, its author recognises that this prejudice does not imply support for a Jewish conspiracy argument. Whilst medical antisemitism will be examined in greater depth at a later point, it must be suggested that the MPA's popularity was generally *despite* its antisemitism. Only if the deep fear of government intervention into the medical world amongst the majority of British GPs (and the conservative BMA) is taken into account, can the MPA's success be explained. Feeding off this fear, the MPA managed to inject a conspiracy theory into the argument, one that was at first explicitly antisemitic. In such a way, arguments which might be considered to be outside the mainstream of ordinary belief – such as the Jewish origins of Hitlerism and Israel Moses Sieff's control of British life – were introduced to a wider public. The MPA might not have stopped the implementation of the National Health Service, but as a pressure group it was successful in augmenting opposition to planning in the medical world.[74]

In general, extreme antisemites in Britain were not so positive as the MPA in their attempts to stop the tide of 'Jewish' planning. A resigned pessimism is more typical of the attitude of such individuals. Writing in the *Social Crediter*, J. Dell of The Britons commented on an article by Harold Laski in July 1942. Laski had suggested that the war offered opportunities for revolution and counter-revolution. To Dell this was tacit admittance of the essential message of *The Protocols* and he commented 'Has the Jew become so confident that he does not mind whether cats are let out of the bag?' Francis Yeats-Brown believed himself an optimist in thinking that 'the Jews will not rule the world, as they confidently expect'. Certainly, with Hitler defeated and a general left-wing transformation of British society, the right-wing antisemite had little to be cheerful about. Even Jewish atrocity stories offered little comfort, for these were generally seen by such extremists as propaganda designed to help Jewish control of the world by getting Gentile sympathy.[75]

In summarising antisemitic ideology in the Second World War, it is important firstly to stress how it contained a dynamic element. Although constant reference was made to an older antisemitic tradition, new factors evolving from developments in the war itself were constantly added. Secondly, although emphasis has been put on some of the ideological agreement of these groups, conflict must also be taken into account. Distributist attacked social crediter, crank dismissed crank as crank, and antisemite dismissed antisemite as 'Jewish'. To some, Catholicism was the answer to the Jewish Peril, to others the two were in league with the devil. Even Arnold Leese's attack on Mosley's 'kosher fascism' did not end with the start of the war.[76] The third point to note is the varying solutions they offered to the 'Jewish problem'.

Supporters of a Nazi-inspired racial antisemitism were rare in Britain, and no one in the war *publicly* advocated extermination. Arnold Leese, who had earlier put forward 'the lethal chamber' as the solution to the Jewish problem, was vaguer in the war itself, suggesting only that 'the Jew must be taken out of Europe'. Leese's other suggestion, that of sending Jews to Madagascar, found support from both the Social Credit Secretariat and The Britons. The idea of exporting Jews also appealed to the BUF. Perhaps one of the most revealing aspects of the papers relating to Mosley's 18B interrogation was his reported willingness to carry out this policy when he had power. Rather than keep the Jews in Ghettos, as 'an eternal irritant within the body politic', Mosley was happy to remove all foreigners. Asked if this included the Jews, Mosley replied: 'Quite right.'[77]

Not all the extreme right went as far as to demand the expulsion of the Jewish minority. Some, while agreeing with Mosley that the Jews were 'a nation within a nation', wanted to recognise that fact legally, with ordinances controlling Jewish activities. However, even here there was a tendency towards supporting expulsion if such apartheid failed. However, extremist support for 'zionism' – of the Jews achieving redemption on the soil of their own lands – did not apply to Palestine. Paradoxically, although those in the extreme antisemitic world were race conscious to a high degree, they still championed the Arab cause in the Middle East. Rather than being simply the backing of the Jews' Palestinian rivals, this support came out of a genuine philo-Arabism. The fact that Arabs were also 'semites' was conveniently ignored.[78] It will be interesting now to examine how important 'race' was in British antisemitic ideology.

How far were genetic explanations of Jewish behaviour accepted by extreme antisemites? Only a few isolated groups like the IFL were open supporters of racial antisemitism, but racial explanations also played their part in other extremists' ideology. For example, although Mosley emphasised in his first 18B interview that the BUF, unlike the Nazis, did not attack Jews on racial grounds, his arguments on the Jews *were* based on an ethnocentrism that at times became deterministic. Mosley later argued that his antisemitism came from a long British tradition coming from the soil, and that antagonism to Jews was 'probably latent in the racial . . . consciousness of a great many [English] men'. As Richard Thurlow has suggested 'It is sometimes difficult in practice to distinguish between "scientific" and "common sense" variants of a [belief] system' on racial matters. Generally speaking, the BUF's views on Jews were Lamarckian rather than Darwinian. E. D. Hart in the *BU Quarterly* of spring 1940 suggested that culture, not race, was the essence of the Jewish problem, and that the solution was to end the Jews' nomadism and to settle them on the soil. Similarly, in the Social Credit movement, the opposition to Jews was theoretically limited to Jewish financial activities. However, yet again the matter is more complex, for not only was a form of conspiratorial antisemitism employed, but also biological explanations were given by Social Crediters for Jewish activities. Jews, according to C. H. Douglas 'have a . . . race consciousness which is perhaps unique'. What is more, the Social Credit guru also praised the Nazi ideology of 'Blut und Boden'; each culture should be racially related to the soil, argued Douglas. Others in Britain during the war supported such a volkisch outlook. Groups connected to Lord Lymington such as *New Pioneer*, the English Array, English Mistery and the League of Husbandry continued to hold summer camps. They also distributed literature attacking the malevolent alien Jewish influence on the English race, and advocated a return to the land.[79]

As a whole, antisemitic ideology in Britain during the Second World War continued its earlier pattern with a greater emphasis on conspiracy ideas. There was also a tendency to replace racialist attacks on Jews with language that was explicit, being based on a more ethnocentric approach. Some ideologists such as A. K. Chesterton abandoned their earlier support for more Nazi orientated antisemitism, and concentrated on the threat to British national sovereignty from the alleged international Jewish influence. Whatever their stance, all extreme antisemites had to re-examine their beliefs in the war against Hitler. Although a few did not change their outlook at all in the 1939–45 period, most had to modify their ideology to some extent. The absurd results that some came up with – such as the Jewish origins of Adolf Hitler or Julius Streicher – show what a desperate time the Second World War was for Britain's antisemitic fringe. Nevertheless, it also shows how flexible and durable conspiracy ideas have been in British society.[80]

Extremist antisemitism thus took many forms in Britain during the war. One final vital question needs to be asked: what was their impact and importance in British society? As far as organised political groups are concerned, one has only to examine the pathetic showing of movements such as the BUF or the ENA in the war by-elections to prove how distant they were from electoral success. A total of 1,549 votes in four contests does not indicate a mass following. However, as Stuart Rawnsley has perceptively pointed out, groups like the BUF could exert more influence than mere membership figures would suggest, especially over certain issues. In the Second World War, the constant fascist opposition to Jewish refugees and to the Jews' War made their impact on British society. As late as 1943 the social commentator, James Hodson, reported on a survey of new recruits and what they thought they were fighting for. The response 'I am fighting because Jewish international financiers wanted a war,' was not isolated. Indeed, Hodson commented that there were many such replies 'of which this is representative'. However, it is doubtful whether other aspects of fascist propaganda, such as the need for a corporate state, made any impact on the public either in the 1930s or in the war.[81]

Part of the BUF's limited success came from its pragmatism. Whereas its rival, the IFL, was a one trick pony with a limited appeal of its physically and verbally violent antisemitism, the BUF adapted to local 'needs'. In Bristol it was anti-Welsh, and in Liverpool and Cardiff it was anti-black. In East Anglia it concentrated on rural issues. Its British Traders Bureau, aimed at lower middle class malcontents, enjoyed some success, especially in North East London, here the Jewish issue being used successfully. Used effectively, on a street level, antisemitism remained one of the BUF's best crowd pullers. The organised fascist and antisemitic groups thus helped Britain to remain Jew conscious into the Second World War.[82]

What of the power of the antisemitic word in the 1939–45 period? In 1940 John Hooper Harvey, a man previously associated with the literary committee of the IFL, wrote *The Heritage of Britain*, an Aryan history of Britain. Harvey believed that the knowledge contained in the book could 'yet save the British nation from the downfall which awaits those who lose race consciousness, and who mix their blood with that of lesser breeds'. It is doubtful if an unsuspecting member of the public who by chance managed to read one of the few hundred copies of *The Heritage* would have been impressed. Even the *Weekly Review* remarked that Harvey's book was nonsense, 'based on the undigested reading of anthropologists'. Harvey's work obviously belongs to the world of the lunatic fringe and his activities with his wartime ally, Count Potocki, would seem to confirm this judgement.[83]

Potocki was pretender to the Polish Crown and his 'court' in Little Bookham, Surrey, in March 1943 was the scene of one of the most bizarre incidents in the war. Frederick Bowman, ex-18B and supporter of the Duke of Bedford, was to be knighted by the 'king' for his services to the crown. Harvey, dressed up in a Robin Hood tunic, played his flute, whilst Potocki 'as high priest of the sun' lit the incense, intoned a prayer and knighted Bowman.[84] Can Potocki or Harvey be taken seriously given the nature of these events, and the obscurity of their publications?

The answer, perhaps surprisingly, is yes, for on the one hand Harvey was in the process of becoming an eminent architectural historian and on the other, Potocki's activities were not limited to sending 'court circulars' to fellow eccentrics. The intriguing aspect about John Hooper Harvey was his ability to work at many different levels. His 'gutter antisemitism' letter to Arnold Leese in April 1940 has already been mentioned, yet with *The Heritage* he could produce more reasoned 'Aryan' antisemitism. Moreover, although he had contributed to *The Fascist* in the 1930s, at the same point he had written respectable academic articles. In the war itself, Harvey's first major book, *Henry Yevele*, managed to combine both this academic respectability and Harvey's 'Nordic' philosophy. In it Harvey praised the Gothic (which he had earlier stated was the same as the Aryan), attacked cosmopolitism and planning and advocated a Golden Age of the fourteenth century.[85]

His next work, *Gothic England*, completed at the end of the war, was a similar mixture. Whereas in *The Heritage of Britain* he had bluntly praised Edward I's treatment of the Jews, in *Gothic England* the phraseology was more guarded. Here Harvey stated that 'England had been given back to the English by Edward I', the same message – but a respectable tone. This was the great danger of Harvey, the ability to communicate an anti-Jewish message in a publicly acceptable manner. In his most famous book, *The Plantagenets*, Harvey did this at the most sophisticated level. Again he praised 'the statesmanship of Edward's decision to remove the whole Jewish community', but in this case Harvey actually managed to suggest that the Jews had indeed committed ritual murders in twelfth and thirteenth-century Britain. The subtle way in which Harvey was able to bring in the medieval blood libel against the Jews is shown by the fact that it is only now, nearly forty years later, that this book, a school best-seller, has been suppressed by its publishers.[86]

Harvey thus succeeded in bringing extremist antisemitic ideas into mainstream British society. However, he was not alone. Antisemitic periodicals like the *Social Crediter*, *Weekly Angles* or *The Vanguard* had a circulation of up to 2,000. *The Patriot* may have had up to 5,000 subscribers. Their individual influence was thus not great. In 1940 the Home Secretary, John Anderson, suggested that the twenty or so fascist or antisemitic periodicals 'circulate among the same limited groups of people'. As will be shown shortly this in itself did serve a function, but these figures show the limited appeal of such antisemitism. However, the ideas contained in them were not exclusive to these periodicals. Again a system of diffusion into wider society operated. In the war, both the periodical *Truth*, located in most 'respectable' clubs and with links to the Conservative Party, and the popular publicist, Douglas Reed, were putting out similar ideas to those of *The Patriot* or the *Social Crediter*. The language was less hysterical but the message was similar. Reed and *Truth* attacked 18B as Jewish revenge; the Beveridge Report, PEP and Federal Union were seen in terms of Jewish conspiracy, as was the black market; and both doubted the stories of Jewish persecution in Europe. Reed even went as far as suggesting the Jewish origins of Hitlerism, the same view held by the Social Credit Secretariat. The impact of Reed and *Truth* on British society will be left to later chapters, but at this point it is necessary to point out that both were ways that extreme antisemitism managed to percolate into wider society.[87]

What then of Potocki? Whilst the total eccentricity of his behaviour and appearance paradoxically made him an acceptable literary figure in the 1930s, the political impact of the *Right Review* and his Polish Royalist Associated was negligible. However, the war gave Potocki a certain prominence despite his obvious crankiness. The antisemitic world was short of outlets to print its material, and the mad Pole, with his primitive press, became a vital link in helping extremist groups to get their message across. In 1942 he published the literature of the 18B Publicity Council, and a year later, after he had fallen out with the latter group, Potocki printed the second edition of Alexander Ratcliffe's *The Truth About the Jews*. A *Jewish Chronicle* reporter suggested it was 'probably the vilest antisemitic pamphlet yet produced in Britain'. In it Jews were blamed for 90% of all crimes, pornography, birth control, and the war. Perhaps the worst feature of the book was his claim that 'there is not a single authentic case on record of a single Jew having been massacred or unlawfully put to death under the Hitler regime'.[88]

The book became notorious and although only several thousand were produced, according to the Glasgow police '100,000 copies could easily have been printed and sold.' The circulation of *The Truth About the Jews* also illustrates how closely knit the antisemitic world was in Britain during the war. The Potocki-Ratcliffe link was only one of several connections. The book was also sold by Essential Books, an antisemitic distributor and publisher of Taunton, and by Edward Godfrey, the English National Association leader. John Hooper Harvey's home itself acted as a nucleus keeping an antisemitic coterie alive in Britain. Potocki, Alfred Day and Frederick Bowman were just some of the extremists given refuge by Harvey in the war. Journals such as *The Vanguard* and *The Patriot* (whose offices were also a meeting place for ex-18B detainees) also kept individuals in touch with one another in this most difficult of periods. Such antisemitic coteries were not limited to the organised extremist groups and papers. In Durham, a viciously antisemitic Mass-Observer spent the war attacking Jews along with her husband, friends, coalman and grocer![89]

These coteries also performed the function of keeping antisemitic ideas alive in Britain. Indeed, in November 1941, *The Patriot* launched a desperate appeal for funds to keep the journal going, stressing 'the need for an organ devoted both to exposing the undermining of the country's social structure and to providing ideas for maintaining intact the heritage which has come to British people'. Elsewhere other groups fulfilled the same function. It is highly ironic that the Britons Publishing Company produced two new editions of *The Protocols of the Elders of Zion* in the war, at the same time as the Germans were using it as a major propaganda weapon against the Allies.

At the very end of the war, Douglas Hyde could write that 'there is now a growing network of [antisemitic] bookshops [in Britain] stretching from Liverpool to Taunton'. Hyde was exaggerating to an extent because there were few in between, but his point that the antisemitic and fascist world had re-established itself by May 1945 is a sound one. By the efforts of the extremist organisations and journals the antisemitic world in Britain had been maintained during the war. Limited in size, it was still large enough to keep the government worried about a fascist or antisemitic threat to British society.[90] Whilst the government's fears may have been exaggerated, it is true that the foundations had already been laid for the post-war fascist revival. Under the guise of the League of Ex-Servicemen and later Mosley's Union Movement, fascist violence, so prominent in the 1930s, was to return to the streets of the East End of London after the war. What had happened to the East End Jewish-Gentile relations in between these two periods will be the subject of the next chapter.

2

The East End and evacuation experiences

The East End had been of central importance in modern Anglo-Jewish history up to the declaration of the war. The Aliens Question, the riots of the First World War and the battles with the BUF in the 1930s were all staged at their most dramatic level in this concentrated part of the Metropolis. Indeed, when in late 1938 Mass-Observation decided to undertake a detailed study of antisemitism in Britain, it decided to base its study in Stepney.

The complexity of Jewish-Gentile relations in the East End has not stopped contemporary or modern observers making unsubtle generalisations about the subject. As a *Times* correspondent perceptively pointed out at the height of the BUF campaign in 1936: '[they] have seen what they would have liked to see and heard what they wanted to hear.'[1] The Mass-Observation survey was no exception, with Tom Harrisson's anthropological background coming to the fore. To Harrisson, the East End was like another foreign expedition, with the tribes concerned being Jewish or Gentile, or perhaps Lascar and Chinese. Jewish behaviour patterns were observed and compared to their 'Cockney' equivalents. The complicating factor that some Jews saw themselves as Cockneys, and that there were 'Irish' cockneys as well as 'English' cockneys never occurred to 'these innocents abroad'.[2]

However, the thorough report did provide an indication of the position of Jews in East End society in the period immediately before the war. Socially Jews and non-Jews did not mix very often and the image of the pub as a Gentile preserve was not without foundation. East End Jews, contrary to popular belief, were not flashier than 'Cockneys', although they *were* smarter. Generally, what emerges from the study is the similarities, rather than the differences, between the two communities. Both liked the cinema, music-hall, boxing and billiards and although there were peculiarities distinct to each community, there was also common ground. The reading of newspapers most clearly indicates this point. The Yiddish (but Anglicised) *Jewish Times* was a Jewish preserve, as were the Irish papers on the 'Cockney' side. Yet the *News Chronicle* was the most widely read paper marking 'the meeting point of politics' of the two communities. This could be seen in local politics with a right wing Labour group dominating Stepney Borough council, made up of Irish Catholics but also of moderate Jews. Further to the left was a group of more radical Jewish councillors, including (from 1938) a communist named Phil Piratin.[3]

The Stepney Communist Party was not totally dominated by Jews; in fact, it aimed to give the impression of Jewish-Gentile co-operation. Of 500 members in 1939 'half or more were Jewish'. However whilst the Catholic world was largely anti-Communist in the East End, the Jewish Community was at least tolerant of the Communist Party. In Whitechapel Library, the *Daily Worker* was read eighteen times more by Jews than by Gentiles. With the Stepney Tenants' Defence League, the Communist Party did succeed in uniting Jews and non-Jews in political action, and by June 1939 its membership had risen to 7,500. Up to £45,000 had been refunded to Stepney tenants with rent and rates rebates, proving that it was not true that the working class Gentile cockney 'recoiled from active combination' with Jews, as *The Times* had claimed three years earlier.[4]

Thus by the summer of 1939, Jewish-Gentile co-operation was as common, if not more significant than the conflict represented by the clashes with the BUF. However, within the East End there were other factors which complicated the overall pattern of community relations. The Mass-Observation Survey of 1939 found that women were less antisemitic than men, and that 13% of females compared to 2% of men actually liked Jews socially. Moreover, both men and women were capable of ambivalence on Jews and families could often be split on the subject; a resident of Ernest Street felt that antisemitism 'was a shame' even though her husband was a Mosleyite. The most common response (16% women and 9% men) was 'live and let live'. A resident of Maryland Street who 'did not agree' with antisemitism, but 'didn't like Jews' was typical of many East Enders' attitudes, showing both the strengths and weaknesses of toleration.[5]

On top of individual and gender issues, the Mass-Observation survey showed how antisemitism could vary from street to street. Poplar, an area which had given strong support to the British Brothers' League's anti-alien campaign at the turn of the century, still remained a hostile region, as did Bethnal Green. The threat of a Jewish 'invasion', or perceptions of Jewish entry into these areas remained strong and antagonistic. However, even in Bethnal Green the Mass-Observation team did not really find the blatant antisemitism that they had expected to find.[6] As a Jewish East Ender put it: 'those who *like* are as abnormal as those who *hate*, and the average absence of *liking* must not be interpreted as the presence of *disliking*.' In areas of Jewish concentration such as Stepney, social relations were good and the BUF was despised because it was 'trying to destroy the feeling of neighbourliness'. In other areas, such as Bethnal Green where Jews remained on the periphery of society, the BUF was generally tolerated. However, despite the higher tension, Bethnal Green Jews were largely left alone. A comment of a thirty year old Bethnal Green woman that the Jews have 'as much right to live in Bethnal Green as any other foreigner' shows the social distance between the two communities, but also the limitations to hostility.[7]

The success of the BUF in the East End in the middle 1930s showed the potential for organised antisemitism in the area. By 1939, however, the Mosleyites were in general retreat from the East End, having failed to permanently mobilise the economic and social tensions of this poorest of areas. The earlier crisis in the East End at the time of mass immigration had also showed the possibilities for antisemitic agitation. Would the Second World War, which had such a devasting impact on East London, bring another wave of antisemitism to the area?

The initial impact of the war was to bring some chaos to East End life. The population of Stepney, which had stood a fraction under 200,000 before September 1939, declined to 139,000 by the end of that month. The fall in numbers was largely attributable to the evacuation of children and women, and although many of these were to return by Christmas 1939, the general population of the borough was never to recover. Indeed by 1942 at 72,000 it was at a level of just over one third of the pre-war total. It seems doubtful that East End Jews left at a greater rate than their non-Jewish neighbours (despite the fascist rumours of a Jewish panic from the metropolis). Given that the Jewish population had been declining faster throughout the 1930s, a liberal estimate of the Jewish population until mid-1940 would be around 60,000, or 45% of the Stepney population. By the end of the war only 25,000 to 30,000 Jews would remain in what had been the heart of the immigrant quarter just half a century earlier.[8]

Whilst the war was to show the disorganisation and corruption of Stepney Borough Council, it also had a compensating effect. As the official government historian was to write: 'unsuspected, and hitherto unused resources of leadership were thrown up in the back streets of Stepney.' Amongst this grass roots movement were to be many Jews. Whilst the First World War had shown the general isolation of the Jewish population in the East End, the start of the Second showed that Jewish East Enders, as the *Jewish Chronicle* gladly pointed out, were 'playing their part'.[9] How then were Jews accepted in the local civil defence forces?

Corresponding to the variations in the concentration of Jews in the East End, some ARP stations were either totally Jewish, Gentile, or a mixture of both. The first category was shown by Wardens Post C125, Poplar. In its satirical organ *Ye Olde Belle and Rattle*, it made fun of its own ethnic make-up demanding 'Freedom for the Aryan minority in Burcham Street' – showing perhaps not only a strong self-confidence but also a high degree of acceptance from amongst the surrounding population. Jews were undoubtedly prominent in the civil defence forces of the East End. However, the estimate given by the Jewish Defence Committee, that they represented some 85% of all such workers was probably an exaggeration. Relations between Jewish and non-Jewish units appear to have been generally amicable, although there was also a competitive edge that could contain an element of antisemitism.[10]

In 'mixed' civil defence units in the East End relations were more complex. Jack Miller, an ARP man in Brick Lane, where 75% of the station was Jewish, stated that the atmosphere was 'excellent'. In White Horse Lane Auxiliary Ambulance Service Station 101, Bert Snow commented on the interesting variety of Jews and Christians, and the general harmony within the unit. Despite ideological differences between Jews and Catholics, antisemitism was 'an interesting and valuable topic for discussion at Station 101'. With the first Christmas of the war the Jewish members of the unit came forward to man the station so that their colleagues could celebrate the festival. Such co-operation was not unique to Station 101.[11]

Elsewhere such harmony was not so evident. Fascists within civil defence units often succeeded in creating antisemitic friction. Several were reported as saying that 'I shan't help Jews who get hurt, don't you worry', whilst a section of an AFS station was found to be spreading rumours about Jews and the white slave traffic. Within these units, antisemitism was not necessarily aimed at fellow Jewish workers. An antisemitic AFS man was reported as stating 'you'll never convince me that Yids ain't bastards. Mind you, I don't say there aren't exceptions, like young Solly here and Nat.' Nevertheless, in the same unit the Jewish instructor came in for a great deal of racial abuse. To further complicate the pattern, in another AFS unit in the docks, where 75% of the Station was Jewish, relations were generally good, although the Company Officer was a Mosleyite![12]

Up to the blitz, the relations between Jews and Gentiles in East End civil defence units were influenced by two generally conflicting factors. Firstly, the negative force of past prejudices against Jews (and also of Jews for Gentiles) carrying on into the war. Secondly, contact between the two elements within the stations which acted as an integrating force and to an extent counteracted hostilities. As a generalisation, the involvement of Jews in East End civil defence duties helped to improve relations *within* these units. However, up to the blitz, this integration was not a model for the East End as a whole. In the phoney war period, morale in Britain was probably at its lowest ebb. This was reflected in the East End where government reports indicated that although 'Mosley ha[d] lost substantial ground . . . anti-Jewish feeling appear[ed] to be growing.'[13]

The very presence of substantial numbers of Jews in the civil defence groups of the East End created tensions. A largely Jewish AFS unit in the dock area was greeted by onlookers by the shout 'Windy Yids', showing that the image of Jews as army dodgers in the earlier conflict had not been forgotten. The tensions of waiting for the war to begin 'properly' were reflected in other adverse ways as far as the Jewish community was concerned. With only 30,000 shelters provided for a population six times that size, the already tense relations between landlord and tenant in the East End were made even more fraught. By the first few months of the war, this conflict was assuming an antisemitic air as Jewish landlords were being selected for attack in their failure to provide air raid protection. Realising that this was an issue which the fascists could favourably exploit, the Stepney Tenants' Defence League (STDL) organised rent strikes until satisfactory air raid protection was provided. That such action was generally successful is shown by the rise in membership of the League to 11,000 in the summer of 1940. Attacking both Jewish and non-Jewish landlords, and being based on inter-community co-operation, the STDL helped to minimise the racial aspect of complaints about housing and shelters.[14]

Other economic based tensions threatened to endanger the relations between Jew and non-Jew in the East End. By the second month of the war there were also rumours of profiteering by Jewish shopkeepers. Although the STDL did its best to stop such abuses and the allegations, the idea that Jews were making financial gains from the war persisted to well after the blitz. The difficulties the war created for small shopkeepers were also exploited by fascists, despite the similar problems faced by Jewish traders.[15]

Up to August 1940, whilst the war had united the East End in some ways, most clearly shown by co-operation in civil defence units, it had not brought the Jewish and Gentile communities closer in general. Indeed, the petty tensions of the phoney war period helped to create more strain. Even on the spiritual side there were problems between Jewish and Christian clergymen. Clarence Kaye of the East London Tabernacle stated that such relations were 'decidedly frigid in the first part of 1940'. As one observer in the East End put it 'Antagonism between Jews and Christians was one of the evident but less admirable aspects of life.'[16]

In February and April 1940 Mass-Observation carried out two surveys on attitudes to Jews in the East End districts of Silvertown and Limehouse. In the former, an area of very few Jews, 31% were categorised as 'definitely antisemitic'. In the latter, where more Jews resided, 15% were placed in this category. Only 27% of Silvertown's population was pro-Jewish compared to 40% in Limehouse. Such figures give an indication of the fact that the level of antisemitism did not necessarily correspond to the proportion of Jews in the population of East London. However, the intensity of antisemitic feeling *was* higher in Limehouse, giving some credence to those that believed that the bombing of the East End, with its high Jewish population, was bound to lead to an antisemitic reaction. Would the blitz create a further deterioration of Jewish-Gentile relations as many people feared?[17]

How the East End Jews would behave under intensive bombing was a question that created widespread concern even at a governmental level. At the height of the invasion fear in May 1940, Home Secretary Anderson told the Cabinet that in the East End, with its large 'alien' population, 'it was of value to have some aliens in services like the Warden's in order to pacify and calm their fellow aliens in time of emergency'. Frank Lewey, mayor of Stepney in the blitz, believed that 'there was a pretty prevalent belief among numbers of Londoners that the Jews would panic if ever raiding became very bad'. Thus when the blitz began in earnest in early September 1940, there were both fears of how the 'volatile aliens' of the East End would behave, and also of the possibility of 'anti-Jewish riots' from their non-Jewish neighbours.[18]

By the end of September it was clear that these two pessimistic forecasts had been proved wrong. However, all was not sweetness and light. Of all the domestic episodes of the Second World War, memories of the blitz have become the most mythical. Part of this process of distortion has been to emphasise the cheerfulness and unity that was born out of the constant aerial bombardment. It actually began in the war itself and can be found in the contemporary descriptions of Jewish-Gentile relations in the East End. Leading the field in this matter was what could be called the Toynbee Hall approach, summarised by its warden, J. J. Mallon, in an article written in 1942. Mallon, talking of the blitz, referred to 'a common sympathy, a common humanity in which differences, including the differences between Jews and Gentiles were submerged and lost'. The reality was more complex.[19]

The pressure cooker effect of war on minority relations was to be seen at the clearest level, as far as the Anglo-Jewish community was concerned, in the intensive bombing of the East End in September and October 1940. The first raid was on 23 August 1940, but the real blitz did not start until 7 September. In this two week period tempers were frayed and the strain of waiting led onto some unpleasant antisemitic incidents. Quarrels broke out in queues for the shelters with the Jewish origins of anti-social offenders being unnecessarily brought into the arguments. On 7 September, the night that the suspense finally ended (now known as 'Black Saturday'), antisemitism did not disappear. One observer heard curses against Jews as the occasional Jewish shopkeeper left to escape the area in a taxi – 'Another Yid saving his skin'. The image of the cowardly selfish Jew running away or monopolising shelter space was to persist throughout the blitz.[20]

If antisemitism was to reach serious proportions in Britain, the conditions in Stepney in September 1940 were to offer its best chances of success. In London as a whole there were 76 continuous nights of raids after 'Black Saturday', with 27,500 bombs. From 7–14 September, 6,000 people in the capital were seriously injured or killed. Stepney was to bear the brunt of this attack, and well over a quarter of its population were left homeless for over a day. Conditions in the big shelters, such as the Tilbury warehouse, were appalling and added to the general misery. The blitz itself provided the potential for antisemitism and there is much evidence that the East End community was at times divided on racial lines. Late in September, an incident occurred outside a Stepney shelter where 500 people were waiting to get in. Two non-Jews of Cable Street, Mary Cini and Mary Owen picked fights with Jewish women claiming that 'You Jews are all the same pushing and shoving.' Despite the fact that the two women were deliberately trying to start trouble, the crowd took sides, the non-Jewish minority siding with Cini and Owen. Such incidents were not isolated; according to a JDC report there were countless other examples in the tubes and shelters.[21]

However, the Toynbee Hall-type analysis was also not without foundation. Despite Lord Haw-Haw's threats, German bombs could not distinguish between Jew and Gentile, and the obvious common suffering of both communities did make an impact on their inter-relationship. An AFS officer reported that the previous antisemitism of his unit 'failed to survive the first month of the blitz'. Those that had said they wouldn't help Jews 'learned sense at the fires in Whitechapel'. Within the shelters, close contact between Jew and non-Jew brought tensions, but it also proved that despite their differences, the two communities had much in common. By the end of the first month of bombing, the East End Jewish community had shown that it was as able 'to take it' as well as the non-Jewish population. Idiosyncrasies remained. One young Jewish warden, whose shelter had just been hit, 'suddenly burst into Yiddish' as he shouted instructions, showing that old world influences had not disappeared from the East End, even amongst the younger generation. Yet Jews and non-Jews were also discovering what they had in common. A conversation reported by Mass-Observation found that whilst Jews referred to bombs as 'somebody dropping potato ludkies', to the 'Cockney' it was the same, only with peanuts being dropped. Adversity could create harmony.[22]

Even with the notorious Tilbury shelter, where up to 15,000 found refuge from the bombs, no prolonged antisemitism occurred. Blanche Dugdale visited this shelter on 12 September 1940, when sanitary conditions and general organisation were at their worst. She reported that 'morale . . . was perfectly good and enquiry elicited no sign of antisemitism due to present conditions'. Indeed, one observer found that the race feeling at Tilbury was not so much Jew versus Gentile, but white against black, with the Indian contingent being the centre of attack from both the white communities. However, antisemitism was not absent, and it would appear that the awful environment was responsible for the occasional outbursts aimed at the Jewish shelterers, who were roughly half of Tilbury's residents.[23]

At first the only medical services at Tilbury were provided voluntarily by one Jewish doctor and three Jewish nurses, but as the blitz progressed conditions slowly improved. At the forefront of the movement to improve shelter conditions was the Stepney Communist Party. The Communist campaign for adequate air raid protection had begun in 1937 and it had continued throughout the war. Given the success of the Tenants' Defence Leagues, it is not surprising that the Stepney Communist Party set up committees in all main shelters aimed at protesting to the authorities about the conditions. These shelter committees operated on two levels, firstly aiming to improve the state of the shelters by organising food and entertainment, secondly by publicising the conditions of the East End to the outside world. In late September, the most famous incident of the latter policy occurred with the march of one hundred East Enders to the Savoy Hotel. Although the immediate impact of this protest was negligible owing to an all-clear, the message struck home with the Cabinet, and a Committee was set up to improve conditions and ensure such demonstrations did not recur.[24]

In this way, through the actions of the local Communist Party, (which was, according to its secretary, 'tempering the Party Line to the needs of the people'), anger at the conditions of the shelters was channelled not at an immediate scapegoat, but at its real cause – the authorities. The Communist Party was not alone in fighting for better conditions; the Settlement movements and the Churches were also active. However, within the last category there was tremendous hostility to the activities of the Communist Party, especially from the local Catholic Church. This antagonism, following earlier Catholic opposition to left-wing East End activities, was soon to be identified with antisemitism.[25]

Reflecting on the impact of the blitz, Tom Harrisson wrote that it 'confirmed hatred already felt by some, extended others, leaving many more barely touched'. The first two categories certainly apply to certain aspects of Catholic relations with Jews in the East End. In the *Catholic Herald* in October 1940, two priests launched an attack against Jewish Communist activities in the shelters, on the grounds that such activities were ultimately defeatist. Further articles accused the East End Jews of cowardice and low morality – the latter due to the fact that Jews were 'Oriental' and had thus a different attitude to sex! Jews, as has been pointed out, were prominent in the local Communist Party, but they by no means dominated the shelter committees. Indeed, such activities were consciously split between Jews and non-Jews. This was illustrated by the Savoy March where there were equal numbers of Jews and non-Jews, the Communist Party attempting to present an image of working class unity.[26]

This was only one aspect of Catholic-Jewish relations in the East End, for there was also a great deal of co-operation. Food, clothing, and buildings were shared, and religious leaders of both communities helped each other to organise services. The Mayor of Stepney, observing this positive side of the blitz, contrasted it to their previous relations when 'they had long been a byword in Stepney as mortal opponents'. However, the antagonism to what was seen as Jewish communism did not disappear from the Catholic community. As late as 1943, Father Groser – once of the Tenants' Defence League – reported that one priest, formally sympathetic to Jews, was becoming antisemitic due to their activities in the East End shelter committees. There were thus limits to the new understanding between Jewish and Christian communities.[27]

With the improvement in shelter conditions and with better all-round planning, Jewish-Gentile relations fell into a more settled pattern after the initial blitz. Visiting Liverpool Street, one of the biggest deep shelters in London, the Marquess of Donegall was impressed with the good organisation and co-operation within the shelter. At this point in early October 1940, Liverpool Street had its own Rabbi, although there were also common prayers delivered by all the clergy. To some this co-operation was not just a passing occurrence but 'was a promise. Here was humanity – internationally at peace. Mixed races, foreign languages, were not used as barriers. Here was a new brotherhood, and a common heart.' Such comments appear idealist given the concomitant misery that the blitz created, but it shows how far the East End was from the antisemitic riots that some had feared. Rather than panicking aliens, the bombings produced stories of Jewish bravery and courage. Of the first list of George Crosses, two out of thirteen were awarded to Jews. If Jews admitted to nervousness at the start of a raid, so did Gentile East Enders. Although antisemitism did not disappear, it never succeeded in being more than localised and aimed at individuals rather than at the whole of Jewry. Those who attempted to spread the rumour of the Jews' War were laughed down, and the aggression created by the shelter conditions was channelled towards the authorities and not against the Jewish population.[28]

After the intense bombing of September 1940, the next two months saw an overall decrease in air raids. Moreover the East End, which had borne the brunt of the initial blitz, was not seriously bombed again until July 1941. Whilst at the peak of the attacks 177,000 Londoners were sleeping underground, only 4% of them were using public shelters at the start of 1941. Life in the East End shelters, where 'it was one big happy family', proved to be a short-lived experience. To the novelist Bernard Kops, the blitz had completely destroyed the sense of community in the East End. Although the shelters created 'superficial friendliness', it was only temporary, and 'the world as I knew it had passed away'.[29]

Kops was not alone in sensing the general depression of the post-blitz Stepney. A report on the morale of the area in January 1941 pointed to the overall gloom of the people who were tired and miserable. Antisemitism persisted in the shelters: some of it encouraged by fascist elements; some of it brought on with persistent shelter problems and some of it simply part of a Saturday night exuberance. However, the *Jewish Chronicle* at the same time was able to report on an increased philosemitism due to the success of Jewish entertainers in the shelters. Indeed co-operation and harmony was a more regularly reported phenomenon in 1941 than the reverse. Even the community spirit that the destruction or damage of the vast majority of East End houses brought was not totally destroyed. Inter-faith reciprocity continued, and in April 1941 a Passover Service in the Tilbury shelter was marked by Jews singing religious songs and Gentiles English folk songs. The Yiddish poet A. N. Stencl was deeply impressed by 'the brotherhood of the people in Whitechapel in those days'. A similar service took place in Micky Davis's Shelter with the chairs supplied by the Convent of Mercy.[30]

Despite these touches of humanity, the East End was changing irreversibly. By the middle of 1942, Stepney, which at one point was home for a quarter of a million people, had only 72,000 residents and its once vibrant street life had disappeared. The borough was 'a ghost of its former self' and only in the shelters and clubs of the area was there any sense of community. A worker in Toynbee Hall recalls its rest home in Sussex where elderly Jewish and non-Jewish East Enders came to escape. Despite their strong ties to Stepney these people 'were sick of war and glad to get out'. With the hardships of the war and the general social isolation of East Enders, most people, as a Jewish Bethnal Green resident remembers, 'were too busy to worry about the Jews'.[31] However, old tensions mixed with new factors still persisted. These can be best illustrated by a study of Jewish-Gentile relations in the districts immediately to the north of original Jewish settlement area of the East End.

The war itself intensified two trends which had affected Jewish life in the East End from the 1920s. The first was the movement north to such areas as Hackney and Dalston. The second was a diversification of the Jewish occupational structure. The residential shift beyond the area of primary settlement had accelerated in the 1930s, with the receiving population tending to be highly antagonistic to the Jewish arrivals. Indeed in 1939, when the BUF's East End support was in decline, it was in areas of North East London such as Stoke Newington, Bethnal Green, Dalston and Hackney, where fascist gains were made. With the war it was in this northern part of the East End that violence and tension against the Jewish community was to be found at its highest level. It was here that fascist activity was at least tolerated, and at times actively supported.[32]

In the first few weeks of the war, Jewish shop windows were smashed in Bethnal Green and the pattern of violence continued throughout the war. In late May 1940, another such shop in the same area was destroyed, and the next month 'retaliations' were made against Jews for the fascist internments. Even with the blitz the violence continued, Jewish wardens being attacked in Hackney and Stoke Newington. When attempts at a fascist revival were made in the middle of the war, much of the evidence for it was found in Bethnal Green where Jewish shops were covered in the sign 'PJ'.[33] However, housing and employment remained the two most contentious issues with regard to general Jewish-Gentile relations in the area. It was over the former matter that the most serious violence occurred.

Just as the most extreme and concentrated attacks against the Asian population in 1980s Britain have occurred at the periphery of its settlement area in the East End, so it was with the Jews in North East London. In Hackney the Jewish population had been increasing considerably since the 1930s. Indeed, the MP for Hackney North estimated in May 1943 that 60% of his electorate were Jewish. He was convinced that there was 'ill-feeling between the Jews and the Christians in the constituency', and his analysis was proved to be correct by incidents in the area a few months later. A new housing complex, the Pembury Estate, was the scene of much antisemitic violence. Non-Jews were in a majority in the estate, and through the use of intimidation an element within the Gentile community wished to make the new housing area free of Jews. Jewish women were beaten up, children attacked going to school and slogans were painted on Jewish houses. Some Jewish residents did apply to leave, but generally incidents were not reported because the victims feared 'even worse manifestations of antisemitism'. Eventually the police and the local MP intervened and the outward manifestations of hostility subsided. Although an extreme case, the Pembury Estate issue showed the strength of local feeling against the Jewish movement into the area. Another report of a large flat complex in South Hackney, where 20% of the residents were Jewish, pointed out that none of the Jewish occupants had mezuzot on their door for fear of drawing attention to themselves.[34]

In analysing the course of this victimisation, the Jewish Defence Committee suggested that 'the *Hackney Gazette* has much to answer for'. It was not alone in attacking this right-wing local paper which even managed to attract the support of *The Patriot*. During the war the *Gazette* carried on a continuous campaign against Jewish gaming clubs, accused the Jews of cowardice in the blitz, supported discrimination against Jewish tenants, and generally opened its letter columns to those antagonistic to the local Jewish population.[35] Such a policy from this popular tri-weekly paper cannot have helped inter-community relations in North East London, but the antipathy that it played upon was not just of its own making. East End papers, like all such papers had to be sensitive to local opinion, and the *Hackney Gazette's* outlook is important in that it was a mirror of the community in which it served. However, other East End papers showed the need for taking account of changing circumstances in their localities. The *East London Advertiser*, which at the time of mass immigration was generally anti-alien, was now opposed to race hatred. The *East London Observer*, which had attacked aliens in the 1914–18 conflict, was now happy, in its editor's words, 'to put the Jewish point of view'. Finally the *East End News*, which had supported the British Brothers' League in the 1900s, was at worst neutral on Jewish matters in the Second World War.[36]

That the *Hackney Gazette* was isolated in its antipathy shows the local character of antisemitism in the East End. Yet even within its circulation area of North East London all was not hostile. Within the shelters, although at first there had been violence against Jewish officials, the blitz created a sense of camaraderie between Jew and Gentile – even in Hackney. The leader of its ARP commented that the differences between the communities 'had been wiped out by the war', and it would appear that the actions of Jewish ARP men did do something to dispel the latent antipathy towards Jews. The warden of Bethnal Green's Victoria Park trench shelter commented on the 'wonderful spirit' between all the different races and nationalities – this is an area which had at one point been a definite Jewish no-go area. A Jewish chemist of Hackney recalled that 'the only tiffs I heard during the blitz in the shelters were *between* Jewish people'.[37]

However, it was in the area of North East London in 1943 that the most serious single event of wartime domestic antisemitism occurred. On the evening of 3 March 1943, in a panic at the entrance of the Bethnal Green tube shelter, 173 people were killed. Although news was suppressed about the disaster, rumours soon spread across London about the causes of the tragedy, prevalent among which was the idea that it was due to a Jewish panic. Why this slander developed will be discussed at a later stage, but it will be necessary now to examine the Jewish East End aspects of the disaster.[38]

As the accident was in the East End it was assumed by many people that it took place in a Jewish area. This was in fact inaccurate for although there were streets or parts of roads such as Blythe and Teesdale Street (Jews'

Island) that were predominantly Jewish, and close to the tube station, the area was largely Gentile. Moreover, the Jewish population of the area was declining proportionally to the non-Jewish as the war progressed. Perhaps the most ironic aspect of the Jewish slander was the fact that the shelter was the heartland of Bethnal Green's BUF. Despite this qualification, there is still a small question mark concerning why the Jewish death toll in the shelter was so small. Only five Jews, or fewer than 3% of the total casualties, were killed in the tragedy, yet an estimate just after the war put the Jewish population of Bethnal Green at one tenth, or roughly three times higher than the shelter proportion.[39]

Why were so few Jews among the victims of the tragedy? According to one antisemite, it was because the shelter was already 'packed full of Jews a couple of hours before the disaster'. The reality was more complex. As early as the start of the blitz in 1940, there had been reports of antisemitism in the Bethnal Green tube, and it would appear that 'the unpleasantness' that the Jews 'were always subject to' put many off using the shelter. Fascist bullying, or the fear of intimidation made many Jews prefer the Liverpool Street shelter, which although further away, was more Jewish orientated. The few Jews that used the shelter at Bethnal Green, such as the Kops family, felt 'strangers in a strange world'.[40]

If there was antisemitism associated with the shelter before the disaster, then the same cannot be said of the locality after the tragedy. Whilst the rumours that it was a 'Jewish panic' spread across all parts of London, this was not true of Bethnal Green, where according to Home Intelligence 'there is full knowledge that any such statement is untrue'. One or two individuals in the area attempted to spread rumours against the Jews, but local opinion in the East End realised the absurdity of such lies. More credence was given to the idea that the disaster was instigated by fascists. Generally, however, in Bethnal Green the grievances and blame were directed towards the local Council, which was regarded as having been negligent over the safety aspects of the shelter. In Stepney an awareness of the small Jewish population of Bethnal Green also acted as a barrier to the success of antisemitic rumours, and one had to go to the outlying areas of the East End, such as West Ham to find any belief in the 'Jewish panic' libel. This again confirms the impression that it was areas on the edge of the concentrated Jewish population where prejudice was most profound – a clergyman in West Ham the year after the disaster commented that in his parish 'the Jew is anathema'.[41]

The Jewish question was one of popular discussion in wartime Britain, and the Bethnal Green disaster simply underlined how 'Jew-conscious' the public had become. Was the Jewish question of much concern in the East End in the Second World War? In late 1939 a public meeting in Stepney on this issue resulted in a lively response, with many non-Jewish East Enders giving 'petty and malicious' reasons for the existence of antisemitism in the locality. At Warden's Post 13, just outside Whitechapel, the four most popular issues discussed were racing, the war, religion and finally antisemitism. Moreover, in April 1943, a reporter in the dock area of Stepney commented that 'several people complained to me, unprompted about Jews'. However, Jews or the Jewish question was not the burning issue in the war that might have been expected from this area with such a long tradition of hostility. The new warden of Bethnal Green's Oxford House was surprised how few manifestations of antisemitism there were in the area, considering its previous Mosleyite success. Generally speaking, apart from the start of the blitz, the non-Jewish East Ender was too busy surviving to worry too much about the Jew in his midst. Only when faced in intimate contact would the Jewish issue come to the fore, and as has been noted with the shelters and the local civil defence, such mixing could often be beneficial.[42]

In one area however there was potential for friction. Particularly in Stepney, but also to a lesser extent in the neighbouring areas, Jews were prominent as shop owners. In a war where there was strict rationing, especially in food, shopkeepers could quickly become unpopular figures. As early as the third week of the war the *Jewish Chronicle* was reporting that a Jewish food shop in Stepney was creating antagonism amongst both communities by its profiteering. Indeed, throughout the war there was evidence of East End hostility to Jewish shopowners who exploited the shortages for their own financial ends. The image of the East End Jewish black marketeer was soon to replace that of the simple profiteer, and there was strong antagonism to those who were seen to have 'got rich' with the conflict. Nevertheless, all was not negative in this respect. Firstly, although some people were hostile to the small trader, there was also sympathy to the plight of the 'little man' in his fight for survival against the big shopping chains. Representative of this sympathy was a petition signed by all the inhabitants of College Buildings in Whitechapel (half of whom were non-Jewish) when three local Jewish shopkeepers were interned in June 1940. All three were old residents of the area who had never been naturalised, and their internment caused 'regret, indignation and sorrow' from their neighbours. Secondly, many East Enders realised that not only Jews were to blame for the local rackets. The mayor of Stepney, Councillor Pritchard, defended the Jewish traders. He believed that considering their prominence in the locality, their proportion of offenders was surprisingly low. Finally the black market also served to meet a demand, and in this respect Jewish offenders were offering a service. Indeed one resident was hostile only to West End Jews who were said to spoil the local illicit market![43]

In economic terms the East End was in a state of turmoil in the Second World War, and it was thus not only the black market that created a potential financial conflict between Jews and non-Jews. The heavy bombing and the acute shortage of male labour acted as a catalyst to trends which had been in motion since the late 1920s. Two major features were thus outlined in the war. Firstly, there was a move away from Stepney by local industry, either to North London or as far away as the Home Counties. Secondly, industries such as tailoring were becoming less specifically Jewish. The new demands of war, and the need for any sort of labour, thrust Jewish and non-Jewish workers together in areas that had previously been preserves of either section of the community. A Toynbee Hall report found that some employers were not happy about using Jewish workers, fearing them to be either communistic or lazy. One East End firm actually refused to employ Jews due to the hostility of its staff. This was not the whole picture however, for elsewhere there was satisfaction. Several businesses actually decided that they would stay in Stepney because of the Jewish labour supply. Within the workforce, although there were reports of inter-ethnic conflict, co-operation in the desire to help the war effort would seem to have been more common.[44]

Harmony was also present within the Borough Council which had been the battleground of earlier Irish-Jewish clashes. At the end of December 1942, a special meeting was arranged in sympathy with the Jews of Europe, with the Council passing a resolution asking the government to do all that was possible to help the persecuted. Several months later an extraordinary meeting was held to counter 'antisemitic activities' in the borough, with the government being asked to pass legislation to make antisemitism illegal. Also in November 1943, the Council unanimously denounced the government's action in releasing Mosley. Although it was usually (left-wing) Jewish councillors that brought these issues into consideration, it was a sign of the new co-operation that all the Council acted sympathetically to them. There were still signs of conflict, such as unfair accusations that the Jews of Stepney were not pulling their weight in fire watching duties, but generally such squabbling was put aside for the duration of the war.[45]

Typical also of this co-operation were the clubs and settlements of the East End. With a reputation of elitism and of being patronising, the war helped bring these 'outside' organisations more fully into East End society. The settlements became prominent in the war, giving services in and after the blitz. They also offered entertainment in an area that was desperately short of social amenities. Yet even the most famous of these, Toynbee Hall had only a very localised appeal and it is easy to overestimate their importance. However, within Toynbee and the Bernhard Baron settlement there is little doubt that Jews and Gentiles mixed freely and that social relations were excellent. One East End Jew, Alexander Hartog, remembers that the atmosphere at Toynbee in the war 'was truly magical'. Even the Jewish youth clubs were practising a policy of integration, and in such clubs as the Hackney Jewish, Oxford and St George and Cambridge Jewish it was reported that 'Christian boys were mixing harmoniously with Jewish boys'.[46] Such fraternity was also evident in the slightly less establishment world of Stepney Communist Party. A document of 1944 summarised its approach – 'Jew and Gentile Together' – aimed at 'Tommy or Issy, Sarah or Jane'. Within the local Party there was 'great comradeship' according to its Secretary, and 'no barriers' either politically or socially. Although a specific attempt was aimed at winning over the Jewish electorate, Phil Piratin's Communist victory at Mile End in the 1945 election was also based on a joint communal campaign.[47]

How typical was the 'Toynbee' or Communist Party model in regard to the integration of Jews into East End society? There is no doubt that both the settlements and the Stepney Communists were enjoying much popularity by the end of the war, the latter having one thousand members by 1945. However the free social mixing of these institutions was probably in advance of its time, even if the war had removed some social barriers. Jews and Gentiles were in closer proximity at work and in the shelters, but the home largely remained an ethnic preserve. An incident in the Troxy Cinema in Stepney at the close of 1944 perhaps emphasises the need for caution with regard to evaluating the positive integrative force of the war. At the showing of Louis Golding's *Mr Emmanuel*, a disturbance developed where elements of the non-Jewish section of the audience shouted approval at the scenes of Nazi persecution of Jews. Like earlier cinema scuffles in the 1930s, and like incidents in the shelters four years earlier, the audience divided and fought along Jewish-Gentile lines.[48]

This qualification is just one of many needed to show the difficulties in weighing the impact of the war on communal relations in the East End. If, as has been suggested, there were many 'East Ends' in a geographical sense, it was true also of its institutions. A perspective from a Gentile, Toynbee, Communist, religious, trade unionist, Zionist or whatever point of view would produce different results. Each one (or more often, more than one) had its own bearing on the individual. Yet the task of the historian is to generalise, and in the final analysis the verdict has to be that the war pushed Jews and non-Jews in the East End closer together – more than it pulled them apart. If it is slightly ironic that it was German bombs that were largely responsible for this, it must be remembered that the humour of the situation is largely lost due to the simultaneous physical destruction of the East End. The sense of community in the area was a war phenomenon and was paid for both in human terms as well as in the damage to property. Death remained a feature of East End life right until the end of war – the last V2 rocket fell in Stepney in March 1945 killing 130 people, 120 of whom were Jewish.[49] The overall harmony of Jewish-Gentile relations in the area during the Second World War must thus be seen as temporary, for after 1945 the Jewish East End had largely ceased to exist.[50]

From this localised study of concentrated ethnic relations it is now necessary to look at a parallel development, one that was spread across the whole of Britain.

Jewish evacuees in the Second World War

By 3 September 1939, 3·5 million people were either officially or privately evacuated from their homes in Britain. Although evacuee numbers were never to reach this level again – either in the blitz of autumn 1940 or in the flying bomb raids of 1944 – as a social experiment in mixing people of different class and background, evacuating cannot be regarded as a successful exercise. Despite long term planning and the experience gained from the evacuation around the Munich Crisis, government and local authorities were not prepared to deal with the issue of selecting the right evacuees for the right areas – the priority was to shift the population in bulk. The experience of Jewish evacuation in the war must therefore not be seen as an isolated phenomenon, for although it created unique problems, it was also part of a troubled social dislocation in Britain.[51]

The idea that the Jewish population would panic out of the cities at the threat of war had been rehearsed in the 1938 Crisis. The BUF had claimed that the Jews had fled London like 'a flowing river of grey slime'. With the start of the real conflict the accusation revived. The imputation was neither limited to the capital nor was it only made by extremists. In the north of England, Lake Windermere was known locally as 'the Sea of Galilee' and in Wales, Llandudno as 'Jerusalem by the Sea'. Mass-Observation and other sources show that the image of the timid Jew, running to a safe billet, was quite widespread among the British people.[52] However, taken in aggregate terms, there is no evidence that Jewish evacuees proportionally outnumbered their Gentile equivalents. Indeed, in the East End there was evidence that the reverse was true. As more than one observer noted, there was something of a contradiction in arguing that London Jews crowded not only the shelters but also the safe seaside zones. Yet, looking at the question qualitatively, it is true that there was a concentration of Jews in the Home Counties, the Lake District, and the West Coast of England. Even if Jews did not dominate these areas, their presence in fairly large numbers made them conspicuous.[53]

However, although Jewish evacuees may have been at times conspicuous, this does not imply that antisemitism against them was therefore 'well-earned'. As will be stressed shortly, Jews had often never been seen before in evacuation areas, and thus they became even more prominent than they would have been as mere evacuees. Moreover, as the latter themselves were strangers, it was easy to label all evacuees as Jews, or at least to overestimate the proportion of Jews in the new arrivals. This explains why as Arthur Marwick has suggested 'the words "evacuees" and "Jews" were used interchangeably'. Such generalisations hid the complexity of evacuation experiences which varied not only over time – September 1939, September 1940 and summer 1944 representing three separate developments – but also over locality, often on a village to village basis. It was also an intensely personal experience, so much depending on the individual. In London alone 14,000 Jewish children were evacuated in September 1939.[54] To make sense of so many individual histories it will be necessary to concentrate on several areas of Jewish evacuation – the Home Counties (especially Bedfordshire and Oxfordshire), East Anglia and the coastal resorts. At the same time, a dynamic approach will be maintained, for although evacuation was a short-lived temporary development, it was also subject to constant change.

The first evacuation of September 1939 was not a success either in social or governmental terms. By the New Year, 66% of the evacuees had returned to London, and the country as a whole was reverberating with horror stories about the state of the evacuees. The Jewish community itself was fully aware of the difficulties that could follow with 'the introduction [of] the Jewish problem into many areas in which no Jews had been seen before'. The *Jewish Chronicle* warned its readers to behave if they were away and the community was prepared for outbursts of rural antisemitism. Such fears were exaggerated, for although there was at times strong feeling against the Jewish evacuees, it rarely broke into violence.[55]

The initial evacuation did create tensions that were specifically linked to the new Jewish arrivals. At a farcical level, rumours were heard in the Home Counties concerning Jewish prostitutes seducing the innocent village bumpkins of Hertfordshire, or of Jewish pawnbrokers ruining the local inhabitants. Neither had any foundation. Such exotic stories were not as common as other misconceptions about Jews which, for a while, created a barrier between host and evacuee. In Chatteris, Cambridgeshire, 700 evacuees swelled the normal population of 5,000, 85% of the new arrivals being Jewish East Enders. There were initial conflicts due to the difference in habits between town and country dwellers, and also class problems, even between the agricultural and industrial poor. On top of this, however, the strangeness of the previously unknown Jews strengthened the division between newcomer and host. However, by November 1939 most of the initial difficulties had been ironed out. In Shefford, Bedfordshire another large influx of Jews, this time schoolchildren, was being experienced as this became the new location of the Jewish Secondary School for the duration of the war. Over 500 children were billeted in and around this village, the potential for conflict being increased by the fact that most of the children were German refugees. As in Chatteris, the pattern was one of initial tension, Shefford being totally unprepared for this Jewish invasion. Jews had been seen previously either in biblical terms or less complementarily as 'mean merchants', or even occasionally in demonic terms with horns on their foreheads. The presence of these well-behaved schoolchildren overcame some of the more bizarre beliefs about Jews, but their strict orthodoxy over ritual created much misunderstanding. However, with tact on the side of the school and communal organisers, a regular and peaceful pattern was soon established in this remote village.[56]

Elsewhere this initial harmony was missing. In Little Eversden, Cambridgeshire, a Mass-Observer commented that its North East London Jewish evacuees were generally 'unloved', and that the locals were happy when they started to disperse in October 1939. If the evacuation of the Jewish Secondary School turned out to be a model of success and integration, then its rival Jews' Free School had a disastrous evacuation experience. One refugee worker remembers the influx of these East End schoolchildren 'as a real cross to bear'. Ely in Cambridgeshire was the setting for the Free School's evacuation, and whereas organisation had been strong in Shefford, it fell apart in this area of East Anglia. The strong adherence to orthodoxy in the former school broke down in the latter, whose pupils were more rebellious concerning tradition. With a lack of mediators on the Jewish side, local animosity grew unabated and many children, after an unhappy few months, returned to the East End, or to other areas.[57]

In general, the East Anglian counties seemed less tolerant of the Jewish evacuees than did those in the Home Counties such as Bedfordshire. The better organisation prevailing in the latter explains some of the discrepancy in treatment, although there is evidence that Norfolk, Suffolk and Cambridgeshire suffered more intensely from xenophobia and insularity than most rural areas. R. M. Titmuss in his official war history felt it necessary to comment that 'Jewish customs were unknown and misunderstood in the rural areas of East Anglia, long settled in their habits and hostile to "foreigners" though they might only be strangers from a neighbouring county.' A farmer in a village near Ipswich epitomised this parochial attitude, telling a Jewish East Ender, 'London? I've been there once.' One East Anglian observer felt that the Jewish evacuees who came to her village at the start of the war were 'as completely Oriental and foreign to our northern green as so many exotic black parrots'. In another such village, the novelist Hugh Massingham commented that the Jewish evacuees were being blamed for the black market and the housing shortage as well as being enemy agents! Similarly, in a Norfolk village it was the Jewishness of the evacuees that was objected to when several newcomers allegedly misbehaved. Writing in January 1940, the pacifist J. M. Murry believed a few trivial incidents involving the evacuees had led to 'the rumblings of antisemitism' in the wilds of Norfolk.[58]

If Ely was typical of the strained relations between Jewish evacuees and hosts in East Anglia, then the small town of Bedford was an example of the relative harmony in the Home Counties. Bedford's pre-war Jewish population was limited to one or two isolated families, and thus the arrival of fifty-five Jewish refugee children and a London secondary school that was over 20% Jewish, could well have created problems. However, as in Shefford, integration was aided by Jewish organisers, in the case of Bedford it being Mr and Mrs Harris. They were able to establish close contact with the local population and to set up a Jewish evacuation centre, Harris House. In early 1940, the local population provided facilities for Passover and Arnold Harris confided to his diary 'the "goyim" are indeed exceptionally accommodating. I marvel at their spontaneity to help us in all our good work'. The success of the Bedford experience thus owed much to the Harrises; as one of his charges later commented: 'it is impossible to overestimate their importance'. However other factors were important. Compared to Ely, the Jewish evacuees were much smaller in number and were generally better behaved than their Jews' Free School contemporaries. Polite and disciplined, they made ideal evacuees. On the host side, several ex-Bedford evacuees have commented on the nonconformist tradition in Bedford which they felt helped the acceptance of the Jewish arrivals. This certainly contrasts with the more narrow minded view of Jews in East Anglia.[59]

Bedfordshire and East Anglia can thus be seen as ideal types representing positive and negative features of the initial evacuation. However, it is necessary to repeat that evacuation was a very personal experience. One Jewish schoolgirl had a miserable time being shifted from billet to billet in Bedford, whilst other Jewish schoolchildren had the times of their lives in East Anglia. Bearing in mind these complicating factors concerning generalisations, what was the overall impact of the phoney war Jewish evacuation?[60]

The first point to note is that it is difficult to avoid noticing the shock aspect of the Jewish influx. Stories about Jews being asked about their horns abound – an indication of the lack of knowledge of the rural population as far as Jewish matters were concerned, in this pre-mass-television age. The confusion created by the fact that Jews were actually human quickly subsided, but other stereotypes were more persistent. The image of Jews as purely Biblical characters was as strong, as the writer Chaim Bermant found out. As a Glaswegian refugee in Dumfriesshire, Bermant remembers being regarded 'with something like awe, as if I was a close relative of Jesus Christ'. Whereas he was very religious, his fellow Jewish refugee was totally lax as far as observation of Jewish diet and other rituals was concerned. This created confusion, for as Bermant suggested 'I at least seemed to conform . . . to what they knew of the Jew from their reading, but they were never quite sure what to make of him.'[61]

If some of the rural population were discovering that the Jews had an absence of horns, others were finding out that many were just normal people, who often did not care for any Jewish ritual. Many friendships developed between evacuee and host where the Jewish origin of the former was simply unimportant – for either side. Whether this development broke down any latent prejudices is debatable. Respect for the individual or the family did not necessarily mean a liking for their Jewishness. Nevertheless, it is highly unlikely that such intimate harmonious mixing acted as a negative force on the ways in which Gentiles viewed Jews as a whole.[62]

What happened when Jewish evacuees became more prominent through a desire to be religiously observant? In both Shefford and Bedford, the local inhabitants definitely took a pride in the way their religious orthodox children adhered to tradition, to the extent of chastising them when they appeared to be slackening in their ritual. Yet in both these centres, the Jewish community helped to provide kosher meat and made sure that the hosts had little need to worry over the religious requirements of their guests. There was at least respect for the religious beliefs of the children in both Bedford and Shefford, and cases of attempted proselytisation were very rare. In the case of Chaim Bermant and others, the respect for Jews was even stronger, based on a fervent religious philosemitism. He remembers that the practising Christians, who were his hosts, 'were grimly determined to keep me Jewish'.[63]

However outside the minority cases of religious philosemitism, or where the Jewish community could keep a close eye on its children or offer financial help to the billets, the story was less happy. Food was the obvious source of conflict. Some Jewish evacuees were happy to be unleashed from the restrictions that Judaism created on their eating habits, but others dreaded the prospect of having to consume forbidden meat. To some children, being forced to eat rabbit or pork was a greater grievance than any physical maltreatment, and consequently many Jewish children had a totally miserable evacuation experience. Often the price of being accepted into a family was to abandon Jewish ritual and to join the Sunday school. There could thus be a strange ambivalence; a liking or even a loving of a Jewish evacuee child but an antipathy to Jews as a group. Lily Joseph, who was billeted in Welwyn Garden City, was subjected to antisemitic jokes every mealtime, yet the couple she was billeted with were desperate to adopt her. Forced proselytisation was rarer than Jewish children joining the Church of their own desire. Despite this, the orthodox Jewish community was involved in some melodramatic incidents, kidnapping Jewish children who were seen to be at risk in Christian homes.[64]

Therefore on purely religious grounds, the Jewishness of the evacuees did create its own problems, though occasionally it could produce positive results. Such problems as there were could usually be ironed out, either by tact and understanding, or by moving billet. There were, however, other sources of conflict. Some of these were because Jewish evacuees were largely urban and usually poor. In this though, the Jewish evacuees were not unique, for the whole evacuation experience was based on a city-country cultural clash. This universal aspect of evacuation could in fact work to the benefit of the Jewish community, for although the East End Jews were poor and dirty by middle class standards, they were probably less so than their Cockney neighbours. In Egham, Surrey, 80% of the evacuees were Jewish East Enders (hence its nickname Eghamstein), yet

Jewish schoolchildren were often preferred because they were better spoken and cleaner than their Christian counterparts. As the historian Norman Longmate has stated (although exaggerating slightly): 'the evidence is unanimous that Roman Catholic evacuees were by far the dirtiest, the most ragged, and since they tended to come in large family groups, the hardest to place . . . Jewish evacuees, by contrast, caused little trouble.'[65]

Generally speaking, in the first year of evacuation the city-country clash was a more powerful source of conflict than the Jewish-Gentile one, with the former tending to subsume the latter. Chaim Bermant, when beaten up by local bullies in Annan, was delighted in the fact that his injuries 'were not incurred from the fact that I was Jewish, but that I was a town boy, a Glaswegian'. Similarly the Hallgartens, evacuated to Kings Langley in Buckinghamshire, found that the locals did not like them at all: 'it was not that we were Germans, and it was not that we were Jewish. It was that we came from London.' However, at times a degree of antisemitism was brought into the conflict. A young Jewish girl, evacuated into a South Wales village, found herself on the side of the evacuee when they were attacked by the locals, but there were also occasions 'when both groups united to attack me as a rotten Jew'. Antisemitism from fellow evacuees was also not an uncommon experience.[66]

The first evacuation was not a success in national terms, and in that sense the Jewish experience mirrored that of the country as a whole. Organisation was often found wanting, the sheer scale of the operation proving to be a formidable barrier. However, where some stability was achieved, especially in the case of child evacuees, it was not a total disaster as far as the Jewish community was concerned. Good relations and contacts were gradually built up, and problems such as those associated with food were overcome. It was the short-term contact between host and evacuee that was the most fertile ground for antisemitism. It was for this reason that there was more antagonism towards Jewish adults, who either as visitors to their children, or as part-time evacuees, attracted much hostility.[67] It was in the seaside areas such as Brighton, Bournemouth, Blackpool and Llandudno, or in safe zones such as the Peak District, the Lake District or the West Country, that antagonism to Jewish evacuees was most pronounced *throughout* the war. This antipathy was of a totally different variety from that which confronted East End Jewish evacuees, for it was based not on opposition to their poverty, but to their alleged opulence, ostentation, vulgarity and cowardice. Summarising this approach, the novelist Andrew Soutar, wrote to the *Western Morning News* complaining about Jews paying extortionate rates in hotels, buying up property and keeping 'their heads and civilian suits, while all about them are losing theirs'.[68] Although not all these nouveau-riche Jews were a figment of Soutar's literary imagination, the distortion and prejudice inherent in his letter was typical of the misunderstandings and antipathy that were felt in holiday areas against Jewish evacuees. Unfair accusations that the Jews were not pulling their weight in war charities in both Torquay and Blackpool, and the policy of refusing Jewish guests in Bournemouth and Margate hotels were just a few of the symptoms of a wider antisemitic undertone in the coastal resorts of Britain.[69] There were thus two levels of antagonism to Jewish evacuees that had emerged by the summer of 1940; firstly against the poor 'Whitechapel' type Jew and secondly against the alleged ostentatious 'Golders Green' nouveau-riche Jew.

Taken as a whole, negative reactions to Jewish evacuees by no means predominated in the first evacuation. However, the second dispersal at the time of the blitz was to bring into greater prominence both rich Jew and poor Jew antisemitism. With the military crisis of the summer of 1940, the increased threat of aerial bombardment led to a return to the evacuation areas, but this movement did not become a flood until the actual bombing began. However, only 500,000 people left London in September 1940 which was much less than in the original evacuation at the start of the war. In the period from September 1940 to May 1941 there were only 181,000 official evacuees. Taken as a whole, the blitz evacuation was more successful than the earlier attempts. Organisers had gained experience and both the host and evacuee had learned to be tolerant of each other. However, as far as Jewish evacuees were concerned the reverse appeared to be true. In order to explain this paradox, one that generally did *not* operate in the first evacuation, the experience in Oxfordshire and the Home Counties will be examined.[70]

At the height of the blitz, the Chief Constable of Buckinghamshire reported that the sight of London refugees had 'aroused considerable indignation and pity'. Paradoxically, at the same time the *Jewish Chronicle* was reporting that whilst antisemitism was on the decline in the East End, it was rising in the Home Counties.[71] Were then the Jewish evacuees bringing antisemitism with them, as the fascists liked to claim, or were the Jewish newcomers simply fulfilling their age-old role as scapegoats?

A strong case for the latter was made by Tom Harrisson who believed that in September 1939 hosts tended to put the blame on all evacuees. With the obvious distress caused by the blitz, the average evacuee was no longer a permissible target to attack for the difficulties that such large population influxes inevitably created. A more specific outlet was needed and thus Jewish evacuees were blamed collectively for any problems that arose. Harrisson's model is useful in that it explains the report by Home Intelligence, that antisemitic feeling against evacuees 'was out of all proportion to the Jews arousing it'.[72] It does, however, oversimplify the complexity of the issue, for in areas like Oxfordshire, the Jewish presence *was* significant.

The intensity of the blitz in London, and particularly in the East End, led on to a spontaneous unofficial evacuation in September 1940. On 15 September 1940 alone, 25,000 such evacuees left for Berkshire, Buckinghamshire and Oxfordshire. The latter county, and particularly its major town, was the centre of this movement and by the middle of September up to 20,000 evacuees had arrived in Oxford. Many of these were East Enders, half of whom were probably Jewish.[73] As most of the arrivals were unofficial evacuees, Oxford became chaotic, its former sleepy existence transformed into a confused state with a dire shortage of accommodation. This problem spread to the small villages such as Chipping Norton and Woodstock. In some of the latter, the local population blamed the lack of room available on the Jewish evacuees. Feeling was strong, a resident of Banford commenting 'round here "East End Jews" are words of abuse'. It was not only poorer Jews who were the subject of hostility. In Oxford, the luxurious Randolph hotel had guests, who were, according to its receptionist, 'unfortunately Jews'. Indeed the editor of the *Oxford Times* felt that the antagonism from the local population was not aimed at the poorer Jewish evacuees, but at 'the very large numbers of the wealthy, purse-proud and pushful type'. Sometimes all Jewish evacuees were lumped together and attacked because of their 'extraordinary bad manners – noisy, aggressive, loud and tactless'.[74]

There is no evidence that Jewish evacuees, even rich Jewish evacuees, were any more vulgar than non-Jewish evacuees. However, those that did fit the nouveau-riche image soon came to typify the whole community. One local Mass-Observer tried to analyse her own hostility to the new arrivals. She admitted that she could not 'help feeling anger at well-dressed Jews and Jewesses' in her district, stating that 'if they weren't Jews I shouldn't notice them' and that there were plenty of non-Jewish evacuees whom she ignored. In this process of distortion, the term evacuee and Jew could be used interchangeably, and Jews were blamed for all problems that evacuation had caused. However one should not ignore the genuine conflict that could exist between the host and the Jewish evacuee.

Many of the latter found the countryside backward and tedious, and were not afraid to air their complaints. In this they did not differ dramatically from non-Jewish town evacuees. In Oxfordshire, the higher concentration of London evacuees, added to the larger Jewish presence than in equivalent evacuation areas, gave the potential for a stronger local antisemitic feeling. In other Home County areas, where conditions were generally better, and Jews less prominent as evacuees, relations were more congenial, and hostility aimed more at the evacuees as a whole.[75]

The Jewish evacuation experience by the end of 1940 had thus created three problem areas in a geographical sense – seaside and resort regions as a whole, East Anglia and Oxfordshire. However, even in these problem spots, the dynamic nature of evacuation needs to be taken into account again. Throughout 1941, there was a general improvement in Jewish-Gentile relations in evacuation areas. Again there was a settling in period, the most unhappy evacuees went home and as the blitz lessened in its intensity, more people returned. By February 1941, Mass-Observation noted that only a minority of both the hosts and evacuees continued to hold grievances, which were no longer part of mainstream evacuation life. As part of this improvement in relations, antisemitism had subsided.[76]

In general, if host and guest could get through the initial traumatic period, then their relationship would, in the words of a Jewish evacuee to Berkhamsted, 'mellow'. Certain areas might have a sudden rash of antisemitism if there was a new influx of Jewish arrivals, but as 1941 progressed these became rarer. In the problem areas such as East Anglia and Oxford, a similar pattern was being followed. The Jewish community would gradually set up evacuation centres and difficulties would be ironed out. In East Anglia, a report in 1944 suggested that the earlier problems had been settled and that Jewish-Gentile relations were now 'natural and friendly'.[77] Where there was conflict it tended to be on specific questions, such as food or business matters. As regards the former, the problem of evacuees having much time and little to do could create tension. Jewish evacuees were particularly eager to queue early for such kosher commodities as fish, and thus it was often reported that queues were the sources and the scene of antisemitism. Jewish evacuees attempting to set up businesses also created local antagonism, usually based on exaggerated fears. However, although antisemitic incidents were reported in evacuation areas in the years from 1941–3, they were sporadic and should not overshadow the general harmony that existed in the small towns and countryside.[78]

In 1944 the final stage in evacuation occurred. The gradual and near complete return to the cities was reversed as over a million Londoners sought refuge from the macabre threat of the flying bombs. The reactions to Jewish evacuees the third time round is interesting and it generally emphasises the degree of integration that had taken place by 1944. Mass-Observation believed it to be the most successful of the evacuations. Moreover, unlike the 1940 blitz period, the Jewish experience seems to fit into this wider pattern. Jewish representatives stated that there were very few problems in 1944, giving the reason that 'since 1940 there are few areas in Great Britain which are not now accustomed to have Jews as residents and neighbours'.[79] There were minor reports of tensions, and regional variety – Northampton, Nottingham and Luton had good relations, despite the doubling of their Jewish population, whilst Leicester was regarded as being fairly antisemitic. The Board of Deputies believed that the latter was due to past fascist activities, which had made the local population hostile, whereas a town like Luton welcomed Jewish evacuees, who could provide business and jobs. The amount of Jewish public relations work was also much higher in Luton than in Leicester.[80]

Another negative aspect of a generally bright picture was the continuing hostility to Jews in holiday areas. Some improvement in attitudes had occurred since the 1940 blitz. For example, surveys from Blackpool and the Lake District reported no problems in districts which had been bitterly hostile. In Brighton, local antagonism continued with rumours that Jews were monopolising all available goods, local housing, petrol and even the cinemas. Across the coast in Devon, a member of the Torquay District Council reported 'a general increase in feeling against Jews', an analysis shared by a Mass-Observer. It must be suggested that these Southern resorts, within easy reach of London, were subject to virulent antisemitism against evacuees because, unlike many rural evacuation areas, the Jewish presence in these coast towns was unsettled, and thus there was less time for good relationships to be built up. With the Jewish population in these resorts constantly changing, there was more room for misunderstandings about the evacuees. Another factor explaining Brighton's reaction to Jewish evacuees, was the existence of an antisemitic tradition in the town, fostered as in Leicester by the BUF.[81]

The Brightons, Oxfords, Torquays and Leicesters must not disguise the national trend, which by 1944 was one of good integration of Jewish evacuees into the reception areas. In the last months of the war, the population returned once again to its own homes, yet by then strong bonds had been formed by many Jewish evacuees with their hosts. In Shefford, many tears were shed when the refugee children finally returned to London in the summer 1945, a far cry from the hostile response they had received at the outbreak of war. Often evacuee and host would remain lifelong friends – a sign of some of the positive results of Jewish evacuation. Was this typical of the overall impact of Jewish evacuation, and how did evacuation change people's perceptions of Jews?[82]

Drawing a balance sheet of Jewish-Gentile relations is always difficult and also a dangerous pursuit. Generalising even about an area or a town is hard enough, given the diversity of human responses. Applying this on a national scale becomes near impossible. One cannot subtract the antagonism of a Brighton from the harmony of a Shefford and come up with a final net result. Nevertheless, a Board of Deputies summary of evacuation suggested that although it had created some problems, it had also 'demonstrated that the Jew is very much the same as his Christian neighbour'. This was a basically sound analysis, especially in areas where locals previously 'possessed thoughts that the Jew was born to do harm only'. However, several qualifications need to be made to this. Firstly, good relations often depended on a degree of permanence of the Jewish arrivals, and where the Jewish numbers were great, good organisation was also important. In areas such as Oxfordshire where neither factor really operated, a long standing grievance against the evacuees could result. Also, as children were more likely to stay in one place than adults, Jewish youngsters were often better received than their parents. Secondly, close and harmonious relations did not necessarily change overall attitudes to the Jewish people. With the Jewish Secondary School in Bedfordshire, despite the love of the children and the respect for their religious observance, a social worker still found that there were problems from the householders stemming from 'prejudice against the Jews'. Some villagers could not accept that the school was short of money and resources, believing that the Jewish community was inherently wealthy. Similarly in Staines there was a strong Jewish presence in the town throughout the war. However, as late as 1944 there were complaints against the local Yeshiva, with 'the somewhat unusual appearance of the students' causing local suspicion.[83]

Nevertheless, even in areas where relations between Jews and non-Jews were bad, violence was rare and limited. More commonly, hostility was manifested in a refusal to give billets to Jewish evacuees. The village pogrom in Hugh Massingham's fictionalised account of Jewish evacuation, *The Harp and the Oak* never materialised or even looked a likely possibility. However, evacuation could still be a traumatic time for Jewish evacuees. In East Anglia, a group of English born Jews were so unhinged by evacuation that at first they would speak only Yiddish and were taken to be refugees.[84] Others attending non-Jewish schools for the first time were 'first made aware more starkly of being Jewish'. Given the pressures of living in a totally Christian atmosphere, and with the near impossible task of organising children right across Britain, the Second World War years were disastrous as far as Jewish education was concerned. The legacy of these absent years is still felt today and it has been suggested that 'the damage done . . . at that time is incalculable'.[85] However, little of it was done by deliberate malice from the Gentile population, indeed the Jewish children were often happy to drift into a secular or Christian world. Although some Jewish children suffered miserably in the war trying to preserve their background, many more were happy to follow the path of integration. Another category found themselves accepted fully as Jewish children, whose foster parents encouraged their religious beliefs.

If evacuation tended to integrate the Jewish population, often at the cost of religious observance, it also acted as a catalyst in breaking down the areas of Jewish concentration. As the Jewish East End disappeared new areas of settlement emerged, such as Leicester, Northampton and Nottingham.[86] Both the blitz and its concomitant evacuation thus pushed Jew and Gentile into close proximity. The net result was that barriers and prejudices on both sides were overcome. Yet this process was not an easy one and its price was high. In the case of the East End, it came through tremendous physical and human destruction, and in the evacuation areas often at the cost of Jewish tradition. Both blitz and evacuation brought tensions which created antisemitism, some of which, like the hatred of the parvenu Jewish evacuee, persisted after the war. Yet taken as a whole, these two great domestic war developments pushed Jews more firmly into the wider British community. It is to the question of how British society as a whole viewed its Jewish minority in the war that we must now turn.

3

Jews in British society (1)
The Jewish question in Britain 1939–45

In the first week of the war Tom Harrisson decided to terminate Mass-Observation's survey on antisemitism in Britain. Writing to the Board of Deputies, he suggested that 'all our work points to the present conflict as pointing away from antisemitism'. Harrisson's common sense belief that a war against the Jew-persecuting Nazis was bound to end domestic prejudice is one that still persists nearly half a century later. However, as Mass-Observation were themselves to find out shortly, the reality was somewhat different. An observer in London, writing in October 1939, referred to an 'almost universal anti-semitic feeling' in the capital. It was soon apparent that the Jew-consciousness of the late 1930s was going to continue throughout the war. Whilst rarely a total obsession, the Jewish question was one that was to recur frequently, albeit in many different forms, in the years between 1939 and 1945.[1]

A brief examination of the quantity of contemporary debate on the Jewish issue will illustrate how widespread public concern was over the subject. Two anthologies were produced – *Gentile and Jew* and *The Future of the Jews* – both with wide-ranging ideas from many contributors. In addition much of the contemporary press, from the *News Chronicle* to the *Dundee Evening Telegraph*, presented major debates on the subject. Indeed no major periodical in Britain was free from heated arguments on the Jewish question. George Orwell, who himself wrote regularly on antisemitism, commented that the issue was 'discussed interminably in the press'. So great was the public interest in the area, that anyone daring to mention Jews in print, however indirectly, was besieged by a flood of letters. Adding to this general fixation on matters Jewish, the war saw a proliferation of Jewish defence literature. Some of this was produced by Jewish organisations, but much of the defence material came from left-wing elements in British society. This anti-antisemitic literature will be dealt with separately, but it will be sufficient now to point out that it was just one of many elements that made up an atmosphere where 'Jews were news'.[2]

The vast amount written and spoken on the Jewish question in Britain during the war necessitates a clear analytical framework for its evaluation. Otherwise there is a danger of losing sight of the many heterogeneous attitudes that were present, but which could be lost in the sheer volume of material. It has been pointed out that it is important to differentiate between forms of antisemitism, and the constant presence of antisemitism in the war should not hide the fact that this antipathy took a wide variety of forms.[3]

Attempts to draw a clear political spectrum from right to left are always fraught with danger. The ideologies of both organised antisemitism and fascism illustrate this point. Although most readily identified with the extreme right, antisemitism has not been absent from liberal and socialist circles. Furthermore, it is difficult to subsume the antipathy of Jewish power from either the Chesterbelloc circle or the BUF under the category of conservatism. To quote a virulently antisemitic follower of the former school: 'What am I? Anything but Tory.' As Lord Rothermere and others were to find, Mosley's organisation was not simply an anti-communist bulwark, but was a radical movement in itself.[4] However, if caution is employed, it is possible to divide attitudes to Jews into the three categories of right, left and centre. It is by no means the only way in which hostility towards Jews in British society can be compartmentalised nor is it a watertight model. However, as long as the others factors which cut across these subdivisions – such as class, sex, age, religion and locality – are taken into account then it is satisfactory to use it as a working model.

In the dogma of the extreme left, antisemitism was identified as a reactionary force, being an indirect attack on the workers and a 'secret weapon of the Ruling Class'. As even the *Daily Worker* was to realise, antisemitism was not just a monopoly of the right, but nevertheless it remains a fact that much of the most blatant attacks on Jews in the war could be identified with conservative sources. The grounds of the Right's attack on Jews were based on two central objections containing one essential ingredient – the ultimate loyalty of the Jews. Firstly, Jews were identified with radical and revolutionary world forces, and secondly, they were perceived as essentially un-British.[5]

As we have seen, after 1918 the leading spirits of High Toryism – *The Times*, the *Morning Post* and *The Spectator* – were quick to accuse Jews of being the central force behind Bolshevism and a generally malevolent world power. After the discrediting of *The Protocols* in 1921, the identification became less respectable and by the outbreak of war both *The Times* and *The Spectator* were more liberal on Jewish matters, and *The Morning Post* had ceased to function. However not all conservative organs had forgotten the issue by 1939.[6]

At the forefront of the campaign against the subversive Jewish influence was *The Patriot*. Although priding itself on its widespread presence in Conservative clubs, this weekly journal, which continued to peddle the argument of *The Protocols* throughout the war, cannot be seriously regarded as part of mainstream British society. Slightly more respectable were the ultra-patriotic and reactionary British Empire Union (BEU) and National Citizens Union (NCU). Both had dabbled in Jewish conspiracy arguments in the late 1930s but by the outbreak of hostilities had generally stopped attacking Jews as international revolutionaries. Nevertheless, the BEU's journal, *Empire Record*, whilst attacking German persecution of Jews, reminded its readers that 'the great majority of the founders of Bolshevism in Russia were German Jews'. Similarly, the *National Review* denounced Nazi antisemitism but suggested that history 'will perhaps not hold a subversive Jewish element blameless – Communism has much to answer for.' Its long standing antagonism against German Jews continued through the war, this respectable journal attacking 'the Communism daily spoken to Germany in the rich Jewish voices of the men Hitler flung out six years ago'.[7]

The only other major grouping that consistently blamed Jewry for Communism centred around the right-wing *Catholic Herald*. A long standing thorn in the side of Anglo-Jewry, it did little to modify its attacks on Jewry in the war. It dismissed the stories of Jewish persecution, and preferred instead to open its columns to a lengthy debate over Jewish responsibility for the Russian Revolution. In so doing, the paper revealed the strong interest on the subject from a sizeable proportion of the Catholic population and its intelligentsia.[8] Elsewhere, social commentators such as Wickham Steed, Arthur Keith, Arthur Bryant and Douglas Reed revived the Jewish–Bolshevik myth, but generally speaking, outside the Tory diehard and right-wing Catholic worlds, the matter had ceased to be one of public concern. Whilst Mass-Observation's numerous social surveys on Jews between 1939 and 1943 revealed widespread fears about Jewish power in society, not once did this include the Jewish–Communist bogey.[9]

If Tory diehard thinking on the Bolshevik revolution was becoming anachronistic, it did not follow that Conservative antisemitic conspiracy thinking was also a thing of the past. In the war, the Conservative Party was split in a similar manner to that of the 1980s, with a dominant nineteenth-century individualist section, but with a significant social reform group in opposition. It was within the former section that an influential grouping could be found, which was centred around the weekly *Truth*, and in opposition to the alleged Jewish influence in Britain. The Conservative Party had close financial connections to *Truth*, which were the subject of anti-fascist scrutiny in the war. In addition there is evidence that the deputy editor of *Truth*, the ex-BUF director A. K. Chesterton, was employed by the Conservatives in 1945.[10]

It was within *Truth* that right-wing opposition to any form of government planning was most clearly articulated. Its two leading contributors, Collin Brooks and Sir Ernest Benn, formed two pressure groups in the war – Aims of Industry and the Society of Individualists – both set up to preserve free enterprise. The latter claimed 10,000 members in 1942 and George Orwell was not alone in believing *Truth* to be a dangerous and 'distinctly influential paper'. Antisemitism had become prominent in the weekly from the late 1930s and, throughout the war, *Truth* 'indulged lavishly in it'.[11]

Its hostility to Jews was based on the belief that Jews were essentially foreigners and a dangerous force in society. These two elements were forged together in an article, 'Contrasts in Patriotism', where the war record of a group of Conservative peers was compared to that of three left-wing Jews – Gollancz, Laski and Strauss. The resulting heavy libel fines did little to stop *Truth*'s innuendos which suggested that the British were fighting so that alien Jews would gain at home. Following in the path of the Chesterbelloc circle, *Truth* deemed that Jews, whether they had arrived in Britain recently or several centuries ago, were essentially alien to British life. To Collin Brooks, its editor, the real Jewish question was whether an alien race should be allowed unlimited power and influence over society. It is revealing how in 1940 *Truth* saw the Hore-Belisha case in terms of the Dreyfus affair. Again in Belloc's footsteps, Brooks saw the solution in terms of a form of apartheid where Jews 'would, metaphorically, wear the Star of Judah proudly . . . and withdraw from the normal life of the nation'. If this was not carried out then the Jews would face an antisemitic backlash and be expelled from Britain again.[12]

There is no doubt that *Truth* was widely regarded as 'a reputable weekly periodical', but in Jewish matters how far was it reflecting public opinion? Claude Claremont, an anti-Freudian, declared his conversion to Belloc's analysis in a major work in 1940, but as a Mass-Observation survey in 1944 showed, his views were fairly isolated. Out of 155 people questioned, only three believed that Jewish activities should be circumscribed as they were a danger to the country. Yet the same sample showed that up to 10% believed that Jews were a power in society. Furthermore, other similar surveys showed that Jews were seen as un-British by a large proportion of the population. A Mass-Observation report on attitudes to foreigners in 1943 brought the response 'I cannot understand the inclusion of Jews' from one man, but it was one of only two out of a sample of sixty-eight.[13]

It would thus seem that only a small minority of the population actually wanted laws against Jews in Britain. Yet paradoxically, a similarly small percentage considered, as did one Mass-Observer, that Jews 'were no different to other people' or that 'British Jews' were 'British'. In failing to differentiate between alien and Jew, *Truth* was in tune with the views of much of the population. In suggesting apartheid or expulsion it was satisfying the desires of only a fragment of the British public.[14]

In its attitude to government social policy, *Truth* found itself in a difficult dilemma. On the one hand, it represented a strong segment of Tory opinion, on the other this feeling was swimming in the opposite direction to public opinion. Whilst *Truth* accused Beveridge of wanting 'to force securities upon people whose sole desire is for risk and adventure', 88% of the population disagreed. In this area *Truth* represented what Home Intelligence saw as a small 'hostile minority', compared to the general nationwide support for the Beveridge report. *Truth*, in blaming PEP for the success of planning in the war, and in suggesting, as Sir Ernest Benn did, that this organisation was 'sinister, semi-secret' with a pronouncedly 'Jewish influence', was probably only preaching to a small, already converted minority. Nevertheless, it succeeded in presenting Jewish conspiracy ideas and warnings about Jewish power to a large public in the war.[15]

Realising that there was little chance of getting the paper to change its policies, the Board of Deputies attempted to get the government to suppress *Truth*. Herbert Morrison, the Home Secretary, whilst agreeing to keep a careful watch on the paper, decided that banning *Truth* would be too great an interference with the liberty of the Press. An attempt was made to get the Conservative Party to renounce *Truth*, because, in the Board of Deputies' words, 'there is still a very strong feeling that the Central Office is interested in that paper'. No such repudiation came from the Conservatives.[16] Indeed, there is some evidence that the Conservative Party had encouraged *Truth*'s antisemitic attack on Hore-Belisha in 1940. Moreover, it has been suggested that the sacking of the Jewish War Minister was due to 'Conservative Party unwillingness to resist antisemitism in the Foreign Office and among the army generals'. It is significant that the Tory Chairman, Sir Thomas Dugdale, told the editor of *Truth* in 1942 that 'The [Conservative] Party had no press at all – either daily or periodical – *Truth* being nearest to a dependable organ.'[17]

The Conservative Party was more troubled by the activities and imprisonment of one of its MP's, Captain Ramsay. Although Ramsay was never disowned by the Conservatives, he was, even in terms of the Conservative antipathy towards Jews at the time, 'clearly in a class of his own'. Ramsay, by the end of the war, was becoming an electoral embarrassment and his local Party had no qualms about replacing him. Although Ramsay's constituents had rejected his conspiratorial antisemitism, there is no evidence that other Conservative constituency parties were restraining social prejudice against Jews. For example, in 1937 Daniel Lipson had been refused the candidateship of the Conservative Party at Cheltenham due to his Jewish background. It has been suggested that throughout the 1930s and 40s given that local constituency parties had more control over the selection of candidates (who had previously nominated themselves via personal finance), that the demise of the Jewish Conservative was ensured. It is significant that in the 1945 election there were no Jewish Conservative MPs elected at all.[18]

The problem of Conservative antisemitism was great enough even to stir the Board of Deputies into action. Despite its past reluctance to involve itself in Party politics (to the extent of refusing to attack the BUF), its President Selig Brodetsky approaching R. A. Butler in 1943 on the issue. Butler, representing the more liberal element within the Party, told Brodetsky that he would consider getting the Conservatives to tell its members of the dangers of antisemitism. It would appear however, that Butler's more progressive attitude was not typical of the Party as a whole. A group of Conservative MP's, who claimed to be representative of the Party, wrote to the Prime Minister in February 1940, giving an indication of Conservative antipathy to the Jews in Britain. They wrote hoping that the refugees present in Britain would not be naturalised as it would 'result in a permanent increase of our already over-large Jewish population. Most of us feel that we would rather hand down to posterity a slowly denuding number of people of British stock than provide new material for increasing the stock of Jewish or Jew-British population.' The latter was already 'a most unhealthy symptom in the body politic. The Jewish vote is so strong in some constituencies that the Member has no freedom of action'.[19]

With this sort of attitude, it is not surprising that the prominence of Harold Laski in the Labour Party, as Chairman of the Labour Party

Conference in 1945, attracted right-wing antisemitic hostility. The *National Review* commented 'anything less like the British working man than an international Jew could not well be imagined . . . he has so much contempt for this country . . . with no idea about the land he happened to be born in, save to make a revolution in it'. Lord Croft, the old man of Tory diehardism followed suit, writing in the popular press that Laski was 'a fine representative of the old British working class'. This was the sort of language that had been used after the end of the First World War, but nevertheless a change had taken place in Conservative thinking on the subject. Churchill, who had been at the forefront of the attack against Jewish–Bolshevism after 1918, now warned Croft to 'be careful, whatever the temptation, not to be drawn into any campaign that might be represented as antisemitic'. It would appear that Churchill, although sympathetic to Croft's remarks, realised they were no longer respectable in a political climate that was discovering the Nazi concentration camps.[20]

In any evaluation of antisemitism along a political spectrum in the war, one must agree with Orwell, who wrote in 1945 that 'antisemitism comes more naturally to people of Conservative tendency, who suspect Jews of weakening national morale and diluting the national culture'. In the press world it was the Conservative Rothermere, Beaverbrook and Kemsley empires that showed the greatest hostility to Jews in the war, and, via *Truth*, respectable Toryism and antisemitic extremism were given a common platform. Moreover, just as the 1980s have seen a degree of entryism from National Front supporters into the Conservative Party, so in the 1945 election the latter received support from ex-BUF members.[21]

Orwell's belief that antisemitism was mainly associated with the Right did not blind him from acknowledging that 'People of Left opinions are not immune to it'. However, Orwell's self-critical stance on his fellow Socialists has not been one that has gained many followers. It has recently been written that 'any attempt to raise even a discussion about the antisemitic nature of . . . socialist practice is almost invariably met with apoplexy and vilification. It is virtually a taboo subject.'[22]

Whilst Orwell was happy to generalise that within the right wing 'neo-tories and political Catholics are always liable to succumb to antisemitism', he was unsure why those on the left indulged in it, generally ascribing it to irrational personal prejudice. There is some truth in this argument, James Robb, for example, in his post-war survey of antisemitism in Bethnal Green, found no difference between liberals, socialists or conservatives in regard to personal prejudice. In the BUF by-elections, Mass-Observation found that Labour supporters in Silvertown 'were frequently strongly anti-Jewish' and that in Leeds antisemitism was as common in Labour voters as 'amongst the general average'. In the former, 31% of the population were 'definitely' antisemitic, in the latter, 14%. Nor was pathological prejudice a monopoly of the extreme right. Recently released Home Office papers have revealed that the Labour MP Richard Stokes was a member of Captain Ramsay's antisemitic Right Club, and Labour Party archives disclose that a Labour supporter from Stoke was active in the equally extremist Militant Christian Patriots.[23]

It would thus seem that socialists were not immune from the prevailing antipathy in British society towards Jews, nor were certain individuals free from severe anti-Jewish complexes. Can one go further, however, and suggest that there was a form of antisemitism specifically associated with the Left in Britain? I have already commented on the need for caution when discussing the possibility of a socialist antisemitic tradition in Britain.[24] Nevertheless, the persistence of this strain of thought into the Second World War shows the necessity of taking the matter seriously. However, it is important to evaluate the nature and extent of this hostility, and then to see if it has any unique features.

In June 1939 the radical ILP supporting journal, *The Forward*, attacked the 'Jewish control of British foreign policy'. This onslaught on the alleged power of international Jewish finance bears a resemblance to the left-wing campaign at the time of the Boer War. Indeed it has been described as 'striking a radical theme of earlier times'. However *The Forward* had not made up its own mind. In July 1939, when answering the question 'Do Jews Want War?', it suggested that even if they did 'Jews are everywhere an unimportant and far from determining factor in such cardinal questions as war and peace.'[25]

The journal's ambivalence continued throughout the war, attacking the international financiers – 'the Shylock-in-waiting' – for promoting war, the House of Rothschilds, and 'the Hebrew leaders of the Money-lending business', yet dismissing as 'absurd' the idea of 'our financial system being dominated by Jews'. *The Forward* was unable to give up a long standing antipathy to the bogey of international Jewish finance. At the same time, however, it was incapable of putting this in the context of the Nazi persecution of Jews.[26]

The attack on Jewish financiers was not one specifically linked to the left, indeed it was one of the most prominent aspects of the propaganda of the BUF and other fascist and antisemitic groups in the 1930s and 40s. However, these latter organisations did not attack the Jewish financier in isolation, for it was seen as only part of the international Jewish power, which was directly linked to Jewish Communism. To all groups on the left, to attack socialists such as Harold Laski and Manny Shinwell as international Jewish Bolsheviks was anathema. Despite this vital difference, left-wing groups such as the ILP and the United Socialist Movement, which were hostile to the war could co-operate with quasi-fascists like the Duke of Bedford and John Beckett. Indeed in 1939, there was talk of a coalition between the ILP and the BUF.[27]

In the words of the Duke of Bedford, 'adversity can make strange bedfellows' and the major pacifist organisation, the Peace Pledge Union (PPU), saw the involvement of the extremes of left and right in the war. Although the PPU had a strong connection to the ILP, it also received the attention of Nazi appeasement groups ranging from the antisemitic Link and Nordic League to the slightly more moderate British Council for Christian Settlement. The conflict between left and right, between socialist pacifists and those sympathetic to the Nazis, threatened to split the PPU. The editor of *Peace News*, John Middleton Murry, wrote in 1942 that he was 'astonished by the apparent intolerance displayed by pacifists towards one another'.[28]

Nevertheless, although some socialists abhorred the linking of PPU to individuals such as Bedford, others were willing to co-operate. As we have seen, prominent members of the ILP supported the latter's peace mission to Ireland, and John McGovern MP was active in getting the government to release Nazi sympathisers interned under 18B. Bedford's links with Guy Aldred's United Socialist Movement were even stronger. Bedford was allowed to contribute financially to this socialist-anarchist organisation. In addition, he was permitted to attack Jewish financiers in its journal, *The Word*. Stranger still were the contributions of Alexander Ratcliffe to *The Word*. Ratcliffe's antisemitic anti-war *Vanguard* was circulated by the Anarchist Federation. There were thus some peculiar contacts made between the extreme (but anti-Soviet) left wing and the antisemitic fascist appeasement movements in Britain.[29]

These connections could be dismissed as a result of the desire for peace at any price, but there was to an extent some ideological agreement. Whilst *Peace News* opened its columns to attacks on international Jewish finance from quasi-fascists such as Edward Godfrey and the Duke of Bedford, there were similar sentiments expressed by Murry himself and the novelist Ethel Mannin, both of whom had ILP connections. Furthermore, Murry's other journal, *The Adelphi*, a Christian socialist–pacifist review, engaged in what Orwell called 'Jew-baiting of a mild kind'. It is important not to overstress the connections between the pacifist left and appeasement right over the Jewish question – a significant socialist element in the PPU were active in fighting antisemitism inside and outside the movement. However, to a prominent group within the peace movement there could be co-operation between the left and the right. To these individuals, attacks on international Jewish finance were perfectly acceptable.[30]

No such contact was ever considered in the more orthodox Marxist world of the Communist Party. Even so, antisemitism directed at rich Jews did not disappear amongst its supporters. In 1940, Malcolm Muggeridge wrote that 'when a Rothschild was spoiled of his possessions in Vienna, socialists must complain'. The *Daily Worker* did not seem to agree, launching bitter attacks on the Barons Maurice and Edouard de Rothschild when they arrived in Britain from Europe in 1940. The fact that the European Houses of Rothschild had been destroyed by the Nazis, and that they had arrived in Britain having lost most of their possessions (and nearly their lives) did not occur to the Communist Party's organ. Instead, the *Daily Worker* attacked the support which other sections of the press gave for the Rothschilds. It saw this press sympathy as an indication of who the real enemies of Britain were. The *Daily Worker* believed this was not Germany, but those who wanted to set up fascism at home – the defenders of international finance.[31]

This crude 'social fascist' argument did not stop the *Daily Worker* from attacking antisemitism, which it had done consistently from the 1930s. However, until its suppression in 1941 it continued to attack Jewish finance. To the *Daily Worker* 'bankers [were] bankers and business [was] business', regardless of the Nazi persecution of all types of Jews. Even so, the Communist Party did find it necessary to warn its members that not all Jews were capitalists and that Jews did not control international finance.[32]

Fears that Communists and fellow travellers harboured such views would appear to have been justified. Many left-wingers could simultaneously attack fascism and antisemitism yet show strong signs of rich-Jew antisemitism. One Mass-Observer wrote in 1940 that 'as a Communist [I do] not like Jewish influence and activity in finance and industry . . . I think the Jews as capitalists are a nuisance and require strict control.' Many other examples could be cited of Communists who were as 'obsessed with "Jewish capitalism" as [was] Hilaire Belloc'. Some went further believing 'Jews have too much power as so many of them control finance and finance . . . controls us.' Others blamed international Jewish financiers for the war.[33]

Douglas Hyde, who was the anti-fascist correspondent for the *Daily Worker*, remarked after the war that 'nowhere will one find a more cynical antisemitism than in the [Communist] Party itself'. Hyde's remark needs to be put in the context of his bitter attack on his former employer, but it would seem to contain an element of truth. The association of Jews with finance capitalism (despite the historical inaccuracy of this belief by the 1930s), would appear to have been deeply ingrained into the communist mentality in wartime Britain. Nevertheless, the Communist Party did change its attitude in the latter part of the war. Walter Holmes, who had earlier attacked the refugee Rothschilds in the *Daily Worker*, was now forced to admit that in Dachau concentration camp, rich Jews had been killed as well as their poorer brethren. Within the Communist Party a section for sympathetic Jewish businessmen was set up, although not without strong opposition. The Communist Party had begun to realise that Nazi antisemitism knew no class barriers and that Jews as a whole should be enlisted in the fight against reactionary forces.[34]

However, it is important to stress that not all on the left wing had come to realise that a simple class analysis could not explain antisemitism. To many, Jews were not victims but oppressors and thus they could not suffer from Nazi attacks. At worst only working class Jews would be victims. Thus some left wing anti-war organs cast doubt on the accuracy of the atrocity reports. They suggested, when the news of the Nazi extermination programme first became public at the end of 1942, that 'exaggerations can only harm Jews', and that the reports were just propaganda justifying an imperialist war. The Trotskyite *Socialist Appeal* showed its total failure to grasp the nature of Nazism when it claimed, after the liberation of Belsen, that the worst victims were the German working class. Mass-Observation surveys confirm that left-wing distrust of Jewish atrocity stories was not uncommon – one correspondent suggesting that they were in fact organised by rich Jews. Others believed that the Jews deserved the treatment they were getting because of their role in finance, and that it was 'a great pity that the opposition to the Jews in Germany has been so emphasised to the exclusion of socialists, anti-Nazis, liberals and anti-Nazi Christians'; the latter being examples of those who deserved genuine sympathy.[35]

Confusion over whether the Jews were the exploiters or the exploited produced an ambivalent response from the British trade union movement at the time of the alien's debate. Fears of unfair alien competition led the TUC to call for the restriction of alien immigration in 1892, 1894 and 1895. At the same time, however, Jewish immigrants in Britain were encouraged to become trades unionists, though usually in their own organisations. Rivalries and tensions persisted but, by the time of the First World War, most Jewish trades unions had amalgamated with non-Jewish ones to form integrated organisations such as the United Garment Workers' Trade Union, founded in 1915.[36]

Such integration indicated to an extent an easing of ethnic friction in trades such as tailoring and furniture making. In 1939 the United Ladies' Tailors Trade Union united with the National Union of Tailors and Garment Workers. The former, whose membership was largely made up of older Yiddish speaking workers, recognised that it had 'too much "Jewishness" in it to be able to attract the English workers'. Thereafter, the only specifically Jewish trade union was the London Jewish Bakers.[37]

Amalgamation, however, was not a strong enough weapon to fight the economic pressures of the inter-war years, especially in trades of Jewish concentration. The strains of the depression led to renewed ethnic conflict. In the garment trade 'differences arose between Catholics and Jews' in the union movement. Moreover, the old accusations that Jews were responsible for sweating were raised again in the 1930s, particularly in the furniture trade by the National Amalgamated Furnishing Trades Association (NAFTA). This hostility did not end with the outbreak of war. In early 1940, William Zak, London district secretary of NAFTA was 'concerned about the growth of antisemitism in the Furnishing Trade'. The Assistant General Secretary of the Union believed 'that a lot of the antisemitism in the Furnishing Trade was due to the attitude of certain employers, most of whom were Jews'. Indeed, so strong was union hostility to alleged Jewish 'sweating' that, in November 1940, the Asquith Committee on aliens was dissuaded from releasing too many refugees from internment because of the advice of a 'labour source' that 'every Jewish employer would take advantage . . . to obtain sweated labour.'[38]

Indeed, with regard to Jewish refugees from Nazi oppression, the trade union movement revealed an ambivalence not unlike its response to the aliens half a century earlier. There was general abhorrence of the Nazi regime and a 'profound sympathy with the victims of Fascist oppression'. Nevertheless, this sympathy was tempered by hard economic realism. Some prominent socialist and trade unionist refugees were aided by the TUC, but generally the response was one of extreme caution. In 1939 the General Council of the TUC, whilst recognising 'that some practical expression' should be given to the sympathy felt for the persecuted, urged that 'the number of refugees admitted to this country in any one year shall be limited'. The government responded to such union pressure, making work permits for refugees a scarce commodity. Union caution on this issue applied not only to the highly skilled professions such as medicine, but also to those at the other end of the scale who applied to come to Britain as domestics. Even the General Secretary of the TUC, Walter Citrine, admitted that he had 'many times regretted that we were not able in our . . . movement to be perhaps a little more generous in respect of providing opportunities for such people to obtain employment in this country'. Particularly stringent against the refugees was the Medical Practitioners' Union. It opposed any refugees being given permission to practice medicine, welcomed mass internment in 1940 and demanded the removal of all aliens in 1945.[39]

Generally, however, in the war itself, union opposition to the employment of refugees subsided. The shortage of manpower meant that refugee labour was welcomed by the government, although many refugees still faced hostility – both anti-German and anti-Jewish – from their workmates. Antagonism was also felt by second generation British Jews. In the inter-war years, antisemitism, or the fear of antisemitism, kept many Jews in all-Jewish workplaces. This was changed by the demands of the war economy which thrust Jews into the mixed environment of Munitions' factories. For some Jews it would be their first confrontation with antisemitism since schooldays. It was a traumatic experience which could only be overcome by a return to 'Jewish' employment. Many others welcomed the new opportunities, and the chance to escape the hardships of the traditional trades. Thus some employment divisions between Jews and non-Jews were overcome in the war, but the process was not an easy one.[40]

Overall, there was a persistence of union and workforce suspicion of Jewish economic activities, but this had declined by the end of the war. Indeed, a prominent Jewish labour historian, writing in 1946, suggested that the antisemitism associated with the Medical Practitioners' Union was 'certainly the exception' in the union world, and that the 'trade union movement in Britain is concerned with the combatting of all types of antisemitism'.[41]

We must now return to the original question: how unique was socialist antisemitism and how extensive was it? With the first point, we have seen how it was only the left that attacked international Jewish finance, not as an attack on world Jewry, but as an assault on the capitalist system. This socialist antisemitism was part of a general attack on the rich, but Jewish capitalists were specifically singled out for being particularly vulgar and powerful. Elsewhere, socialist antisemitism was generally part of a wider hostility to Jews. In the war itself one Labour MP attacked Jews for their Communist activities, and another prominent Labour official, in a fit of xenophobia, told his Jewish colleagues to 'go back to Palestine'.[42]

Turning to the extent of socialist antipathy it is vital to point out that the above instances were fairly isolated. Whilst the Board of Deputies was forced to make a general appeal to the Conservative Party to try to control its antisemitism, it was only concerning specific instances that complaints were made to the Labour Party; ones that shocked the latter as much as the Jewish community. Also, although the identification of Jews with international finance was made across the Labour movement, it appears that it was only prominent amongst the extreme left wing. Journals such as *The Forward*, which regularly made this linkage were becoming rare, contrasting dramatically to the position in the left-wing press forty years earlier. Finally, although we have been warned against drawing 'a balance sheet with any form of racism', it must not be forgotten that the left-wing movement was at the forefront of the battle against antisemitism in Britain. This will be dealt with in a separate chapter, but it is necessary to point out at this stage that if left wing hostility to Jews is to be directly compared to that of the right in the war, not only was Socialist antisemitism of a less intensive nature and also more sporadic, but Conservatives, with a few notable exceptions, played little part in fighting antisemitism.[43]

If, for a significant section of the right-wing world, the Jew could never be an Englishman (at best he would be 'Jew-British'), and he was furthermore a diluter of the 'Anglo-Saxon heritage', then the converse was believed by both liberals and socialists. To many Conservatives not only should Jews remain Jews but they should be recognisable as such. Changing a 'Jewish' name to an 'English' one was 'an outrageous state of affairs.' Amongst more progressive forces in Britain, the solution to the problem was seen in terms of not more, but less Jewishness.[44]

It has been suggested that 'the liberal compromise offered emancipation in the expectation that Jews would cease to be Jewish and move closer to British society'. Such an interpretation of emancipation was not accepted by all liberals, nor by the established Jewish community itself. However, it remained true for the nineteenth-century (and also for the first half of the twentieth-century) that those who wanted to be totally accepted in British society had to adopt Christianity.[45]

In the liberal creed there was theoretically neither room for antisemitism nor a distinctively Jewish population. In practice liberals have not been immune from various forms of antisemitism. In the Eastern

Crisis of the 1870s, and the Boer War agitation at the turn of the century, liberals were prominent in attacking what was seen as the undue Jewish influence. At a more local level, several Liberal constituencies discriminated against Jews. Even as late as 1944, the Tottenham Liberal and Radical Working Mens' Club deemed it necessary to ask its members if they were 'of Jewish birth'. Indeed, there is no evidence that liberals were any less prone to personal prejudice against Jews than other sections of the British population, despite the official Party line that 'antisemitism was against the principles of Liberalism' and that the Party would 'always denounce antisemitism'.[46]

However, it is not on these more universal forms of hostility to Jews but on the more specific 'liberal' objections to Judaism that we must now concentrate. There is a paradox that the most extreme forms of antisemitism and the mildest attitudes to Jews have the same long term goal – the ultimate removal of Jews from society. Whilst most liberals abhorred the Nazi extermination programme, there was simultaneously a macabre (though self-ashamed) satisfaction at Hitler's attempt to solve finally the Jewish question. Most people repressed such thoughts and were genuinely moved by the suffering of European Jewry. Nevertheless, such feelings were often ambivalent and there was 'a tendency', in the words of a liberal novelist, 'to think serve them right before one can catch oneself up'.[47]

Such attitudes came not so much from cold-heartedness but from the liberal critique of Jewishness. Implicit in this belief was the idea that antisemitism would only end when society started to tolerate Jews, and for the Jews to subsequently give up their religion. The corollary of which was that the survival of antisemitism in a tolerant society, such as Britain, was due to the Jews themselves. The premise that Jews, by refusing to fully integrate into society, were responsible for the hostility towards themselves, is an example of the 'well-earned' theory of antisemitism; part of what Bill Williams has recently called 'the antisemitism of tolerance'.[48]

From the social surveys, diaries, literature and even government records of the war years it appears that the most dominant feelings about Jews were not of their being an unassimilatable foreign body in British society, but of the reverse. Jews were attacked for refusing to integrate, for being clannish and for ultimately creating antisemitism. A survey carried out in April 1943 on 'the means of overcoming antisemitism' found that all the replies amounted 'to a statement that it was up to the Jews themselves to combat antisemitism.' Most of the suggestions to the Jewish community were that they should 'mix freely with the inhabitants of the country of their adoption'.[49]

In the attacks on Jewish exclusivity, the ideas of H. G. Wells were often cited. In Wells's world-view the idea of any 'chosen people' was anathema, and his works, right up to his death, reveal a deep antipathy primarily towards Catholicism but also towards Judaism. Wells had no time for Nazi antisemitism, but then regarded it (in such books as *The Fate of Homo Sapiens* and *All Aboard for Ararat*), as a response to the Jews' claim to be the Chosen race. Although Wells's influence as a socialist was on the wane by the Second World War, his attitude to Jews appears to have gained popular support. Furthermore, when General Sikorski quoted Wells – in support of his belief that it would be playing the Nazi game in treating Jews as a separate nationality – both Ministry of Information and Foreign Office officials were in full agreement.[50]

Other 'liberal' socialists, such as George Bernard Shaw and George Orwell, were united with Wells in his opposition to Jewish exclusivity; the former remarking on several occasions in the war that Nazi antisemitism was a natural development from Mosaic Law. Wells went further than simply attacking the exclusive tendencies of Judaism, to him it was the only factor that kept an essentially anachronistic people together.[51] Again the public would seem to have agreed. That Judaism had nothing worthwhile to offer as a religious creed after the arrival of Christianity was an assumption that most of the public shared. A small minority of the population had a genuine interest and admiration for Jewish religious customs, but more typical was the reaction of novelist Hamilton Fyfe, who admonished Jews to 'give up their Kosher meat and their worship of a bloodthirsty, revengeful, anthromorpic deity . . . [Your] troubles are due to [your] exclusiveness'. At the end of an anthology on the Jewish question, the editor, Chaim Newman, despairingly made a plea for a solution 'in which the Jew can face the world with pride, confidence, peace of mind and remain a Jew.' In this symposium of over twenty replies, only two contributors made it clear that the Jewish religion had a legitimate future. The rest adhered in varying degrees to a strict interpretation of the emancipation doctrine, that is the ultimate disappearance of Jewishness. Attempting to counter this, Newman suggested that 'there must be . . . toleration which does not expect rigidity'.[52]

Although these attitudes to the Jewish religion show the important difference between tolerance and acceptance, it must not be forgotten that the former still operated as an effective barrier against attacks on Jewish religious freedom. As will be shown later, the Government bent over backwards to make sure that the hardships imposed by war did not hit the Jewish community unduly. Moreover, the general disdain of the public against

Judaism in no way affected the rights of British Jews to practice their religion. In only one sphere, Jewish ritual slaughter (shechita), was there anything like an organised campaign against Jewish religious practice.

The subject of minorities and their religious slaughter of animals is one that has produced an emotional public reaction in the 1980s, a reaction that shows certain similarities to opposition to shechita in the late 1930s and the Second World War. Then, as now, animal rights enthusiasts have been accused of racism, a matter made more complicated due to the involvement of antisemitic and fascist groups in the general campaign. Both have occurred in an atmosphere of general race tension, and in each case the attacks on ritual slaughter have suffered from serious distortion.[53]

In the recent debate, the potential accusation of antisemitism has been a source of embarrassment and, to an extent, a stumbling block to animal welfare organisations. In the 1930s and 1940s this was not the case, indeed such groups used the fear of creating antisemitism as a weapon against shechita. Writing to the Board of Deputies in June 1939, the chairman of the RSPCA claimed that in 'the last couple of years there [has been] growing up a very strong feeling of antagonism towards the continuation of the Jewish method of slaughter in this country'. At a meeting in June 1939 a mini-emancipation contract was proposed by the RSPCA, who claimed that if the Jews voluntarily gave up shechita it would improve Jewish relations with the wider society.[54]

Part of the 'very strong feeling of antagonism' that the RSPCA had referred to had been deliberately stirred up by antisemitic organisations. At the forefront of this campaign was the Nordic League who were distributing a German antisemitic anti-shechita film in public meetings. Adding to the emotional atmosphere, a speaker referred to 'Jewish Ritual Slaughter, or call it Ritual murder if you like: it is one and the same thing' carried out by 'sadistic, armenoid, mongroid aliens'. Links were made via such activities between respectable animal rights groups and the extremist Nordic League. As a result, antisemitism entered the shechita debate quite freely. In a 1944 pamphlet M. Dudley Ward, who had connections with the RSPCA and the Animal Defence Society, could write in language inspired by *The Protocols* concerning ritual slaughter. Suggesting that most Jews would be against shechita 'but they [were] dupes of a crafty and obdurate rabbinical ring and mass hypnotism', she believed that 'there is money in Kosher – oodles of it! Plenty of plums; itching palms; ferocious vested interests.'[55]

The war itself created negative and positive factors as regards the maintenance of shechita. On the one hand, the RSPCA decided to delay any attempt at banning religious slaughter until the end of the hostilities; on the other, the dispersion of the Jewish population with evacuation brought shechita into prominence in new areas. It was particularly in the Home Counties that shechita became a major issue, with arguments raging in both the Northamptonshire and Oxfordshire press. In the latter a heated debate continued for four months, giving some insight into how far antisemitism was a factor in the anti-shechita camp. Not surprisingly, the latter denied any such intent, yet several correspondents enlarged their attack on shechita to a general assault on Judaism. It was indicated that the Jewish religion was as outdated as shechita, and, as the latter was barbaric, it should be outlawed.[56] As was the case with the RSPCA, the emancipation contract was indirectly cited. To quote one correspondent: 'Jews have sanctuary and protection in this country and they should therefore be compelled to toe the line, and to adopt British methods of slaughter', or else in the words of another 'a general feeling of resentment is likely to arise against *any* body of alien[s] [which] . . . do[es] not . . . conform to the standard of public opinion'.[57]

The Board of Deputies was in little doubt that opposition to shechita was strong in wartime Britain. Two defence leaflets on the subject were produced and its concern would appear to have been justified. A *News Chronicle* debate on antisemitism in 1943 found that many of the 'reasoned' antisemitic letters were based on a hostility to shechita. The shechita debate itself reveals the limitations of liberal attitudes to Jews. For although liberalism was opposed to antisemitism due to its intolerance and the threat it posed to democracy, the threat of antisemitism could also be used to control the freedom of the Jewish community. This ambivalent approach in some ways offered the greatest threat to Britain's Jewish minority, for although it ensured that the State would be opposed to violent manifestation of antisemitism from the far right, it also suggested that a form of appeasement would operate to forces hostile to Jewish activities in Britain. The government wanted to make sure that amorphous antisemitism did not become an organised threat to liberal democracy. We will see later that such thinking operated in government circles in regard to such issues as the black market, Sunday Trading, domestic antisemitism, internment of aliens and policy to European Jews.[58]

Most people in Britain theoretically wanted Jews to stop being separate. Was it possible for Jews to have assimilated if they had wanted? In other words, it is important to analyse the strength of the barriers to the entry of Jews into the social and economic life of Britain. This is an attempt to ask: was the emancipation contract honoured from the non-Jewish side?

So far we have concentrated on attitudes and hostilities associated with specific political standpoints. However, when social attitudes to Jews are examined closely, such categorisation is impossible to maintain. The sentiments of Lady Mosley's blunt statement to the Advisory Committee in 1940 that she was 'not fond of Jews' was shared by many on the left. Mass-Observation found that many Communists 'nevertheless confess a secret contempt or dislike' of the Jews. In the more moderate Labour world, Hugh Dalton could describe Barnett Janner as 'a malodorous Jewish solicitor'. It could be argued that although Dalton and Lady Mosley were on opposite sides of the political spectrum, they shared the same upper middle class background, where it has been claimed 'antisemitism was very common'. Indeed Mollie Panter-Downes, the London correspondent of the *New Yorker* wrote at the start of 1940 that antisemitism was strong in Britain, 'especially in the upper classes'. However, it must be pointed out that Panter-Downes moved predominantly in such circles, and observers had a tendency of locating antisemitism in groups with which they were most familiar. Thus George Orwell believed the working class – or more specifically Irish labourers – to be the most antisemitic, whereas Cyril Connolly confined it to the middle classes. Mass-Observation went as far as concluding that personal dislike of Jews could be found equally among 'working class, middle class and upper class Observers, for all ages, sexes, areas, occupations, political views, educational standards'. Nevertheless, it has been shown that in some districts of the working class East End, relations between Jews and non-Jews were very amicable. One had often to go to upper class preserves to find blatant social discrimination against Jews.[59]

A. J. P. Taylor has commented that many were 'annoyed at having to repudiate the antisemitism which they had secretly cherished' because of Nazi persecution of Jews. Taylor was referring to the 'quiet' antisemitism of the golf club or the public school, yet there is no evidence that any such change took place either in the 1930s or the war itself. Clubs such as Les Ambassadeurs in Mayfair refused Jewish members as late as 1943. Many golf clubs followed a similar policy and a numerus clausus operated in some private schools. The persecution of European Jewry was not likely to remove deeply ingrained social snobbery, especially in an age where the notion of privilege was under serious attack. However, discrimination could also be found lower down the social scale particularly in middle class preserves such as medical schools. Indeed a case could be made that the most serious antisemitism was located amongst the lower middle classes, who felt threatened by the increasingly mobile Jewish population in the professions and in occupations such as shopkeeping, taxi driving and clerical positions.[60]

It is difficult to quantify the exact impact of job discrimination on Anglo-Jewish development in the period around the war. A refusal to employ Jews occurred in many sections of the economy. Indeed such discrimination was probably increasing during and after the war. It would seem this had a net effect of both slowing down the entry of the descendants of the East European Jews into the professions, and of encouraging Jews to continue a tradition of economic independence. In the housing sphere, blatant discrimination against Jews ensured that the movement from primary or secondary settlement areas would follow an explicitly Jewish pattern. Areas such as Golders Green, Didsbury in Manchester and Moortown in Leeds thus became in some ways 'gilded ghettos', anglicised but not totally integrated into the wider society. This pattern can be expanded to cover Anglo-Jewry as a whole in the war. The hostilities opened up social and economic opportunities, but continuing hostility to Jews meant that Anglo-Jewry would remain in many ways separate, though more equal members of British society.[61]

We have thus seen that although antisemitism cut across class barriers, there were still unique features in social prejudice. For example, working class social snobbery against Jews was not necessarily the same as the middle class variety. However, two other factors need now to be taken into consideration in qualifying the nature of social prejudice in Britain. The first is one that has been emphasised before – that it is vital to take into account ambivalence both regarding attitudes and behaviour to Jews. Social surveys on Jews in the war found that only one in a hundred people could be said to be totally pro-Jewish, and the same could be equally said of the reverse. A study of Mass-Observation's war diaries reveals that only one diarist out of 500 showed constant negative attitudes to Jews. Indeed, other surveys carried out by this social survey group suggest that up to 50% of the population were as philosemitic as they were antisemitic. The reply that whilst some Jews were 'nice' but that 'there [were] others that even I would liquidate' was typical of many. Comparisons between cultured intelligent Jews like Freud, and 'fat, greasy assertive second hand Jews' were also common. Another favourite dichotomy was to show sympathy of European Jews whilst attacking the alleged malpractices of those in Britain.[62]

Adding confusion to this picture was the fact that many people who admitted their antisemitism still mixed intimately with Jews. Some were consistent, their private hostility reflected in their exclusively non-Jewish company, or in an unsympathetic attitude to persecuted Jews, typified by the army exploits of Evelyn Waugh. Others, like Harold Nicolson, warned publicly against the dangers of antisemitism at any level, yet privately hated the very presence of Jews. Thus no clear equation can be drawn between thought, speech and behaviour patterns, which was probably to the advantage of the Jewish community itself. Purely 'private' hostility to Jews was widespread, if the alarming findings of Mass-Observation are to be believed (with over 55% of the population feeling in some way antagonistic to Jews). However, this antipathy does not seem to be reflected as far as public behaviour to Jews was concerned. A restraining factor was often at work, typified by the actions of a Scottish novelist and her friends, who attacked Jewish refugees in private 'so that one can get it off one's chest and not say [it] in public'.[63]

This same author also revealed another aspect of attitudes to Jews when she added that 'I try never to feel anti-Semite [sic]'. This indicates the second qualification that needs to be made as regards social antisemitism in the war – its dynamic element. Whilst Nazi antisemitism succeeded in making Britain more Jew-conscious (and possibly actually increased domestic prejudice in some people), it also made a significant part of the population rethink its attitudes to Jews. It has been written that 'it was the Second World War . . . which really precipitated Orwell's critical reappraisal of his attitudes to Jews', yet Orwell was not alone in this, for a large number of Mass-Observers showed similar tendencies. Like Orwell they were not always totally successful in overcoming their prejudices, but as a report in 1943 indicated, although 'many people dislike Jews . . . the majority . . . feel uncomfortable and ashamed of feelings that they recognise as having little basis'.[64] Thus although philosemitism changed little between surveys carried out in 1940 and 1943, unfavourable attitudes to Jews declined by half, and were replaced in the latter year by a greater ambivalence. To some people, the impact of the news of Nazi extermination of Jews in December 1942 lasted only a couple of hours, to many others it was part of a slow realisation that antisemitism was a dangerous problem and that efforts should be made not only to attack its political, but also its personal manifestations. It is significant that individuals such as T. S. Eliot, Lord Alfred Douglas and John Buchan, who were at the forefront of British antisemitism in the 1920s, had repudiated such sentiments by the Second World War.[65]

There was thus a private form of censorship as regards antisemitic sentiments in the war, but how far was antisemitism unacceptable in society as a whole? There is no doubt that some change had taken place in the respectability of antisemitism in Britain by the war compared to a generation earlier. In Oxford University, before 1914 overt antisemitism was almost the norm amongst students, whereas in 1939 an undergraduate at Cambridge could write that whilst many were still privately disdainful of Jews 'it is almost blasphemy in the University to be openly antisemitic'. However, it is easy to be too optimistic as regards society's intolerance of antisemitism, for as Angus Calder has written about the Second World War 'the connection between Nazism–Fascism and antisemitism was not widely grasped in Britain'.[66]

The career of Douglas Reed illustrates the need for caution when evaluating the unrespectability of antisemitism in the war. We have seen, in the case of John Hooper Harvey, how it was possible for an extreme antisemite to successfully move from the world of fringe fascism to wider society. In the case of Douglas Reed the reverse process is observable, yet not until well after the war was this popular author dropped by his publisher, Jonathan Cape. Cape's reluctance to dispose of Reed in some ways is not surprising, for his *Insanity Fair* of 1938, which predicted the Anschluss, was one that gained tremendous public interest, with up to one hundred reprintings before the war. Yet Reed's work was also marked by a blatant antisemitism, one that pervaded throughout even his early books for Cape. His publishers were well aware of his hostility to Jews, and in *Disgrace Abounding*, published in 1939, Reed had been told to rewrite certain sections of the book because of its antisemitism. Cape was satisfied with Reed's revisions; this seems surprising in view of the final product. As in *Insanity Fair*, Reed warned that Jews were trying to take over London as they had Berlin, he cast doubt on the authenticity of German antisemitism and suggested that the public should be more worried about the power of Jews in England.[67]

In the war itself, Reed's work became even more obsessed with the Jewish peril. Influenced it would seem by extremist social credit ideas, Reed became convinced that the *Protocols* were being enacted, 'the evidence becomes too strong to ignore'. The idea of a combined Jewish–Fascist–Bolshevik conspiracy appeared in his work, justifying his belief that antisemitism was a total sham, and that atrocity stories were a plot to gain sympathy for the Jewish cause. All this was mixed in with an infantile gutter antisemitism with Jews being accused of panic, cowardice, the cultural degeneration of Britain and of controlling the black market. Reed was the source of much anger and alarm in the Jewish community, but there was little they could do to stem the flow of Reed's antisemitism. By the middle of the war, Reed had become a convinced antisemite and it is doubtful whether he would have responded to attempts to curb his hostility. However, there is no evidence to suggest that Cape even tried to restrain Reed. Indeed, in their journal *Now and Then*, Reed was still being warmly promoted by his publishers.[68]

Turning to the impact of Reed, a *Jewish Chronicle* editorial commented that his war books had 'gained praise from unexpected quarters'. It is true that many reviewers took Reed to task for his antisemitism, but others were either silent or supportive of his views on the Jews. As far as the public was concerned, Reed himself commented that 'the only antagonism [my books] met was directed against the parts of them which deal with the Jewish Question'.[69] However Reed also gained much support on this issue. Predictably, the extreme antisemitic world became increasingly impressed by Reed, but he was also quoted by many respectable commentators such as the Reverends Bulman and Huxley-Williams (of Cricklewood and Brondesbury) in their campaign against aliens in North West London. To some, Reed merely confirmed their belief that Jewish atrocity stories were false and that 'the Jewish menace will continue to grow', but his writings also shaped attitudes. A Mass-Observer in 1943 commented that he had no opinion on Jews at all until reading Reed, and that 'I now have decided views about them . . . In short I don't like Jews.'[70]

By the end of the war Reed was, like John Hooper Harvey, working in several milieux, being Foreign editor of Kemsley newspapers, yet at the same time forging links with fringe antisemitic organisations. On some occasions he only hinted at the existence of the Jewish conspiracy, at others he used his reputation as an able journalist to give explicit warnings about Jewish power to a wide audience. Reed's continued success, and the refusal of his not unprogressive publishers to remove him, suggests strongly that Nazi persecution of Jews had not made manifestations of antisemitism necessarily beyond the pale in wartime Britain.[71]

Cape was not alone in giving a public forum to an antisemite in the war. In February 1943, the *Daily Dispatch* opened its letter columns to J. B. Rothwell, who accused Jews of controlling the black market and all the war rackets, refusing to join the fighting forces and warned of an anti-Jewish backlash in Britain. The letter, according to Mass-Observation, gained some support although it also led to mass protest meetings in Manchester. The editor of the paper defended his decision to publish the letter, urging that it was necessary to give 'full expression . . . to both sides of a case'. This reason was given by several editors who felt the Jewish question was one that could be legitimately aired, and that it was only fair to give a platform to the antisemitic side of the argument. Characteristic of this approach was a review of Reed's *Lest We Regret* in *The Spectator* by

D. W. Brogan. Brogan attacked the antisemitism of the book, but believed this was no reason to silence Reed, who should be allowed to have his say. The campaign by the Communist Party and the NCCL to make antisemitism a libel offence appears to have been similarly unpopular with the public, who wanted the right to remain antisemitic, regardless of what was happening in Europe. Illustrating this attitude, when Blanche Dugdale went to see the Secretary of State for the Colonies, Oliver Stanley, concerning antisemitic remarks made by Lord Gort, High Commissioner for Palestine, Stanley remarked 'Not everybody likes Jews'. Thus even in government circles, social antisemitism was no reason for being refused office, even when one was directly concerned with Jewish matters.[72]

It is thus unwise to conclude that 'Hitler . . . put an end to the casual, innocent [!] antisemitism of the club-man.' Nazi persecution of Jews at best made an element of the British population rethink its attitude to Jews, but it did not put an end to social antisemitism or make (non-fascist) hostility to Jews unacceptable. Those publishers that removed antisemitism from books, those individuals such as E. M. Forster that refused to have any social contact with antisemites, and those actors that portrayed Shylock in a sympathetic manner, were still in a minority in Britain at war – despite the prevailing anti-fascist spirit.[73]

Antisemitism in Britain cannot be measured therefore simply by looking at the success (or lack of success) of organised fascist and antisemitic groups during the war. It is still necessary, however, to evaluate the strength of hostility to Jews and to see how near domestic antisemitism was to being a serious problem. Measuring antisemitism, whether on an individual or a societal level is always fraught with danger. To talk of levels of antisemitism in British society also ignores the fact that there were many types of hostility to Jews in the six years of the war. There were forms of antisemitism associated with the Jews' War accusation; with the blitz and evacuation; with the refugees; with the black market and army dodging; with literary and social forms of prejudice; with the various political antipathies to Jews; as well as with unique events such as the Bethnal Green tube disaster and the assassination of Lord Moyne. All were in some way related, but many were such distant cousins that direct comparison makes little sense.[74]

However, if caution is applied, a tentative chronological map of war antisemitism can be drawn. At first the nervous tensions of the war, with the anticipation of what was to come – in addition to the nuisance of restrictions such as the blackout – seem to have created antisemitism. It would appear that Jews were blamed for the problems of the 'phoney war' period because they were seen to be also somehow responsible for the war itself. This was the time when 'morale' was probably at its lowest in Britain. It was largely for this reason that Leslie Hore-Belisha was not offered the Ministry of Information, in case his appointment would give any support to the defeatist Jews' War line. Defeatist antisemitism was also one of the reasons for the government's suppression of the BUF, although it needed the threat of invasion to make the Cabinet act on the matter. Nevertheless, in the first six months of the war, although antisemitism had certainly not decreased compared to the pre-war period, it was not a serious problem for the Jewish community.[75]

However, in the months from April to August 1940 the fifth column panic threw Jews, and particularly alien Jews, into the spotlight; the general xenophobia affected the whole Jewish community. Government fears of riots against alien Jews at this time were possibly exaggerated, although attacks on Italians in June 1940 show the need to take such a possibility seriously. The period was also notable for the disintegration of liberal forces within British society. This hostility to aliens continued during the blitz in the autumn of 1940, and maintained its earlier antisemitic character. Before the blitz, it was thought that intensive bombing might lead to an antisemitic reaction. In the event, however, although it did create a general feeling of hostility to Jews in London (with accusations that Jews were crowding the shelters), the East End remained calm. The evacuation associated with the blitz was a more important factor in creating a higher level of antisemitism in Britain, but its dispersed nature limited its potential as an organised feeling.[76]

Throughout 1941, food and other shortages created growing bitterness amongst the British public, and in turn a scapegoat figure was sought out. As with the initial problems of the war, Jews were blamed, but this antisemitism was essentially sporadic until the following year. The year 1942 saw the crystallisation of the concept of the black market, public hostility to this being encouraged by the government. Before long Jews were being strongly identified with the black market, a linkage that was to be the dominant factor determining the strength of antisemitic sentiment in Britain for the rest of the war. The ogre of a black market in itself acted as a safety valve mechanism, releasing the tension caused by rationing. Within this feeling Jews, and particularly alien Jews, became a hate figure, enabling a 'foreign' scapegoat to be blamed for all shortages.[77]

The suggestion that the antisemitism associated with the black market was due to a scapegoat mechanism does not imply that there was no Jewish involvement in it, for as will be shown later, this was substantial. However after 1943, when the black market ceased to be of public concern, antisemitism seems to have generally declined, yet there is no evidence that Jewish black marketeers became any less prominent. It was thus in the periods when the black market was at its most unpopular – in the spring of 1942 and in the winter of 1942 – that antisemitism was most commonly reported to be at its highest level. In the latter period, the news of the extermination of European Jewry appears to have increased Jew-consciousness in Britain, creating on the one hand sympathy, but on the other, increased hostility especially aimed at Jewish black marketeers. This ambivalence would explain the apparent contradiction found by BIPO in January 1943. At this point, according to BIPO, 25% of the population believed antisemitism was increasing, whilst 16% thought it was on the decrease – the highest levels for both categories throughout the war.[78]

It was in early 1943 that the Jewish community became most concerned about the dangers of domestic antisemitism. However, with the military progress of the Allies throughout the rest of the year, the attention of the public moved away from the domestic problems and more to worrying about the post-war world. Antisemitism thus seems to have tailed off by the end of 1943 and to have become sporadic by the following year. Only in 1943 did it appear to have become dangerous, and it would probably have needed a large military disaster to make it very serious. As it was, the Bethnal Green Tube disaster led to widespread accusations against the Jews, but this heated reaction never became physical. Similarly, the assassination of Lord Moyne in November 1944 brought antisemitic comment back into prominence, but again there were no violent disturbances in Britain such as those which followed the Hanging Sergeants incident in 1947.[79]

With hindsight, one can see that the government's fear, which operated throughout the war, of an organised antisemitic feeling in Britain gaining strength, was a long way off happening on a national scale. However, was there a possibility of a local reaction? Late in 1943, a Foreign Office official reported Home Secretary Morrison's concern of 'the growth of antisemitic feeling in certain towns'. The most obvious centres for this would be the cities of Jewish concentration such as London, Manchester, Leeds and to a lesser extent, Glasgow. However, it has been noted that the strength of antisemitic sentiment does not necessarily correspond directly to the number, or concentration, of Jews in a particular locality.[80] Whilst all three of these provincial towns witnessed some antisemitism, especially against Jews who were trying to advance economically and socially, nothing like an organised movement came into existence. Only in North West London, at the end of the war, did this take place. Here the 'Hampstead petition movement' aimed at removing the 'aliens' from this area of London, and a strong degree of antisemitism was linked to this popular organisation.[81]

It would appear that antisemitism was actually higher in towns with a small Jewish population such as Sheffield, Liverpool or Oxford. The lack of familiarity with Jews could create the opportunities for serious misunderstandings. In Sheffield, Jews were accused of evading fire watching duties and of profiteering in blitzed property, both of which allegations were totally without foundation. Criticism of Jews appears to have been a regular occurrence, although there were only 2,200 Jews in the city. Nevertheless, despite personal insults and social ostracism, the local Jewish representatives could report that 'overt antisemitism in Sheffield is not particularly troublesome'. Again, even on a localised level, there was a limit to how far hostility to Jews could be channelled. However the Hampstead movement (admittedly in unique circumstances) shows that Morrison's fear was not totally without foundation.[82]

The relative lack of violence should not lead us to believe that antisemitism was of no consequence in wartime Britain. The Jewish question was to the fore in this period, yet the solutions that were offered were contradictory and left Jews in an impossible dilemma. An element of the population told the Jew to remain separate, a more powerful section urged him to stop being exclusive. Yet Jews who attempted to move freely in British society found that there were still substantial barriers in their way. Faced with a hostile atmosphere in the war, Jews were told that antisemitism was their own fault. Not surprisingly a degree of neuroticism, verging on self-hatred could develop in the Anglo-Jewish community. Thus Nathan Laski was pleased that Hore-Belisha was sacked, as it removed a potential target for antisemites, Lord Rothschild could refrain from sending his children to America lest 'the world should say that seven million Jews are cowards' and Lewis Namier would 'hope to God the fellow is not a Jew' when reading a black market report.[83]

Nevertheless, Nazi antisemitism had some impact on British attitudes to Jews. On an individual level, more progressive people were rethinking their opinions on the issue, and even some Conservatives were beginning to realise that open antisemitism was unacceptable by 1945. At the other extreme, the Communist Party was also reassessing its attitude to Jews, and, with the setting up of its National Jewish Committee in 1943, it started to reject a totally assimilationist approach to the subject. Yet one can overplay the impact of the Nazi factor. Many actually doubted the authenticity of Jewish persecution, and fears about Jewish power persisted throughout the war. As late as 1944, a survey showed that 9% of the British population felt threatened by Jews. Antisemitic stereotypes thus had a strong degree of persistence and it is necessary now to see how the Jewish image as a whole changed in British society during the war.[84]

4

Jews in British society (2) The Jewish image in Britain in the war

Commenting on the survival of medieval stereotypes in the modern world, Norman Cohn has stated that 'myths do not necessarily disappear with the circumstances that first produced them. They sometimes acquire an autonomy, a vitality of their own, that carries them across the continents and down the centuries.' The Jewish stereotype, it has been suggested, possesses a 'massive durability' – the popular belief that Jewish evacuees would have horns would seem to illustrate the point. Nevertheless a dynamic factor is still present in the historical imagery of Jewry.[1] Whilst some stereotypes disappeared or became insignificant over the course of time, others adapted to changing conditions (without necessarily becoming any less unfavourable) and new categories came into existence, though often not without reference to earlier images. In the Second World War it is possible to see this complex process at work in British society; to examine how the stereotypes of 'massive durability' stood up to powerful economic and social change and to evaluate the new imagery of Jewry that emerged from the tension of the war.

The source of much British thinking on Jews in the war predated even the medieval times and rested on the Bible itself. Yet even here there was a typically ambivalent attitude illustrated neatly by the novelist Dorothy Sayers. Sayers remarked that Jews underwent a transformation 'in the blank pages between the Testaments: in the Old, they were "good" people; in the New, they were "bad" people – it seemed doubtful whether they were really the same people'. To a small section of the population, admiration for Biblical Jews carried on to Modern Jews. Visiting a synagogue for the first time in 1942, Blanche Dugdale was moved to write in her diary 'these are indeed The People of the Book . . . two thousand years seemed but as yesterday'. Eleanor Rathbone's philosemitism had similar roots, being drawn by 'the romance of the prophets'. More common, however, was to contrast the 'pure clean-cut Semite' (of which Jesus was a fine example) of the Old Testament, with the modern Jew and his 'sallow complexion, coarse black hair and beard . . . and distinctive hooked nose', as did the Headmaster of Marlborough School in a school religious text.[2]

Sayers herself suffered from no such ambivalence, stating in the war, that she was 'hopelessly allergic to Old Testament characters'. It is thus not surprising that Sayers' radio plays based on the life of Jesus, *The Man Born to be King*, showed a continuing hostility to New Testament Jews. Matthew is described as 'as vulgar a little commercial Jew as ever walked Whitechapel' who behaves like an ancient black marketeer. Moreover, the plays were notable for the way in which Sayers portrayed the crucifixion. With an audience in the millions, this BBC play (which was broadcast from November 1941 to October 1942 and repeated in Easter 1943), upset the Jewish community. The latter believed that the bloodthirsty Jewish demand for the death of Jesus, as depicted in *The Man Born to be King*, would create antisemitism.[3]

Sayers' unsympathetic account – the Jewish mob chants 'Crucify! Crucify! Crucify! A'rrh, A'rrh, A'rrh' – highlights the fact that this charge of deicide against the Jews was still commonly being made nearly 2,000 years later. A reader of *Tribune* was shocked to hear a five-year-old tell a Jewish friend 'you are a naughty girl – why did you kill our Jesus?' However, many other Jewish children suffered at school, especially at Easter, from this accusation.[4] Nor was this a monopoly of the immature. After a broadcast in 1941 on Christian attitudes to Jews, W. W. Simpson was sent a variety of antisemitic letters, many from clergymen, some of whom attacked Jews for killing Christ. Similarly, a Mass-Observation survey just before the war found that several correspondents believed that Jews 'must and will (always) be guilty' and that 'they are now suffering for their actions'. Many still believed that economic rather than religious reasons were more important in explaining modern antisemitism, but it would appear that, up to 1945, Christian attitudes to Jews had not significantly changed.[5] W. W. Simpson, as secretary of the Council of Christians and Jews (CCJ) from its formation in 1941, believed that although some Christians were beginning to re-examine their approach to the subject in the war, the CCJ was still ahead of the time in being sympathetic to the Jewish religion. There was still widespread religious belief that Jews were responsible for antisemitism, even in its German form, and that this was somehow related to the Jewish responsibility for the Crucifixion, and for the subsequent refusal of Jews to recognise Jesus as the Messiah. Indeed, some went further, denying that Jesus was actually a Jew – a Mass-Observer being rebuked for even suggesting this for 'He was the son of God apparently.' Nevertheless, philosemitism associated with the image of Jesus as a Jew did exist, one Jewish soldier having his bed made by a Welsh Methodist for this reason![6]

Despite, or even because of, its early Jewish origins, the early Church had become anti-Jewish and medieval antisemitism was essentially Christian. Through the Gospels themselves, the Jew as Christ-killer was transformed into the Jew-Devil or anti-Christ. With such thinking, the Blood Libel myth was able to appear for the first time, in Norwich in 1144 and a century later in Lincoln where, due to 'the cruel distortion by myth of reality', nineteen Jews were hanged for the alleged ritual murder of a child. Yet, like the Christ-killing Jew, the Jew-Devil imagery was another medieval legacy that survived into the Second World War.[7]

No new fresh cases of ritual murder accusations were made in Britain from the Lincoln case in 1255 until the eighteenth-century. However, through Chaucer's 'The Prioress's Tale' and seventeenth- and eighteenth-century pamphleteers, the idea was kept alive in Britain. As the nineteenth-century essayist, Charles Lamb, wrote 'Old prejudices cling about me. I cannot shake off the story of Hugh of Lincoln.' Chaucer's account of the latter was also converted into a popular eighteenth-century ballad called 'Sir Hugh' or 'The Jew's daughter'. To quote Jennifer Westwood 'old legends die hard' and the late nineteenth-century witnessed a revival of the accusation in Britain, with the Ripper Murders not being free of this medieval charge. These continued sporadically in the 1920s and 30s, when the charge was made by both respectable Catholics and the more marginal Arnold Leese.[8]

However, we need to keep a delicate sense of balance over the importance of blood libel accusations in Britain by the Second World War. On the one hand, one must agree with an Edgware vicar who in 1940 claimed that whilst antisemitism was widespread 'most people had not heard of Ritual murders'. Even the English oral tradition was not impervious to change and it is significant that twentieth-century versions of 'Sir Hugh' have been sanitised from antisemitism, if not ritual murder. Nevertheless, on the other hand, occasional claims were made during the war that Jews may have committed such crimes in the past, one even being made in the House of Lords. Also we have already seen how John Hooper Harvey managed to put the charge in a mainstream school history book, whilst the popular commentator, Douglas Reed, praised Chaucer's 'Hugh of Lincoln' in 1942. By 1945, it was slowly being recognised that the ritual murder accusation was unrespectable – though it took until 1959 for a plaque of the incident at Lincoln to be removed from the Cathedral. Characters such as Harvey have kept the myth alive in postwar Britain, and it is thus understandable why objections have been made recently to satirical accounts of ritual murder in the magazine *Punch*. The charge is not so dead as to be regarded as a joke.[9]

Neither should the blood libel accusation be examined in isolation, for it is part of a wider imagery that suggests the essential evilness of Jewry. It has been noted how shechita was linked to ritual murder, and how the former was a result of 'Jewish Cruelty'. Similarly, animal rights' groups specifically attacked the involvement of Jews in the fur trade, stating that the infliction of pain involved in the industry was essentially un-British. Medical groups also attacked vivisection and even vaccination as products of the inhuman Jewish mind. It is thus important to remember that whilst few believed explicity in the blood libel, or in the extremist Alexander Ratcliffe's idea that Jews were part of 'the synagogue of Satan', Mass-Observation found that over 60% of the population 'were convinced that Jews were in some way evil'. The horned, fanged and bearded devil-Jew of Ratcliffe's propaganda was simply a more direct descendant of the medieval image than the more popular concept that Jewish evacuees were envisaged to have protuberances on their heads. The legacy of the middle ages had thus survived, albeit more commonly in a watered down and confused form.[10]

A parallel development can be found in another aspect of the Jew-devil link – the sexual fear of Jews. It has been perceptively pointed out that the antisemitism associated with Jewish white slave traffickers at the turn of the century, with its suggestions of demonic Jewish influence, 'represented a sexualization of the ritual murder accusation'. Moreover, it was a charge that continued in Britain in the Second World War (despite the total demise of this trade). Again, we can see a process where only a few extremists and the occasional popular author actually raised the Jewish white slave issue, but where fears of Jewish sexual power were much more widespread.[11] The death of Freud in October 1939 brought forth comments about his obsession with sex and his 'unwholesome influence on the inter-war years.' On a more personal level, a young Jewish refugee was told that the only reason she wanted to go to the city was for carnal purposes – 'Man mad – you dirty Jew bitch!' Harold Nicolson assumed, without any evidence whatsoever, that a group of girls accompanying some American soldiers in 1944 were East End Jews. He commented in his diary 'I am all for a little promiscuity. But nymphomania among East End Jewesses and for such large sums of money makes me sick.' These series of leaps in imagination show how the process of distortion could occur, and how antisemitic sexual imagery could make its impact on even such an urbane and sexually liberated character as Nicolson.[12]

The image was certainly one that continued in popular literature. In John G. Brandon's *Death in Duplicate* (1945), although Isaac Levant is a 'dirty, greasy rat', he also had a 'strange power over women', a predator who had teeth 'like those of a man-eating denizen of the deep.' In the hugely successful novel by the Manning Coles, *Drink to Yesterday* (1940), it is not sensuality but sheer money power that allows the 'Jew-boy' to buy off two nice young Aryan girls who are simply 'hungry'. However, whilst the 'greasy Jew' is a threat to 'white' women in such novels, the Jewess, in typically ambivalent fashion, is often beautiful, possibly wicked, but totally acceptable to the Gentile. The war thus did little to break down these long held literary and attitudinal sexual stereotypes, as is illustrated by the remarks of the daughter of a well known novelist. Despite the persecution of Jews and a knowledge that she was herself prejudiced, she could not help thinking of Jews as 'Shylocks . . . or else beautifully wicked Jewesses who are mistresses of millions of men . . . the women never grow old and the men are never young.' It is now necessary to turn to the first part of her equation – the 'greedy old men huddled over their moneybags, and lending money at enormous interest'. That is the less exotic, but more prevalent, legacy from the Middle Ages – the image of the Jew as usurer.[13]

It is clear that, even in the medieval period, Jews by no means dominated money-lending, yet by 'the twelfth-century the words "Jew" and "usurer" had become almost synonymous'. In Britain the usury issue was used as a pretext for the expulsion of the Jews in 1290. Yet despite the absence of Jewish money-lenders in Britain for the next four centuries, the image of usurer continued either in literature (of which Marlowe's Jew of Malta and Shakespeare's Shylock are only the best known examples of a common portrayal), the Church or in folk tales. As a literary convention, the Shylock figure has been 'persistent . . . international [and] fairly static', and this seems to have been reflected in popular thinking. In Manchester in the 1880s, although Jews played only a minor role in money-lending in the city, a local journalist, Walter Tomlinson, believed that the identification of Jews with extortionate usury was 'extensively believed in'. Indeed, the historian of British antisemitism has concluded that up to 1914 the image of the Jew as Shylock was one of the two dominant perceptions of Jewry, and one that was to continue in the inter-war period. Did this change in the Second World War?[14]

A study of the Shylock image in the war reveals the complex way in which stereotypes change during periods of economic and social upheaval. Firstly, we need to recognise the tremendous persistence of the image and of the cultural forces that promoted it. The depth of the antisemitic tradition in the area of usury was illustrated by Captain Ramsay's attempt to revive the Statute of Jewry of 1290 in the Commons at the end of the war. Ramsay's admiration for Edward I's campaign against Jewish extortion and exploitation was shared by the '27 July 1941 movement' – one that wanted this day (that of the expulsion of the Jews) to become a national holiday. However, outside the extremist world, the source of beliefs linking Jews to usury were more obvious. They stemmed largely from a childhood reading of *The Merchant of Venice*, written when hardly any Jews lived in England. A survey on the major influences affecting people's attitudes to Jews found that Shakespeare's play was one of the most important.[15]

Nevertheless there was change, and the second point to note is that the Shylock image had altered from its original form. A satirical work on English attitudes to foreigners published in 1935 suggested that although 'Jews . . . are undoubtedly very cunning and get the better of Christians . . . no one expects nowadays to come upon funny business with pounds of flesh'. In literature it is rare to find an actual Jewish money-lender by the 1940s. What was more common was the offspring of Shylock's younger 'cousin' – Fagin or, more frequently, Shylock in modern garb, the Jewish financier. We have seen how fear of Jewish finance permeated British society in the war, and the same image emerges in popular literature, reinforcing long-held stereotypes. So strong were these that they actually affected relations with ordinary Jews. A Jewish soldier reported in the war that 'I had a most difficult job in explaining to one of my room mates that I [was] not an International Jewish Financier.'[16]

The all-powerful Jewish financier was not a new literary development in the war, indeed it was a stereotype that had been strongly rooted since the late nineteenth-century, especially in authors such as John Buchan. What is interesting is how this figure continues into the war in the works of several popular novelists – regardless of Nazi persecution of Jews. Elizabeth Kyle's *The White Lady* (1941) has a Jewish financier, Julius Hermani, who was 'not so much a man as an expression of power'. As well as dominating single-handed 'the commercial life of Central Europe', Hermani controlled the balance of European political power and he eventually organises a peasant revolution. How deeply this literary stereotype had become ingrained is illustrated by a review of this book in the liberal (and philosemitic) *Time and Tide*. The reviewer did not attack the portrayal of Hermani but commented merely that he was 'a Jew financier', assuming that the journal's readers would know what this meant. In the work of Anthony Parsons, the hero, Sexton Blake, is pitted against a Jewish financier, Simon Levey, and the yellow peril in the form of Si Lung, a tea magnate. Levey, via an international currency swindle, is controlling both the Bank of England and the Bank of China. Interestingly, the Jewish peril is shown to be greater than the yellow, for we later find out that Blake has only one enemy, for Si Lung is in fact Levey in disguise![17]

We thus see the perpetuation of the international Jewish financier image but a third and final point about the development of the Shylock image needs to be made. It has been shown that the usurer stereotype was transformed into that of the financier, but there was also a positive change by the time of the war. By 1940, authors like John Buchan had studiously avoided using Jewish financiers in their stories, some theatres were beginning to treat Shylock sympathetically and it would seem that a Mass-Observer, who was starting to question her image of the Shylockian Jew, in the light of 'Hitler and Streicher', was not alone. Even so, the belief that Jews were obsessed with money was still perceived by the British public to be the dominant Jewish trait in the war. In an opinion poll carried out in 1940, 38% of the comments on money-mindedness were connected to Jews. Exactly the same percentage of the sample saw Jews as predatory; statistics showing that Jews were not only linked to money, but were also, and because of this, perceived as a malevolent powerful force in British society.[18]

This was most blatantly portrayed in *The Protocols of the Elders of Zion*. It has been noted how The Britons circulated two editions of this document in the war, and how fascist and antisemitic groups referred to them increasingly throughout the conflict. However, it has also been shown how through such publicists as Douglas Reed, or the organ *Truth*, conspiracy ideas reached a wider public.[19] It is now necessary to examine how widespread the image of the all-powerful Jew was across British society.

Writing in the late 1960s about the history of antisemitic conspiracy theories, James Parkes pointed out that 'there was a time when it would have been unnecessary to explain what *The Protocols* are, for they were blazoned over the national press, and agonised discussions were held as to whether they were genuine or not'. This was certainly true of the early 1920s and although a change had taken place by 1939, it is remarkable how often *The Protocols* were discussed in the war. Excluding extremist sources, the authenticity of this document was the subject of lengthy correspondence in the *Catholic Herald, The Scotsman* and more briefly in the *London Teacher*.[20]

Moreover, *The Protocols* found an outlet through the influence of the social credit movement. Professions such as medicine and the building trade, which were prone to resorting to money-lending, were susceptible to this ideology. Thus *Medical World* and the *Builders' Merchants Journal* contained antisemitic conspiracy ideas in the war. Adding to this picture was the British Israel movement. Whilst it is easy to dismiss as cranks the believers of the theory that Britons were the real descendants of the Chosen People, it is evident that in the war British Israelitism was extremely popular, to the extent of causing the government concern.[21] Some of their literature merely suggested that modern Jews had no connection to those of the bible, but a significant section, headed by the prolific Basil Stewart, went further. They argued that *The Protocols* outlined how the real Chosen People had been usurped by Ashkenaci (sic) modern Jews, who were 'racially neither Jewish nor Semitic but mongrel breeds of minor Asiatic races'. The sales of such pamphlets, according to George Orwell, were enormous.[22]

When added to the fact that the Nazis were using *The Protocols* in their propaganda and, according to Goebbels, by 1943 devoting between 70 to 80% of their broadcasts to antisemitism, it is not surprising that Maurice Samuel could write in 1943 that 'today *The Protocols* are embedded in the minds of millions as genuine revelations'. Nevertheless, Mass-Observation surveys on Jews reveal that explicit reference to *The Protocols* was rare. The comment that 'I always see the Jews as a huge *octopus* with its tentacles spread over the wealth of the world, and *nothing* but *chopping* will get those tentacles separated from the *wealth*' being an exception. Yet out of a sample of sixty-eight replies in October 1940, twelve (17%) expressed concern over Jewish power in society, of whom four (5%) believed that Jews actually controlled Britain.[23]

Thus the influence of *The Protocols* was more indirect, perhaps most popularly expressed in the 'Jews' War' argument, but also in the common belief that Jews controlled public opinion via the press, or culture via dance bands, comedy and the cinema.[24] The latter was the most serious complaint, with Jewish finance (the alleged controller of the screen), being blamed for destroying the Christian Sabbath, or, in more Svengalian imagery, for 'producing a type of robot mind'. Ironically, the claim that Jews controlled culture (a 'fact' according to the *St. Helens Reporter* 'which is accepted as naturally almost as nightfall and dawn'), was being made at a time when Jewish influence over the cinema and theatre was declining rapidly.[25] Yet, in the distorting atmosphere of a society where the concept of Jewish power was almost taken for granted; where intelligent observers could seriously 'never understand why world Jewry allowed Hitler to get away with [persecuting their brethren],' and where 12% of the population believed that there were more than three million Jews in Britain (and 42% could overestimate the real figure of 400,000); one can understand how the mistaken belief that Jews culturally dominated Britain could become a prejudice, unchanging when exposed to new knowledge.[26]

The concept of Jewish power was but another aspect of the legacy of medieval antisemitism, with the magical and demonic Jew transformed to meet the needs of modern society in the shape of the Learned Elder, the international Rothschild, or the Hollywood Mogul. There now remains, after having examined the image of the Jew as Christ-killer, Demon and world power, the need to consider the final aspect of the medieval contribution to modern antisemitism; the idea of the Jew as the perpetual alien. In the modern period, a dual process operated whereby a durable stereotype of the Jew as foreigner was reinforced in both the late nineteenth-century and the 1930s by a new influx of Jewish immigrants. Ironically, at both points the established Jewish community had become Anglicised. For this reason, the new arrivals were often badly received by their co-religionists who feared that the alien Jewish image was being given new ammunition. Nevertheless, old and new Jews *were* differentiated in Britain; as one satirist put it; 'Oriental Jews wear beards and occidental Jews wear diamonds.' The former was portrayed in Warwick Deeping's *The Dark House* (1941) – described as a 'Yid' who 'cringed and whimpered', '*it*' had 'a huge bowler hat, a long black overcoat almost down to its feet. It had a sallow face, and a hook nose, and a black retriever beard. It lisped.'[27] This was part of the 'Jew-boy' image, the Whitechapel Jew, whose other half had semi-contradictory features. His alter ego was just as physically unattractive and as oily but was not cringing but 'flashy', 'suave, well-dressed, financially successful and without scruple'. The 'Aldgate' Jew could simultaneously be very rude whilst 'cringing to an extent that is almost indecent'.[28]

Having escaped from the East End to the more affluent pastures of North West London, the Jew-boy is transformed, but not beyond recognition. He may, or may not have lost his lisp en route, but in the process he had acquired even more diamonds for his podgy fingers, along with some bright plus-fours and patent leather shoes. The nouveau-riche Jew may have entered Hampstead but he was 'of any nationality save English'. Thus in Hugh Massingham's *The Harp and the Oak* (1945), a well-meaning Jewish doctor causes havoc in a country village because, despite his wealth, he was not 'a real gentleman' but 'like a showman at a fair, displaying the [pound] notes with expansive negligence'. By 'ram [ming] Semitism' down the villagers' throats, Dr Abrahams becomes the hate figure and eventually an antisemitic riot occurs. Massingham attacks both the excesses of village prejudice *and* the Jewish irritant in society – the 'assimilated Jew' is still not an Englishman.[29]

As the Jewish bourgeois was still in a way an alien, it enabled an attack to be made on materialism without it being an assault on wealth itself. In the war, the sin of being ostentatiously wealthy could be blamed on the Jews; many believing (quite falsely) that Jews predominated in all the expensive haunts of London. The press pandered to such ideas, most notoriously in the case of Isaac Wolfson, the head of Great Universal Stores. Wolfson was portrayed in the *Daily Express* in 1943 as a tasteless, money-obsessed parvenu. Although his home had a great library (like a country gentleman's), he had no time to read the books. Indeed his home was not really English, it was more 'like an ambitious Hollywood film set'. A similar assault was attempted on Leslie Hore-Belisha, emphasising both his ostentation and his Jewishness.[30]

The alien Jew stereotype thus proved to be both persistent and malleable. In the 1930s, however, it gave birth to a new image, one created out of changing conditions but, as ever, with strong linkages to the past – the Jew as refugee. By the time of the war, the quantity of books depicting the plight of Jewish refugees was itself creating hostile comment, even from liberal elements within British society. *Tribune*'s Daniel George stated that he was 'getting sick of them', and Orwell remarked in 1940 that 'for the time being we have heard enough about the concentration camps and the persecution of the Jews'. The refugee Jew image had thus arrived, but it is vital to stress that this was not necessarily the positive or sympathetic happening as might at first be assumed. It is true that Britain prided itself on its supposed liberal and humanitarian history of allowing the oppressed to enter, and that the categorisation 'refugee' itself implied less negative qualities than that of 'alien', but even the former term did not imply total innocence.[31]

However, in some of the literature of the war, a philosemitic image of refugees does emerge, most clearly seen in the works of Phyliss Bottome. Bottome, who along with her husband had worked 'night and day to help refugees escaping from Hitler', portrayed Austrian and German Jews not just as victims, but as people. In *Within the Cup* (1943), the Austrian Jewish narrator, Rudolph, pointed out that 'people think of refugees as unfortunate people who have lost their homes, suffered various painful experiences . . . driven out of their country in a moneyless and embarrassing condition . . . but we are something quite different. We are human beings changed in essence'. Similarly, in Peter Mendelssohn's *Across the Dark River*, published just after the war, the narrator refers to an Austrian–Jewish innkeeper, Mr Schapiro, who is being increasingly persecuted. Schapiro is described as being 'just an ordinary man like myself. So what?'[32]

This seemingly obvious point was not grasped by other pro-refugee writers. Ada Jackson won the Greenwood Prize for poetry in 1943 with her 'Behold the Jew', nineteen pages of verse which likened persecuted Jews to 'driven birds and badgers baited to their deaths and bulls that . . . bleed for strutting matadors . . . otters slain for wantonness'. In similar patronising fashion Geoffrey Johnson compared 'the world-wide-wandering Jew' to the 'foxes and birds of the wild' both 'seeking a hole to nestle in'. Rebelling against this sort of approach, Phyliss Bottome's refugee concludes that 'I am not like a bird. I am a man who loves a home, who has once had one, and been deeply rooted.'[33] Yet Jackson's furry mammalian imagery was more prevalent than that represented by Phyliss Bottome. In real life interaction the same was true – refugee adults receiving a muted welcome but 'the children evoking pity'. Those like Eleanor Rathbone, who were filled not with pity for the refugee but with 'pleasure in his company', were comparatively rare. As the editor of an anthology on the Jews pointed out in 1945, 'so long as they are looked on as one looks at freaks at a fair or animals in the zoo, the future of the Jews will be dark indeed'.[34]

However, the very fact that refugee Jews were human – with all the faults this naturally entailed – created problems for the poet Louis Macneice. Hoping that the experience of persecution would enrich the character of the Jews, Macneice was disappointed when he found that they remained ordinary people. Thus in his poem *Refugees* (1940), in the words of his biographer; 'exiles flee to be themselves'. Macneice described the refugees in uncomplimentary terms, referring to their 'prune dark eyes, thick lips' or elsewhere as 'hawk-like foreign faces the gutteral sorrow of the refugees', 'resigned Lazaruses who want another chance'. The idea that the refugees simply wanted to go to America to start again anonymously disgusted Macneice who already hated the loss of individuality in the modern mass world. Nevertheless, if the poetry of Macneice or Ada Jackson denied the refugee Jew the freedom to act as a human, their underlying feeling was one of sympathy for the exiles. To others, perhaps the majority, the refugee was not necessarily a victim.[35]

The point is well illustrated by a social survey in October 1940. Of all comments concerning oppressed people, 47% were directed towards the Jews, yet only 18% felt Jews were deserving sympathy. Such a dichotomy can also be found in literature. Eunice Buckley's *Family From Vienna* (1941) has a group of refugees who were a 'paradoxical mixture of tragedy and arrogance, resignation and discontent', who have 'a regrettable likeness to those of the Jews caricatured in Nazi newspapers'. In Sarah Campion's *Makeshift* (1940) the refugees are equally repulsive, one admitting 'they're awful: we're awful, but we live!' Lip service is paid to the evilness of Nazi antisemitism, but the refugee is not therefore seen as innocent. In *Men in the Same Boat* (1943), an old German Jew escaping to America rues the fact that if it had not been for the Nazis 'he would not have been a successful man and made money . . . If it were not for them, the Jews would have become the secret rulers of the earth, by controlling all the money markets.' The Manning Coles detective hero, Tommy Hambledon, is also split between the need to destroy the Nazi racket in confiscating Jews' property, and the knowledge that the Jew 'had battened on the miseries of Germany in the bad years'. This approach explains why the Government was reluctant to use Jewish persecution in its atrocity propaganda. 'Horror', pointed out a Ministry of Information memorandum in 1941, 'must be used very sparingly and must deal always with treatment of indisputably innocent people. Not with violent political opponents. And not with Jews.'[36]

However, in a significant number of cases, the refugee Jew was not only unpleasant but actually seen as a threat to British society. To explain how this could be believed it is necessary to refer back to the Jew-alien image – the Jew as an undesirable element who knows loyalty only to himself. The refugee Jew could thus be a fifth columnist, *despite* Nazi antisemitism. The spy scare gave the cheap thriller in Britain a new lease of life, and often a Jewish character was present in these books. Tom Harrisson, who studied such literature, found that 'half worked in a Jew somehow or other, and only in one case was the reference not unfavourable'. In the *Black Cripple* (1941), Karl Mendel, a 'swarthy, Jewish-looking man', was the Gestapo chief in Britain, who 'knows everything'. Andrew Soutar also warned against alien refugee agents who 'had insinuated themselves into trusted positions'. *Truth* was not isolated in warning against the 'Refuspy'. The novelist, Somerset Maugham, commented that 'the Gestapo is known to have had spies among refugees, and these have not seldom been Jews'.[37] A film *Next of Kin*, and a radio play *Music for Miss Rogers*, all contributed to an atmosphere where refugee Jews were not only disliked but actively mistrusted. Without knowledge of this background image, it is impossible to understand the public reaction to the refugees in the summer of 1940. However, the impact of Nazi racialism had one positive impact on the thriller genre; antisemitism revealed by a character was often an indication of being an enemy agent – a technique paradoxically used by many authors who simultaneously attacked refugee Jews.[38]

A brief examination of the situation in North West London during the war reveals a close similarity between the Jewish refugee image, and the manner in which refugees were actually treated and regarded in an area of high refugee concentration. At the start of the war, 14,000 aliens – the vast majority of whom were Jewish – lived in Hampstead, Golders Green and Hendon, and it is probable that the number increased throughout the conflict. However, in Hendon alone there were 145,000 people. The idea of an alien takeover in the area of what Douglas Reed called 'St Johanns Wood, Finchley Strasse and British West Hampstead' was far-fetched.[39] Nevertheless, refugee Jews were prominent in the area, a fact that some locals appreciated – a Hampstead man commenting 'I like them being here. For the first time London feels like a cosmopolitan city.' Others expressed sympathy, admired their artistic talents or simply liked the refugees as people.[40]

However, there was enormous hostility to alleged refugee behaviour in North West London. Refugees were supposed to have been rude and aggressive, especially in the local shops. It was a feeling supported by local papers – the *Hampstead and Highgate Express*, the *Hendon, Finchley and Golders Green Times* and the *Kilburn Times* echoing the earlier hostility of all East End papers to the Eastern European newcomers.[41] Despite close personal contact, local refugees were accused of being foreign agents, one sympathetic Hampstead resident writing that 'I have heard it said that one-half the refugees are dangerous elements — spies, Nazis and whatnot, who never ought to be allowed at liberty in this country.' Internment was both urged and then welcomed in 1940. The *Hampstead Express* went as far as saying it was 'a blessing in disguise' as it gave a chance to clear the area of refugees. Brief mention has already been made of the Hampstead petition movement which became a formal organisation at the end of the war. The feeling it represented had been growing throughout the conflict, with several whispering campaigns against the refugees reported in 1943.

Progressive elements in North West London attacked the petition movement as antisemitic and Nazi-inspired, but over 2,000 residents supported the attempt to remove the 'aliens' from the area.[42]

North West London thus represented a microcosm of the whole refugee stereotype – admired by a few, pitied by many, but disliked and feared by an even larger number. Both the heated feelings in Hampstead at the end of the war on a local scale, and the national reaction in the summer of 1940 show the need to take the hostility to Jewish refugees in Britain seriously. The 'new' image of refugees owed much to earlier hostile attitudes to Jews, and thus did not improve the position of Jews in society as a whole. The same could be said with even more conviction for the most dominant image of Jews in the war – one that was created in the conflict but owed much to practically every earlier Jewish stereotype; the Jew as black marketeer.

The identification of Jews and the black market in the war was almost as strong as that between Jews and usury in the medieval period. Discussion of either topic usually brought in the other and, as has been illustrated, levels of domestic antisemitism were strongly correlated to the relative unpopularity of the black market. In the introduction it was stated that to understand antisemitism one needs to examine four questions. Firstly, what was the prevalent Jewish image in society? Secondly, who was attacking the Jews? Thirdly, what was the social and economic background to the attacks, and finally what was the Jewish role in society? To explain why the Jewish black marketeer image became so prevalent, we need to examine all these issues in turn to produce a total picture.[43]

Firstly, the Jewish image. In many ways the Jewish and black marketeer stereotype coincided. The black marketeer was inevitably money-minded and unscrupulous in the way he made his fortune, corresponding neatly to the Shylock image. He was also foreign, dark and 'evil-faced' and an internal threat to Britain. Again popular stereotypes of Jews could easily be applied to fit the role, especially as Jews were often linked to villainy in traditional British attitudes. The black marketeer was also seen as a power in society, and it comes as little surprise to find that it was popularly believed that Jews were 'at the bottom of the conspiracy in almost every black market prosecution', with over 70% of the population believing that there was an organised black market. Even Jewish attempts to deal with the black market were viewed in a conspiratorial light, the *Daily Mail* referring to 'the black tribunals' asserting 'a tremendous influence' and *Truth* to a 'racial Sanhedrin'. Lastly, the black marketeer was closely related to the war profiteer. In the 1914–18 conflict Jews had been accused of making money, while the boys were away fighting. The idea that the Second World War would help Jews could also easily be adapted to suggest that the war would financially benefit the Jewish community.[44]

It was with the knowledge that the war was likely to bring about such accusations, that the *Jewish Chronicle* warned its readers in September 1939 not to indulge in any profiteering. It believed that such activities would lead to the whole community being charged with misbehaviour. In the same month, the *Jewish Chronicle*'s fears were borne out with the BUF launching an attack on aliens seeking to make their fortune out of the war. This brings us to the second question – who linked Jews to the black market?[45]

It is not surprising that organised fascist and antisemitic groups did their utmost to stress the Jewish involvement in the black market. This was done by literature, leaflets, whispering campaigns and letters to the press, of which J. B. Rothwell's was only the most infamous. Rothwell's letter also circulated as a leaflet and it was popularly received. Nevertheless extremist activities, although reinforcing the Jewish black marketeer stereotype, did not alone create the spontaneous public feeling on the issue. Even at the start of the war, 'Beachcomber' of the *Daily Express* could write 'Here lies the profiteer Kosteufelstein, Called latterly Fitzwarren, There is some corner of an English field, That is for ever foreign.'[46]

Throughout the war this identification continued, present in radio plays, the House of Commons, popular literature, comics, even in a 'brainteaser', where contestants had to work out the prison sentences of Messrs. Abrams, Brody and Cohen![47] The Jewish black marketeer very nearly made an appearance in a Ministry of Food propaganda film. However, most important of all was the role of the press in promoting this stereotype. Major attacks were launched on Jewish involvement in black marketeering in papers ranging from *Time and Tide* and the *Daily Mirror* to the *Spectator*. Many had lengthy correspondence on the subject, where it was claimed that up to 90% of all offences were committed by Jews. Yet more vital than this was the selection of black market prosections chosen by the press. In May 1941, of 2,000 Ministry of Food cases, forty were reported in the national press. Of these, twenty (50%) were Jewish. Similarly in March 1942, *The Grocer* reported forty-eight cases, only three of which involved Jews, yet it was these three and only a few others that received national attention.[48]

When the Jewish community accused the newspaper world of antisemitic bias in reporting the black market, vigorous denials were made.

Nevertheless, it is hard to resist the conclusion that the press was pandering to popular taste on this matter. Home Intelligence commented in 1942 that 'satisfaction is reported where [black market] activities and prosecutions can be traced to Jews'. The press which, in Herbert Morrison's words, had now shown 'any undue tenderness . . . to black market offenders' made the most of this Jewish unpopularity.[49]

The Jewish image was suited to being converted into a black marketeer stereotype and it was widely employed across society in the war. However, these factors alone did not mean that the 'Jewish black marketeer' ogre was an inevitable occurrence. To explain why it came into prominence the precise economic and social background needs to be taken into consideration. It has been shown that the black market, which in reality was fairly insignificant, operated as a scapegoat mechanism; the Jews becoming a scapegoat within a scapegoat. When the press and public became bored with the subject in the latter part of the war it was not due to any decline in the black market, which paradoxically probably increased. With a decline in interest in the black market came a decline in the domestic antisemitism associated with it – although the Jewish black marketeer did not disappear. Does this mean the Jewish role in the black market was irrelevant?[50]

The answer is complex. On occasions, including several prominent court cases, a Jewish involvement was suggested where none existed. However, this must not disguise the fact that there was a significant Jewish involvement in the black market. A study of offences committed between April 1942 and May 1943 revealed that 10·9% of over 2,500 Board of Trade and Ministry of Food prosecutions were carried out by Jewish offenders. This proportion rises to 24% if the figures are limited to the five major trades where the black market occurred and to six of the major urban areas of Britain. Given that the Jewish population of Britain was less than 1% of the total, the figures at first sight seem alarming. However, another survey revealed that Jews owned up to 15% of firms in Britain, and that if the same trade and location factors are imposed, a figure of 23% is obtained.[51] In other words, the Jewish involvement in the black market was closely related to the proportion of Jews in the British economy. The pronounced Jewish presence in the black market reflected not a lack of business morality, which was so often assumed, but a stage in the socio-economic development of Anglo-Jewry, where small business ownership was common.[52] The prominence of refugees in the black market can also be explained without reference to their alleged naturally ingrained dubious business practices. Involvement in the black market was largely due to the dire financial position of many of these foreign Jews in the war, added to their difficulty in understanding the complex rationing regulations. Even so, a Home Office survey in 1941 found that the alien Jewish involvement was only fractionally above what was statistically expected.

On purely rational grounds, therefore, the British public was inaccurate in accusing Jews of undue involvement in the black market. However, in the real world of a British society fraught with domestic tensions, it is not surprising that the public was motivated more by emotion rather than cool statistical analysis. Although the Jewish black marketeer stereotype was principally generated by a scapegoat mechanism – and the Government participated in this – the Jewish involvement *was* relevant to the question. Real Jewish offenders confirmed past prejudices, and it would seem that some exceptionally bad cases in which Jews were involved generated particularly strong antisemitism.[53]

Black market antisemitism was probably the most important element of British hostility to Jews in the war. Nevertheless, no Jewish black marketeers were ever physically assaulted, although there is evidence that Ministry of Food officials particularly sought out Jewish shopkeepers to prosecute and that the courts were more severe against Jewish offenders. Certainly some Jewish refugees received rough justice by being re-interned for petty war regulation crimes; in other words, Jewish myth was transformed once again into a real world situation. Yet aside from the problems imposed on the Jewish community, the bogey of the Jewish black marketeer helped to raise morale in society as a whole, enabling a safe scapegoat to be used to deflect attention from the problems of rationing.[54] However, Jews were rarely accused of black marketeering alone – they were almost always simultaneously alleged to be avoiding their military duties. Taken together, these dual accusations were a diluted form of the Jews' War argument.

On pure statistical grounds there was again no basis for the Jewish war shirker image to come about. To explain its pervasive appeal one has, as usual, to examine the past Jewish stereotype. The most significant aspect in this respect was the combined image of the cowardly and non-physical Jew. According to a London headmaster, Jews were 'naturally cowards', a view shared by much of the population. There were widespread accusations that the Jews were running away at the start of the war (rumours that were also made in the First World War), or joining the 'safe' civil defence units. As has been shown with the blitz, there were rumours that Jews were both fleeing the city and crowding the tube shelters; even in government circles there were fears of an alien panic.[55]

Secondly there was the question of loyalty. The 1914–18 conflict had re-emphasised the alien quality of the Jewish immigrants. It would appear that memories of the Alien Military Service problem persisted into the Second World War. The belief that Jews were not actually entitled to fight for Britain was not uncommon; Elsie Janner was told that 'I didn't know there were any Jews in the forces.' More prevalent was the idea that Jews simply did not want to help the war effort, and apart from the army dodging issue, Jews were accused of avoiding firewatching duties, Jewish women of escaping war work, and young men of not being Bevin boys. Thirdly there was the ever present conspiracy argument; Jews were said to be at the forefront of the military service ramp.[56]

The combined image of Jews as weak, cowardly, alien and powerful were all strongly ingrained in the public mind. Indeed the strength of such imagery is highlighted by the experience of Jews in the British Forces during the Second World War. As was the case in the 1914–18 conflict, a disproportionate number of Jews joined the Forces – 15% of Anglo-Jewry or 60,000 men and women compared to 10% of the population as a whole. The age and occupational structure of Anglo-Jewry partly explain its over-representation. However, it is also possible that a heightened sense of patriotism amongst second generation British Jews was another factor explaining why the Jewish military war effort was so great. Typical was a Manchester Jew born in 1912 who joined the army immediately when war broke out because he 'love[d] this country'.[57]

The existence of such motives was beyond the understanding of many non-Jews in the Forces. A soldier in a Tank Regiment in Italy found that his friends refused to accept that he was Jewish – they simply thought there were no Jews in the army. Similarly, many Jews in the Forces found themselves subjected to the verbal antisemitism of colleagues who were unaware of the Jewish origins of the recipients of their vitriol. It was a situation that could lead to deep embarrassment on the one side, and hurt and anger on the other. Often, however, Jews were confronted with personalised antisemitism. Reactions to this hostility varied. Alexander Hartog, an East End Jew, was so overwhelmed by the number of antisemites in his unit 'that in the end I had to ask to be released'. Others found resistance less impermeable: 'at first, when they knew I was a Jew, they were not so friendly, but after a week or so they treated me the same as anyone else'.[58] Jewish refugees encountered particular problems, with the RAF and Royal Navy being effectively closed to them. Nevertheless nearly 10,000 men and women refugees served in the Pioneer Corps and later in the mainstream British army. Suspicion against them broke down as the war progressed.[59]

Although individuals such as Hartog were not unique in finding antisemitism in the Forces intolerable, it appears that most Jews were accepted in their units. Indeed the comradeship between men, which it has been suggested can be understood only 'in terms of love', was also experienced by Jews in the Forces. Jews and non-Jews according to Basil Henriques were 'just brothers in arms'. Individual Jews were liked for their personal attributes and respected for their military skills. Nevertheless, even in this most intense atmosphere of human co-operation and fellowship, it must be doubted how much change was made in overall attitudes to Jews. The Jewish soldier was often confronted with the challenging statement: 'but you are different'. Such limited toleration forced some to either downplay or overplay their Jewishness. On the one hand, they could change their name and 'pass' as gentile, on the other hand they could attempt to overcome on their own the stereotype of the cowardly Jew by volunteering for all the most dangerous jobs. Both responses indicate how prevailing stereotypes of Jews in the Forces made it difficult for individuals to be totally accepted *as Jews*.[60]

Similar to the experiences of the blitz and evacuation, the close mixing of Jews and non-Jews in the Forces helped remove some of the grossest of misunderstandings of the latter towards the former. Friendship could remove previous hostility. A Sergeant told a Jewish soldier that 'before joining the army I was a real Jew hater but since meeting you, I've changed my opinion'. However more typical was the statement of another Sergeant: 'You know I hate Jews . . . if all Jews were like you they would be a wonderful people.' A Jewish soldier confirmed a more pessimistic assessment when he asked after 1945 whether 'the word "Jew" [has] lost any of its degrading meaning in the war, except in the few cases where our lads in the Forces have convinced their Gentile comrades that Jews haven't got horns, don't all wear gold watches, smoke cigars and own thousands of pounds?'[61]

One reason for the persistence of hostile Jewish stereotypes was that literature and entertainment for the Forces presented imagery that reinforced old antipathies – such as quips about Jewish pawnbroker battalions. Thus the real presence of Jews in the army, navy and air force was to an extent counteracted. Moreover, the War Office was reluctant to address the issue of antisemitism in its educational programme. It believed that to do so would only make matters worse. Nevertheless in disciplinary cases, where Jewish servicemen were attacked by superiors simply for their Jewishness, the military authorities did not tolerate such antisemitism. The Jewish question, as was the case with the rest of British society, was one of popular discussion in the Forces. Generally, however, it was not confronted by organisations such as the Army Bureau of Current Affairs (ABCA). The net result was that antisemitism in the Forces, despite the personal popularity of Jewish members, exhibited the same tendencies as society as a whole – reaching a peak of intensity in 1943.[62]

Within the structure of the Forces themselves, it is clear that efforts were made to provide the minimum of religious facilities for Jews. Inevitably, however, given the pressures of fighting in a total war, it was difficult, if not impossible for Jewish combatants to remain strictly observant. In terms of different responses to Jews from the army, navy and air forces, more research is required. Tentatively, it must be suggested that the degree of snobbery was stronger in the last two and that this was reflected in a greater hostility to Jews. Even in the army, in its officer class and higher echelons, social animosity, as occurred in the case of Hore-Belisha, was present. This possibly partly explains the relative absence of Jews at the very top of the army structure.[63]

Across British society as a whole, some improvement in the military image of Jews can be detected as the war progressed. In early 1940, false accusations that there were very few Jews in the British Expeditionary Force were not contradicted, whereas four years later the same rumours concerning the Arnhem invasion were widely condemned. In addition, the BBC from 1943 did its utmost to stress the military contribution of Jews to the war effort. Louis Macneice in 1943 and J. B. Priestley in 1944 wrote plays with Jewish war heroes.[64]

Yet these self-consciously positive attempts at stereotyping could not be said to represent the dominant Jewish image. With notable exceptions, the press ignored the Jewish background of soldiers such as Majors Wigram and Kisch. In literature, including Richard Hillary's classic war novel, *The Last Enemy* (1942), the Jew remains a cringing coward, as does the dance band musician, Jackie Kraus, in Geoffrey Cotterell's *Then a Soldier* (1944).[65] Indeed, the persistence of the Jew-coward stereotype was amply illustrated by the Bethnal Green tube disaster and the Polish Jewish army question, both of which occurred towards the end of the war.

The local antisemitic impact of the disaster has already been examined. It is now necessary to examine why the canard of the Jewish panic gained national credence. A Board of Deputies report suggested that, within hours of the announcement of the disaster, antisemitic allegations were being heard as far away as the West Country. In Manchester a member of

Toc H, the Christian fellowship society, related how, in a meeting of twelve professional people, the Jewish slander developed. At 6 pm all that was known was that the disaster had taken place in London; at 6.30 pm the Jews had been deemed 'probably responsible'. Forty minutes later the Jews 'were definitely responsible' and after more discussion it was agreed that the Jews had 'panicked blindly'. Similar developments happened inside London and across the country.[66]

The strength of the past Jewish image goes a long way to explain the speed with which the Bethnal Green rumour gathered pace. However, it is possible that earlier memories of a disaster in 1918 – when seventeen people died in a rush to an air raid shelter in the East End – were remembered. This alleged panic was again blamed on the Jews, an automatic reflex that operated throughout the Second World War. As with the black market, Jews were held to blame for behaviour that was seen as 'un-British'. The Bethnal Green accident also occurred at a bleak time in the war, and it is significant that an equally horrific incident in America at the same time was also blamed on the Jews.[67]

Even after the government's denial of the Jewish panic explanation in April 1943, antisemitic rumours still persisted. The full scale emergence of the Jews in the Polish Army question the following year showed that the cowardly Jew image continued unabated. The reasons for the desertion of over 200 out of 800 Jews in the Polish army were highly complex and will be dealt with in greater detail in the next chapter. However, it is clear that to a significant section of the War Office, the main reason was not fear of antisemitism, or political reasons but 'the approach of active operations'. Although one Foreign Office official rejected the army shirker explanation, another remarked that Jews 'have not shown themselves [to be] very good military material'. It was fortunate for these Polish Jews that other questions of diplomatic relations saved them from the severe punishment that they would have received as deserters.[68]

In conclusion, despite the heroic actions of Jews in the Allied Forces and in such instances as the Warsaw ghetto rising, the war did little to dispel the 'timid' Jew image, one that was 'compared unfavourably with the fighting reputation of the Arabs'. One Mass-Observer was irritated by Jews in the war, not due to the black market, but because they would not fight back like the IRA but preferred 'to suffer'. It must be suggested that not until the successes of the Israeli army in the post-war world has the cowardly Jewish image been put to rest.[69]

One aspect of the Jewish stereotype that has not been examined so far is the important question of the Jewish self-image. Not surprisingly, the

Jewish community was much concerned with its own image. In the tense Jew-conscious atmosphere of the 1930s and 1940s, it is understandable why there was a simultaneous tendency both to internalise Jewish stereotypes from the wider society, and to rebel against it with an alternative, defensive viewpoint. This dual process can be seen most clearly in an article in the *Sunday Pictorial*, October 1940 'I am a Jew, but – ' by Denis Myers, possibly one of the most blatant press attacks on the Jewish community in the war.[70]

Myers started the article by claiming he was writing against all Jews and in this he could claim to have succeeded. The first attack was made on 'the Jews who ran away', rich Jews who by 'their intrigue, their trickery' had managed to escape the war to make their fortune in America. In accusing his own people of a lack of courage, Myers was not alone. Alfred Perles, a refugee, accepted that the Jews were naturally nervous, and the *Jewish Chronicle*, in constantly referring to the exploits of Jewish soldiers, at times appeared to be attempting to convince itself, as well as the non-Jewish population. There was an element of surprise in its blitz headline 'London Jewry's Splendid Fortitude. Death Roll Slightly Above Average.' Even the Board of Deputies' *British Jewry in Battle and Blitz* (1943), an impressive account of the Jewish war effort, did not impress Cecil Roth, because the record was 'not by any means sensational'.[71]

Myers then went on to attacking ostentatious Jews taking over the English countryside, transforming it 'to the babble and waving palms of an Eastern bazaar'. Again Myers was not just reflecting general attitudes but also those of much of the Jewish community. A complaint about Jewish behaviour on the Great Western Railway, of loud talking, flaunting of rings and wealth and bad manners was accepted by the *Jewish Chronicle* without thought. Indeed, one of the major Anglo-Jewish novels of the war years, Richard Ullmann's *The Kahn's Progress*, portrayed a grotesque nouveau-riche Jewish family, whose older members know no social constraint. In attempting to buy a country estate the father provokes antisemitism. Only in abandoning Judaism and 'rouge and lipstick . . . jewellery' and loud dresses, do the younger members of the family escape the real problem that Jews create in British society.[72]

Myers was also one of the first to suggest that Jews were profiteering in the war. The following year when the black market issue developed, the Board of Deputies' Trades Advisory Council (TAC) appears to have accepted the view that Jews were particularly responsible. One member wrote that the antisemitism associated with the black market was 'to a great extent due to the conduct of the Jews', and another that food restrictions had 'attracted many weak and wicked Jewish traders into the black market'. Alleged Jewish sharp economic practice was accepted by the Board's Sidney Salomon, and the *Jewish Chronicle* launched a careers campaign against 'the get-rich-quick-mania' in business.[73]

Myers' final attack was on the refugee Jews, who in response to English generosity, 'flaunt themselves, openly, aggravatingly, ungratefully'. In language nearly identical to that of Douglas Reed, Myers suggested that 'each corner of this English field on which they bred became forever Israel. They turned Golders Green into the Ringstrasse; they elbowed the interloping English out of the way; they spoke . . . the German or Czech of their native land abroad where they had been outcasts'. Here Myers was on even firmer ground as far as the Jewish community was concerned. Through groups such as the Hampstead Vigilance Committee, the Board of Deputies tried to stop the 'anti-social behaviour' of the refugees. Speaking in foreign languages was frowned upon and even the loyalty of the refugees was put into question. As will be shown, sections of the Jewish community, including the refugee organisations, did little to oppose mass internment in the summer of 1940.[74]

What was unique about Myers' onslaught was the concentration of his attack. Whilst the individual allegations were part of the Jewish self-image, taken together they were far too negative for the community to accept. Thus Neville Laski, who had launched many attacks on Jewish behaviour himself, was forced on the defensive. Laski replied in the *Sunday Pictorial* a week after Myers, writing about the Jewish war effort and charitable endeavours.[75]

The final aspect of the Jewish self-image is the development of the Anglo-Jewish novel in the war. It has been suggested that until recent times Anglo-Jewish writers have attempted either to present Jews in a sympathetic light, as respectable Englishmen, or alternatively, to rebel against the emancipated bourgeois Jew ideal of the established community.[76] In some respects, all the Anglo-Jewish novels of the war were examples of the latter, although several had the aim of defending the Jewish community, or at least sections of it.

In the 1930s, a new breed of Jewish writers came into prominence. Young, left wing, second generation East End Jews started to write about their surroundings. Simon Blumenfeld was the first to emerge, and his second book, *They Won't Let You Live*, was published soon after the start of the war. The bad West End Gentile capitalist, a money-lender, is contrasted to the good poor Jews and non-Jews of the East End. In the end both the Curries and the Rothsteins are united, but are oppressed by the capitalist system, and forced to commit suicide. Similarly, in Barnett Sheridan's *King Sol*, published at the same time, East End Jews, blacks, Catholics and Chinese are united against fascism at Cable Street. Again the Jews are portrayed as good proletariats.[77] In Willy Goldman's *East End My Cradle* (1940) the Cockney picture is harsher; Jews are selfish and Gentiles drunk, but ultimately the story is one of a local society unified by poverty, not just of 'a poor Jewish family' but of 'all the human family'. However, in Richard Ullmann's *The Kahn's Progress* (1940) and to a lesser extent in Max Mundlak's *Journey Into Morning* (1941), the lifestyle of both working class and middle class Jewry is rejected as 'un-English',[78] Jewish self-perceptions were thus formed from a mixture of the acceptance and rejection of Jewish stereotypes in wider society. It is now necessary to examine how important these Jewish stereotypes were in the major public forums in Britain during the war.

With the temporary demise of television, the most important influences on public opinion in the war were the press, the radio, the cinema and, to a lesser extent, literature and drama. Of all these the press was the most vital with regard to the Jewish image. Even so, Angus Calder has suggested that apart from *Truth* and the *Catholic Herald* 'there was little overt antisemitism in British publications during the war'. On a national level, if the *National Review* is added to this list, then Calder's statement is supportable, in so far as no other mainstream organs followed a consistently antisemitic policy in the war. However, on a local and provincial level the situation was less happy. Papers such as the *Hackney Gazette*, the *Hampstead and Highgate Express* and the *Porth Gazette* were continuously hostile in the war. Returning to the national scene, the Beaverbrook, Rothermere and Kemsley empires, whilst making token gestures of friendliness to British Jews, simultaneously and consistently attacked refugee Jews; the *Sunday Dispatch* was particularly virulent.[79]

If the British press had a commendable record as far as reporting the persecution of Jews in Europe was concerned, this cannot be said of its handling of the domestic black market question. It is difficult to evaluate how far newspapers were responsible for antisemitism associated with this issue. On the one hand, press reports were constantly given as justifications for antisemitism; on the other, the press was responding to what was seen as a more newsworthy aspect of such offences – a Jewish or alien name. That there was 'copy' in this during the war explains such ridiculous headlines as 'Jew alleges robbery in Oxford field' or more blatantly, in regard to a conscientious objector, 'The Jew'.[80]

The reinforcing, if not innovative, tendency of the press was also shown in its repeated discussion of the Jewish question. Hostile statements, either from journalists or in letters, were used to bolster antipathetical attitudes of a wider public. In this they operated in a similar manner to Douglas Reed, who also reached a large audience with his antisemitic writings. The press therefore kept alive a public outlet for discussion of Jewish matters, and helped to maintain the Jew-consciousness of the period. In the refugee and black market issues it was at the forefront of the feeling against Jews, but in neither case did it create, on its own, the original hostility.[81]

Less impact on Jewish matters was made by the two other major popular media, the radio and the cinema. In the case of the former, strict BBC censorship ensured that hostility to the Jews on the radio was rare. A special effort was made to avoid news stories involving Jewish black marketeers, although an occasional mistake was made in this issue. Only 'The Man Born to be King' caused serious offence. Countering this, several Christian broadcasts were made attacking antisemitism (although they simultaneously attacked Jewish behaviour).[82]

Throughout the 1930s, the film industry had been thwarted by the British Board of Film Censors in its attempt to produce anti-Nazi films. As part of its appeasement policy, the Board refused to allow any scenes involving persecution of Jews as 'it undoubtedly comes definitely under the heading of political propoganda [sic]'.[83] With the war, this policy reversed, although certain towns like Brighton still refused to show the anti-Nazi film *Professor Mamlock*, as it would 'enhance hatred against Germany'. When this and other such films like *Pastor Hall*, *The Great Dictator* and Louis Golding's *Mr Emmanuel* were actually shown, scenes of persecution, especially of Jews, were not always greeted with enthusiasm by the audience. Also, unlike America, the British film industry made few films in the war which referred to Nazi antisemitism. *Mr Emmanuel*, the story of a Manchester Jew's discovery of Nazi antisemitism, was not produced until 1944.[84] Moreover, whereas several American films emphasised the Jewish war effort, no such attempt was made in Britain. *Hold Up Your Head, Comrade* (1942), a Ministry of Information propaganda film about the refugee Pioneer Corps, was the nearest approximation to this. However, its impact was lessened because it could not show the alien volunteers in action against the Nazis. In addition, government sponsored films sympathetically portrayed Jews as bombed out evacuees and as East End Social Workers.[85]

On the negative side, complaints were made about the portrayal of Jews in several religious biblical films. Alex Comfort also complained in 1944 of 'the increasing antisemitism of films' in Britain, with 'baddies' represented with a 'facial character such as blackness, a moustache, or a Yid nose'. One Mass-Observer suggested that one of the major influences on his attitude to Jews came from films, where Jews 'are slimy, hooked nosed and twisting'. Nevertheless, whilst the cinema in this way contributed to negative images of Jews, it does not seem to have been as important a factor as either literature or popular entertainment.[86]

In 1945 George Orwell claimed that in Britain, since the rise of Nazi antisemitism, 'anti-Jewish remarks are carefully eliminated from all classes of literature', and to 'put an unsympathetic Jewish character into a novel or short story came to be regarded as antisemitism'. Doubt can be cast on both these statements. Turning to the second, whilst Roy Fuller's *Fletcher*, a story of a cowardly intellectual Jew, was attacked by Cedric Driver as 'subtly antisemitic', similar characters such as Evelyn Waugh's Ambrose Silk, Richard Hillary's Neft and Geoffrey Cotterell's Jackie Kraus aroused no such comments in what were important war novels.[87]

Referring to less serious works, Orwell claimed that there was less antisemitism now 'than there was thirty years ago. In the minor novels of that date you find it taken for granted, far oftener that you would nowadays, that a Jew is an inferior or a figure of fun'. Again Orwell oversimplified. Contemporary observers, such as Tom Harrisson and Alex Comfort, believed that antisemitism in thrillers and the like continued at a high level in the war, or even increased. The reason was supplied by Orwell himself in an article on Boys' Weeklies. Orwell commented on how little the stereotyped figures had changed, how the year could be 1910 or 1940 'but it is all the same'. Thus, whilst John G. Brandon made the occasional comment to indicate that his novels were now in a war background, his general content of Jewish and Yellow perils differs little from that of Sax Rohmer's at the turn of the century. However, there were faint signs of change in this genre, shown in the works of the Manning Coles. In *Drink to Yesterday* (1940), in little more than half a page a Jew is introduced who is a war profiteer, an army shirker, physically repulsive and a sexual predator. However, its sequel, *Pray Silence*, published in the same year, reluctantly attacked the Nazis for their excessive antisemitism, and actually introduced a minor Jewish war hero.[88]

Orwell can also be attacked for his belief that 'after 1934 the "Jew joke" disappeared as though by magic from postcards, periodicals and the music-hall stage'. Yet again, one is confronted with the 'massive durability' of these stereotypes in these worlds, though occasionally indirect reference was made to German antisemitism. In a Donald McGill postcard, a hooked nosed stereotyped Jew is pictured in a nudist club: 'The girls all took him for a Jew, This saucy old Barbarian, But since he joined the Nudist Club, They see that he's an "Airyun".'[89] In another war joke, Cohen manages to sell Goering a left-handed tea service! However, generally one is struck by the lack of change in war jokes about Jews. Jews are portrayed as cowards, as money-obsessed, foreigners and twisters, with Jewish comedians often being the worst offenders.[90] Jewish jokes did not dominate music-hall humour, but neither did they disappear. In comics, mean Jews continued to be portrayed, especially by *The Dandy*. As an American comic executive stated in 1944, 'We are interested in circulation primarily. Can you imagine a hero named Cohen?' In periodicals, anti-Jewish cartoons still appeared, Fenwick drawing one for *London Opinion* depicting Jews illicitly getting petrol. When accused of antisemitism he replied: 'When I see these Jews going round still in large cars, in civilian clothes, it makes me long to do some really unpleasant cartoons.' We thus see the continuation of antisemitic stereotypes but the realisation that a degree of constraint was now necessary.[91]

How much influence did these various literary and oral portrayals have on British attitudes to Jews? There is much evidence of the offence they caused to the Jewish community, but did they actually make an impact on general public thinking? With certain qualifications, it is possible to recognise an impact. Even with ethnic jokes, which are often assumed to be harmless and lacking any real malicious intent, a real influence can be found in the Jewish variety.[92] A Mass-Observation survey which examined the way attitudes to Jews were formed, found that jokes were one important way antisemitic stereotypes were introduced to the public, and the NCCL was convinced that comics 'were responsible for a lot of antisemitism amongst children'. ENSA (the Entertainments National Service Association) quips in the war, according to a Jewish sergeant, had 'more than a passing effect' and music-hall portrayals of Jews, along with their accent, clothing and behaviour, were seen as typical of Jews as a whole. Orwell himself could not escape from his perception of Jews as 'comic-paper cartoons'. Popular literature also influenced attitudes to Jews; a (non-Jewish) soldier remarking at the end of the war that 'so many people talk the same old claptrap because it is what they once read in some rag'. It was these sources as much as the classic Shylock or Fagin characters that influenced the Jewish image in Britain.[93]

However, whilst it is important to consider these printed aspects of a cultural tradition of hostility in Britain, it is possible that oral sources were even more important. Attitudes were often learned at an early age and were, in consequence, often hard to shake off. An East End Gentile related that from his earliest memories he was told 'that a Jew is our natural enemy and must be treated as such'. Another East Ender recalled how a four-year-old boy was told by his uncle that the Jews were evil, unclean and 'certainly not British. He was teaching the boy antisemitism.' In the case of fascists such as Oswald Mosley and the Duke of Bedford, one can trace a family history of antisemitism, yet the same process operated amongst the wider public. It was because the individual not only had to face the influence of literature, press, radio and other forms of entertainment, but also of family and friends that Jewish stereotypes were so impervious to change. The Mass-Observer who could not stop himself making 'rude jokes about Jews', although he was ashamed about it, was not a unique phenomenon.[94]

In conclusion, the most remarkable aspect of the Jewish image in the war is the lack of change that took place, despite the background of Jewish persecution in Europe. Past Jewish stereotypes readjusted to the needs of war, most obviously with the black marketeer image. Even in the case of the Jewish refugee, past attitudes ensured that this would not be a totally favourable concept. Although six years of conflict, involving intense mixing of Jew and non-Jew, helped the reassessment of British attitudes to Jews, by 1945 the two basic Jewish images of Shylock and alien had still not been overcome. Even medieval libels such as the blood accusation occasionally surfaced in the war.

In studying the Jewish image, it has been vital to see that stereotypes did not exist in watertight 'mental' compartments, but actually impinged on the life of real Jews, directly or indirectly, positively and negatively. This process can be seen at its most important and clearest level in British government policy on Jewish matters, to which we must now turn.

5

The British government and the Jews

The attitude of the State is perhaps the most vital factor affecting the well-being of a religious or racial minority. For the Jews this has been particularly true. In modern history the severest antisemitism, in late Tsarist Russia and Hitlerite Germany, has been state-sponsored. In medieval Britain, as elsewhere across Europe, the Jewish community depended on the protection of the state. When this was removed, either because popular opinion was excessively hostile, or the Jews were no longer of economic value to the government, expulsion could quickly follow as in England in 1290.

By the Second World War, this medieval relationship between Jews and the State had changed beyond recognition. Illustrating the point, Sir Alexander Maxwell commented on a scheme of 1941, whereby the government made arrangements for the maintenance of Jewish refugees in Britain, as one 'which will reverse the historic practice by which governments have borrowed money from the Jews and will introduce a new procedure by which the Government will lend some money to the Jews!'[1] Nevertheless if the 'Court Jew' world had disappeared, the British government had still a vital role to play in Jewish matters at home and abroad.

It must be suggested that all the government departments would have been a lot happier had there been no Jewish aspect to complicate domestic and foreign questions which were already difficult. Yet Jews and antisemitism were factors that could not be ignored in the war. The manner in which the British government approached issues ranging from the providing of kosher cheese to the rescue of European Jewry reveals much about the strengths and weaknesses of a liberal democratic state. In the discussion that follows we will examine how the government approached Jewish matters. It will be necessary to analyse whether elements of antisemitism, or indeed philosemitism, explain state policy. However, the state will not be viewed in isolation, for it will also be important to examine how far the government responded to public opinion on Jewish matters.

In 1943 the Board of Deputies suggested that the British authorities had maltreated Jews in Tripoli. The accusation brought forth a violent denial from the Foreign Office. An official replied 'His Majesty's Government does *not* discriminate against Jews (indeed, rather the reverse).' In other words, it was unthinkable that the government or the British people could in any way be antisemitic, for this was against the principles of liberal democracy. However, in private the various government departments feared what they saw as increasing domestic antisemitism. Nevertheless this was not publicly admitted to be the case.[2] In official government statements it was assumed that the British public, as well as the state, was free of antisemitism. Was there a similar policy as regards Jewish religious matters in Britain?

As will be shown later, a vital aspect of government policy on European Jewry was to deny consistently that Jews were in any way a separate entity. As one official put it: 'Jews must be treated as nationals of existing states and are not to be regarded as having a distinct Jewish nationality.' To do otherwise would 'perpetuate the very Nazi doctrine which we are determined to stamp out'.[3] Jews were simply foreign nationals of a different religion. In this the British government was at least consistent in its treatment of its own Jewish citizens. Whilst in theory the emancipation 'contract' might have encouraged the state to weaken Jewish religious bonds, in practice the particular war needs of the Anglo-Jewish community were either granted, or given serious attention, by the government.

The most obvious and important requirement of Jews in Britain was for special food. According to the Ministry of Food, kosher meat was an 'extraordinary knotty problem'. This was due to differences in pricing and weighing techniques compared to normal meat. Apart from the problems it created with the rationing system, there were also strong protests from the public. Some believed that they were 'required to eat fat pork for the ration when they know that the best quality beef is going to the Jews'. Nevertheless, according to a Ministry of Food memorandum in December 1943, it was 'the policy . . . to provide, so far as the supply position permits, Kosher meat for those Jews who want it'.[4]

In other food matters, the Ministry was equally as helpful. Despite the shortage of vegetable oil, Jews were allowed to swap their bacon coupons for margarine, and matzos for Passover was exempt from regulations concerning biscuits. As a result of pressure from Sir Robert Waley Cohen, and the sympathy of Lord Woolton, the Minister of Food, arrangements were made (at considerable costs in terms of bureaucracy) to alleviate any hardships that might have occurred for observant Jews.[5] Only in one area, that of kosher cheese, were these difficulties not overcome. Although a petty matter, the Ministry of Food's response on the subject is revealing about wider governmental attitudes on Jewish matters.

Only a section of the orthodox Jewish community, estimated by officials as at most 10,000 people, actually required kosher cheese. However, with pressure from Waley Cohen, the Ministry of Food again attempted to satisfy this minority demand. According to the Ministry, 'very considerable administrative difficulties' were created by this problem, yet this was not why the project was finally abandoned. The seemingly bizarre reason given by the Ministry of Food for its refusal to give Jews kosher cheese, was that the product was 'very delicious'. In the words of an official 'other things being equal', the Jewish community should have kosher cheese. However, unlike kosher meat 'other things [were] not equal'. Whereas kosher meat could be hidden from the public through distribution by Jewish butchers, this was not possible with cheese. The Ministry's policy was 'as a matter of principle . . . to avoid ever giving a concession to Jews as such and labelling them'. The Ministry became convinced that the distribution of kosher cheese would lead to serious antisemitism, it would create jealousies and accusations of 'favoured treatment being meted out to Jews'. The problem became a 'terrible one' to the Ministry and Waley Cohen was politely turned down after two years' struggle.[6] The government thus spent an enormous amount of administrative and scientific time in the war, trying to ensure that a small section of the Anglo-Jewish community did not suffer too harshly from the food regulations. Yet when faced with a situation where it could have been accused of favouritism towards the Jews, it quickly reversed its policies. Government consideration for Jewish dietary needs had thus a strong limiting factor.

No such restrictions were imposed on the Jews' right to practice their own religion. Indeed, the government allowed and even encouraged the public presentation of the Jewish religious point of view. In 1941 the Ministry of Information approved the establishment of a Jewish section of its own Religious Division. However, there was a strong proviso that it would 'be concerned only with religious questions and [would] not touch political problems' (by which was meant either Zionism or solutions to antisemitism). A monthly periodical, the *Jewish Bulletin*, was financed which ran until the end of the war. The BBC followed a similar pattern, for although Jews, along with other religions that denied the deity of Jesus, were not officially allowed broadcasts, unofficially two religious programmes were allowed every year – usually given by the Chief Rabbi. The BBC allowed these out of a 'great sympathy to Jewish listeners'. Judaism also featured in a Ministry of Information film *Religion and the People* (1940). It featured a service held at the Great Synagogue in the City of London, where attention was particularly drawn to the prayer for the Royal Family. This was an attempt to show the patriotism of the Anglo-Jewish community.[7]

The other great issue of government policy that affected the Jewish minority was related to education. By 1939 the majority of Jewish children were receiving their education in non-denominational schools. Under the 1902 Education Act, the state paid for secular but not religious education in voluntary Jewish schools. However, in the war a major rethink of the education system resulted in the Butler Act of 1944, one that was to make a large impact on Jewish education in Britain. Butler found that his major problem over the proposed legislation was Catholic opposition. Nevertheless, he felt it necessary to consult the Jewish community about its educational requirements, despite it further complicating his task. Butler, sympathetic to Jewish needs, told the Chief Rabbi that he aimed 'to be as helpful as he [could] . . . in the matter of promoting religious instruction for Jewish children for whom Jewish schools were not available'. With, in addition, increased state aid for its voluntary schools, the Jewish community was pleased with both the attention that Butler had accorded it, and with the opportunities the new Act created.[8]

Overall, therefore, in strictly religious matters, Anglo-Jewry found the government both sympathetic and supportive. Only when the state believed that antisemitism may have resulted from such a policy, was its helpfulness put into doubt. In the course of the war, however, domestic antisemitism became a major preoccupation of the government, and its attitude to this subject must now be examined.

Throughout the war the government used all its sources of information to monitor levels of antisemitism in Britain. It was viewed as a weapon of the enemy, an 'extremist activity' which must be avoided at all costs. Jewish and left-wing anti-fascist organisations were in full agreement with this analysis. Yet paradoxically, when these groups pressurised the government to use its resources to attack domestic antisemitism, it refused.[9] A close examination of why this was the case again reveals government ambivalence on the Jewish question.

The first priority of the government was to avoid the creation of antisemitism. In the words of a Foreign Office official, antisemitism 'always affords a good opportunity for enemy propaganda and it is therefore to our own interest to discourage it at all points'. This was a policy that was to be a mixed blessing for the Jewish community. The major aim of the government was to ensure that latent antisemitism in Britain did not become politically organised. Yet, simultaneous with this was the constant fear of being identified with the Jews as a whole, for in the government's policy anything that supported the idea of a Jews' War was to be avoided. Hence the Foreign Office's refusal to have a Jewish propaganda Minister in the shape of Leslie Hore-Belisha. Taken together, these policies ensured on the one hand that the government would refuse to launch a blatantly pro-Jewish or anti-antisemitic campaign. On the other hand, the government would attempt to appease what it saw as the potentially antisemitic British public.[10]

The latter side of the equation can be seen most clearly in Ministry of Food policy on the rationing week. Up to July 1942 changes in rationing were announced on Sunday, coming into operation the following day. There were complaints, especially from the National Federation of Grocers, that this system benefited Sunday traders – hence the Jews – and was therefore leading to antisemitism. Due to this pressure the rationing week was changed to begin on Sunday. Yet the National Federation of Grocers now claimed that Jewish traders were gaining from being open on the first day of the 'week', and were 'creaming off the new points and coupons'. The Ministry of Food was again ready to appease any antisemitic sentiment by changing the rationing week. The Jewish community was also willing for this to take place. However, after investigating the issue, the Ministry found that shopkeepers were not gaining from being open on Sundays, nor was there any serious antisemitism being created. It therefore decided not to change the rationing week. Nevertheless, what is interesting about the question is how Herman Kent, the secretary of the National Federation of Grocers, attempted to exploit the government's fear of antisemitism. It was a tactic that worked once and would have worked a second time had there been any real antisemitism to appease.[11]

The other aspect of government policy – its refusal to directly combat antisemitism – is well illustrated with the black market question. In 1942 and 1943 the Board of Deputies criticised the Ministry of Information for merely measuring antisemitism, stating that it was 'not sufficient to receive reports as to whether antisemitism had increased or not'. The

Board wanted the government particularly to counter the allegations about Jews and the black market, especially in the latter part of 1943 when it had the results of its own survey, disproving the canard. Brendan Bracken, the Minister involved, refused to make use of the Board's figures believing that the public would not accept them.[12] However, unbeknown to the Board of Deputies, the Home Office had carried out a similar enquiry at the end of 1941.

It was launched by Herbert Morrison in response to demands from two antisemitic Conservative MP's. The latter wanted naturalisation to be revoked in the case of alien-born subjects who had been convicted of war regulation offences. Morrison seems to have shared these sentiments, minuting that he was 'furious' about these people breaking the law. Despite complaints from his civil servants, the investigation was carried out, with disappointing results for Morrison. Alien Jews were not found to be the principal offenders. However, rather than publish the figures, which would have dampened the real public antagonism to Jews, Morrison refused further action.[13] Indeed a year later, when news of the report had apparently leaked out, a left-wing campaign to secure the release of the survey was also unsuccessful. The most the government would do on the question was to ensure that the BBC, or other official agencies, did not publicise the misdeeds of Jewish black market offenders, and unofficially, to tell the press to do likewise.[14]

Neither would the government allow any official discussion or attacks on antisemitism. The subject was banned from the popular Brains' Trust and efforts to air the subject on other BBC programmes were constantly thwarted. Even though the Ministry of Information shared the Board of Deputies view that antisemitism was a sign of low morale, it refused to acknowledge publicly that the problem existed. In Brendan Bracken's words, any attempt to issue denials of antisemitic allegations would do 'more harm than good'.[15] This was a philosophy based on the government's mistrust of both the British people and the Jewish minority, and a general fear that the government would be seen as pro-Jewish.

A similar attitude can be found in the question of making antisemitism a libel offence. The matter arose in 1943 in response to Alexander Ratcliffe's pamphlet *The Truth about the Jews*. This pamphlet, apart from containing the usual antisemitic attacks, also denied that any Jews were killed by the Nazis. A senior Home Office official, Frank Newsam, felt that its sentiments were dangerous and could lead to serious antisemitism. It would at least create 'animosity towards one section of His Majesty's subjects'. However, Herbert Morrison did not follow Newsam in wanting a libel law against antisemitism. In Morrison's view, any attempt by the government to protect the Jewish population would 'have an effect contrary to that intended'. To summarise, the refusal of the government to officially recognise that the Jewish community was anything other than a religious minority meant that, logically, it could not give Jews special treatment, apart from over purely ritual matters. Given that antisemitism, by its very nature, singled out Jews, it could not therefore be dealt with by the government.[16]

Occasionally however, the government's embarrassment about the existence of antisemitism in Britain could work to the advantage of the Jewish community. The question of Polish Army antisemitism, which came to a climax in 1944, has already been touched upon. Considering the widespread and profound hostility to Jews in Poland, it is not surprising that accusations of antisemitism against Polish soldiers in Britain were made from the start of the war. These continued from 1941 to the beginning of 1943, in which period seventeen Jews deserted from the Polish army. There is little doubt that this antisemitism was of a serious nature, causing real distress to the Jewish soldiers. It was reinforced by a Polish paper, *Jestem Polakiem*, which was believed to have been provided with newsprint by the *Catholic Herald*. It was also supported by other right-wing British Catholics and antisemites.[17]

In the latter part of 1943, and the first half of 1944, the matter came to a head. Over 200 Jewish soldiers deserted and the British government was forced into action. Why it happened at that stage *is* complicated. The War Office and certain Foreign Office officials believed it to be due to Jewish cowardice on the eve of battle; the *Catholic Herald*, the Polish Ambassador and Winston Churchill believed it was part of a left-wing 'conspiracy to malign Poles'; and left wingers believed it was due to increased Polish and fascist attacks on Jewish soldiers (including death threats).[18] The last two analyses in combination probably give the real explanation. The Polish-Jewish soldiers were generally sympathetic to the Soviet cause, and there is little doubt that the Communist Party and some fellow travellers wished to stress the antisemitism of the Poles, and so discredit their government-in-exile, especially at a time of a serious split in Soviet-Polish relations. However, there is also strong evidence that the introduction of pro-German Poles, captured by the British in Tunisia, into the Polish Army seriously increased the level of its antisemitism. There were violent incidents and much of the sympathy and agitation on behalf of the Polish Jews was genuine and not of an opportunist nature.[19]

The most startling aspect of this affair was the manner in which the War Office – which made no secret of its hostility to the Polish-Jewish deserters – allowed the transfer of these men to the Pioneer Corps in record time. Tom Driberg, the left-wing Labour MP at the forefront of the campaign on behalf of the deserters, believed the War Office decision was largely due to public pressure.[20] The reality was far more complex. What the government wanted to avoid was any discussion on the subject whatsoever, for it believed the subject could discredit the Polish government in both Russian and British eyes. The government realised that to admit having an antisemitic ally on British soil would have been disastrous from a propaganda point of view. Therefore the War Office reluctantly agreed to the transfer due to 'serious political considerations'. In addition, the Home Office was, as ever, wary of an increase in antisemitism, which it believed the Poles might spread to Britain. It was a fear not without foundation. The Home Office also wanted to encourage harmonious Polish-Jewish relations so that, in the post-war world, Jews would be happy to return to Poland, again removing antisemitic potential from British soil.[21] In the case of the Jews in the Polish Army, the British government's fear and embarrassment concerning antisemitism worked to the advantage of the Jewish community, whose response to the issue will be examined later. As has been shown, this was not always the case – the government's inability to confront the issue of domestic antisemitism directly revealed the limitations of a liberal democracy. However, the state had to confront an even more serious 'foreign' question in the war – its treatment of refugees, most of whom were Jewish and of enemy origin. More than any other issue, this was to reveal the strengths and weaknesses of British tolerance and intolerance. In addition, it illustrates the relationship between governmental action and public opinion on Jewish matters.

It has been suggested that mid nineteenth-century British goodwill to refugees depended on two factors – the lack of a severe threat to the well-being of society and the support of public opinion. In the self-confident Victorian era the latter was an assumed fact – asylum for refugees was part of the dominant liberal philosophy. At the turn of the century, with the loss of this confidence and an increasingly hostile public, asylum came under increasing threat. With the 1905 Aliens Act 'what once [had] been impossible now became normal, right became privilege'.[22] Nevertheless 'liberalism', as an almost self-contained concept, did not totally disappear as a factor in the complex equation that determined policy towards refugees. Neither did the other earlier elements – the perceived threat to society and public opinion. All three aspects combined in the Second

World War; their various strengths dictating refugee policy at any given time.

Bernard Wasserstein has portrayed Britain's refugee policy 'as an alloy of the elements of xenophobic restrictionism and liberal hospitality traditional (at different periods) in British politics'. However, it is also important to stress that these two elements have existed simultaneously – whilst their relative power has varied, they have both existed constantly. Unless this is recognised it becomes impossible to explain the violent changes that took place in the treatment of refugees in the war. In what follows, no attempt will be made to give a detailed account of the mechanics of the government's internment policy, for this has been dealt with adequately elsewhere. Rather it will trace the pattern of tolerance and intolerance and will examine how far a 'Jewish' factor influenced government policy.[23]

Government policy on refugees in the Second World War owed much on the administrative side to the experience gained in the earlier conflict. Even so, the fact that the enemy aliens were of a different nature to those in the Great War did make an impact on the initial treatment of the refugees, especially at the start of the war. On 4 September 1939, Sir John Anderson, the Home Secretary, made this point stating that 'a large proportion of the Germans and Austrians at present in this country are refugees and there will . . . be a general desire to avoid treating as enemies those who are friendly to the country which has offered them asylum'. At this point, the government was following a self-consciously liberal policy which it exploited for propaganda purposes. The BBC was encouraged to report a tribunal to decide the status of an alien. This would show, in the words of the Home Office, 'British justice at work'. By differentiating between the treatment of the refugees in a democracy and in a dictatorship, the government hoped to impress world public opinion, especially in America.[24]

Although a system of tribunals to categorise the aliens into three groups was instigated – Category A whose loyalty and reliability the tribunals doubted, B of whose loyalty the tribunals were not absolutely certain and C of whom there was no doubt – refugee organisations were impressed by the sympathetic manner in which they were carried out. The public, as John Anderson's biographer has pointed out, were at this stage generally contented with government precautions. Whilst Norman Bentwich was exaggerating when he stated that 'the current of humanity ran strong and warm in England like a Gulf Stream', it was true to say, as one observer did in October 1939, that 'the spy mania of the last war is not so far being repeated in this one'. If there was any concern over the refugees, it was linked mainly to fear about jobs rather than security matters.[25]

However, it is vital to emphasise that even in this 'liberal' period, a strain of hostility continued against the refugees. Some of this hostility was of an antisemitic nature. This antisemitism came most blatantly from the BUF and their campaign against the 'refujews'. However, more respectable far right journals such as *Truth*, *Empire Record* and the *National Review* continued an opposition to alien Jews, which in the case of the latter had its origins in the pre-1914 era. It is also important to note that the Kemsley, Beaverbrook and Rothermere press empires also maintained their hostility to the refugees, which had been a feature of the 1930s. In the *Daily Mail* in October 1939, G. Ward Price warned of the danger 'of the aliens in our midst'. To Ward Price, Jewish refugees were simply enemy agents in disguise, and he attacked the tribunals for not dealing severely enough with them.[26]

Ward Price may have been correct in believing that overall the tribunals were being sympathetic to the aliens, yet even in the 'humane' period problems were arising. In some ways the very liberality of the government's approach caused difficulties, for the almost casual approach of the tribunals, and the lack of firm guidelines allowed personal prejudices and local confusion to produce inconsistent results. Over 1,600 male aliens were put into Category B, representing 10% of all those examined by 1 January 1940. These were generally arbitrary decisions that were to become vitally important in the summer of 1940.[27] Already over 200 aliens had been interned, the most surprising feature of this being the inclusion of many Jewish refugees in Category A. Why leading Jewish anti-Nazis such as Eugen Spier, Ewald Stern, Jurgen Kuczynsky and Alec Natan were interned at this early stage will remain a mystery until the relevant Home Office papers are released. However, it must be suggested that in the conspiratorial world of the security forces, being Jewish and anti-Nazi was no proof of loyalty to the British cause. Stern seems to have been interned merely because MI5 were interested in him as the Gestapo had expelled him from Germany.[28] The Security forces had been in the forefront of the campaign to link Jews with international bolshevism in the post-war world, and it does not seem that their views had totally changed in the Hitlerite period. Maxwell Knight, in charge of MI5's spying network in the war, could distrust an agent simply because she had a Jewish lover. Knight's biographer claims that his antisemitism sprang from 'a fear of the unknown'.[29]

Nevertheless, in the first few months of the war, liberal elements were strong enough to force those hostile to the refugees into relative impotence. The threat to British security was seen as minimal and public opinion was relatively indifferent, if not sympathetic, to the alien question. Britain could still congratulate itself on the success of its liberal treatment of the victims of Nazi persecution. By early 1940, however, the balance appears to have been moving slowly away from the dominant tolerant position. In January 1940, right-wing Sunday papers such as the *Sunday Express*, *Dispatch* and *Pictorial* were increasing the concentration of their attacks on the refugees, and starting to demand a policy of mass internment. Accusations of spying and sabotage were made, the *Sunday Pictorial* commenting on how few aliens had been interned. It warned that 'the public is worried' – an attempted self-fulfilling prophecy. The press campaign gained momentum in February 1940 as the phoney war period came to an end. The Home Secretary wrote at the start of March that 'the newspapers are working up feeling about aliens. I shall have to do something about it.' At this stage Anderson was more concerned about public hysteria than any real threat posed by the refugees. However, by March 1940 one element in ensuring liberal treatment of refugees – the goodwill of the public – was coming under increasing attack, due to the campaign of the 'less reputable papers'.[30]

In April 1940, any restraints that might have operated in the press world disappeared. The *Sunday Dispatch*, at the forefront of the campaign, proudly announced its intolerance: '[we] offer no apologies to namby-pamby humanists for having been the first to voice these demands [for mass internment].' In April 1940 these 'namby-pamby humanists' were still offering strong resistance to the anti-refugee movement, Sir Norman Angell commenting that it 'plays completely the game of Hitler and Goebbels'.[31] The public had also to be convinced. Although a Mass-Observation report on the fifth column, at the end of April, revealed that the press was an important influence on those who wanted mass internment, interestingly, another survey indicated that the press campaign had not yet percolated through to the masses. Only one in a hundred interviewees 'spontaneously suggested that refugees should be interned en masse'. Anti-refugee feeling was widespread yet it was 'predominantly for economic and financial reasons'.[32]

Public opinion, as was the case with the British fascists, turned violently against the refugee aliens immediately after the fall of Holland in the middle of May. In a couple of days antisemitic anti-alien talk 'gushed up into the open [and] became the currency of respectable talk'. In May 1940, opposition to internment melted away – the previously pro-refugee *Manchester Guardian*, *Spectator*, *Time and Tide*, *Daily Herald*, and even the *Jewish Chronicle*, all supported government measures on aliens. Only just over 1% of the public felt the actions taken were too strong – in such an atmosphere both the left-wing *Tribune* and *New Statesman* decided to keep silent on the issue. The independent 'liberal factor' as a barrier against antisemitic forces had simply disappeared – almost overnight.[33]

By mid May the government had responded by interning all male Germans and Austrians aged sixteen to sixty in certain protected areas. In the latter half of the month this was expanded to cover all Category B aliens, and by 11 June 1940 Category C aliens were added, making a policy of mass internment complete. At the peak 27,000 enemy aliens were interned, with over 7,000 sent overseas. Why did this happen?[34]

As with the internment of the British fascists, the basic reason for alien internment was the change in the military situation. By the end of May 1940, invasion was a strong possibility and the country was in a period of crisis. On its own however, this factor does not explain the extent and direction of alien internment, for it should not be assumed that mass internment was inevitable. Indeed, as late as 24 May 1940, the Cabinet rejected a request by the War Office 'for the internment of all enemy aliens'. Furthermore, when the decision was taken several weeks later, it was against the wishes of the Home Secretary, John Anderson.[35]

It is vital therefore to weigh the various forces involved in the issue, and to examine how important any Jewish factors were in the ultimate decision. The military and security forces were strongly on the side of those who wanted wholesale alien internment. To the War Office and MI5, the refugees 'were simply enemy aliens' who needed to be locked away for the safety of the realm. Writing to the Foreign Minister in February 1941, Herbert Morrison stated that 'one of the main reasons for the policy of a general internment . . . was the insistence by MI5 that they were unable to give any information' about the aliens.[36] The security forces claimed this was due to lack of resources. However, tribunals had investigated all the refugees by January 1940, and it is hard to resist the conclusion that the military and security forces 'shared the prejudices of enemy aliens expressed in the press campaign in the spring of 1940'. Contemporaries including H. G. Wells, Kingsley Martin and F. Lafitte, and some modern commentators have gone even further. They have suggested that there was in fact a conspiracy between the popular right wing (and former appeasement) press and sections of the military forces, which played up the alien threat to divert attention from the real homegrown fifth column. It is perhaps better to explain the frantic desire for alien internment from these sources as a climax to an anti-Jewish refugee campaign that had its roots in the 1930s. These military, security and press groups had never trusted German or Austrian Jewish refugees. Therefore, one does not need to be conspiratorially minded to understand that the military crisis in the summer of 1940 merely gave an opportunity to transform previous hostility to refugees into restrictive policy.[37]

However, until the Dunkirk evacuation and the fall of France, at the end of May and early June, the Cabinet could resist these pressures, and maintain its policy 'not to undertake mass internment'. Nevertheless, the new Prime Minister, Winston Churchill, had already been converted to the War Office/MI5 position by mid May. At this stage, the only major governmental force against internment came from the Home Secretary, Anderson. As an individual, Anderson consistently deplored a policy of general internment. However, as an important Cabinet member, he was willing to be dictated to by the arguments of the security forces and also the mood of public opinion.[38] The government was closely watching popular and press reactions to aliens. It does not seem that the government simply used popular demands for internment as 'a red herring', as has recently been suggested. The mood of the public in late May and June was becoming ugly and the Cabinet's desire to implement internment to protect the refugees from an anti-alien/antisemitic reaction appears to have been genuine. Public opinion was thus an important factor in the process of decision making on internment. However, in refugee matters it was not just a negative factor. John Anderson was aware that widespread internment would be welcomed 'in many quarters', but he was worried about a sharp reaction against it once the threat of invasion had passed. Concern about such liberal niceties was wiped away in early June. Yet what is revealing is how Anderson made no effect to calm down the fifth column fear, despite being urged to do so by the Ministry of Information's Home Morale Emergency Committee. Indeed the government did the reverse, allowing the British minister at the Hague, Sir Nevile Bland, to make an alarmist broadcast on the BBC. Bland stated his belief that refugee fifth columnists had been responsible for the collapse of Holland, and told the public to suspect anyone of German and Austrian connections.[39]

To summarise: the military crisis in the summer of 1940 allowed the intelligence forces to demand mass internment. Public opinion, inflamed by a lengthy press campaign, and finally by government propaganda, shared this demand as the crisis intensified. At this point, liberal opposition to internment disappeared in an alarming manner. As far as the Jewish aspect was concerned, although the aliens were not interned because they were Jewish, neither was their Jewishness irrelevant. Despite the fact that the vast majority of the aliens were refugee Jews, the security forces were not convinced of their disloyalty to Nazi Germany – partly as a result of a long-held distrust of Jews as a whole. Similarly, the press campaigns of the Rothermere, Kemsley and Beaverbrook empires against the aliens were not free of antisemitism, nor was hostile public opinion from the latter half of May 1940. The severe crisis of the summer of 1940 allowed previously unrespectable antisemitism to come to the fore, and so influence policy. The British government, people and press were shown to be vulnerable to intolerance, a reminder of the dangers of relying on the bulwarks of British liberalism and decency as permanent barriers against antisemitism. After the fall of Holland, as Mass-Observation reported, it was suddenly 'quite the done thing' to publicly express antisemitic sentiment.[40]

Nevertheless, as soon as mass internment had been carried out, a policy of reversing it was put into action, as liberal forces re-established themselves in alien matters. After having demanded some form of internment in May 1940, the *Manchester Guardian* then published fifty-four editorials attacking government policy on aliens by the end of 1940. *The Daily Herald* at the start of July also reversed its earlier demands, and ridiculed the waste and stupidity of mass internment. With the fear of invasion fast fading in July 1940, liberal public opinion reasserted itself. This was aided by the revulsion caused by the loss of life on the Arandora Star, a ship transporting Italian and German internees to Canada. The drowning of over 650 aliens on the Arandora Star helped to focus criticism from what Home Intelligence referred to as 'middle class intellectual circles'.[41] Nevertheless, polls carried out in mid July found that 55% of the public according to Mass-Observation, and 43% to BIPO, still demanded the internment of all aliens. Even so, Mass-Observation believed that the violent feeling against the aliens of late May and June was now to be found only in a small minority of the population. By early August anti-alien sentiment had declined even further, with only 33% wanting mass internment and 15% suggesting that no aliens at all should be interned.[42]

On a parliamentary level, Eleanor Rathbone, who had refrained from attacking the government in June 1940 – owing to the mood of the country – launched a powerful attack on internment in the Commons on 10 July 1940. With the security threat diminishing and public opinion losing its ferocity, a White Paper was produced at the end of July specifying categories of release. By November 1940, over 7,000 aliens were freed with another 2,000 released by the end of the year.[43] However, two major problems still faced the refugees who were still interned – the camp conditions and the government's inconsistent release policy.

Concerning the first, the two immediate difficulties were the physical conditions (especially in the temporary transit camps such as the notorious Warth Mills near Bury), and the indiscriminate mixing of pro-Nazi and anti-Nazi/Jewish aliens in the camps. The former improved at a greater speed than the latter, the release and deportations allowing a more settled and humanitarian system. However, the mixing of hostile groups was not sorted out until the middle of 1941, revealing how the government was reluctant to differentiate between different types of enemy aliens. Nevertheless, after six months to a year, the Isle of Man camps became more in keeping with the holiday atmosphere of their setting. Married camps were created and restrictions were generally lax. Yet for those remaining there was still the lack of that essential ingredient, freedom, and the stigma that went with being a long term internee.[44]

The government's release policy was as erratic as the manner in which it had rounded up the aliens. Although there were eighteen categories under which internees could apply for release in the July 1940 White Paper (to which was added a nineteenth – political refugees – in August), the system was still a lottery. Releases, which appeared to be random decisions, had the effect of unsettling those still interned. Those in Category C could apply to join the Auxiliary Pioneer Corps. By January 1941, over 4,000 aliens had been accepted into this non-combative section of the army. However, others refused to join the Pioneer Corps, believing that they were being forced unfairly into 'buying' their freedom.[45]

Generally the government's policy – pursued by the new Home Secretary, Herbert Morrison, from October 1940 – was to release the aliens within a restrictive framework that catered for the prejudices of both the Security forces and public opinion. In November 1940, Morrison was aware that 'the vocal elements of public opinion [were] in favour of a more liberal policy'. Yet this was not seen as important, for what was necessary was to appease the then silent part of the public who might, at a later date, again demand restriction. As will be shown, Morrison's philosophy was always to satisfy the lowest sentiments of public opinion on matters Jewish or alien. Morrison was also unwilling to oppose the views of the Security forces who continually demanded that there should be no relaxation of the internment policy. Indeed, Morrison shared the view of the Joint

Intelligence Committee that 'the ruling factor must always be the security and military needs of the country' – a view that even Churchill had rejected by the end of 1940.[46]

Two rival committees, the Council on Aliens and the Asquith Committee, were set up by the government to deal with the problems of mass internment. Designed to be complementary, with the former concentrating on alien morale through improving camp conditions, and the latter with release policy, the two in fact were mutually incompatible. Lord Lytton, as chairman of the Council on Aliens, realised that morale could be maintained only by a liberal release policy, which MI5 were obstructing. Contrary to this, the Asquith Committee refused to question the judgement of the Security Forces who, it admitted, distrusted 'a large number of the internees . . . especially the refugees who constitute 80% of the Germans and Austrians in internment'. Encountering what Churchill himself admitted was the 'witch-finding activities of MI5', Lord Lytton resigned in January 1941. However, with its painfully slow but continuous release policy, the numbers interned dropped to under 9,000 by August 1941, of which 6,000 were in Canada or Australia. A year later less than a thousand were interned on British soil, and by 1944 overseas internment had effectively ended. Only a few refugees were left on the Isle of Man – some of whom had been re-interned for minor criminal offences.[47]

What then was the overall impact of internment? To the infirm and elderly refugees, the camps, especially in their earlier days, did create serious physical difficulties. These included many long resident East End Polish Jews who had never been naturalised. Nevertheless, the major problem was more psychological, especially to those refugees who had suffered in the German concentration camps during the 1930s. Needing security, instead they were given more barbed wire to face. Although not common, suicides did occur, a sober qualifying factor to the tendency to view internment, a generation later, in almost nostalgic terms.[48] Although many did accept internment as a necessary temporary measure, others were embittered by the slur on their loyalty – a factor that encouraged some refugees to leave for America after the war. Although Inspector Cuthbert at the Rushen camp was sympathetic to the refugees, his predecessor, Dame Joanna Cruickshank, was not. Cruickshank had difficulties, according to several internees, in 'grasping the differences between German Jews and Nazis' – an analysis with which the Home Office agreed. One Manx lady felt 'the ones she could trust were real Germans and not German Jews', a philosophy shared by the Army commander of the Dunera, the ship transporting the internees to Australia. He contrasted the 'honest' Nazi Germans with the German and Austrian Jews who could 'only be described as subversive . . . they are definitely not to be trusted in word or deed'. Not surprisingly, given this attitude, some of the worst abuses of the whole internment experience took place on the Dunera.[49]

It was the nightmare quality of being a victim who was still distrusted that caused the greatest hardship of internment. As one refugee worker put it: 'these men are more deeply hurt by being treated as "enemies" than by anything else of all the ignominies and harshness they have suffered.' By 1941 camp conditions had become excellent, indeed a few refugees actually requested to remain interned.[50] However, the policy of mass internment and its slow reversal is one for which the government can be justifiably criticised.

After the crisis in the summer of 1940, public opinion on the refugees returned to the economic, rather than the security, threat of the refugees. In the height of the blitz, anti-alien fifth column feeling returned briefly. Indeed, allegations that the refugees were spies continued sporadically until the end of the war. Nevertheless, such beliefs were overshadowed by concern that refugees were taking jobs that belonged to the British servicemen.[51] Yet again, government policy was to appease such sentiment.

The Home Office appears to have taken a sympathetic view of the needs of the refugees to find suitable work. However, it refused to take on the powerful resistence to alien employment from many sections of British society. This was possibly strongest in the British Medical Association, whose secretary, Dr G. C. Anderson, was described by the Home Office as 'a violent anti-alien.' At the start of the war Dr Anderson objected to the use of refugee doctors in the war effort. He used the threat of violent opposition from the medical profession if these aliens were allowed to settle and profit, while 'Britishers' were away fighting. At this point, although the Home Office regarded Dr Anderson's position as unreasonable, it bowed to the fear of anti-alienism. 'Refugees should be allowed to volunteer for military service', in the view of Sir Alexander Maxwell, Permanent Under-Secretary at the Home Office, 'otherwise there may be an outcry that the refugees are getting soft jobs while the British youth is being conscripted.'[52] As the war progressed and a dire shortage of specialist skills developed, work restrictions were lifted on the refugees. Nevertheless, the Home Office was anxious that as many as possible of the refugees should leave after the war. As one official wrote in 1944, 'We do not want an outcry during demobilisation that foreigners have taken the jobs of the British soldiers – which incidently might lead to a revival of the antisemitism fermented by the BUF with consequent disorders.' Herbert Morrison was particularly concerned about this sentiment, stating that he was 'sure there will be trouble if all possible refugees do not go after the war'. The Home Office even refused to consider naturalisation for the industrialists who had created thousands of jobs in the special estates of South Wales and the North East. There was pressure on this matter due to a desire to ensure that these industrialists would stay permanently in Britain, but the Home Office refused to commit itself.[53] At the end of the war, it stated that 'the primary consideration which influences [it] is that nothing shall be done which carried with it an implication or may be used as an argument for permanent residence in this country'. In individual cases the Home Office could pursue a more liberal policy, but in general they were willing to comply with any pressure from trade unions or the Ministry of Labour to restrict the refugees. As a Board of Trade official wrote after the war, 'they [the Home Office] are almost pathologically anxious to have full powers to "tie up" any foreigner who wishes to do anything at all in this country'. Although the later years of the war brought greater job opportunities for the refugees, they also saw an increase in their insecurity about their own future in Britain. It was an insecurity that appears to have been well justified.[54]

Overall, government policy concerning the refugees in Britain was an outcome of a liberal stance from the Home Office (one which acknowledged both the problems and the contribution of the refugees in the war), being tempered by an obsessive desire to appease anti-alien sentiment from the public, the trade unions or the security forces. The result was that the Home Office, which had expected to intern only 'a small proportion of the total', ended up administering the reverse policy. In the issue of alien employment, the Home Office refused to consider naturalisation for refugee industrialists whom it had, a decade earlier, actively recruited from Nazi Germany. That there was actually a refugee problem to consider, with up to 250,000 present in Britain in the middle of the war, shows the strength of liberalism in Britain. That many of these refugees ended up interned, or denied the right to settle or work permanently, shows its limitations. It also reveals the power of British anti-alien/antisemitic sentiment.[55]

However, during the war years, the British government not only had to consider Jewish refugees on its own soil, it also had to deal with the plight of European Jewry. It was not a prospect that it welcomed, indeed the government did its utmost to avoid facing the problem. However, the sheer dimension of the European Jewish tragedy, and the centrality of antisemitism to the Nazi regime forced some sort of response from the British government. The study of the Allied response to the Holocaust has recently become a growth industry.[56] These historical works give detailed accounts of the workings of governmental and Jewish bodies with regard to events in Europe, therefore it will not be necessary to cover this ground again. What will be attempted, is an evaluation of the importance of a Jewish factor (including antisemitism) in government thinking on helping the Jews of Europe, and to examine in detail the relationship between government and public opinion on this matter.

The most direct way open for the government to help European Jewry was to allow refugees entry onto British soil. Excluding those foreigners who came to Britain as members of the Allied Forces (including some Jews – as with the Polish troops), over 70,000 refugees arrived in Britain during the Second World War. However, out of the latter total, the Jewish proportion was 'quite small', probably amounting to only several thousands. Of these it is not unfair to say that they found refuge in Britain despite, rather than because of, government policy. Although it is true that no refugee was refused entry after reaching British shores (despite a boat carrying forty refugee children being fired upon in Cornwall), it also remains that the government made no effort to help such Jews reach Britain.[57]

Why was this the case? From 3 September 1939, the government made all pre-war visas granted to refugees invalid. Moreover, the War Cabinet Committee on the Refugee Problem agreed not to differentiate between refugees and German nationals with regard to entry to the United Kingdom. Occasional exemptions were made, but the general policy was to refuse any admissions.[58] This was based firstly on security grounds. The government believed that any refugees arriving after the start of the war would have needed the approval of the Germans. There were thus fears that these refugees could be enemy agents. As with the fifth column scare, this fear turned out to be totally groundless. However, it was used to great effect by the Colonial Office to refuse Jews entry into Palestine. The head of its Middle East Department, H. F. Downie, went further, believing that illegal immigration into Palestine was 'a conspiracy', facilitated by the Gestapo and the Jewish Agency. Downie himself wrote that he regretted 'that the Jews are not on the other side in this war'.[59] R. T. Latham, of the Foreign Office, was convinced that Downie regarded 'the Jews as no less our enemies than the Germans', and that he tried to link the two by 'secret and evil bonds'. If this was the case, then it is more than possible that Downie was influenced by *The Patriot*, the violently antisemitic and pro-Arab weekly, which was putting forward such a view in the war. The 'spy' argument was revived in early 1942 against allowing the refugee ship, the Struma, entry to Palestine, with the net result that the vessel sank in the Black Sea, leaving only one survivor. Whilst Foreign Office officials generally came to doubt the refugee-spy argument, the Colonial Office persisted in it. It was a reflection of the latter's distrust of Jewish refugees, and its belief in Nazi-Zionist collaboration.[60]

The other basis for a restrictive war refugee policy was due to the government's concern over public opinion. More than any other issue, government fear of domestic antisemitism ensured that any measures for helping European Jews to escape to Britain would be highly limited. As early as December 1939, it was decided that Jews still in Germany could not be 'admitted here as refugees' because if any were given permission 'we are bound to receive a flood of applications'. Only very exceptional cases were to be considered 'in order to keep the numbers small'.[61]

In early April 1940, the reasons why such an influx was seen to be unwelcome were made explicit. R. T. Latham was concerned that the Jewish refugees in Belgium and Holland were creating dangerous antisemitism in these countries, and that if they could leave for Britain or Palestine it would be 'a set back to local Nazis'. Another Foreign Office official disagreed, stating that 'I am inclined to think that the danger of antisemitism in this country is as great as in Holland and Belgium.' What all officials were agreed upon was that National Socialism had 'gained many supporters merely by exploiting antisemitism'.[62] When Herbert Morrison became Home Secretary in October 1940, the domestic antisemitism argument became even more powerful against the entry of Jewish refugees in the war.

It has already been noted that Morrison was adamant that the refugees already in Britain should be removed as soon as possible after the war, and he was equally anxious to avoid any new Jewish refugees adding to the problem. In October 1942, with news of the fast deteriorating situation of European Jewry spreading to Britain, Morrison was forced to meet a pro-refugee deputation. He told them that although 'the general body of public opinion in this country was humanitarian and deeply sympathetic of the plight of the refugees . . . there was also a body of opinion which was potentially antisemitic'. Morrison warned them 'not to ignore the existence of this feeling'. The immediate subject under discussion was whether any help could be given to Jewish refugees in unoccupied France. Sir Herbert Emerson suggested up to 1,000 visas should be issued to these Jews. However, Morrison wanted to restrict it to children and the elderly with relatives in Britain, estimating it would save 300–350 people. This was soon changed to children with parents in Britain, limiting the number to not more than twenty. By November 1942 the issue became academic as the Germans occupied the area administered by the Vichy government, ending any possibility of the refugees reaching Britain.[63]

It is important to note the refusal of Morrison to consider allowing (as he told the Cabinet Committee on the Reception and Accommodation of Jewish Refugees in its first meeting in December 1942), more than 'a limited number of refugees, say from 1000 to 2000' into Britain. 'There were', according to Morrison, 'already 100,000 refugees, mainly Jews, in this country' and 'there was considerable antisemitism under the surface in this country. If there were any substantial increase in the number of Jewish refugees . . . we should be in for serious trouble.' It was a warning to be repeated many times by Morrison and his government colleagues, especially in the Bermuda Conference on refugees in April 1943. Were the fears that anything other than a 'token entry of Jews' would provoke serious antisemitism justified?[64]

Many liberal minded people in Britain thought this was not the case. Rumours that the government had refused 2,000 Vichy Jewish children on these grounds were regarded as 'a slander against the British people'. Realising that Morrison was so concerned about domestic reactions, pro-refugee personalities, such as Victor Gollancz and Eleanor Rathbone, set about mobilising public opinion in support of a more liberal policy in rescuing the Jews of Europe. Through Gollancz's hugely popular *Let My People Go* and pamphlets issued by the newly formed National Committee for Rescue from Nazi Terror, considerable pressure was put on the government to change its policies. In February 1943, the National Committee commissioned the British Institute of Public Opinion to carry out a poll on whether the British government should help any Jewish refugees who could get away. The outcome was that 78% of the sample felt they should. Only 13% were against giving succour, some giving antisemitic reasons for their opposition. However, the poll also revealed that only 55% wanted 'as many as can come' to be let in. Fewer than 10% wanted those arriving to be received indefinitely. The poll therefore showed strong public sympathy to the refugee plight, but also limitations on the amount of hospitality that should be given to them.[65]

Mass-Observation's surveys on Jews also confirm that there was much sympathy for the Jews of Europe, although this was often followed by indications of personal hostility to Jews. Harold Nicolson was not alone in disliking Jews, yet doing his utmost to help European Jewry. On the whole, the Mass-Observation survey in March 1943 reveals disgust at the lack of government action on the matter. Private prejudices did not generally interfere with a demand for a generous refugee policy.[66]

Therefore, whilst the government was not mistaken in believing that there was antisemitism in wartime Britain, it made the error of not differentiating between types of antisemitism. It also did not allow for public ambivalence on the subject. As a symptom of this, it is important to note that the Ministry of Information's Home Intelligence was not interested in recording pro-Jewish/refugee sentiment in the war – only the reverse. The government's aim was to pacify any possible anti-alien/antisemitic feeling in Britain and to avoid giving in to the demands of 'humanitarian' opinion as far as was possible. The net result, as far as helping Jews to escape was concerned, as a contributor to the *New Statesman* realised, was that 'fear of antisemitism [was] as restrictive of compassionate activity as antisemitism itself'.[67] Fearing a flood of foreign refugees into the Allied countries, Britain and America effectively decided against any measures that would have facilitated a mass exodus. The Allies' Bermuda Conference on refugees in April 1943 was thus doomed from the start. It was designed only to attempt to satisfy liberal opinion that something was being done. As a Foreign Office official wrote several months after the conference: 'from our point of view, fortunately, the German Government appear to be intending to persist to the last in their refusal to allow Jews to leave Germany'. Hitler had called Jewish refugees 'a valuable hostage to me'. In this, his analysis was correct, for the Allies had decided that they could not cope with a large influx of Jews in the war.[68]

The fear of domestic antisemitism was at the bottom of the government's refusal to allow anything other than a trickle of refugees into the country. It was based on a distrust of the British people, but also of the Jewish refugees themselves. The latter was particularly true of Herbert Morrison, whose strict line and fears of antisemitism even brought criticism from his colleagues. A close examination of Morrison's attitudes bring into doubt his previous image as being 'favourably inclined to Jews', a man without a 'tinge of antisemitism'. There is no questioning Morrison's disgust at political antisemitism either in Britain or in Germany. Moreover, his approval of Socialist-Zionist experiments in Palestine cannot be doubted.[69] Nevertheless, his analysis of the causes of antisemitism reveal a less favourable picture. In October 1936, in a meeting with Neville Laski and the Communist Harry Pollitt to discuss the threat of the BUF in the East End, Morrison had suggested that Jews should stop their activities as sweated employers and bad landlords and estate agents; they should be '100% economically clean'. Furthermore they should avoid being too prominent in local politics, which was, as Geoffrey Alderman has pointed out, close to demanding that Jews should 'accept second class status'. It was a sign of Morrison's belief in a 'well-earned' theory of antisemitism, which he was to develop further in his position as Home Secretary in the war.

Morrison's unjustified criticism of alien Jewish black marketeers has already been commented on. What is interesting in this context is Morrison's reply to his Under-Secretary's plea that revoking naturalisation of alien offenders would only strengthen antisemitic forces in Britain. Unimpressed with this argument, Morrison replied that 'these [foreign Jewish black market offenders] people [were] creating the anti-alien feeling'. There is little doubting what a leading British Zionist called Morrison's 'anti-refugee attitude' in the war. It was an attitude which led him to restrict entry of aliens in the war and to urge the removal of refugees from Britain after it, so as not to provoke what he regarded as justified antisemitism.[70] Morrison's own distrust of Jews led him to distrust the public's attitude to the refugees. It thus ensured that no effort would be made to identify the government with pro-Jewish refugee sentiment.

Although Morrison's views were probably less generous than other government officials, little opposition was put forward to his restrictive stance. Despite pressure from groups such as the National Committee for Rescue from Nazi Terror, the Home Office and Foreign Office constantly refused visas for refugees who had reached neutral countries, but whose lives were still in danger. Only those who could help the war effort were given permission to come to Britain. Rather than satisfy humanitarian feeling in Britain, the government chose to appease any possible anti-alien sentiment. Thus in the Parliamentary debate on refugees after the Bermuda Conference, the Cabinet put pressure on Whips so that the speeches would not be biased in favour of free admission of refugees to Britain. Rather than discussing any possible ways of helping the refugees, the debate became a repetitive discussion of the strength of antisemitism in Britain. With this attitude, it is not surprising that those who had attempted to prove the pro-refugee sympathy of the British people came to regard themselves as at war with the stone-walling policy of the relevant government departments, particularly with Morrison and the Home Office.[71]

Had the government wished to pursue a more generous policy in allowing refugees into Britain, it must be suggested that the British public would not have been in opposition. However, public opinion surveys also show the limitations of sympathy towards Jewish refugees. Any mass influx would have needed powerful backing by British propaganda agencies to ensure that hostile sentiment did not increase to a dangerous level. Such a policy would not have been considered, however, for throughout the war years the British government constantly refused to identify with the Jewish cause, as its propaganda policy concerning the fate of European Jewry indicates.[72]

At the very start of the war, the government considered issuing a White Paper on conditions in the German concentration camps. Sir Alexander Cadogan, Permanent Under-Secretary at the Foreign Office, offered two objections to this proposal that were to recur throughout the war. Firstly, the 'hair-raising reports about Jewish concentration camps' came from Jews themselves, 'who were entirely unreliable [?] witnesses'. Secondly, 'the Germans will only say that this is further proof that the British Empire is run by international Jewry. And I am sure that sympathy with the Jews hasn't waned very considerably during the last twelve months.' The matter would have been left to rest, but a few days later the Germans revived accusations about British South African concentration camps in their atrocity propaganda. Therefore the go-ahead was given for the British White Paper which was published in October 1939. However, although the White Paper included documents on atrocities on Jews, prominence was given to less 'sensational' cases involving, in a Foreign Office Official's words, 'perfectly good Aryans such as Niemoller'. The aim was to avoid giving Goebbels 'an opportunity of talking once again about the influence of international Jewry in this country'. It was necessary, at all costs, to avoid anything that would give strength to the Jews' War accusation.[73]

Although the White Paper sold well, and the British press (with a few notable exceptions), was in support of it, the government believed it to have been a failure – dismissed by the public as atrocity propaganda. After it, there was a reluctance to use any atrocity propaganda, and care was made not to single out Jews as suffering any more than other victims of the Nazis. Although aware that Jews were suffering particularly, one official in April 1940 remarked that 'as a general rule Jews are inclined to magnify their persecution. I remember the exaggerated stories of Jewish pogroms in Poland after the last war which, when fully examined, were found to have little substance.'[74]

'Jewish sources', as another Foreign Office official noted, were 'always doubtful' – as were the Jews themselves. A broadcast in January 1941, which referred to refugee Jews as 'the friends of all that we were fighting to preserve', was objected to because the two did not 'follow inevitably'. It was also wrong 'to emphasise the mainly Jewish character of our refugee population', as there was 'so much antisemitic feeling in the world'. The Ministry of Information's instructions in July 1941 have already been noted, stating that atrocity propaganda 'must deal with undisputably innocent people. Not with violent political opponents. And not with Jews.' Although exceptions were made to this instruction, it was generally obeyed. However, by the latter part of 1942, it was becoming a very difficult line to maintain as the reports of the dire fate of European Jewry became too numerous to ignore. A Polish Bund report in June 1942, which had outlined how over 700,000 Polish Jews had perished, was followed by a telegram in early August which detailed the Germans' Jewish extermination plan. Thereafter, 'almost every day', in Martin Gilbert's words, 'news of the killing of Jews on a massive scale began to reach the Allies'. Nevertheless, until December 1942, the government resisted attempts to use the extermination reports in its propaganda.[75]

This reluctance was based on the same premises that had controlled policy on Jewish atrocity stories since the start of the war. There was a distrust of what H. Downie of the Colonial Office called the 'Jewish technique of atrocity propaganda', or J. Bennett of the Foreign Office referred to as 'Jewish Agency "sob stuff" '. The report of the extermination plan was, in another Foreign Office official's words, a 'rather wild story' and thus the government's Political Warfare Executive refused to use it. Although Sir Herbert Emerson, the Director of the Inter-Governmental Committee for Refugees, was in 'no doubt that it is the policy of Germany literally to exterminate all Jews . . . of all nationality', his government colleagues disagreed. To accept that would be to accept a particular Jewish problem in Europe, which was contrary to the 'view [of] His Majesty's Government that Jews must be treated as nationals of existing states'.[76]

In early December, the Polish government-in-exile challenged this position, demanding Allied publicity on the extermination of Polish Jewry. Anthony Eden, the Foreign Secretary, who was actually to make this Declaration on 17 December 1942, did not want to pursue this policy, due to what Lewis Namier referred to as 'a general fear of contaminating himself by pronouncing the name of Jew'. However, the pressure became too immense and Eden announced to the House of Commons that 'the German authorities . . . are now carrying into effect Hitler's oft-repeated intention to exterminate the Jewish people in Europe'. Eden warned that those carrying out 'this bestial policy of cold-blooded extermination' would not escape retribution. The Commons, according to 'Chips' Channon, 'was deeply moved' – as were the British people as a whole.[77] Yet, the Declaration was regarded as a mistake by the Foreign Office, for it raised public expectations of government action in aiding the Jews of Europe, when no such policy was intended. Thereafter, no declaration was made on behalf of the Jews, who were again relegated to a non-special treatment category. When the Jewish Agency, in July 1943, asked the government to recognise that Jews were in greater danger in German-occupied countries than other people, the Foreign Office response was that although 'the argument ha[d] some foundation in fact, [it] would meet with the strongest opposition were any attempt made to use it'. Likewise, the Bermuda Conference several months earlier, although devoted to the *Jewish* refugee problem, refused to acknowledge this fact publicly. Refugees were to be referred to by nationality rather than by race. Even when the concentration camps were liberated, the government's policy of ignoring the Jewish aspect continued. The recently rediscovered government film on the subject had the instruction that it was 'especially desirable to document the extent to which non-Jewish German nationals were the victims of the German concentration camp system'. The final script referred to Jews only three times and, in regard to Buchenwald, did not mention Jews in the thirty-one categories of those killed there.[78]

Similarly, doubts of the atrocity stories – based on distrust of Jewish sources – continued in government circles until the end of the war. V. Caventish-Bentinck, chairman of the Joint Intelligence Committee, doubted a report on the use of gas chambers because 'The Poles and to a greater extent the Jews, tend to exaggerate German atrocities in order to stoke us up.' One official noted the need to take allowance for the 'Jewish tendency to superlative', another bemoaned the amount of time wasted in the Foreign Office 'with these wailing Jews'.[79] Even as late as January 1945, a Foreign Office official could note, with regard to atrocities, that the 'sources of information are nearly always Jewish whose accounts are only sometimes reliable and not seldom highly coloured. One notable tendency in Jewish reports on this problem is to exaggerate the number of deportations and deaths.' James Parkes, in his autobiography, remembered how the Foreign Office responded to a draft that he had written throughout the war on the Jewish problem. He originally put down that 50,000 Jews had been murdered, but the Foreign Office crossed off one of his noughts. The same happened with his second draft, which used a figure of half a million, and finally towards the end of the war with his last estimate of five million Jews killed. At this stage Parkes gave up.[80]

Certain government officials therefore joined the select group of authors and journals such as *Truth*, the *Catholic Herald, Peace News, Socialist Appeal* and Douglas Reed in doubting atrocity stories *because* they were Jewish. In this they seem to have again been more cynical than the public, the majority of whom it must be suggested, accepted the veracity of the reports of the destruction of European Jewry. Due to a great reluctance of the government to single out the Jews for special propaganda treatment – a policy reinforced by doubts of the intensity of Nazi persecution of Jews – only on one occasion, at the end of 1942, did the British government acknowledge the plight of European Jewry. As with the rescue of Jewish refugees, pro-Jewish propaganda was not a priority of the British government in the war.[81]

In summarising the government's record in helping the Jews of Europe, what role did antisemitism play in its inaction? Bernard Wasserstein has concluded that 'certainly there was a tinge of antisemitism in the words of some British officials and politicians . . . But antisemitism does not by itself explain British conduct.' More important, in Wasserstein's opinion, was bureaucratic indifference to the Jewish fate, where helping 'the Jews of Europe was seen as a low priority'. Wasserstein is right to suggest that direct antisemitism was rare in government circles, except perhaps in the case of the Middle Eastern Department of the Colonial Office, who, in the words of R. T. Latham, regarded 'the Jewish world as a sort of secondary enemy'. Yet there is possibly more antisemitism, albeit of an indirect variety, in the bureaucratic indifference than Wasserstein allows for. It is true that, in the example of the bombing of Auschwitz or the railway lines leading to it, even requests from the Prime Minister could be ignored by civil servants. Nevertheless, it could be argued that one of the major bureaucratic reasons behind the refusal to consider a rescue policy – the fear of domestic antisemitism – had its roots, like the refugee spy scares, in a fundamental distrust of refugee Jews themselves. This was particularly true of Herbert Morrison, who was largely responsible for the policy of restricting entry into Britain in the war, but also of many of his colleagues. One Home Office official noted late in the war that many more Jewish refugees could have been accepted into British society without creating serious antisemitism 'if they were not so gregarious and not so assertive'. More blatantly, J. Bennett of the Foreign Office gave his reasons for not helping European Jewry: 'Why should the Jews be spared distress and humiliation when they have earned it?'[82] Distrusting Jews themselves, it was only natural for these officials to distrust the British public as a whole. Thus the government chose to ignore the genuine sympathy that the persecution of the Jews had created in the war. Whilst the possibilities of helping European Jewry were limited, the British (as did the American) government chose to do as little as possible. The government refused to identify with the Jewish cause, thus failing to come to terms with the most barbaric aspect of its enemy's policies. The study of British government reactions to the plight of European Jewry reveals the limitations of a liberal democratic state, where, as Richard Breitman has written, 'Western humanitarian values were unable to prevail over the antisemites and pragmatists who stressed the risks of giving evidence to support German charges.'[83]

A Foreign Office paper, just after the war, gave instructions on how to deal with accusations that Britain had been responsible for many Jewish deaths by its policy of restricting the entry of Jews into Palestine and elsewhere. The answer was simple: 'His Majesty's Government were not responsible for countless Jewish deaths and suffering. The Nazis were responsible'. This fact needs to be remembered, and the British response to the holocaust should be kept in this perspective. Yet this does not rule out criticisms of government policies.[84] The government line that Jews were to be regarded as 'a purely religious community, on the same national footing as their fellow citizens', and that subjects 'must not be discriminated against because of their religious faith'[85] *were* fine liberal sentiments. Nevertheless, they were irrelevant in the light of an enemy who persecuted the Jews simply because of their race. Thus with the help of sympathetic ministers, such as Lord Woolton and R. Butler, the Jews could be granted their particular religious demands. However, the more vital requirement of succour to the Jews' co-religionists abroad could not be dealt with; it was more than just a religious matter.

The emancipation contract demanded that Jews, in return for equality, would cease being Jews. At worst they would be 'Englishmen of the Jewish faith'.[86] Antisemitism was seen as being incompatible with liberalism; the former's survival was viewed as the Jews' own fault. Thus in the war, the government refused publicly to admit the existence of antisemitism and therefore was unable to deal effectively with domestic hostility to Jews. Its failure to differentiate between forms of antisemitism (and thus its exaggeration of the danger of domestic antisemitism), was a reflection of the inability of liberalism to deal with the problem of those who did not regard Jews as 'nationals of a different religion'.

When under threat, whether from the 'enemy within' (as with the internment crisis in the summer of 1940), or the 'enemy without' (as with the fear of a mass influx of Jewish refugees, had Britain agreed to help European Jewry), humanitarian considerations, as an independent factor, soon disappeared from the governmental outlook. The only restraint then operating on the government came from outside pressure from, or on the behalf of, the Jews. It is with the strength of these pro-Jewish or anti-antisemitic forces in the war that the final chapter will deal.

6
The response to antisemitism

The war not only generated dramatic antisemitic developments in Britain, but also produced an equally lively response from Jewish and anti-fascist bodies. New organisations such as the Council of Christians and Jews came into existence, both the Communist Party and the National Council for Civil Liberties launched major campaigns against antisemitism, and there were important changes in the response of Jewish communal institutions. With regard to Jewish defence literature, the bibliographer of Anglo-Jewry has commented that 'the wartime period . . . brought with it a spate of publications on antisemitism, the Jewish problem, the refugees and allied subjects'.[1] The purpose of this chapter will be to examine the relative strength of groups such as the Council of Christians and Jews in British society, the impact of their activities and propaganda on the public and the government, the relationship between the groups and an assessment of their tactics. An attempt will also be made to analyse the attitudes of these groups towards Jews. Both external and internal limitations of British philosemitism and anti-antisemitism will be critically evaluated.

As it is possible to trace an antisemitic tradition in Britain over the past hundred years – albeit one that has varied immensely in its strength – an anti-antisemitic tradition can also be found. Attacks on antisemitism in Britain have not been confined to Jews. Nevertheless, by the period of mass immigration from the 1880s, a wide range of Jewish organisations had been established which were aimed at protecting Anglo-Jewry. The Board of Deputies of British Jews, founded in 1760, had become the quasi-official representative body of the Jewish community. In 1871 the Anglo-Jewish Association was formed, aimed at ensuring the well-being of Jews across the world. Just over a decade earlier, the Jewish Board of Guardians had come into existence. This organisation, whilst directly aiming to help the 'deserving' Jewish poor, was indirectly an attempt to make the poorer members of Anglo-Jewry less visible in society – thus removing a potential threat to the well-being of the richer brethren. The community was also served by an important national paper, the *Jewish Chronicle*, an English language organ which has run continuously since 1841.[2]

When the mass influx began in the last quarter of the nineteenth century, it was, therefore into an already well organised Jewish community. However, despite the strength of this bureaucracy, there remained powerful self imposed restraints in how far the community would combat domestic antisemitism. Responding to the unwritten demands of emancipation, the Board of Deputies in particular refused to regard the Anglo-Jewish community as anything other than a religious grouping. Political action was limited to ensuring the freedom of English Jews to practice their faith without restriction. Much energy was thus spent in defending shechita in the 1900s when it was under strong attack, and likewise exemption from restrictive Sunday trading legislation which would have also badly affected the Jewish community.[3]

Antisemitism was not a problem that should have existed after emancipation in the official thinking of the Board. Therefore, no attempt was made to counter the literary antisemitism of the Chesterbelloc school, nor of the works of Joseph Banister, and other antisemites. Indeed, in the South Wales riots of 1911, the initial official Jewish response 'was to play down the Jewish aspect', with most leaders 'refus[ing] to believe that antisemitism had been a factor' in the disturbances. In the Limerick riots seven years earlier, the blatant antisemitism and subsequent anti-Jewish boycott had forced the Board of Deputies to take some action. However, the Board preferred behind the scenes diplomacy; a tactic utterly unsuited to the problem that was faced. When confronted with violent opposition such as that from the British Brothers' League, the immigrant Jews could not rely on their 'official' representatives for help. Left exposed, an alternative grass roots response to antisemitism developed as early as 1902, with the formation of an Aliens Defence Committee consisting of East End Jewish and non-Jewish trade unionists.[4]

Likewise, with the issue of alien restriction, the Board of Deputies made little effort to fight the Aliens Bill. As Geoffrey Alderman has suggested 'outright opposition to the measure . . . was left to a group of radical Liberals . . . and to the immigrants themselves'. Here the class aspirations of the established community acted as another limiting factor as far as barriers to antisemitic forces in Britain were concerned. Sharing and reinforcing the government's fear of antisemitism, the Board of Deputies wished to stop a mass influx of alien Jews into Britain. Its sister organisation, the Jewish Board of Guardians, co-operated with the authorities in deporting 50,000 Jews in the immigration period.[5]

Opposition from non-Jews to the aliens agitation should not be minimised. Liberal papers, such as the *Manchester Guardian* and *Tribune*, consistently opposed the Aliens Act in the 1900s, as did most socialists. Nevertheless both these worlds, whilst opposing antisemitism on principle, also demanded of the Jew that he cease being exclusive and that he should ultimately disappear into British society. This was another limiting factor of the forces of anti-antisemitism, and a reminder that the latter is not necessarily always a form of philosemitism.[6] However, in the early 1900s, the government preferred to appease anti-alien feeling and to ignore the ever present humanitarian anti-restrictionist sentiment in Britain. It was a pattern that was to become familiar as the century progressed.

The First World War witnessed interesting developments in response to what was an intensely antisemitic period. Faced with continuous anti-Jewish press attacks, the Board of Deputies was forced to take some form of public action and responded with its first major leaflet campaign. Internal struggles involving Zionists and the Balfour declaration had the net effect of opening up the Board, which by 1918 had become a slightly more democratic organisation. Nevertheless, the old restraints on direct action remained strong and there appears to have been no response from the Board of Deputies to the antisemitic riots of 1917. Again, the immigrant community was forced to rely on itself, through such organisations as the Foreign Jews' Protection Committee, made up of Jewish socialists, anarchists and trade unionists. East End Jews and non-Jews also joined together to defend the aliens in the British Socialist Party. In contrast, the Board of Deputies refused to use its governmental contacts to complain about alien Jewish internment, fearing that any such protests would give the appearance of disloyalty.[7]

However, in the post-1918 world the Board of Deputies was a slightly different animal – becoming involved in public denunciations of the Jew-Bolshevik libel and actually complaining to the Home Office throughout the 1920s about government treatment of Jewish aliens.[8] Although the 1930s were again to show its limitations, the Board had responded to the criticisms that it was doing nothing about antisemitism.

The generally harmonious 1920s also saw two interesting developments with regard to the response to antisemitism. Firstly, the British far left involved itself in violent clashes with the early fascist movement as early as 1926. In addition, a strong link had been forged between young Jews in the immigrant areas and the Communist Party. Secondly, and of significance for the future, 1927 witnessed the formation of the first major Jewish-Christian goodwill body, the Society of Jews and Christians. Thus by the 1930s, there were already a variety of Jewish and non-Jewish organisations ready to face the antisemitism of this troubled decade.[9]

At the forefront of the opposition to the BUF in the 1930s was the Communist Party (CPGB). Unlike the Labour Party, the CPGB did not shy away from direct confrontation with the fascists, a policy that helped attract even more Jewish support to the Communist cause.[10] Yet again, the Board of Deputies refused to protest directly against the antisemitic threat to Jews, and the working class Jewish community was forced to deal with the problem itself. In 1936 a genuine left-wing popular front organisation, the Jewish People's Council (JPC), was created out of a coalition of Communist and Jewish labour groupings. Its willingness to use physical force against the fascists, most clearly seen at Cable Street, was anathema to the Board of Deputies. Moreover, the hostile relationship between the two defence groups reveals other limitations of the Board's approach. Any co-operation was ruled out for the Board objected to the full title of its rival organisation – the 'Jewish People's Council Against Fascism and Antisemitism'. In a demonstration of the absurd lengths to which the Board would go to honour the emancipation contract, it refused to accept any 'political' involvement. As a result, it was stated in a memorandum, 'we cannot declare ourselves against Fascism per se.' Any attempt, in the words of the Board's secretary, to 'get the whole Jewish community [to be] anti-fascist' would prevent 'the very object which it seeks to achieve', which was political invisibility. Not until 1939 did the Board realise the unreality of its approach and actually begin to defend democracy.[11]

The Board, it must be emphasised, was not inactive in fighting antisemitism, indeed its Jewish Defence Committee (JDC) was formed for this purpose in 1938. Yet its approach was to negotiate behind-the-scenes, using governmental and other high level contacts. Occasionally successful pressure could be put on journals and organisations to change their attitude to Jews. However, this was of limited use when confronting papers such as *Truth*, whose editor was, in the words of a judge in 1941, 'obsession[al] with regard to the Jews'. The Board also managed to infiltrate extremist organisations like the Nordic League and pass on the information to the Home Office or Scotland Yard. Such contacts gave the Board opportunities denied to grass roots organisations like the JPC, yet its privileged position was not necessarily of advantage to the whole Jewish community. Feeling insecure of its own position, the Board of Deputies helped to reinforce the government's fear of domestic antisemitism and thus failed to challenge, for example, the cautious policy of allowing refugees to enter Britain in the 1930s.[12]

This insecurity was reflected in the spate of defence literature in the late 1930s, from Jewish and non-Jewish writers. Writing in an apologetic vein, these authors bent over backwards to give both sides of the case. The net result was that defence literature could become 'sugar coated antisemitism'. Only Louis Golding was brave enough to declare that 'the Jewish problem is in essence a Gentile problem'. Even he was to criticise Jewish behaviour towards the end of his book on antisemitism, which was published by Penguin in 1938.[13] This lack of confidence in the official Jewish world, and the refusal to confront domestic antisemitism directly were to become important factors in the response of the Jewish community in the Second World War years, as will shortly emerge.

By the outbreak of war, Jewish defence had become as much a feature of British society as antisemitism itself. Although lacking unity, there were both Jewish (official and grass roots) organisations against antisemitism, and non-Jewish ones such as the Communist Party and the National Council for Civil Liberties (NCCL) which had fought antisemitism and fascism since its formation in 1934.[14] The changed circumstances of war were to reshape the policies of some of these organisations and also to create new groups opposed to antisemitism. It is to consider how they tackled the problem of domestic fascism in the war that we must first turn.

After the bitter struggle between the Board of Deputies and the JPC, it is ironic that by the second month of the war, informal co-operation could take place between the two groups in an East End anti-defamation campaign. At first, the Board of Deputies ignored the street activities of the fascists in the war, stopping its open air defence campaign 'in order not to embarrass the government'. Instead, unsuccessful attempts were made to persuade the Ministry of Information to suppress fascist antisemitic anti-war literature. However, influenced by a continuation of fascist public meetings, and pressure from the independent *Jewish Chronicle*, the Board took a more public stand against domestic fascism by the end of 1939.[15]

The Board's new found support of democracy led it to take an increasingly militant position against the BUF. By the Leeds by-election in March 1940, it was circulating leaflets in support of the democratic parties, and warning that the BUF meant 'Concentration Camps for You!' Paradoxically, the change in the Board's tactics in the war were simultaneous with a muting of the Communist Party's attacks on the BUF. Although distancing themselves from the BUF's peace campaign – especially at the Silvertown by-election – the Communist Party generally ignored the Mosleyites in the phoney war, preferring to attack the 'fascist bosses in this country'. However, clashes between fascists and left-wing Jews did not disappear. A mass meeting in Wilmslow in December 1939 led to particularly violent scenes.[16]

The turnabout in responses to domestic fascism was also reflected in the reaction to the new defence regulations in May and June 1940. The Board of Deputies passed all its information on BUF members to Scotland Yard and welcomed the restrictive measures, whereas the *Daily Worker* warned that the real threat to the country remained: 'the workers are not blind to the fact that those who interned Mosley are the very people who have introduced Mosleyism into this country'. This 'social fascist' analysis was also applied to domestic antisemitism by the Communist Party in the summer of 1940. The *Daily Worker* claimed antisemitism was not due to Hitlerism or mere Mosleyism but was in fact the 'secret weapon of the ruling class', who were trying to divert the attention of the workers away from 'a dying system'.[17] However, with the Nazi invasion of the Soviet Union in July 1941, and the transformation of the conflict from an 'Imperialist' to a 'peoples' war, the Communist Party also changed its attitude to domestic fascism and antisemitism.

With its reappearance in September 1942, the *Daily Worker* devoted much space to the post-18B fascist revival in Britain. Indeed the Communist Party as a whole became almost obsessive about the danger posed by these tiny groups. Why was this the case, and how did the Board of Deputies receive this renewed Communist interest in domestic fascism? Douglas Hyde became the anti-fascist correspondent of the *Daily Worker* during the war, and in his cynical post-war account of the CPGB he explained the interest in the domestic fascist revival. 'Here was the chance once again to come out as the great anti-fascist fighters,' Hyde claimed, even though these 'obscure neo-fascist organisations' were 'very much a question of bricks without straw.' Can this analysis be accepted?[18]

There is little doubt that the Communist Party, through mass protests and rallies, elevated groups (such as the 18B Detainees Fund and the British National Party), to an importance that their membership did not justify. Yet Hyde himself later admitted that although the CPGB's campaign contained an element of opportunism, there was also genuine concern of a fascist and organised antisemitic revival in Britain. It was coupled with a fear that the war would be transformed into an anti-Soviet crusade, when 'these groups would then gain importance'.[19] The public opposition to these fascist groups from the far left must also be put in the context of the Board of Deputies' response. Although the Board had been vocal in its attack on the BUF in 1940, by 1942 it had returned to its earlier, non-public tactics. It refused to attack the 18B publicity groups, claiming that to do so would 'play into the hands' of those who were suggesting that regulation 18B was simply an attack on antisemites. When the BUF was revived in 1944, in the form of the League of Ex-Servicemen, the Board refused to confront it directly. Instead, the Board merely got 'in touch with the relevant authorities' to register its concern. Although some unofficial links with the CPGB existed, the Board was not happy with Communist involvement in anti-fascism, claiming it was making 'a lot of mischief'.[20]

The clash between the two approaches was most clearly seen in the reaction to Mosley's release in November 1943. The Communist Party was at the forefront of the opposition to Herbert Morrison's decision. It helped to articulate the 'storm of indignation' across the country where 90% of the population were opposed to Mosley's release. The Board, however, remained silent, a policy that was not unnoticed by the Jewish population. As in the 1930s the Board of Deputies had shown itself to be out of touch with the feeling of most Jews in Britain, including the *Jewish Chronicle*, and in 1942 the 'Friends of Jewish Labour' was formed in opposition to it. In 1944 and the immediate post-war years, many Jews would look to militant Jewish and left-wing organisations in the fight against fascism rather than their 'official' organisation.[21] Although organised antisemitism and fascism was of a limited nature in the war, both Jewish and Communist groups had revealed major weaknesses in their opposition to it. A similar pattern can be found in the reaction to the wider problem of domestic antisemitism in the war.

By late 1942, the Board of Deputies Jewish Defence Committee (JDC) was beginning to realise that its defensive position on antisemitism – rebutting attacks on the community and at the same time demanding better behaviour from Jews – was not necessarily working. Nevertheless, the dominant aspect of the JDC's response to antisemitism throughout the war continued to be that of an apologetic stance. At the beginning of the conflict, it urged the Jewish community to volunteer for the defence of the country so as to present an image of 'a solid wall of loyalty and courage. We must stand in line with the best elements of the whole of the country.' The fear that this would not be the case haunted the JDC, and in 1940 it decided to devote its resources 'to the internal causes of antisemitism'. At that stage in the war this was mainly the behaviour of Jewish refugees or evacuees; two years later it would largely be concerned with the Jewish involvement in the black market.[22]

In 1940 a formal body, the Trades Advisory Council (TAC), was formed from within the Board's JDC to maintain 'harmonious relations between Jew and non-Jew in trade and industry'. One aim was to solve disputes between and against Jewish traders using diplomacy, in which it had some degree of success.[23] More problematic was its desire to deal with Jewish offenders in the economic world. In 1942 and 1943 the TAC launched a major attack on Jewish black marketeers, one that was to lead to a serious split in the Board of Deputies. The Zionist takeover of the Board in the war is well known. However, a by-product of this development remains to be explored. Amongst the Zionists who had entered the Board were several prominent members of the British section of the World Jewish Congress; left-wing in politics, they included Noah Barou and Maurice Orbach, both of whom became prominent members of the TAC. It was perhaps their socialist outlook that explains the violence of the language used by the TAC against Jewish offenders. Its public attacks were, it seems, a response to the quiet approach that typified the Board as a whole. It is thus not surprising that the TAC was at loggerheads with the JDC, its original creator, for the latter part of the war.[24]

Despite the different tactics of the TAC from its parent body, the net effect was the same – to concentrate its efforts on the internal causes of antisemitism. At the same time the Board of Deputies became obsessive about answering any antisemitic accusation in the war. Well over a million of its defence leaflets were circulated, the impact of which will be examined later. The desire to answer antisemites rationally could lead to absurd results. When considering an answer to *The Protocols*, the JDC's Sidney Salomon even suggested pointing out that the eventual goal of the forgery was 'the happiness and well-being of all'.[25] Yet the apologetic position of the Board was not without a challenge, for in 1943 both the Communist Party and the NCCL launched major campaigns against domestic antisemitism.

Neither the NCCL nor the Communist Party were newcomers to the fight against antisemitism, for it had been part of their anti-fascism in the 1930s. Nevertheless, their previous opposition does not account for the level of importance in the 1943 campaigns, or their widespread nature. Unlike the Communist Party, the NCCL continued to attack the BUF's antisemitism in the phoney war period. Even so both groups continued to attack non-organised hostility to Jews. However, despite its opposition to fascism, the NCCL also attacked the defence regulations, especially 18B for its denial of habeas corpus. This policy was maintained until 1942 when the NCCL had come heavily under the influence of Communists, especially since the death in 1941 of its Secretary Ronald Kidd. The NCCL's increasing interest in fighting antisemitism later in the war cannot be explained by Communist influence alone however. It seems to have been largely the work of the NCCL's new secretary, Elizabeth Allen – a member of the Women's Liberal Federation Executive Committee. It is significant that the NCCL produced a leaflet 'Fight Against Antisemitism! What *You* Can Do' in 1941, at a stage when the Communist Party was taking little interest in the subject.[26]

Allen, whose background had been in Jewish refugee work, became increasingly concerned at the level of antisemitism in Britain, her philosophy being that 'It Shall Not Happen Here.' She supported the demands to use Regulation 18B against the revived fascist groups, as their activities had 'grave consequences for . . . the larger civil liberties of the rest of the country'. At its Annual General Meeting in March 1943, the NCCL recorded its 'growing alarm' against increasing antisemitism in Britain, and called for the government to make the disseminating of antisemitic propaganda a criminal offence. A month later a national conference was organised, which launched the NCCL's campaign against antisemitism. The major plank in the NCCL's programme was to change the libel laws to include attacks on Jews as a whole, but its other solution to solving antisemitism was to educate the public. Allen, with a faith in public reasonableness, believed that antisemitism could be removed by discussion, which could 'do nothing but good'. Public meetings and press debates on antisemitism were sponsored by the NCCL, the impact of which will again be analysed later. The NCCL also attempted to deal with all forms of antisemitism, with Elizabeth Allen launching an attack on publishers of children's and adult literature that included hostile references to Jews. In addition, she urged the public to counter any private manifestations of antipathy.[27]

The Communist Party was in full support of the NCCL campaign, indeed in the same year it made the antisemitism/libel offence issue a major element in its programme. Was Douglas Hyde right to suggest that the Communist Party cynically and 'deliberately . . . us[ed] the Jewish fear of fascism and antisemitism for [its] own political ends', or was its interest in combatting antisemitism a genuine attempt to solve a serious problem? The answer is complex. As the *Daily Worker*'s Walter Holmes suggested late in 1942, the Communist Party's opposition to antisemitism had sprung from the 1930s, and its present policy was 'in logical sequence to a long and consistent line of policy'. Nevertheless, Hyde's remarks contained an element of truth, for the National Jewish Committee of the Communist Party saw the outcry following the release of Mosley in November–December 1943 as an opportunity to 'make of the Jewish people an active element of the Democratic life of the country'. Yet the very existence of the National Jewish Committee (NJC) indicates that the Communist Party's interest in its Jewish membership was more than just cynical opportunism.[28]

Formed early in 1943, the NJC was a subsection of the Communist Party's International Affairs Committee. This reflected its anti-Zionist stance and also its attempt to link the fight against fascism and antisemitism in Britain to the struggle of European Jewry. Using the NJC, the Communist Party encouraged 'Jewish work' from Jewish Party members. It aimed to rectify 'the situation in which Jewish Communists and progressive elements are largely isolated from Jewish life and Jewish organisations' and to lead the Jewish people in the anti-fascist struggle. In the East End particularly, the Party encouraged Jewish work. This culminated in Phil Piratin's election victory in Mile End in 1945, and in several Jewish Communist councillors being elected onto the Stepney Borough Council in the immediate post-war years. In Piratin's campaign 'An Appeal to the Jewish Electors' was issued, with up to half of his votes coming from Jews in a constituency where only one third were Jewish.[29]

The question still remains, was the Communist Party opportunist in its anti-antisemitic campaign? From the tone and volume of its literature, it appears that the Party genuinely feared antisemitism, not simply because it threatened Jews, but because it endangered the whole working class movement by attempting to divide it. Palme Dutt, its general secretary, in a secret memorandum of 10 January 1943, stated that 'antisemitic propaganda' was 'especially dangerous' and it would seem that the Party's concern over the issue was *not* just to attract Jewish support. Furthermore, the NJC and the attempt to win Jewish support to the progressive cause also indicated a desire to help particular Jewish concerns. The NJC was involved not only in the anti-fascist/antisemitic fight but also in strengthening the cultural identity of the community. A close relationship existed between the NJC and the Workers' Circle (the Bundist orientated Friendly Society), and thus Yiddish culture was actively promoted. The Jewish settlement in Soviet Russia, Biro-Bidjan, and the equivalent in Palestine, were praised, marking an end to the purely assimilationist left-wing solution to the Jewish problem. Thus, although the Communist

Party's interest in antisemitism from 1943 onwards was not without its opportunist elements, it also reflected a genuine concern in the Jewish problem, and an increasingly important Jewish involvement in Party activities.[30]

Like the NCCL, the Communist Party's major solution to antisemitism was to outlaw it, following the example of the Soviet Union. We have noted that it was not a policy that appealed to the Home Secretary, Herbert Morrison, or to the public at large. It also brought disagreement in the Jewish and the Labour movements as a whole. The Labour Party was against legislation, believing that 'the remedy . . . would probably have turned out to be worse than the disease', although Poale Zion, the Jewish Socialist organisation, and the Haldane Club, the left-wing legal group, were in favour of making antisemitism a libel offence.[31] In the Jewish community another conflict developed between the more radical TAC and the Board of Deputies as a whole. The matter was one of tactics. The Board was in favour of a change in the legislation, but it did not wish to pressurise the government on the matter. It also wanted to avoid any contact with the Communist Party as it 'would be highly dangerous', and likewise with the NCCL, which was regarded as a 'political' organisation. If the legislation had been implemented it is doubtful whether it would have had a great effect.[32] But the issue was significant for it revealed the difference in approach between the Board and radical Jewish/non-Jewish organisations. Both sides shared the same objective but the Board of Deputies stopped short of a public campaign that might have embarrassed the government.

A similar process was at work in the Polish Jewish Army question in 1944. The major opposition to this Polish antisemitism on British soil was orchestrated by the NCCL along with left-wing supporters, culminating in a mass public meeting in the Stoll Theatre in May 1944. Although the Board of Deputies had been concerned about Polish Army antisemitism since the early part of the war, and was at that stage involved in negotiations with the War Office, it refused to support the NCCL public campaign. Selig Brodetsky, the President of the Board, told Elizabeth Allen that it could not 'take part [in] or . . . send a message to a meeting of a general political character'. Tom Driberg, one of the main organisers of the public meeting, who also asked questions in the Commons on the matter, later remarked that these activities were 'against the advice – the almost lachrymose pleading – of the official spokesman of the Jewish community in Britain. They felt that any publicity about this might lead to more antisemitism, perhaps directed against their own flock.' It also seems that, again, the Board did not wish to embarrass the government, as it felt 'obliged', as Zvi Avital has suggested, 'to demonstrate its patriotism'.[33]

In the case of the Polish-Jewish soldiers, the dual behind-the-scenes official Jewish approach and public left-wing campaign actually complemented each other successfully. On the one hand, in its search for a diplomatic solution, the Board of Deputies found a responsive War Office. On the other, the government's fear of adverse publicity made the NCCL's public campaign a valuable weapon in forcing a quick change of mind. There were thus times when the Board's non-public tactics could pay off. The Board's behind-the-scenes negotiation policy was particularly successful in sorting out misunderstandings involving Jewish evacuees.[34] Nevertheless, there were limitations in the quiet and apologetic approach of the official Jewish organisations as the internment question reveals.

On 23 May 1940, the various refugee organisations met at Bloomsbury House to discuss the crisis and its implications on the refugees. Esther Simpson, secretary of the Academic Assistance Council, was amazed to find that the representatives of the groups, Jewish and non-Jewish, 'one after the other' not only supported the government's internment policy but actually demanded that it be extended. Bloomsbury House as a whole, according to Simpson, was in a state of panic, with the Jewish organisations 'bending over backwards' to be of assistance to the government, as they were 'afraid of increased antisemitism'.[35]

As in the First World War, the official Jewish representatives did not want to criticise the government's policy for fear of appearing disloyal. However, as Esther Simpson indicated, there would appear to have been actual Anglo-Jewish support for internment. In the Commons in August 1940, Edward Winterton claimed this was indeed the case, suggesting that 'certain prominent Jews in this country' had wanted the internment policy, asking him to 'preserve us from the extremist Jewish and Gentile friends of the refugees in the House of Commons and elsewhere'. It was a charge that the Board of Deputies bitterly resented. Nevertheless it appears to have had an element of truth. Hans Gal, a refugee composer interned in Douglas, remembers with bitterness a visit from a leading British Jew to the camp in the summer of 1940. The visitor said that they (the Jewish representatives) 'would do everything for us but we must stay till the end of the war'. Gal believed that these British Jews 'felt somehow endangered by the presence of so many co-religionists who could be regarded as not quite safe and reliable'. Certainly this would follow on from instructions of Bloomsbury House for refugees to spy on one another in the summer of 1940, and the mutual distrust of the refugees for Bloomsbury House.

Indeed one Jewish refugee remained interned, despite the objections of the Home Office Advisory Committee, because 'the German Jewish Aid Committee thought he might be an [enemy] agent.'[36]

It is clear that the policy of the Jewish refugee organisations was not to 'oppose the general policy of internment', but to do all they could to help the refugees in the way of food, clothing and general conditions in the camps. It was left to grass roots organisations, like the Committee for the Protection of Refugee Aliens, to protest against the most blatant abuses of the government's action such as the internment of elderly East End Jews who had never been naturalised. Although the responses of the various Jewish refugee committees need to be put into the context of the disintegration of opposition to internment in May and June 1940, their continued refusal to attack the government's policy throughout 1940 does allow criticisms to be made. A great deal of information on the refugees was available to the refugee organisations, in addition to ready access to the relevant government authorities. However, the refugee organisations lacked ultimate trust in the people they were supposed to represent, the consequences of which were serious.[37]

The role of Jewish and pro-Jewish organisations had an even more important part to play in securing the government's help over European Jewry. This was to be the most severe test of the strength of British philosemitic and anti-antisemitic forces in the war. With a government unwilling to consider propaganda or physical aid for the persecuted Jews of Europe on its own accord, the activities of those sympathetic to the Jewish cause became vital. Only their pressure stood in the way of a policy of total indifference taking place.

It has been shown that the government believed that its White Paper on atrocities, published in October 1939, had been a failure with the British public. The government was under the impression that the public had rejected the stories contained in it as mere war propaganda. There is some evidence to confirm the government's analysis. At this stage, according to Tom Harrisson, 'the stories of Nazi atrocities have had little effect'. In April 1940, *Time and Tide* could write that 'the fate of the German Jews has been forgotten'. Nevertheless, a Mass-Observation survey in October 1940 revealed that the public was still greatly aware of the dire plight of European Jewry. This applied to the antisemitic as much as the philosemitic.[38] Actual disbelief of the atrocity stories was rare, and thus the government's analysis of the public's reaction does not appear to have been correct. The most common response was typified by the liberal Mass-Observer who wrote that she 'would like not to believe the stories about the persecution of the Jews . . . , but I think there is too much evidence not to believe'. Belief therefore was not necessarily a sufficient factor to guarantee action on behalf of the Jews of Europe. As another observer wrote when asked about this question: 'Must you? One had almost forgotten them . . .' In the case of others, however, '[Jewish] sufferings under the 3rd Reich are quite sufficient indictment against the Hitlerian regime. Their deliverance is one of our chief war aims.'[39] Yet this humanitarian sympathy towards European Jewry was of an unorganised nature, and would remain so for the first years of the war.

The most likely way for such sentiment to become institutionalised was through Christian-Jewish organisations. Although the Society of Jews and Christians had met violent opposition from both communities since its formation in 1927, close contacts had been established by the 1930s between Christian and Jewish refugee organisations. Bloomsbury House, the refugee co-ordinating body, was to be a springboard for future Christian-Jewish combinations. As one of its leading members, W. W. Simpson, has written 'it was . . . out of the close, friendly and fruitful co-operation that had developed between Jews and Christians in all that was embodied in the Bloomsbury House experience that the Council of Christians and Jews was born'.[40]

Out of negotiations beginning in November 1941, the Council (CCJ) was officially launched in March 1942, but not without a series of internal crises. The reason for these will be examined later, but now it is necessary to examine why this important organisation came into existence at that stage in the war. The Society of Jews and Christians had been involved in Jewish 'defence' work in the war, especially in evacuation and blitz areas, but it was a small group, generally lacking in influence. By 1941, the global rise of antisemitism, including antipathy to Jews in Britain, stimulated the demand for a more powerful Christian-Jewish umbrella organisation. On the Jewish side there was a desire to gain the support of influential Christians against antisemitism, on the Christian a genuine revulsion against Nazi antisemitism, coupled with a belief that this was also 'part of a general and comprehensive attack on Christianity . . . and on the ethical principles common to both religions'.[41]

The first few months of the CCJ's activities were dominated by problems of domestic antisemitism, with attempts being made to counter black market accusations against Jews. The approach of the CCJ was similar to that of the Board of Deputies – the use of diplomacy wherever possible, and an apologetic response when attacking antisemitism. W. W. Simpson, its secretary, typified the CCJ's tactics in a response to a work that claimed that antisemitism was the Gentile's fault alone. Simpson argued that there were always two sides to an argument and he did 'not like one-sided presentations of any case'.[42]

In many ways the CCJ mirrored the activities of the Board of Deputies, gaining its success in similar areas. Useful work was carried out in evacuation areas, and in dealing with other personal Christian-Jewish misunderstandings. However, with the problem of securing government aid for the Jews of Europe its limitations were to be exposed. Since its inception, the CCJ had been concerned about the plight of European Jewry, but it was not until the major revelations about atrocities on Jews in late 1942 that it was stung into action.[43]

On 17 December 1942, the Allied declaration attacking the Nazi extermination of Polish Jews was delivered by Anthony Eden in the Commons. The day before Eden's Under-Secretary, Richard Law, met a delegation from the CCJ. The Executive Committee of the CCJ had agreed upon such a delegation on 3 December 1942, although there were doubts about what this would achieve. One of the Executive believed 'that the apparent inaction of the Foreign Office . . . was not due to any lack of concern but to the difficulty of deciding what action, if any, could be taken'. It was also proposed that the deputation should ask the Foreign Office to establish 'the authenticity of the reports which had been received from various sources as to the treatment meted out to Jews in Eastern Europe'. Indeed, Selig Brodetsky, who was active in the Executive Committee, remarked shortly after 3 December 1942 meeting, that the disbelief of the atrocities was to be found as much in the CCJ as in the Foreign Office (with the exception of the Archbishop of Canterbury).[44]

With this reserved attitude it comes as little surprise that the deputation was easily deflected by Richard Law. Law wrote after the meeting that 'in spite of the fact that the deputation expressed great appreciation of my alleged sympathetic attitude, I don't think that I gave anything away'. Five days after the Allied Declaration, another delegation from the Board of Deputies, described by the Foreign Office as 'a respectable and reasonable body of British Jews', was received. Foreign Office officials were impressed with the public outcry that the declaration had caused. They believed that this 'new situation' could 'only be met', in the words of A. G. Randall, 'by a new policy, or modification of the present one'. Just a month later, the same official wrote after another delegation 'that the situation can be held'.[45] Were these pro-Jewish deputations partially to blame for the lack of change in government policy in early 1943?

It is evident that the major problem facing the deputations was the unwillingness of the government to consider positive action on behalf of European Jewry – if it could possibly avoid it. Nevertheless, there was an awareness among these groups that the government, especially Morrison's Home Office, were being unreasonably obstructive in considering relief measures. Knowledge that the Foreign Office was of a similar mind was less well known, however. As it became clear that little action had resulted after the December 1942 declaration, the deputations continued. In late January 1943, the two senior officials of the Board of Deputies told Richard Law that 'they were having great difficulty in holding back their co-religionists at bay' with regard to the rescue of European Jewry. A few months later, Law was to write about the 'extreme pressure from an alliance of Jewish organisations and Archbishops', showing the government's concern at the problem of satisfying humanitarian sympathy on the issue.[46] Yet at the same time, after the Bermuda Conference in April 1943, the government had refused to change its position of non-action – apart from the gesture of soothing words. Ultimately, it could afford to do this for the Christian-Jewish representations could be so easily deflected. At a meeting in April 1943 with A. Brotman, the Board of Deputies Secretary, Frank Roberts of the Foreign Office remarked how 'very patient and helpful' Mr Brotman was. He continued that it was 'in our [the Foreign Office's] interest to keep him and his moderate organisation as contented as possible'. Over a year later, with little change in the Foreign Office's position, Brotman was again described 'as always, entirely reasonable'. Norman Bentwich, active in Jewish refugee matters in the 1930s and 1940s, criticised the Board's approach of sending endless memoranda that had 'no hope of serious attention by governments', and that the Board's deputations were marked by 'unreality and impotence'. Was an alternative strategy possible, or was Selig Brodetsky right to say that 'there was little we could do'?[47]

Reference has already been made to the National Committee for Rescue from Nazi Terror, formed early in 1943 as an attempt to galvanise public sympathy for the Jews of Europe into a powerful pressure group. Up to this point, the genuine British concern over the issue had remained amorphous, but the stimulus given by the December 1942 declaration helped to focus it into a coherent pattern. Grass roots organisations, both Church and lay, sprang up and through Victor Gollancz's and Eleanor Rathbone's powerful pamphlets, this spontaneous public feeling was channelled in a co-ordinated manner. Letters were written to the press, criticising the government's inaction, especially its fear of domestic antisemitism. In addition, resolutions were sent to the Foreign Office which tried to prove the public's approval for aiding the Jews of Europe. Yet the government remained unmoved and, by late 1943, the National Committee for Rescue was struggling to keep alive an issue that it had so successfully brought before a receptive public earlier in the year. Whilst less 'reasonable' in its approach than the CCJ or the Board of Deputies, Rathbone's National Committee had thus also failed to change the negative policy of the government.[48]

It has been suggested that Jewish organisations could have followed the example of Samuel Zygielbojm, a Jewish member of the Polish National Council in London, if not in committing suicide as Zygielbojm did in protest against the Allies' inaction, in May 1943, then in a policy of mass civil disobedience against the British government. Was the organisation of, say, a hunger strike in Whitehall a serious option open to the various pro-Jewish groupings? In the reality of the war situation and the attitude of the government this was highly unlikely. As a Foreign Office official put it in June 1941, 'when it comes to the point, the Jews will never hamper us to put the Germans on the throne'. The British government knew that however much the Anglo-Jewish community objected to its Middle Eastern policy, or its failure to help European Jewry, it would not ultimately interfere with Jewish support for the Allied war effort. Jewish and pro-Jewish organisations realised that the major priority had to be to concentrate on an Allied victory, and thus nothing should be done to hinder its progress.[49] Faced with this dilemma, there were tremendous limitations on the freedom of action of Jewish groups, that should not be minimised. Nevertheless, there was still a range of options open to groups such as the Board of Deputies, and internal restraints on their action need to be seriously considered.

Both the Board of Deputies and the CCJ desired official respectability and thus, it must be suggested, did not wish to embarrass the government on the European Jewish question. By March 1943, there were even suggestions within the CCJ that it was spending too much time protesting against Jewish persecution abroad. Thereafter until the end of the war, more time was spent by the CCJ examining domestic antisemitism, and the general question of Jewish-Christian relations in Britain. With the Board of Deputies there was also a lack of confidence reflected in its fear of antisemitism, a fear that it had communicated to the government throughout the war. Both the Board of Deputies and the government shared a private concern about domestic antisemitism, even if in public they denied its existence. It must be questioned whether the Board and other groups such as the NCCL and the Communist Party, were wise in emphasising domestic antisemitism at a time when the government was using its existence as a reason not to help the Jews of Europe. Frightened of its own safety and of appearing disloyal, the Board of Deputies was trapped in its special relationship with the government and thus made impotent regarding European Jewry.[50]

There is no guarantee that even if the Board of Deputies, or other groups had organised mass rallies or hunger strikes that the government would have been stirred into action. Indeed with the protests over Mosley's release, the government, and particularly Herbert Morrison, showed a strong disregard for what was powerful public opinion. In ignoring humanitarian sympathy over European Jewry, the government revealed the weaknesses of British philosemitic forces. Although the government often admitted that sympathy was more numerically important than hostility, it knew that philosemitism, even in a rampant form, offered no threat to law and order. By its very nature humanitarian support for Jews was non-violent. Consequently, the government was more concerned with potential anti-alienism and antisemitism than in satisfying the real existence of philosemitism with regard to rescuing European Jewry. However, if the blame for the lack of an Allied initiative on this question rests mainly with the government, pro-Jewish groups can also be criticised. They failed to secure any concessions to the demands which they made, especially at the Bermuda Conference. The desire for respectability, and particularly in the case of the Board of Deputies, a general insecurity, meant that those in close contact with the government failed to offer it a serious concerted challenge.[51] If the impact of philosemitism was weak on the government, was this true of Jewish defence over the whole of British society in the war?

It is a reflection of the efficient nature of Jewish defence organisations in the war that virtually no accusations against Jews went unanswered. Leaflets, pamphlets, letters and books praised the Jewish war effort, defended shechita, and dismissed claims that Jews ran the black market, international finance or were responsible for the war. The authors of these works were aware that their answers did not necessarily counteract the original charge. Nevertheless can one go as far as one Jewish activist who claimed these defence works 'were all futile'?[52]

Criticisms were made in the war that literature from the Board's Defence Committee was based on the assumption that antisemitism had rational roots, and could thus be removed by logical counter-arguments. It was a problem that the Board acknowledged increasingly throughout the war, as it spent more and more time considering the psychological roots of antisemitism. Jewish groups began to realise that 'there were antisemites who were mentally diseased, who believed that the Jews were in conspiracy against civilisation' and that with these people 'nothing could be done'. Nevertheless, according to the Board's President, their accusations should not go unanswered for 'it avoided the danger of losing by default'. Long and futile press discussions therefore took place with the Board's Sidney Salomon and confirmed antisemites such as Douglas Reed and the journals *Truth* and *The Patriot*.[53]

A reply to Douglas Reed was published in 1942. However, the Board of Deputies was not in full approval of it, believing the book would give Reed publicity, and would not work because 'the antisemitic mind was not receptive' to reason.[54] Whilst this may have been true of Reed himself, it did not necessarily apply to all his wide readership. Moreover, it must be suggested that not all Jewish defence was wasted in the war. Just as the volume of antisemitica in the 1930s and 1940s made its impact by sheer repetition, the same can be argued about defence literature.

In answering antisemitism, the defence organisations had not only to counter the particular allegations made in the war, but also the deep-held traditional attitudes to Jews that gave rise to them. We have seen that the Jewish black marketeer image was an amalgam of earlier Jewish stereotypes, shaped to fit the requirements of war difficulties. Attempts to answer criticisms of Jewish involvement in the black market, through statistical and other logical counter-arguments, ran the risk of being dismissed as Jewish propaganda, but could also be dismissed as they did not match the prevailing stereotype. Indeed, knowledge of the real figures of Jewish involvement in the black market did not necessarily end hostility. Professor A. V. Hill, a tireless worker on behalf of Jewish refugees, preferred 'arithmetic to magic' in considering the Jewish question in Britain. Nevertheless, he continued to believe that Jews were too prominent in the black market when given evidence to the contrary. However, the constant denials of Jewish involvement, particularly in the non-Jewish press, helped at least those sympathetic to the Jewish cause to have ready answers to this most frequent of war allegations.[55]

Repetition was also an important factor in removing misunderstandings based on pure ignorance. Leaflets and booklets outlining Jewish population figures, involvement in finance, the press, politics and the Jewish contribution to the war effort, although bland, could still make 'a very good impression on non-Jews'. Rather than simply preaching to the converted, defence literature could influence a section of the community whose hostility to Jews did not preclude receptivity to fresh information. However, the limitations of an educative solution to antisemitism were revealed by the NCCL's campaign in the last years of the war. The NCCL, like the *New Statesman*, was 'convinced that it [was] useful to bring out into the public mind what antisemitism is, its use by Fascism, and to counter it by deliberate and authoritative statement'. Public meetings to discuss antisemitism were sponsored, and debates in both national and local newspapers encouraged.[56] Neither was a particular success, with the participants merely given the opportunity to repeat anti-Jewish allegations, or to counter them. In the process little worthwhile discussion took place. It would seem that negative comments on Jews made more impact than positive ones, and that the net result was to increase the 'Jew-consciousness' of the public. The weakness in the NCCL campaign was its assumption that antisemitism in Britain was being organised, rather than being part of a powerful cultural tradition. Its solution of bringing the question out into the open, for the public to see its error, was thus naïve, and its results counterproductive. Where educative techniques were used in a more subtle and controlled manner, their results could be more successful.[57]

The great weakness of Jewish defence had always been its easy dismissal as a form of special pleading. The circumstances of the war gave it an opportunity to overcome this limitation, however. Despite its earlier policy, the Board of Deputies stressed in its literature the linkages between antisemitism and fascism, emphasising that Mosley and other antisemites were 'Britain's fifth column'. The fact that other 'Quislings' were also antisemitic gave the opportunity to suggest that antisemitism threatened not just British Jews, but 'the precious lives and liberty of all British citizens'. The example of British fascists such as William Joyce allowed those writing defence literature to draw a connection between 'Antisemitism and Treachery' – much to the annoyance of British antisemites.[58] In the past accused of disloyalty, the Anglo-Jewish community had now the chance to show how antisemitism was a threat to Britain and the whole democratic world.

The identification of antisemitism with fascism was further strengthened by the activities of the British far left. With the Communist Party enjoying enormous support towards the end of the war, with over 50,000 members and the circulation of the *Daily Worker* up to 100,000, Jewish defence was given a strong boost. In its propaganda, the Communist Party not only stressed that antisemitism was 'A Nazi Weapon', a weapon of reaction whose 'real aim [was] an attack on the working class and all democratic forces.' It also attempted to correct the public on simple facts of Jewish involvement in British life. Indeed, in this respect its literature was identical to that of the Board of Deputies.[59] By mass circulation of literature and educative workshops, the Communist Party attempted to identify all forms of antisemitism with fascism. This linkage was not just made by the Communist left. David Low's classic cartoon, 'How the Beastly Business Begins', connecting antisemitic housewife gossip to the Nazi gas chambers, reflected a wider left-wing anti-fascism which also embraced attacks on antisemitism. It even reached the *Daily Express*, with its columnist William Hickey (Tom Driberg) writing in January 1943 that 'anyone who is against the Jews is at least 50 per cent for Hitler, and that if anyone in Britain can legitimately be called a quisling or a fifth columnist it is the man or woman, who helps, even in a slight degree to spread antisemitism'. The business of Jewish defence was thus transformed from a narrow and generally unsuccessful endeavour into that of an important political slogan by the end of the war.[60]

We have so far examined the impact of Jewish defence on the British public as a whole. It is now necessary to briefly analyse how Anglo-Jewry viewed the work done on its behalf. In 1940 the Board of Deputies launched a defence appeal so it could expand its work in the war. Four years later, only a quarter of the amount required had been raised, very little of it coming from the public. It would seem however – and the Board itself believed it was the case – that the failure of the fund reflected not disinterest in the subject of antisemitism, but a disagreement over the Board's tactics. The relative success of appeals for money from Jews for left-wing anti-fascist causes in the war suggests this was indeed the case. Although the Board's Defence Committee believed it had not received the credit it deserved from the Jewish public due to the hidden nature of its work, much of Anglo-Jewry had turned to the left to guarantee its well-being. Criticism of the Board's Defence literature also came from leading Anglo-Jewish publisher, Victor Gollancz, who felt that such propaganda was demeaning and preferred to publish 'positive' books outlining Jewish genius and creativeness.[61]

The exciting developments within organisations devoted to the Jewish cause, or to fighting antisemitism in the war, must not, however, disguise their internal problems and other weaknesses. These limitations are perhaps as strong an indication as any of the success of antisemites at home and abroad in challenging the position of the Jew in society.

We have been warned against over-easy criticism of post-emancipation Jewish leadership, in that insecurity, often based on real hostility, gave communal bodies 'a very limited range of options'. Nevertheless, in seeking to 'rehabilitate' the term 'British Jew', Jewish organisations, such as the Board of Deputies, in the late 1930s and throughout the war 'came very close to appealing to Jews to accept second-class status'. The internalisation of hostile stereotypes by the Jewish community has already been commented on.[62] It was a process that could lead to demands to co-religionists to change their business behaviour, economic structure and social behaviour. This requirement of 'invisibility' was also demanded of the Jewish refugees, which partially explains the paucity of the community's attack on alien internment in 1940. Being Englishmen of the Jewish faith also limited the communal response to the crisis of European Jewry – seen by the British government as merely foreign nationals who happened to be Jewish. Although the Board's Defence Committee saw its future task as spreading the message that 'antisemitism [was] a disease of non-Jews', there was a reluctance to put this into action during the war. Instead, the Jewish community, as the rest of British society, devoted its efforts into demanding 'better' behaviour from its members as the solution to antisemitism. Nevertheless, we have noted that a start was made into investigating the psychological (non-Jewish) roots of antisemitism in the war.[63]

Conflicts within the CCJ in its early years are also indicative of the strains operating within pro-Jewish groups in the Second World War. Forty years on, the CCJ is a well established and respectable organisation, but in the war it had to fight to gain credibility. It is again a reflection of the period that George Bell, Bishop of Chichester, lessened his chances of promotion within the Church due to his refugee and Jewish sympathies. There were also objections to the CCJ from the Jewish side, with the ultra-orthodox Chief Rabbi resigning in May 1942 as he saw it as a 'Society for the Promotion of Spiritual Inter-Marriage between Jews and Christians'. His resignation highlighted the strong tension that still existed between Church and synagogue, for the CCJ had purposely avoided any reference to Christian-Jewish dialogue, which was left to the much smaller Society of Jews and Christians.[64]

Even the CCJ's opposition to antisemitism created problems with James Parkes, the leading Christian writer on the subject, resigning shortly after the Chief Rabbi. Parkes believed that the Board of Deputies wanted to make the CCJ a Jewish organisation under a 'gentile umbrella'. Rather than token Gentiles, Parkes believed what was needed was a powerful group of non-Jews to represent the Jewish case to the government. Parkes thus revealed a marked lack of confidence in Anglo-Jewry. With such external and internal problems, it is not surprising that the CCJ's impact was limited, certainly before 1945.[65]

In his diary in late 1945, Richard Crossman wrote that in 1939 he had been 'pro-Jew emotionally in 1939' as part of his anti-fascism. Crossman believed that after the war he was now 'not *emotionally* pro-Jew, but only rationally anti-antisemitism'. Crossman realised that philosemitism was 'a very different thing' to opposing antisemitism, an important distinction to make in regard to the left and the Jews in the war years. In simply identifying antisemitism as a stage or form of fascism, there was always a danger that its impact on Jews themselves could be forgotten. An example of this can be found in George Sacks' *The Jewish Question* published by the Left Book Club in 1937. Sacks believed that it was legitimate to 'hate the Jew, if you must' but this hatred should not be allowed 'to make you the victim of the Fascist who, on the plea that he also hates the Jew, makes you his accomplice in worse crimes'.[66]

By the war, this crude analysis had to an extent broken down, with the Communist Party particularly emphasising that all forms of antisemitism must be attacked – including any manifestations of left-wing hostility to Jews. There was a parallel development reflected in the attempt to stop 'thinking of Jews as a uniform group', or indeed as mere victims of antisemitism, but rather as a group with its own particular needs. The National Jewish Committee was one major manifestation of this change. However, not all on the left had abandoned simplistic explanations of antisemitism. John Gollan of the CPGB, writing in 1943, conceded that although the fight against fascist antisemitism was vital to protect the working classes, 'dispelling anti-Jewish prejudice' was 'comparatively unimportant'. In addition many left-wingers had not abandoned their position that Jewish survival had been, and would continue to be, dependent on antisemitism alone.[67]

Such limitations within the various pro-Jewish or anti-antisemitic groups and supporters make it even more difficult to draw up a balance sheet between philosemitic and antisemitic forces in Britain. However, it is important to attempt to evaluate the relative place of the former in British society during the war in which two vital factors were operating in favour of the Jewish community. The first was the almost universal anti-fascist feeling in Britain, the second was the similarly pervasive sense of sympathy for European Jewry. With the first, the impact of anti-fascism could only benefit Anglo-Jewry if it was connected to attacks on Jews, and the second only if European antisemitism was connected to domestic events.

Apart from Jewish groups, liberal and socialist individuals, journals and organisations attempted to connect antisemitism to fascism. It was a policy not only of the Communist Party but also of *New Statesman, Tribune, Time and Tide, Reynold's News, News Chronicle*, as well as many individual journalists such as Tom Driberg, Harold Nicolson and Wyndham Deedes, to stress this linkage.[68] The cartoonist Low and the playwrights J. B. Priestley and Louis Macneice all used their artistic skills in the war to make the same point. Yet despite all their efforts it seems that Angus Calder is right to conclude that 'the connection between Nazism-Fascism and antisemitism was not widely grasped in Britain'. A Mass-Observation survey carried out in January 1944 confirms this impression. Whilst only 2% of the sample wanted antisemitism to be 'circumscribed', 24% felt that the future of the country would be harmed if fascists were allowed to continue their activities.[69] Although some of the population were 'pro-Jewish' because 'Mosley was anti', and others felt that 'a nation fighting for democracy [could not] afford antisemitism', the integral connection between fascism and antisemitism had not filtered through to the consciousness of the majority of the British people.[70]

A similar blockage occurred with the question of European Jewry. The news of Jewish persecution did create much sympathy. W. W. Simpson remembers that one of the most exciting aspects of the first years of the CCJ 'was the spontaneous development of other groups doing the same thing [that is organising support for the Jews of Europe] independently and without knowing of the Council.' One such group was an organisation called 'Unity Against Antisemitism'. A largely middle class Jewish/non-Jewish goodwill body, it emerged with the increase in domestic antisemitism and the news of the fate of Europe's Jews in 1943. Although it soon became part of the NCCL, this small group was a reflection of how genuine sympathy to persecuted Jews abroad could improve Jewish-Gentile relations at home.[71]

We have seen that the news of the atrocities against Jews did bring about a slow reconsideration of attitudes to Jews in general in more liberal circles. Sometimes, Jewish defence material could help in this process, one Mass-Observer remarking that she now believed 'that the Jew is as good an Englishman as the rest of us . . . *But*, and it is a big *but*, I am aware that this opinion has been formed only by reading such books as Louis Golding's *The Jewish Problem*, and by making a conscious effort to be fair and tolerant.' Yet for much of the population even this slow self-realisation did not take place. It is again important to stress that the most common form of ambivalence on Jewish matters in the war was made up of a sympathy to European Jewry mixed with dislike of the habits of Jews in Britain.

In the war therefore, whilst domestic fascism and even possibly political antisemitism became disreputable, the various pro-Jewish organisations could not turn the sympathy created by the horrors committed against the Jews of Europe to gain a full amount of support for Jewry as a whole. The deeply ingrained Jewish stereotypes were too strong to be changed by either the extensive Jewish defence campaign or the devastating events in Europe during the war. Thus, although there were impressive developments in the response to antisemitism in Britain during the Second World War, their impact in removing prejudice can be seen only as a positive factor in changing attitudes to Jews in the long term. In the short term, with a government that saw the appeasement of antisemitism at home as more important than the satisfying of humanitarian liberal feeling, Jewish and pro-Jewish organisations were left relatively impotent. As Richard Breitman has recently suggested, 'Adolf Hitler [and one might add in the case of Britain, Oswald Mosley] had succeeded in devaluing the lives of European Jews in the eyes of the rest of the world.' The antisemites of the 1930s and the Second World War had thus managed to dehumanise the Jew. The forces of philosemitism and anti-antisemitism in Britain had only succeeded in starting to reverse this process by the end of the war.[72]

Conclusion

Three million Polish Jews were annihilated in the Second World War, representing 90% of the pre-war total. A similar percentage of Baltic, German and Austrian Jews perished. Elsewhere in German-occupied Europe the proportion varied immensely – from 50% of Rumania's 600,000 Jews to 22% of France's 350,000 Jews and 20% of Italy's 40,000 Jews. Of all the occupied territories only Denmark and Finland maintained their Jewish population intact, contributing nothing to the five to six million Jews who perished in Hitler's Final Solution.[1]

In wartime Britain, over 1,200 Jewish servicemen and women and many other Jewish civilians lost their lives as a result of the conflict, but no Jew was killed by his fellow citizens. Violence was not absent in the British scene – fascists and organised antisemites were responsible for physical attacks on Jews and their property in the phoney war period, and later Jewish evacuees and even occasionally Jewish ex-servicemen were beaten up. There were disturbances in the shelters just before and at the start of the blitz, and even a minor battle between Jews and non-Jews in an East End cinema in 1944. Yet, taken together, such incidents pale into near total insignificance compared with the enormity of Nazi barbarism toward Jews. 'Physical' antisemitism in Britain during the Second World War, when set against the riots of the earlier conflict, appears meagre. Unlike even its great democratic ally, the United States, Britain was free from 1939 to 1945 of major anti-Jewish disturbances.[2]

Nevertheless, in drawing a global picture of antisemitism in the Second World War, as has been pointed out by Michael Marrus and Robert Paxton, 'one runs the risk of comparing the incomparable'. It is tempting to suggest that those countries that managed to save the greatest percentage of their Jewish population did so because they were opposed to antisemitism, and that those who failed to do so supported Nazi treatment of Jews. The reality is more complex. It is true that the deep tradition of antisemitism amongst the Polish people helps to account for the pitifully small number of Jews who managed to survive the holocaust, and that Danish desire to preserve the forces of democracy led to the protection of its Jewish citizens against Nazi orders for deportation. Yet the destruction of three-quarters of Dutch Jewry does not reflect the strength of native antisemitism in Holland (indeed there was much active resistance to Nazi persecution of Jews in the war) as much as the domination of this country by the Germans (added to the difficulty of hiding Jews as a result of geographical factors). Similarly, although France came well down in the league table of the proportion of Jews killed in Nazi-occupied Europe, it was a position that did not reflect the high level of antisemitism in both the Vichy government and the country.[3] What is being suggested is that although 'domestic' attitudes to Jews could be significant, the most important factor in deciding the fate of Europe's Jews was the degree of control that the Nazis exercised in each country. The Jews of the Channel Islands were deported without protest, although as one Jersey resident put it, he 'had certainly never heard a word of either disparagement or detraction' against them. Had the same degree of Nazi control existed in mainland Britain, it is probable that a similar pattern would have developed.[4] The fact that Britain had no death camps in the war, and indeed little violence towards its Jewish minority, does not mean that British antisemitism should be dismissed as unimportant. It is often assumed that British antisemitism has been trivial, 'confined to music hall humour and a form of upper-class joking', in the words of one historian, and leaving 'only a faint and delicate odour in the records' according to another. Aside from 'insignificant' 'golf-club' discrimination, antisemitism is assumed to be foreign – as a 1930s magistrate stated: 'very un-English and very unfair'.[5] In Britain, like America, the antisemitism which existed was just 'one of the many freak details that made up the normal background of everyday life'. Britain, like America, was 'different'. There could be no real antisemitism in Britain, wrote the *New English Weekly* in 1942 for 'the thing is too preposterously contrary to British character'. A closer comparison of British attitudes to Jews with that of Germany and France in the war shows the dangers of such assumptions.[6]

It has been suggested that 'the restrictions under which German Jews had lived in the 1920s were little different from those Jews faced in the United States and England'. In all three countries Jews suffered from economic and social discrimination. It is a reminder that no country had a monopoly over antisemitism. Moreover, the eventual horrors committed against Jews did not seem even a remote possibility just a decade before Hitler came to power. Indeed, in the 1920s France has been categorised as a tolerant society with a 'relatively favourable climate for Jews'. If Britain's treatment of Jews in the 1920s was comparable with that of France or Germany, how much had this changed by the Second World War?[7]

The fundamental aspect separating Britain from, on the one hand, Nazi Germany and, on the other, the collaborationist French was the role of the State. The Nazis carried out extermination whilst the Vichy government, on its own initiative, set about Aryanising France and creating atrocious concentration camps for Jewish refugees. The British government may have temporarily interned its Jewish refugees, shipping many to the dominions; it may have contributed to the dehumanising process in failing to regard the rescue of Jews under Nazi control as a major priority; it may have been suspicious of Jews to the extent of refusing them entry into the higher echelons of the Foreign Office or demanding Aryan film makers for its Air Ministry; it may even have discriminated against Jews as Jews en masse in Palestine and forcibly turned away Jewish refugees from its waters in this area. None of these can be dismissed lightly, yet they are not in the same category as the Nazi government's Final Solution or even Vichy France's anti-emancipation enactments.[8]

Where a direct comparison can be made with France and Germany is in the area of popular attitudes to Jews. In Germany 'during the war a marked worsening of attitudes toward Jews became apparent'. Domestic war tensions also had a negative impact on attitudes in France, but this was also the case in many countries including America, South Africa and, to an extent, Britain. Indeed it is striking how the accusations against Jews in France, particularly foreign Jews, mirrored those in Britain. In the former country Jews were assumed to control the black market, were criticised for not contributing to the war effort and also for ostentation in seaside resorts and country towns. Actual popular violence against Jews was confined to occasional window smashing, carried out by native French extremist groupings. No aspect of this could be regarded as alien to the British experience.[9]

As regards popular support for state measures against the Jews, both the German and French people approved, or were not disturbed by, either quotas or the total elimination of Jews from the economy and public life. Nevertheless, violent measures against Jews were actively supported by only a tiny proportion of the population. However, indifference due to a mixure of fear and antipathy to Jews stopped any major action on behalf of either German or French Jewry. Deportations to the East went unopposed, and although individual Jews were hidden by a minority (who may themselves have been antisemitic) such actions came more from humanitarianism than philosemitism.[10]

In Britain, a small but significant proportion advocated extermination as the solution to the Jewish problem. However, it is doubtful if all this section of the population would have maintained this view had the cruel reality of Jewish persecution been thrust upon them. There was some support for Nazi antisemitism, often described as 'one of the few things in which I agree with Hitler', but general revulsion at Nazi methods. Nevertheless, there was also widespread concern over the alleged power Jews had in Britain, and whilst few actively sought to curtail it, it must be suggested that any legislation to restrict it would not have been unpopular. Deportations, pogroms or death camps were seen as unacceptable solutions by the vast majority of the population, but it seems doubtful whether there would have been mass protests had the Nazis implemented such a policy on British soil. There was a strong tradition of philosemitism and anti-antisemitism in Britain, but the alien internment question in the summer of 1940 showed how easily such forces could fade away in a period of crisis. Had the Nazis been in control in Britain, philosemitic sentiment would have had even less chance of success. In addition, in such circumstances it is possible that domestic antipathy to Jews would have 'helped divert awareness of the scale of Jewish suffering' as was the case in France and Germany. Jews who were prepared to use cyanide capsules in the event of a Nazi invasion of Britain were not necessarily suffering from paranoia.[11]

However, antisemitism in Britain during the war was of more importance than the potential of a counterfactual history, for it had a real impact on the Jewish minority as well as society as a whole. The Nazis constantly warned the Allies that antisemitism would be their downfall. Therefore it is not surprising that the British government was genuinely concerned about domestic antisemitism. Nevertheless, it has been suggested that 'by itself . . . antisemitism . . . was not a significant index of low morale'. Had there been widespread public belief in the suggestion that Britain was fighting the Jews' War – i.e. a war on behalf of international Jewish finance – then it is possible that contributions to the war effort would have declined. As it was, the fear of support for this form of antisemitic propaganda ensured that Britain was denied a suitable (Jewish) Minister for Information in the shape of Leslie Hore-Belisha.[12]

Ironically it could be argued that the idea that Britain was fighting for the benefit of the Jews actually aided morale. This occurred because the public believed in a more watered down version of the Jews' War. It was thought that the Jews were gaining from the war through black marketeering, but not contributing to it due to their alleged army dodging. In both areas the Jews acted as scapegoats for real problems in the war – the shortage of food and other everyday goods and the immense strain of military and other forms of national service. Rather than being divisive, the release outlet of this grumbling form of antisemitism made the British as a whole more cohesive as a nation. However, where Jewish-Gentile co-operation was vital, as in the shelters and the civil defence services during the blitz, common human suffering overcame past latent hostilities in the majority of cases. Overall, therefore, antisemitism did not adversely affect morale in Britain. Attacks on Jews were rarely physical, and thus not a threat to public order. In addition, Jews were a safe outgroup, small in numbers and immensely loyal to the Allied effort. Scapegoating can cause dangerous discord in a wartime society, but in Britain, antisemitism perversely helped the population come to terms with the tensions of the war, without causing serious internal fragmentation.[13]

There were, however, major losses to the British war effort due to direct or indirect antisemitism. Hore-Belisha was one example, but perhaps more significantly was the wastage caused by internment. This arose from both public and governmental xenophobia/antisemitism. Out of the 27,000 interned were many leading scientists, propagandists and industrialists whose skill and future goodwill was of immeasurable benefit to Britain. Although the war contribution of the refugees was phenomenal, its potential was even greater. Their various achievements occurred despite, rather than because of government encouragement. No balance sheet can be drawn up between the 'losses' and 'gains' of British antisemitism in the war, for again one is comparing the incomparable.

There are other issues of importance which are even less quantifiable. Firstly, the war saw the continuation of organised fascism and anti-semitism. The period was one of immense difficulty for these extremists, especially after the government's major measures against them in the summer of 1940. They also faced an increasingly hostile public which began to link their activities more and more to that of the enemy. Nevertheless, the influence of these organisations was not totally negligible. They had some success in linking the Jews to the war in the popular imagination, and they added to the general suspicion and fear of Jewish refugees and caused the government to appease antisemitic sentiment so as to stunt its potential. Furthermore, the survival of organised fascist antisemitism, along with a wide variety of antisemitic journals and literature in the war, indicates the tenacity of this tradition in Britain. Those within the tradition have had a self-conscious desire to preserve it, especially in times of adversity, so that their message can revive in more favourable circumstances. The evidence from the war years would suggest that however strong the atmosphere is against extremist antisemitism, it will continue to survive, even if in a shadowy and feeble form, keeping alive anti-Jewish images and myths for future generations.[14]

Secondly, the war witnessed the continuous use of negative Jewish stereotypes by the wider population. It is important to emphasise that there was a dynamic element in the public's perceptions of Jews – new images such as the black marketeer and the refugee came into existence, yet even these owed much to previous beliefs concerning Jews. The durability of Jewish stereotypes is impressive in the war years. Despite the apparent ease with which the destruction of European Jewry was carried out, fears of Jewish power remained. Both the extreme left and the right linked Jews to international finance although such a linkage was, by the 1940s, nearly half a century out of date. The Jewish refugee, both on paper and in person, was treated not necessarily as a victim, but as a threat to economic and national security. It is also vital to stress that the Jewish image in society did not exist in a vacuum – it could have a real impact on behaviour to Jews. There was no clear relationship between thought, speech or the written word and actual treatment of Jews within the individual, for ambivalence on Jewish matters was the norm. However, it is difficult to argue that personal prejudice against Jews was ever a purely private affair; even if it manifested itself only in reading antisemitic novels, or in telling anti-Jewish jokes, thought could affect behaviour. One cannot understand the internment panic of 1940 solely by the impact, for example, of literature where Jews appear as spies. Yet the latter was part of an antisemitic tradition and culture that (in a period of crisis) allowed the scare to develop.

The most immediate impact of antisemitism was on Anglo-Jewry itself, the effect on which will be examined shortly. Before then it is important to ask firstly why antisemitism existed in Britain during the war. Secondly, we will examine the solutions put forward by the British public to the Jewish question. Turning to the first point, the simplest explanation was that antisemitism had been exported to a country where it was naturally alien. There is some truth in Louis Golding's belief that antisemitism in Britain was 'made in Germany'. Nazi propaganda before the war and during it does seem to have increased Jew-consciousness in Britain, although not always negatively. The Mass-Observer who would have been unfavourable to Jews 'had it not been for [the propaganda of] Hitler and Streicher' was not alone. The Nazis were also not the only 'foreign' influence on antisemitism in Britain during the war. Polish antisemitism is the most famous example of an ally spreading dislike of Jews on British soil, but the French, Dutch and even Americans were not free from such prejudice, although admittedly on a smaller scale.[15]

Nevertheless, the internationalism of antisemitism in the war must not disguise the domestic roots of the British variety. Foreign influences have always been important on British antisemites – whether French in the case of Belloc, or Russian with Arnold White, and German with Arnold Leese and, to a lesser extent, Oswald Mosley. Yet as the last-named told his 18B interviewers in July 1940, there was also a 'long antisemitic tradition in Britain'. It was this, rather than an exotic import that is the more significant factor in explaining the presence of antisemitism in Britain during the Second World War.[16] To understand the degree of hostility to Jews, however, one must examine the social and economic problems of British society in the conflict.

It has been the argument throughout this thesis that it is tensions within British society that explain *manifestations* of antisemitism. Strains of the phoney war, strains due to the threat of invasion, strains due to the hardships of rationing, strains of mass evacuation, strains of war weariness, all needed an outlet and the Jews were often a suitable scapegoat. This suitability was due to several interconnecting reasons. Firstly, Jews had been a scapegoat so often in the past that their selection as modern victims had become an almost automatic reflex. Secondly, the Jewish image, so firmly rooted in British consciousness, was both highly flexible and diverse, and thus capable of adaptation to new needs. Thirdly, in *some* cases there was a degree of Jewish involvement to give sweeping accusations plausibility. Had there been no Jews participating in the black market, it would have been difficult for the press and others to give the impression, widely believed by the public, that Jews controlled this activity. However, the Jewish involvement was distorted to give this picture, even at times to the extent of inventing the Jewish offender. The tensions of the war led to the black marketeer becoming a scapegoat character. The character needed to be un-British, disloyal, powerful and obsessed with money – the past Jewish image fitted smoothly into this role. Jewish involvement in the black market helped to confirm rather than create this powerful war stereotype.[17]

In other instances, as with the Bethnal Green Tube disaster in 1943, domestic tensions and the prevailing Jewish image were enough on their own to create the antisemitic rumours. Here the Jewish involvement was irrelevant, for the 'Jewish panic' slanders that spread across Britain were part of an automatic antisemitic reflex, lacking any connection with the real event. To summarise, the activities of Jews did not affect the overall levels of antisemitism in Britain during the war. This does not mean that the Jewish role should be neglected, for it is often vital in the process of exaggeration and distortion that is the basis of hostility to Jews.

Can antisemitism be put down to a general British xenophobia which is always likely to be intensified by war? The answer is complex. This study has shown that although the Jewish community in Britain had become acculturated by 1939, the vast majority of the population still regarded Jews as foreign. The arrival of Jewish refugees from the continent in the 1930s and during the war, strengthened the 'un-British' image of Anglo-Jewry. In theory a general rise in the level of xenophobia in the war could have also increased antisemitism. This certainly can be seen in the invasion panic of 1940 where the general suspicion against all foreigners led to a rise in hostility to Jews, and in Lord Wedgwood's words 'put a cachet of respectability on antisemitism'. However, even in this period of crisis, hostility to foreigners also took a specific form. Only with the entry of Italy into the war on 11th June 1940 did anti-Italian feeling surface prominently, having an immediate and quite violent effect. A general increase in xenophobia may have adversely affected the Jewish minority in Britain. Nevertheless, when xenophobia was specific against other groups it was also possible that it could have deflected hostility to Jews.[18]

There were over 100,000 refugees in Britain during the war. In addition there was the enormous Irish-born population and American, Polish and other foreign troops on British soil. This had an ambivalent impact on the Jewish community. On the one hand, so strong was the identification of Jew with 'alien' in Britain that the alleged misconduct of any continental refugee or foreigner could be interpreted in an antisemitic light. On the other, the emergence of new out-groups, such as the Americans in the second half of the war, did at times divert attention away from Anglo-Jewry. The stereotype of the American was in some ways similar to the stereotype of the Jew, especially with regard to alleged money-mindedness and ostentation. Although the comparative wealth of the American soldiers brought with it some popularity, it also created jealousy and resentment. It is significant that the Jew-black marketeer linkage was weakened by the Christmas of 1943, with U.S. troops becoming the new scapegoats for scarce goods.[19] Jews themselves could take part in this substitute scapegoating activity – for example, joining up with other white East Enders against Lascars in the shelters during the blitz. Nevertheless, more than one ethnic conflict could exist at one time. In Liverpool and Glasgow Catholic–Protestant tensions did not preclude quite powerful antisemitism, although in Northern Ireland the Jewish community was so small and lacking in prominence that it enjoyed a quiet existence, in this bitterly divided country.[20]

A third factor in the equation of the impact of foreigners in Britain on domestic antisemitism is that their very presence challenged xenophobia. As a senior Home Office official wrote in November 1944 'the traditional insular attitude of the British public towards foreigners has been substantially broken down during the war. British subjects have found foreigners working beside themselves [sic] in munition factories, civil defence, and other wartime occupations, have accepted them in Trade Unions and got used to their presence.' The war opened up many opportunities previously denied to Irish immigrants, who were now accepted into many parts of the economy outside the traditional building or labouring occupations. On a much smaller scale, skilled West Indian workers, despite initial hostility, found positions as engineers in the north west of England. However, one can overstress the degree of integration that took place. Fear of foreign job competition remained and the West Indian workers in particular soon found themselves displaced after the war.[21]

Neither did stereotyped thinking about foreigners disappear with closer contact. Those who had worked or lived with West Indians now knew that the black man did not possess a tail (a widespread belief that parallels that of Jews and horns in the evacuation areas), but other fears, such as the sexual superiority of blacks persisted. Other deeply ingrained prejudices linking the Irish with drunkenness, Italians with cowardice, would remain despite the closer contacts of the war. In short, there is no clear linkage between xenophobia in the war and antisemitism. A general rise in xenophobia could adversely affect the Jewish community, and conversely a decline in distrust of foreigners could benefit it. It is important, however, to stress that there were also individual traditions of hostilities to various national, religious and racial groups in Britain. The existence of a cultural tradition of antisemitism ensured that hostility to Jews was not dependent on xenophobia alone.[22]

Before turning to the overall impact of the war on Anglo-Jewry, it is necessary to examine how Gentiles envisaged the future of Jews in Britain. At the end of 1944, the *Jewish Chronicle* bemoaned the lack of prestige the term 'British Jew' possessed. The goal should be to be British and Jewish, avoiding total assimilation. The *Chronicle*'s concern was justified in that few non-Jews accepted that one could be both and those who did tended to be cultural or religious philosemites. Although the British government respected the religious requirements of the Jewish community, the population as a whole appears to have regarded Judaism as at best an anachronism, at worst barbaric. Judaism was perceived as an excuse for exclusivity, which in turn was responsible for antisemitism. What was needed, according to a Mass-Observation survey, was for Jewish behaviour to 'correspond more to the life and manners of Gentiles'. This then was the liberal compromise. A small section of the population rejected this solution, believing that the only solution was to remove Jews to a country of their own, or (very rarely) to remove Jews altogether.[23]

In theory therefore, most Britons wanted Jews to assimilate into the wider society. Did this take place in the war, and what pressures were there on the Anglo-Jewish minority? As with the Irish, the demands of the war economy opened up many opportunities for Jews. In addition, evacuation, the blitz, military and civil defence duties threw Jew and Gentile into close proximity. Although the classic immigrant trades, such as tailoring and furniture making, would still be significant for the Jewish community well after the end of the war, they would no longer dominate Anglo-Jewish economic history. The original settlement areas such as the East End, Cheetham and the Gorbals would also lose centre stage, the war accelerating their decline as Jewish districts.[24]

Superficially, it would appear that during the war Jews were allowed to enter all aspects of British society, both social and economic. In return, the Jewish community willingly accepted the new opportunities offered to it. However, a closer analysis reveals a more contradictory situation. Many Jews did wish to move closer to Gentile society in that they were looking for non-traditional forms of employment, or housing in non-Jewish areas and leisure outside Jewish circles. Many met blatant discrimination but, more often, there was subtle exclusion. Job discrimination against Jews reached a peak in the last years of the war and those immediately after it. On its own, this discrimination was not enough to stop Jews moving freely in British society, but this hostility confirmed the insecurity of Anglo-Jewry, which was not without foundation. It has been suggested that 'if it were possible to analyse the collective psyche of the Anglo-Jewish community, the deep-rooted hypochondria would be exposed: the fear of antisemitism'. Yet it must be doubted whether this malaise can be called hypochondria, for the fear of rejection from Gentile society has been based on real experiences. It is this that gives the real bite to 'golf-club' antisemitism – not that it necessarily inflicted great hardships, but that it highlighted the fact that Jews were outsiders in British society. In and after the war, Anglo-Jewry responded by moving away from traditional trades and settlement areas, but went on to new Jewish districts and attempted to achieve economic independence, so that potential hostility could be avoided. The strength of British antisemitism in the war was not in its violence against the Jewish community, but that it caught Jews within a vice, demanding that Jews assimilate yet denying them free access to Gentile preserves.[25]

The war did bring changes in the nature of British antisemitism. When Charles Solomon declared in June 1942 that 'antisemitism is no longer respectable' he was not totally mistaken. Extremist antisemitic and fascist groups were handicapped in the war by the public connecting them with the Nazis. Mosley's post-1945 attempts at a comeback were certainly hindered by such linkages. The man who could well have been Prime Minister became a pathetic figure, espousing anti-black racism to ever decreasing audiences. Attitudes to Nazi Germany have also caused problems within the radical right since 1945, leading to a series of splinters and unstable coalitions, of which the National Front was the most prominent. However, the relative success of the National Front in the late 1960s and early 1970s, despite the neo-Nazi careers of some of its leaders, is a warning against relying on the sheer unrespectability of such groups. It is difficult to assess the total impact of the National Front, but apart from causing distress amongst new immigrant communities, it must be argued that the threat of its continued success encouraged rigid immigration control to be imposed in Britain during the 1970s. The comparative ease with which some National Front supporters have moved into the Conservative Party recently also casts doubt on whether such extremists can be regarded as permanently outside the pale of mainstream British politics.[26]

One self-conscious attempt to sanitise neo-fascism is the expanding holocaust denial industry. As this study has shown, it had its roots in the war itself with such protagonists as Douglas Reed and Alexander Ratcliffe, as well as the social credit movement, assorted pacifists, the *Catholic Herald* and *Truth*. Now international, leading members of the National Front and the British Movement have made contributions to the growing 'denial of the Six Million'. Its impact, certainly in Britain, cannot be said to be great at present; the danger lies in the future, as memories fade and it becomes easier to whitewash both antisemitism and National Socialism.

The growing rehabilitation of the reputation of Oswald Mosley can be seen as another, if less important, manifestation of the radical right's attempt to gain historical respectability in Britain.[27]

In the world of non-organised British antisemitism the impact of the holocaust has been less dramatic. The news of the destruction of European Jewry did cause many to reconsider their views towards Jews, but attitudes change slowly and horror at Jewish persecution abroad often did not preclude antipathy to Jews at home. Despite the attempts of Jewish and anti-fascist organisations to link all forms of antisemitism with Nazism, ambivalence on Jewish matters remained the norm in the war. Nor should it be assumed that antisemitism was unacceptable in public forms. Douglas Reed, despite his growing paranoia about Jewish power, remained an eminently publishable social commentator for Jonathan Cape. Starting from the extreme, John Hooper Harvey proved that even medieval myths about Jews could be presented respectably. Dislike of Jews was no barrier to the successful political careers of men such as Lord Winterton, Lord Gort and even Anthony Eden – all of whom had to deal with Jewish matters in their government capacity.[28]

The impact of the revelations of the Nazi concentration and death camps and the Nuremberg trials in 1945 and 1946 on attitudes to Jews can be divided into the short and long term. John Rae has written that 'when the war ended and the secrets of Belsen and Auschwitz were exposed, the Jews enjoyed a brief popularity'. His impression of the brevity of this philosemitism is confirmed by Mass-Observation, who could claim as early as 1947 that 'people are no longer moved by the thought of Jewish suffering in concentration camps'. The anti-Jewish riots in Britain in August of that year – following the hanging of two British sergeants by Zionist extremists in Palestine – would indicate that the initial reaction had indeed been short-lived. The riots occurred in nearly every large British city, and although attacks on persons were rare, the numbers involved in the disturbances alarmed the Jewish community, and damage to property was substantial.[29]

David Leitch has claimed that Jewish terrorism in Palestine in 1946 and 1947 'neutralised much of the sympathy in Britain for the plight of European Jewry'. This was certainly true in the short term, but it is difficult to assess the long term effects of the holocaust on non-Jewish attitudes in Britain. The Churches in particular have shown tremendous sympathy to Jews since the war, the Council of Christians and Jews no longer being ahead of its time in seeking positive relations between the two religions. Whilst the holocaust factor may have put certain restraints on public antisemitism in the last few decades, it has not stopped the occasional manifestation of social prejudice, such as that encountered by Arnold Weinstock during the 1960s in the City of London.[30] Attacks on prominent Jewish politicians as Jews in the 1980s have prompted one Jewish commentator to suggest that 'such . . . antisemitic comments . . . would scarcely have been thinkable a few years ago'. Whilst there is a danger in overestimating the strength of British antisemitism in the 1980s, the antipathy revealed in such cases as the resignation of Leon Brittan serve as a warning of the continuation of prejudice against Jews, and also on the changing acceptability of racism in British society.[31]

The 1947 riots, born out of a mixture of foreign events, despair at post-war austerity, Bank Holiday exuberance and latent antipathy to Jews, were the last mass antisemitic demonstrations in Britain. They were not, however, the last acts of violence against Jews in Britain. The 1960s witnessed fascist attacks on Jewish property, resulting in the death of a Yeshiva boy, and such incidents have continued in the 1980s. Although not on the same scale as violence against the black community, these antisemitic attacks indicate that the presence of West Indians and Asians in Britain has not totally deflected attention away from the Jewish minority. Radical right-wing groups have maintained and indeed appear to be increasing their antisemitism. The presence of other more easily identifiable ethnic minorities since 1945 in Britain has meant that Jews are no longer so readily seen as news. However, it must be argued that the generally high level of racism present in the depressed Britain since the 1970s is also affecting the Anglo-Jewish population. Ritual slaughter is just one issue in which Jews are under attack along with coloured minorities.[32]

When the Jewish shadow Home Secretary, Gerald Kaufman launched an attack on the granting of British citizenship to the South African athlete, Zola Budd, the *Sunday Express* replied that she at least 'had a British grandfather, which was more than could be said for Mr Kaufman'. Here was an example from the 1980s of how impermeable the Jewish stereotype – in this case as an alien – can be.[33] How much then did the close contact between Jew and non-Jew in the Second World War change the perceptions of Jews in Britain?

It has been suggested that whether as evacuees or as members of the Forces, good relations with individual Jews did not necessarily change attitudes to Jews as a whole. Gross misunderstandings such as that Jews had horns were largely removed from British society in the war – it was rare for even the remotest of villages to have had no Jewish contacts at some point in the conflict. Yet post-war studies on attitudes to Jews show that less exotic beliefs about Jews persisted, such as their alleged avarice, clannishness, flashiness and cowardice. On the positive side, Jews were still seen as artistic and intelligent, although the latter category was also seen as a negative attribute. The Jewish black marketeer, the most powerful war stereotype concerning Jews, certainly survived after 1945, being continued in the slightly less negative guise of the 'spiv'. The Lynskey tribunal in 1948 involving Sidney Stanley, the 'super spiv', created a fair amount of antisemitism, and the notorious 1947 editorial in the *Morecambe and Heysham Visitor* referred to 'British Jews, who have proved to be the worst black market offenders'. The Jewish stereotype thus proved to be particularly obdurate, and while many Jews and non-Jews formed good relations in the war, close contact at best only started a process in which deeply ingrained attitudes were re-examined.[34]

In conclusion, what separated Britain from Germany in the 1930s and 1940s in their treatment of Jews, was not so much the failure of British antisemitism but the continuation of British liberal democracy. Yet, paradoxically, it was only the internal weaknesses of liberal democracy that allowed both antisemitism and Anglo-Jewry to survive. In the world in which Jews were emancipated, a separate Jewish community should have disappeared. At the same time, antisemitism should also have ceased. The British government in the Second World War found itself unable to remove antisemitism and thus it set about appeasing those who were hostile to Jews. Indeed, the fear of domestic antisemitism was largely responsible for the government's feeble response to the desperate plight of European Jewry. The government considered that an influx of foreign Jews, however small, would lead to serious problems, an analysis prompted by the belief that it was the Jews themselves who created antisemitism. This was, after all, the argument of the emancipation contract. The genuine fear of antisemitism in British society was used to put pressure on the Jewish community to conform – in other words, toleration had its price. Yet at the same time Anglo-Jewry was also under pressure from those who would not accept them moving closer into society. Thus on the one hand, Britain had avoided the excesses of Nazi antisemitism, on the other, it had failed to produce an environment for the healthy existence of a positive Anglo-Jewish identity.[35]

This study has argued that Britain has had an antisemitic tradition, or to be more accurate, traditions, which continued to operate in the Second World War and made a real impact on the treatment of Jews at home and abroad. This does not mean, however, that the supposed decency, humanitarianism or liberalism of the British with regard to Jews or other ethnic minorities should be rejected as insignificant. The actual belief that Britain was all of these things did affect reality. At the start of the war Britain's liberal treatment of refugees was a self-conscious policy to show the world how decent British society was, especially compared to those countries who had forced out these unfortunate people. Nevertheless, the invasion panic just over half a year later shows the dangers of relying on such decent humanitarianism. Even so, there is a contrast between the treatment of internees in Britain itself, and those shipped abroad. The latter suffered serious indignities and abuse, it could be argued, because they were no longer under the relative protection of liberal opinion at home. In Palestine, events such as the turning away of refugees to almost certain death in Nazi Europe were possible. However, it is doubtful whether this would have been allowed to happen in Britain, because of government respect of humanitarian feeling. The belief in Britain that racism does not exist can thus, at times, circumscribe such antipathy. Nevertheless, there are also great dangers in assuming that racism does not exist. Vigilance is vital with regard to racism or antisemitism in Britain; such caution cannot occur if there is no recognition of the continued existence of hostility to racial and ethnic minorities.[36]

Notes

Preface

1 See particularly B. Wasserstein, *Britain and the Jews of Europe, 1939–45* (Oxford, 1979) and R. Zweig, *Britain and Palestine During the Second World War* (London, 1986).

Introduction

1 L. Langer, *The Holocaust and the Literary Imagination* (New Haven, 1975), p. 7.

2 In the modern period most notably Tsarist Russian and Nazi Germany; T. Endelman, *The Jews of Georgian England 1714–1830* (Philadelphia, 1971), pp. ix–x; M. Salbstein, *The Emancipation of the Jews in Britain* (East Brunswick, 1982).

3 G. Lebzelter, *Political Anti-Semitism in England 1918–39* (London, 1978), p. 1.

4 J. Banister, *England Under the Jews* (London, 1907), p. iii; A. Leese, *Out of Step* (Guildford, 1951), p. 70; M. Zimmerman, *Wilhelm Marr* (Oxford, 1986); J. Robb, *Working Class Anti-Semite* (London, 1954), p. 11.

5 N. Nicolson (ed.), *Harold Nicolson: Diaries and Letters 1939–45* (London, 1967), entries for 13 June 1945, 9 Dec. 1942 and 11 Jan. 1944; G. Field, 'Anti-Semitism with the Boots Off', *Wiener Library Bulletin* (1982), p. 32.

6 *Hansard* HC vol. 356 col. 61–2, 16 Jan. 1940. For a general discussion see A. Trythall, 'The Downfall of Leslie Hore-Belisha,' *Journal of Contemporary History*, XVI, July 1981, pp. 391–412.

7 R. Minney, *The Private Papers of Hore-Belisha* (London, 1960), pp. 17–18.

8 J. Colville, *Man of Valour* (London, 1972), p. 160; Minney, *op. cit.*; pp. 268–75; A. J. P. Taylor (ed.), *W. P. Crozier: Off the Record, Political Interviews 1933–43* (London, 1973), p. 132.

9 I. Macleod, *Neville Chamberlain* (London, 1961), pp. 286–7; D. Dilks (ed.), *The Diaries of Sir Alexander Cadogan 1938–1945* (London, 1971), pp. 241–42; H. Morris-Jones, *Doctor in the Whips' Room* (Bungay, 1955), pp. 114–15 for *Truth*.

10 See for example Dilks, *op. cit.*; Earl of Birkenhead, *Halifax* (London, 1965), p. 447.

11 *Action*, 11 Jan. 1940; J. Higham, 'Antisemitism in the Gilded Age: A Reinterpretation', *Mississippi Valley Historical Review*, 1957, p. 562; K. Feiling, *The Life of Neville Chamberlain* (London, 1946), p. 434; R. James (ed.), *Chips: The Diary of Sir Henry Channon* (London, 1976), pp. 23–24, 120–21.

12 Higham, *op.cit.*; p. 564; Endelman, *op.cit.*; p. 56; S. Spender, *The Thirties and After* (Glasgow, 1978), p. 96; A. Jackson, 'Behold the Jew', *Poetry Review*, July–Aug. 1943, p. 201; anonymous letter 5 May 1943 in NCCL 310/5.

13 C. Holmes, *Anti-Semitism in British Society, 1876–1939* (London, 1979), p. 35; L. Thompson, *1940: Year of Legend, Year of History* (London, 1966), p. 34.

14 O. Mosley, *My Life* (London, 1968) p. 337; R. Skidelsky, *Oswald Mosley* (London, 1975), p. 381; J. Yinger and G. Simpson, *Racial and Cultural Minorities* (New York, 1972), p. 74; G. Alderman, 'Anti-Jewish Riots of August 1911 in South Wales', *Welsh History Review*, 1972–73, pp. 190–200.

15 Holmes, *op.cit.*; p. 100 and 'The Tredegar Riots of 1911', *Welsh History Review*, 1982, pp. 214–25; HO 144/1160/212987/1–13.

16 Alderman, *op.cit.*; pp.195–6.

17 R. Skidelsky in K. Lunn and R. Thurlow (eds.), *British Fascism* (London, 1980), p.84; Holmes, *Anti-Semitism*, pp. 22 and 97; G. Allport, *The Nature of Prejudice* (Reading, Mass., 1954), pp. 245–6; J. Roberts, *The Mythology of the Secret Societies* (London, 1972), pp. 358–9; *Social Crediter*, 27 April 1940.

18 D. Walton, 'George Orwell and Antisemitism', *Patterns of Prejudice*, Jan. 1982, p. 24; E. H. Carr, *What is History?* (Harmondsworth, 1980), pp. 62–6.

19 Holmes, *Anti-Semitism*, p. 141.

20 Holmes, *op.cit.*; chapter 8; J. Bush, 'East London Jews and the First World War', *London Journal*, VI, Winter, 1980, pp. 147–61; A. Smith, 'War and Ethnicity', *Ethnic and Racial Studies*, IV, 1981, pp. 375–97.

21 C. Aronsfeld, 'Jewish Enemy Aliens in England During the First World War', *Jewish Social Studies*, XVIII, pp. 275–83; Bush *op.cit.*; p. 159; J. Jacobs, *Out of the Ghetto* (London, 1978), pp. 58–9.

22 C. Bermant, *The Cousinhood* (London, 1962).

23 For the League see K. Lunn, 'The Marconi Scandal and Related Aspects of British Anti-Semitism 1911–14' (PhD Sheffield University, 1978), pp. 233–60.

24 See H. Pollins, *Economic History of the Jews in England* (Oxford, 1982), pp. 141–6; C. Russell and H. Lewis, *The Jew in London* (London, 1901), p. xiv.

25 See particularly B. Williams, 'The Anti-Semitism of Tolerance' in A. Kidd and K. Roberts (eds.), *City, Class and Culture* (Manchester, 1985), pp. 74–102.

26 D. Cesarini, 'Anti-Alienism in England After the First World War', *Immigrants and Minorities*, VI, 1987, p. 22 for critical comments on the state and antisemitism; Holmes, *op.cit.*; chapter 6; A. White, *The Modern Jew* (London, 1899); J. Bird, 'Control of Enemy Alien Civilians in Great Britain 1914–18' (PhD University of London, 1981), p. 2.

27 Henriques, 19 June 1923 in HO 45/24765/432156/38; Holmes, *op.cit.*; pp. 16–17; A. Sherman, *Britain and the Refugees from the Third Reich 1933–39* (London, 1973).

28 See P. Colbenson, 'British Socialism and Anti-Semitism 1884–1914' (PhD Georgia State University, 1977) and K. Lunn, 'The Marconi Scandal' for the right.

29 Holmes *op.cit.*; chapter 9; Z. Szajkowski, *Jews, Wars and Communism*, vol. 2 (New York, 1974).

30 A. J. P. Taylor, *Beaverbrook* (London, 1972), p. 387.

31 M. Muggeridge, *The Thirties* (London, 1940), pp. 242–3, J. Parkes, *The Jew and His Neighbour* (London, 1939). See R. Thurlow, *Fascism in Britain: A History, 1918–1985* (London, 1987), chapter 4 for the fragmentation of the extreme antisemitic world in the late 1930s; Liverman quoted by G. Lebzelter, *op.cit.*; p. 35.

Chapter 1

1 *Encylopedia Judaica* vol. 3 (Jerusalem, 1971), p. 79

2 Mosley quoted by R. Skidelsky, *Oswald Mosley* (London, 1975), p. 440. See *loc.cit.*; p. 332 for an optimistic membership assessment and G. Webber, 'Patterns of Membership of and support for the British Union of Fascists; *Journal of Contemporary History* XIX, 1984, pp. 578–9 for more accurate figures.

3 Skidelsky, *op.cit.*; p. 442; Special Branch in HO 144/21281/98–102 and HO 144/21429/16–20.

4 HO 144/21429/16–20; S. Rawnsley, 'Fascism and Fascists in Britain in the 1930s', (PhD Bradford University, 1981), p. 208 for Lancs; Trevelyan Scholarship Project 'The British Union of Fascists in Yorkshire 1934–40' (Unpublished ms, 1960), p. 13; J. Brewer, *Mosley's Men* (Aldershot, 1984), p. 78 for Birmingham; Anderson in *Hansard* HC vol. 363 col. 966–67, 25 July 1940.

5 IFL membership in HO 45/24967/37; *New Pioneer* started in Dec. 1938. For a more generous assessment see Webber, *op.cit.*; p. 377. For The Link, see R. Griffiths, *Fellow Travellers of the Right* (London, 1980), pp. 307–11; M-OA: D 5390, 8 Sept. 1939 for surburban support.

6 HO 144/21062 for Joyce; C. Cross; *The Fascists in Britain* (London, 1961), pp. 184–5 for Chesterton; D. Pryce-Jones, *Unity Mitford* (London, 1976), pp. 232–4.

7 'Mosley's Message' in AJA 110/5 and Mosley quoted in HO 144/21429/16–20; Beckett in *Time and Tide*, 16 Dec. 1939, Special Branch *loc.cit.* and HO 144/212811.24–5 for 1938.

8 MEPO 2/3127; HO 144/21429/56–7; JDC report, Sept. 1939 in BD C6/5/1/1.

9 Special Branch, Sept. 1939 in HO 144/21429/4–20; *Action*, 12 Oct. 1939. For restraint see report, 24 Sept. 1939 in BD C6/5/1/1 and MEPO 2/3127; Clarke in *Action*, 30 Sept. 1939; HO 144/21429/100 and A. Calder, *The People's War* (London, 1969), pp. 61–2 for poster disfigurement.

10 MI5 on Joyce's organisation in HO 144/22454/185–8. For the IFL see Special Branch, 16 Sept. 1939 in HO 144/21382/290–6 and BD C6/10/26; HO 144/22454/85–9 for the Nordic League.

11 For Houston see his 18B files HO 45/25713 and HO 283/41 and reports in HO 144/20145/14–7 and HO 144/21062/283; *JC*, 21 April and 19 May 1939; Special Branch report, 4 Oct. 1939 in HO 144/22454/96–7; JDC reports, 24 Sept.–4 Dec. 1939 in BD C6/5/1/1; *Hackney Gazette*, 6 Dec. 1939.

12 Game to Laski BD C6/9/1/3 F3; JDC reports 1–8 Oct. 1939 BD C6/5/1/1; I. Ravensdale, *In Many Rhythms* (London, 1953), p. 147.

13 MEPO 2/3127, Nov. 1939; JDC report, 19 Nov. 1939 BD C6/9/1/3; Mosley in *Action*, 30 Nov. 1939 and *The British Peace* (London 1940), p. 9; N. Mosley, *Beyond the Pale* (London, 1983), pp. 232–3 and O. Mosley, *My Life* (London, 1968), p. 342 for a rebuttal.

14 *Action*, 30 Nov. 1939, 28 March 1940. *New Statesman*, 6 Jan. 1940 reports on the BUF 'refujew' attack; *Action*, 23 Sept. 1939 for alleged profiteering.

15 *New Statesman*, 6 Jan. 1940; INF 1/319; JDC report, 13 May 1940 BD C6/5/1/1.

16 MEPO 2/3127 Dec. 1939–Feb. 1940; HO 45/24895/3 for the conference; Mass-Observation, *War Begins at Home* (London, 1940), pp. 421–2.

17 *JC*, 19 Jan. 1940; JDC reports, 26 Feb. 1940 for Webster and 20 Nov. 1939 and 27 March 1940 for their success; IFL links in BD C6/5/1/1.

18 Special Branch, 20 Feb. 1940 for by-elections and East End campaigns in HO 45/24895/16 and 27; *JC*, 8 March 1940 for women's involvement.

19 HO 45/24895/6; *JC*, 23 Feb. 1940; M-OA: FR 39 'Silvertown'; *Action*; 15 Feb. 1940.

20 *JC*, 23 Feb. 1940; F. Craig, *Minor Parties at British Parliamentary Elections* (London, 1975), p. 12; S. Wlliams, *1939: The Communist Party and the War* (London, 1983), p. 183; M-OA: FR 39.

21 *Action*, 29 Feb. 1940. For Leeds see Craig, *op.cit.*; p. 12; *JC*, 15 March 1940; *Yorkshire Evening News*, 13 March 1940; M-OA: FR A61; *Action*, 21 March 1940.

22 See Allen's 18B file, HO 144/21933 and *Action*, 16 May 1940; *JC*, 8 March 1940.

23 *Action*, 7 March 1940; MEPO 2/3127 Feb. and March 1940; *Civil Liberty*, March 1940 on the press; *New Statesman*, 27 April 1940.

24 MEPO 2/3127 April 1940; *Hackney Gazette*, 8 April 1940; *Yorkshire Post*, 30 April 1940 for Mosley. For the Bureau see Special Branch report, 20 Feb. 1940 in HO 45/24895/16.

25 For the May Day meeting see HO 45/24895/31–4; *Hansard* HC vol. 136 col. 354, 25 April 1940; *JC*, 10 May 1940 and *Action*, 9 May 1940. For later meetings and hostility *Action*, 23 May 1940; Game memo, 14 May 1940, MEPO 2/3127; R. Bellamy 'We Marched with Mosley' (Unpublished ms), pp. 3–4; JDC report 25 May 1940; BD C6/5/1/1 for Dalston.

26 For Middleton see M-OA: FR 154; *JC*, 24 May 1940; INF 1/264 no. 11 (30 May 1940); R. Bellamy 'We Marched', pp. 3–4; CAB 65/7 WM 133 (140), 22 May 1940 for the change in regulation and M-OA: FR 135 for public reaction.

27 For The Link see DOM 56, 4 Sept. 1939 and *Daily Mail*, 6 Sept. 1939. The BCCSE is covered in HO 144/22454/88: *JC*, 13 Oct. 1939 and its link with Mosley in DOM 56, 7–13 Oct. 1939.

28 MI5 report Oct. 1939, HO 144/22454/85–7; Special Branch, HO 144/21382/299.

29 DOM/56, 26 Oct., 22 Nov. and 6 Dec. 1939. For the later meetings see MEPO 2/3127 Jan. 1940; HO 144/22454/112–3; DOM/56 13–29 Feb. 1940 and A. J. P. Taylor, *Beaverbrook* (London, 1972), p. 403 for the Dublin trip and HO 45/25729/860/19/1 for Tavistock's attempt to involve the Duke of Windsor, May 1940.

30 *JC*, 12 April 1940; Marquis of Tavistock, *Years of Transition* (London, 1949), p. 181; Birkett in HO 283/16/93; *Hansard* HC vol. 367 col. 836–9, 10 Dec. 1940.

31 Mosley 3 July 1940 in HO 283/14/84–5; HO 283/18/21, 2 Aug. 1940.

32 DOM/56, 26 July 1939; Special Branch, 25 June 1940 in HO 144/21933/330–1 and Scotland Yard, 24 May 1940 in HO 45/25728/860060/1. For IFL extremists see MI5 report, March 1942 in HO 45/24967/674960/105–8 and the Nordic League, Special Branch, 16 Sept. 1939 in HO 144/21382/298–9.

33 *Action*, 9 and 16 May 1940; *Action News Service*, 14 May 1940 and HO 283/14/91 on the Nordic League.

34 CAB 65/7 WM (28) 40, 18 May 1940 and WM (33) 40, 22 May 1940; P. and L. Gillman, *Collar the Lot*! (London, 1980), pp. 122–3 and A. Masters, *The Man Who Was M* (Oxford, 1984), pp. 89–90.

35 A. Ramsay, *The Nameless War* (Crawleigh, 1968), pp. 99–100; HO 144/22454/103–10 for the leaflet. Wolkoff in Earl Jowitt, *Some Were Spies* (London, 1954), p. 43.

36 Masters, *op.cit.*; pp. 80–9; Jowitt, *op.cit.*; pp. 49–55, 68 and J. Miller, *One Woman's War* (Dublin, 1986) for the Kent affair.

37 Ramsay, *op.cit.*; pp. 73, 102–3 and in *Hansard* HC vol. 360 col. 1378–82, 9 May 1940. The Cabinet's reaction is in CAB 65/13 WM (40) 133, 22 May 1940 and CAB 65/7 WM 133 (40), 22 May 1940.

38 Masters, *op.cit.*; p. 89. MI5, Oct. 1939 referred to 'talk of a military coup' in HO 144/22454/85–7; HO 45/24895/1 for the January meeting.

39 For Churchill see his interview, 22 Oct. 1943 in A. J. P. Taylor (ed.), *W. P. Crozier* (London, 1973), p. 381 and M. Gilbert, *Winston Churchill: Finest Hour* (London, 1983), p. 486.

40 Mosley, 22 July 1940, HO 283/16/82–7; Z. Zeman, *Nazi Propaganda* (London, 1973), p. 144 refers to The Link; N. Longmate, *If Britain Had Fallen* (London, 1972), p. 225 has details of the White List. The prison officer report is quoted in *The Sunday Times*, 18 Dec. 1983.

41 Jowitt, *op.cit.*; pp. 42–5, 68 deals with Ramsey, Wolkoff and Kent. For Marley's accusation see *The Times*, 29 June 1940 and Ramsey's libel action against *The New York Times, The Times*, 1 Aug. 1941.

42 Leese in *Angles*, 9 Sept. 1939; Jowitt, *op.cit.*; p. 66; Harvey quoted by MI5 in HO 45/24967/67.

43 Mosley in HO 283/16/18; MI5, CAB 65/7 WM 133 (40), 22 May 1940. For BUF renegades see HO 45/25799–839 and 'The BUF Roll of Honour' in NCCL 259/2; Morrison in CAB 66/35 WP (43) 148, 14 April 1943.

44 18B numbers in HO 45/24893; Charles Solomon in the *Jewish Bulletin*, June 1942. Cross, *op.cit.*; p. 195 states that 'British Fascism ended in May 1940', technically correct but a rather narrow interpretation.

45 *Action*, 30 May 1940; MEPO 2/3127, June 1940. Lady Mosley comments on the last days of the BUF in HO 144/21995/22. See also HO 45/25713/840436/1; *Action*, 6 June 1940 and N. Driver 'From the Shadows of Exile' (Unpublished ms.), p. 47.

46 *Evening Standard*, 5 June 1940, *Hansard* HC vol. 362 col. 228, 20 June 1940; *Daily Herald*, 10 July 1940 for the whispering campaign and *Sunday Express*, 15 Sept. 1940 for the letters. *New Statesman*, 5 Oct. 1940 refers to the BUF and the tubes.

47 P COM 9/878 for the Council; *Daily Telegraph*, 27 Nov. 1940; *Daily Telegraph,* 17 Oct. 1941; *Daily Worker*, 5 Jan. 1943; CAB 66/35 WP (43) 148, 14 April 1943.

48 See Special Branch, 28 April 1943 on Godfrey, HO 45/25398; Morrison in CAB 66/35 WP (43), 14 April 1943; JDC report, 21 Aug. 1944 in BD C6/2/13e. For protests see *Hackney Gazette*, 5 April 1943.

49 *Acton Gazette*, 3 Oct. and 10 Dec. 1943 and *British National News*, 17 Aug. 1942 for Godfrey's programme.

50 Douglas Hyde (*Daily Worker* correspondent on fascism in the war), interview with author, 15 Sept. 1983; *Daily Worker*, 8–31 Oct. 1942; *New Order* 11 June 1943 for the Potocki link; HO 45/25398/191 for Ratcliffe. *Daily Worker*, 11 Feb. 1943 refers to a cancelled meeting; *JC*, 16 April 1943 for the ENA and Morrison in *Hansard* HC vol. 387 col. 1329–30, 18 March 1943.

51 *Acton Gazette*, 3 and 10 Dec. 1943; M-OA: FR 1983; *News Chronicle*, 9 Dec. 1943 for the campaign; *JC*, 23 April 1943 and *Daily Worker*, 20 April 1943 for Godfrey linkages.

52 *On Guard*, Dec. 1947 for Godfrey's later career; *Hansard* HC vol. 400 col. 2380, 16 June 1944 has 18B figures; PCLP description in Jewish Central Information Office, 'Organised Antisemitism in Great Britain 1942–6' (Unpublished ms.), p. 13.

53 *JC*, 3 Nov. 1939; M-OA: FR 411; *Parliament Christian*, May–June 1942. For Mosleyite support see *JC*, 6 and 27 Nov. 1942.

54 Mosley in HO 45/24891/403–4. For the '18B' groups see *Hansard* HC vol. 404 col. 950, 2 Nov. 1944 and *The Case of G. Merriman* (London, 1942). *The Patriot*, 26 Nov. 1942 gave support.

55 For the BUF revival claim see *JC*, 18 Dec. 1942 and *Daily Worker*, 7–8 Dec. 1942. Antisemitism is revealed in JDC report, Dec. 1942 in BD C6/2/6; Morrison in CAB 66/35 WP (43) 148, 14 April 1943; E. Wrench, *Francis Yeats-Brown 1886–1944* (London, 1948), p. 258. For its activities see *JC*, 26 March 1943, DOM 57, 27 May 1944 and *News Chronicle*, 27 Oct. 1944.

56 *Daily Worker*, 25 May 1943 refers to disagreements; *Hansard* HC vol. 387 col. 1316–7, 18 March 1943 for the memorial; *JC*, 6 Aug. 1943 for Ridley Road. Opposition to Mosley's release is made clear in M-OA: FR 2011, *Daily Worker*, 19 Nov. 1943 and HO 45/24894.

57 JDC report, June 1944, BD C6/2/13J; opposition in Aug. 1944 report, BD C6/2/6. See also J. Hamm, *Action Replay* (London, 1983) p. 136.

58 For Hamm and early meetings see HO 45/25740 and *JC*, 10–24 Nov. 1944. Conflict is outlined in Wiener Library Spector Documents 610 and later careers in BD C6/9/1/3 (7) and C6/3/3/6.

59 Hamm, *op.cit.*; pp. 137–40 and intelligence reports 1945–6 on the National Front in Greenberg papers AJA 110/5.

60 Greenberg papers, *op.cit.*; Spector Documents 610.

61 Ibid and Spector report 1946, microfilm 251/0486 Wiener Library; *People's Post*, Feb. 1954 and M. Walker, *The National Front* (Glasgow, 1977), p. 74.

62 Hyde in *On Guard*, July 1947; journals include *The Patriot, Weekly Review, Vanguard* and *Social Crediter*, companies – The Britons, Boswell Press, Corporate Utilities, Essential Books and Right Review.

63 C. Holmes *op.cit.*; p. 173.

64 *The Patriot*, 14 Sept. 1939; report on the MCP, 16 Sept. 1939 in HO 144/21382/297.

65 *Social Crediter*, 18 Nov. 1939; P. Masson and B. Jenson, *Hitler's Policy* (Liverpool, 1941); *The Patriot*, 21 Sept. 1939 and Webster in ibid. 21 Dec. 1939; Dell in *Free Press*, Nov. 1939.

66 *Social Crediter*, 19 Oct. 1940; *The Patriot*, 7 Sept. 1939; *Free Press*, Oct. 1939; *Weekly Review*, 24 Dec. 1939; Calder, *op.cit.*; p. 57; Leese in HO 45/24967/674960/105–9 and *Social Crediter*, 4 May 1940. His attack on The Britons is quoted by Lebzelter, *Political Anti-Semitism*, p. 82; Ratcliffe in *The Vanguard*, 11 Nov. 1939.

67 *Free Press*, Oct. 1939; Medical Policy Association *Bulletin* I (1943); H. Kopsch 'The Approach of the Conservative Party to Social Policy During World War II' (PhD, Univ. of London, 1970), pp. 43,71 on Conservative anti-Beveridge sentiment.

68 G. Andrews, *For Britain* (Southend, 1939), p. 3; *Weekly Angles*, 30 Sept. 1939 on evacuation; P. Addison, *The Road to 1945* (London, 1977), p. 73 and W. Curry, *The Case for Federal Union* (Harmondsworth, 1939); *Social Crediter*, 7 Oct. 1939, *Free Press*, Nov. 1939 for antisemitic opposition.

69 For general fascist opposition see *New Statesman*, 9 Dec. 1939; *Social Crediter*, 14 Oct. 1939.

70 *Free Press*, Oct. 1939; *The Patriot*, 24 July 1941; Duke of Bedford, *Regulation 18B*, (Glasgow, 1944).

71 Addison, *op.cit.*; p. 218; INF 1/292 No. 114 (1–8 Dec. 1942); C. Douglas, *The Beveridge Plot*, (Liverpool, 1943).

72 R. Northin, *The Beveridge Report*, (Bradford, 1943), p. 2. Only F. Honigsbaum, *The Division in British Medicine*, (London, 1978), pp. 275–83 has examined the MPA.

73 Russell and Basil Steele were linked to *The Patriot*; Bryan Moyniham was a Douglasite – see his *The Problem of the Medical Profession* (Liverpool, 1943) and Alexander Rugg-Gunn a mysticist – see his *Osiris and Odin* (London, 1940) and *The Times*, 7 Sept. 1972. The bulletin is in NCCL 310/6.

74 By Honigsbaum, *op.cit.*; pp. 274–80. For medical opposition to Beveridge see *News Chronicle*, 27 Sept. 1943. B. Steele, letter to author, 29 Aug. 1984 suggests circulation of 2,500 but a wider influence and *The Spectator*, 29 Sept. 1944 and Honigsbaum, *loc.cit.*; p. 274 concur.

75 *Social Crediter*, 25 July 1942; Wrench, *op.cit.*; pp. 257–8. For disbelief of atrocities see *Action*, 2 Nov. 1939; A. Ratcliffe, *Truth About the Jews* (Glasgow, 1943) pp. 15–16; *Social Crediter*, 9 Jan. 1943.

76 *Weekly Review*, 30 Oct. 1941 on Social credit and 16 March 1944 on Ratcliffe; *Social Crediter*, 27 April 1944 on Leese and the latter on Mosley – *Weekly Angles*, 28 Oct. 1939.

77 Anonymous calls for extermination are referred to in *Tribune*, 19 May 1944; Leese in *Weekly Angles*, 14 Oct. 1939; *Social Crediter*, 9 Jan. 1943; Mosley in HO 283/13/40–2.

78 Mosley, *op.cit.* For calls for apartheid see Collin Brooks in *Truth*, 5 June 1942 and Godfrey in *Acton Gazette*, 10 Dec. 1943; pro-Arabism in *The Patriot*, 14–28 March 1940 and *Free Press*, Feb.–March 1940.

79 IFL 'Fascism' in M-OA: TC Politics Box 10 File E; Mosley in HO 283/16/30. R. Thurlow, 'Ideology of Obsession', *Patterns of Prejudice* VIII, Nov.–Dec. 1974, p. 25; Hart in *BU Quarterly*, Spring 1940; C. Douglas, *The Big Idea* (Liverpool, 1942), p. 20 and *Brief for the Prosecution* (Liverpool, 1945), p. 79. Griffiths, *op.cit.*; pp. 317–21 for volkisch groups. See particularly R. Gardiner, *England Herself*, (London, 1943), p. 165 or Lord Lymington, *Alternative to Death* (London, 1943), p. 14.

80 Chesterton in *The Patriot*, 30 Dec. 1942. Even Leese modified his views on Hitler.

81 Craig, *op.cit.*; p. 12; Rawnsley, 'Fascism and Fascists', pp. 25–6; J. Hodson, *Home Front*, (London, 1944), pp. 298–302. M-OA: FR 39 indicates public confusion over Mosley's fascist ideology.

82 *JC*, 16 Feb. 1940; INF 1/319 Jan.–Feb. 1940 on East Anglia, *JC*, 3 May 1940 for the Bureau; INF 1/319 March 1940 commented that the fascists' 'only popular appeal is antisemitism'.

83 *The Heritage of Britain*. p. 6 and BD intelligence file on the IFL, 1937; *Weekly Review*, 11 March 1943.

84 For Potocki, see R. Risk, *It is the Choice of the Gods* (Princeton, 1978); for Bowman, HO 45/25729 and the 'knighthood', *Daily Express*, 29 March 1943.

85 *The Fascist*, July 1936 but also in *Connoisseur*, June 1936; *Henry Yevele* (London, 1944), pp. vi–vii, 77 and *The Heritage*, p. 8.

86 *Gothic England* (London, 1947), p. 15; *The Plantagenets* (London, 1948); *JC*, 16–30 Nov. 1984 and C. Holmes and T. Kushner, 'The charge is ritual murder', *JC*, 29 March 1985.

87 Typical circulation figures are quoted in HO 45/24966/674112/50–4; *The Patriot* figure is in the Spector documents, Wiener Library; Anderson in *Hansard* HC vol. 360 col. 355, 25 April 1940. For *Truth* and Reed see Chapter 3.

88 D. Stanford, *Inside the Forties*, (London, 1977), p. 14 and Morrison in *Hansard* HC vol. 389 col. 1248, 20 May 1943 for Potocki. Douglas Hyde, interview with author, 17 Sept. 1983 stressed the printing link. For *The Truth* see *JC*, 9 April 1943 and Newsam in HO 45/25398/286–7.

89 Glasgow CID, 29 May 1943; HO 45/25398/286–7 and 213–17 for Potocki connections. For Harvey's 'clearing house' home see *Daily Express*, 29 March 1943 and *Surrey Advertiser*, 10 Oct. 1942. DOM 56, 27 Oct. 1943, 1 April, 14 June 1944 for the role of journals; M-OA: DS 296 Sept. 1939, Jan.–Feb. 1943.

90 *The Patriot*, 6 Nov. 1941; for *The Protocols* see *Evening Standard*, 8 Oct. 1943 and L. Lochner (ed.), *The Goebbels Diaries* (London, 1948), pp. 296–7; Hyde in *Daily Worker*, 27 April 1945. Government fears were expressed by Morrison in CAB 45/115 JR (45), 16 May 1945 and by R. Law in FO 371/36731 W6933. See also chapter 5.

Chapter 2

1 Details of the survey are in BD C6/10/26. R. Skidelsky, *Oswald Mosley* (London, 1975), p. 393 ahistorically refers to the East End in the 1930s as 'a piece of Jewish Eastern Europe'; *The Times*, 29 Oct. 1936.

2 See Harrisson television script, 12 July 1939 in M-OA: TC Antisemitism Box 1 File E; Julian Franklyn in BD C6/10/26.

3 M-OA: TC Antisemitism Box 1 File F; *World Film News*, May 1937. Phil Piratin believes the Council was one third Jewish, one third Catholic and the remainder Church of England or Methodist. Interview with the author, 18 July 1984.

4 The CP estimate is from P. Piratin, *Our Flag Stays Red* (London, 1948), p. 49. B. Sokoloff (later the Stepney CP secretary) believes the Jewish proportion was higher. Interview with the author, 1 Nov. 1984. She also states that the Jewish community was generally respectful of the CP. The Library figure is in M-OA: TC Antisemitism Box 1 File F; STDL details in H. Srebrnik, 'The Jewish Communist Movement in Stepney' (PhD University of Birmingham, 1983), p. 69; *The Times, op.cit.*

5 All details in M-OA: TC Antisemitism Box 1 File A.

6 For earlier Poplar reactions see J. Bennett, *East End Newspaper Opinion and Jewish Immigration 1885–1905* (M Phil University of Sheffield, 1979) pp. 212–3, and later antipathy in M-OA: TC Antisemitism Box 1 File A. Bethnal Green is covered in the same survey, Box 2 File F.

7 Franklyn in BD C6/10/26; conclusion of M-OA report, TC Antisemitism Box 1 File A, and the Bethnal Green quote in Box 2 File F.

8 Population figures in D. Munby, *Industry and Planning in Stepney* (London, 1951), pp. 13 and 36; *Action*, 9 Nov. 1939. Post-war figures in A. Levy, *East End Story* (London, 1950), p. 16.

9 For Council corruption see K. Brill, *John Groser* (Oxford, 1971) p. 152 and Srebrnik, 'The Jewish Communist Movement', p. 10; R. Titmuss, *Problems of Social Policy* (London, 1950), p. 106; *JC*, 8 Sept. 1939.

10 '*Ye Olde Bell and Rattle*', Sept. 1939; JDC report, Feb. 1942 in BD C6/9/1 F5; Anon, *The Bells Go Down: The Diary of a London AFS Man* (London, 1942), p. 116.

11 Jack Miller, interview with author, 15 Sept. 1983, H. Snow *In Wartime London* (Imperial War Museum); Abby Levy in the AFS in Wapping also comments on co-operation. Interview with author, 6 Sept. 1984.

12 *JC*, 17 Nov. 1939, white slave traffic allegation in BD C6/9/1/3 F3; AFS details in M. Richardson, *London's Burning* (London, 1942), pp. 33 and 62 and in *The Bells Go Down*, pp. 8 and 171.

13 Sept. 1939 report in HO 144/21429/41 and I. McLaine, *Ministry of Morale* (London, 1979), p. 34.

14 *The Bells Go Down*, p. 23; for the STDL see *Daily Worker*, 12 Oct. 1939 and 8 May 1940, and for antisemitism, *JC*, 29 Sept. 1939. STDL membership figures in *East End News*, 28 June 1940 and impact in *JC*, 22 Dec. 1939.

15 *JC*, 29 Sept. 1939; M-OA: TC Antisemitism Box 1 File H.

16 *East London Advertiser*, 22 Feb. 1941; H. Snow, *In Wartime London*, p. 16.

17 For Silvertown see M-OA: FR 39 and Limehouse FR 78. R. Calder, *The Lesson of London* (London, 1941), p. 70 comments on the fear of antisemitism.

18 CAB 65/7 WM 133, 22 May 1940; F. Lewey, *Cockney Campaign* (London, 1944), pp. 80–81; R. Ball, *The Bull's Eye*, (London, 1942), p. 50 and R. Calder, *op.cit.*; pp. 74–5.

19 A. Marwick, *The Home Front* (London, 1976), p. 10 for blitz myths and J. Mallon in *News Chronicle*, 19 May 1942.

20 Stepney Information Service, 24 April 1950 report in Tower Hamlets Local History Library ref. 081.1 and T. O'Brien, *Civil Defence* (London, 1955), pp. 387–90 for the blitz; M-OA: FR 431 and TC Air Raids Box 9 File T, R. Calder, *op.cit.*; p. 70 and PWE report, 28 July 1941 in FO 898/181 for indications of antisemitism and accusations of Jewish panic.

21 R. Titmuss, *op.cit.*; pp. 257 and 301, T. O'Brien, *op.cit.*; p. 390 for blitz details; *East End News,* 4 Oct. 1940 and BD C6/9/1/3 F5 for antisemitism in the shelters.

22 M. Richardson, *op.cit.*; pp. 64–5 and 137; Home Intelligence reports INF 1/292 No. 1–2 (30 Sept.–14 Oct. 1940), for Jewish and Gentile bravery; Richardson, *loc.cit.*; p. 95 for the Yiddish reference and M-OA: TC Air Raids Box 9 File T for the 'Ludkies' quote.

23 A. Clark-Kennedy, *The London Hospital* vol. 2 (London, 1963), p. 250 for Tilbury; N. A. Rose (ed.) *Baffy* (London, 1973), p. 175 for Dugdale; M-OA: FR 431 for race feeling, and *JC*, 1 Nov. 1940 for antisemitism.

24 B. Donoghue and G. Jones, *Herbert Morrison* (London, 1973), p. 283; N. Branson, *History of the Communist Party of Great Britain* (London, 1985), p. 302; M-OA: TC Air Raids Box 9 File T and FR 431 for STDL shelter activities. A. Calder, *The People's War* (London, 1969), p. 167 has details of the Savoy march, and CAB 65/9 (WM) 250, 16 Sept. 1940 for Cabinet concern.

25 Interview with P. Piratin, 18 July 1984; M-OA: FR 431 for other concern.

26 T. Harrisson, *Living Through the Blitz* (London, 1976), p. 113; *Catholic Herald,* 25 Oct. 1940; Piratin interview, *op.cit.*

27 For co-operation see *East End News,* 24 July 1942; Lewey, *op.cit*; p. 76; John Wills, 1 April 1943 reports on the later Catholic hostility in Kingsley Martin papers 30/1.

28 Donegall in the *Sunday Dispatch,* 6 Oct. 1940. P. Bottome, *Formidable To Tyrants* (London, 1941), p. 86 for the idealist description; S. Salomon letter, 27 Jan. 1944 in BD C6/2/13b for the George Crosses; M-OA: TC Air Raids Box 9 File T for shared nervousness; R. Calder, *op.cit.*; p. 70 for limited antisemitism and *Tribune*, 20 Sept. 1940 for hostility to the Mosleyites.

29 Titmuss, *op.cit.*; p. 257, O'Brien, *op.cit.*; pp. 388–90, 427, Calder, *op.cit.*; p. 184 and Calder, *Carry On London* (London, 1941), p. 59 have details. The 'family' quote is in Imperial War Museum, *World at War* series (tape no. 2819) and Kops in the same series (no. 2718) and *The World is a Wedding* (London, 1963), p. 86.

30 M-OA: TC Air Raids, Box 9 File T; *East End News,* 10 Jan. 1941, and *Bulletin of the Society of Jews and Christians,* Nov. 1941, for antisemitism; *JC*, 10 Jan. 1941 and A. Stencl, 'Whitechapel Spring 1941' *JC*, 1 April 1966; F. Lewey, *op.cit.*; pp. 32–3 for the reverse.

31 D. L. Munby, *op. cit.*; p. 36. The quote is by Piratin, interview with the author, 18 July 1984. See also Clutton-Brock in *The Times,* 28 Dec. 1940. The Toynbee Hall worker is A. Levy, interview with the author, 6 Sept. 1984; the Jewish Bethnal Greener, Lena Barden, interview 20 Aug. 1984.

32 The move north is covered by H. Brotz in M. Freedman (ed.), *A Minority in Britain* (London, 1955), p. 140 and the diversity by H. Pollins, *Economic History of the Jews in England* (London, 1982), pp. 188–90; the BUF in *JC*, 21 July 1939.

33. *JC*, 24 Nov. 1939, MEPO 2/3127 report for May 1940 and *JC*, 14 June 1940. For the blitz see *JC*, 27 Sept. and 4 Oct. 1940, and later *Daily Worker*, 9 April 1943.

34 *The Guardian*, 16 July 1985 editorial; for Hackney's Jewish growth, Brotz, *op.cit.*; and Sir A. Hudson in *Hansard* HC vol. 389 col. 1169–71, 19 May 1943. The Pembury estate hostility is covered in BD C9/4/5; fear in South Hackney in *Jewish Missionary Intelligence*, Aug. 1944.

35 JDC report, 8 Nov. 1943 in BD C6/2/6; *The Patriot*, 22 Feb. 1940. For gaming attacks in the *Hackney Gazette*, 10, 17 Jan. 1940–29 June 1945; accusations of cowardice 2 Oct. 1940; discrimination 5 March 1943; antisemitism correspondence 10 March 1943; 15 June 1945.

36 J. Bennett, 'East End Newspaper Opinion', pp. 174–207 for earlier attitudes. M. Goldsmith, *JC* reporter in the 1930s describes the change in approach – interview with the author, 9 April 1984. Bennett, *loc.cit.*; pp. 128–54 covers the *Observer* as does C. Bermant, *Point of Arrival* (London, 1975), p. 223 for the First World War. In a letter of 27 Jan. 1941 the editor wrote to the Board of Deputies, stating that it wanted to help the Jewish point of view, BD C6/10/43/2. Bennett, *loc.cit.*; pp. 208–29 deals with the *East End News*. For the war see the series attacking antisemitism in March–April 1943 but a hostile article in the issue of 24 Sept. 1943. The *News* stressed left-wing anti-fascism throughout.

37 *JC*, 25 Oct. 1940; comments of Captain Burcher, *JC*, 1 Nov. 1940 and *Hackney Gazette*, 15 May 1944. The warden's comments are quoted in C. Fitz Gibbon, *The Blitz* (London, 1957), p. 143 and the chemists–letter to author from J. Renson, 22 March 1984.

38 For details see HO 199/144 and L. Dunne, 'Report of an enquiry into the accident of Bethnal Green tube station shelter' (London, 1945, Cmd 6583).

39 For population distribution see J. Robb, *Working Class Antisemite* (London, 1954), p. 52 and R. Glass and M. Frenkel in A. Weidenfeld and H. Hastings (ed.) *Britain Between West and East* (London, 1946), p. 40. Roman Road was notorious for BUF support; H. Swaffer in *The People*, 14 March 1943 gives the figure 5.

40 In the NCCL archives 41/7; for earlier antisemitism see Salomon letter to Scotland Yard, 10 March 1943 in BD C6/10/29 and Swaffer, *op.cit.*; Kops, *The World*, p. 108.

41 INF 1/292 no. 127 (2–9 March 1943); for local fascists spreading rumours see *Daily Worker*, 16 March 1943 and Dunne, *op. cit.*; p. 12 for the rumours that the panic was started by fascists. Percy Harris was told that the council was widely blamed–see HAR 158/1/2 diary entry 6 March 1943. The slow percolation to Stepney is mentioned by B. Sokoloff, interview with author, 12 Sept. 1983; for West Ham see M-OA: D 5321, March 1943 and *JC*, 13 Oct. 1944.

42 1939 meeting report in BD C15/3/17, Post 13 in B. Nixon, *Raiders Overhead* (London, 1943), pp. 88–100; Wills report, 7 April 1943 in Kingsley Martin papers, 30/1; Clutton-Brock to Allen, 28 May 1943 in NCCL 311/2; Lena Barden, interview with author, 20 Aug. 1984 comments on the low priority of worrying about Jews.

43 See Orwell in *Contemporary Jewish Record*, April 1945; Wills report, 7 April 1943 quoted in note 42; B. Nixon, *op.cit.*; p. 89. Sympathy for the small shopkeeper is suggested in M-OA: FR 661 and that for the interned aliens in *East*

End Observer, 27 July 1940; Pritchard in *East End Observer,* 31 July 1942; Wills *loc.cit.*; reports on the hostility to West End Jews.

44 Munby, *op.cit.*; p. 186 comments on the move out and H. Llwellyn Smith (ed.), *The New Survey of London Life and Labour* vol. 6 (London, 1934) p. 284 on the deconcentration in tailoring. The Toynbee Hall report is in the Munby papers, Tower Hamlets Local History Library, Box 5610. Loterys and Stepney Laundry did not like Jewish labour, Town Mills, 12 Aug. 1944 and D. Green specifically stayed in the East End for it. *JC*, 30 Jan. 1941 report the outright refusal to employ Jews; *Catholic Herald,* 25 Oct. 1940 suggests conflict, M. L. Richardson, *op.cit.*; p. 150 the reverse.

45 *East End News,* 1 Jan. 1943; Council minutes, 2 March 1943; *East End News,* 26 Nov. 1943. For the fire watching accusation see May 1941 TAC report in BD C6/2/6 File 1.

46 For Toynbee see H. Fagan 'Autobiography' (Unpublished ms), p. 3 and M-OA: FR 431; A. Hartog, *Born to Sing* (London, 1978), p. 44. For club mixing see S. Bunt, *Jewish Youth Work in Britain* (London, 1976), pp. 130–31, *JC*, 29 March 1940 and 24 Aug. 1945.

47 Stepney C.P., *A Stepney to be Proud of* (London, 1944), pp. 4–7; B. Sokoloff, interview with author, 1 Nov. 1984 and J. Jacobs, *Out of the Ghetto* (London, 1978), p. 188. For the election campaign, see the leaflets in the Lazar Zaidman collection.

48 D. Hyde, *I Believed* (London, 1951), p. 187 for the membership figure, M-OA: FR 392 for the lack of social mixing. The Troxy incident is covered in a report to Scotland Yard, 13 Oct. 1944 in BD C6/10/29. B. Kops, *op.cit.*; p. 36 comments on earlier fights.

49 Kops. *op.cit.*; pp. 86–9 comments on the temporary nature of the blitz spirit. For the Vallance Road V2 see A. Levy, *op.cit.*; p. 63.

50 Levy, *op.cit.*; p. 98 comments that by 1945 the Jewish population was down to 25,000, many Jewish landmarks destroyed, but that many Jews would still commute into the East End for work.

51 Titmuss, *op.cit.*; p. 101 has figures and p. 344 makes some defence of evacuation as a safety valve mechanism. See also B. Johnson (ed.), *The Evacuees* (London, 1968) and C. Jackson, *Who Will Take Our Children?* (London, 1985). Titmuss, *loc.cit.*; p. 112 comments on the indiscriminate social mixing.

52 C. Cross, *The Fascists in Britain* (London, 1961), p. 187; *Action,* 23 Sept. 1939. For local variations see the Economic League report, 1941 in BD C6/10/16; M-OA: DR 1345, 1329, 2487 for Oct. 1940.

53 M-OA: FR 392 suggests less Jews left; *National Review,* Oct. 1941. The concentration in the Home Counties and Lake District is suggested by a memo on membership June 1941 in United synagogue archives; R. Broad and S. Fleming (eds.), *Nella Lasts War* (Bristol, 1981), p. 83.

54 A. Marwick, *op.cit.*; p. 70; M-OA: FR 451 comments on the difficulty in generalising even on a local basis. The London figures are in S. Levin, *A Century of Anglo-Jewish Life 1870–1970.* (London, 1970), p. 69.

55 Titmuss, *op.cit.*; p. 174 and E. Halton, *Our Town* (London, 1943), p. 4 on the state of the evacuees; JDC report, 1940, BD C6/2/6; *JC* 15 Sept 1939. For antisemitic violence see *The Citizen*, 23 April 1943; *News Chronicle,* 1 April 1943 and B. Johnston, *op.cit.*; p. 30.

56 J. Parkes, *Voyage of Discoveries* (London, 1969), pp. 172–3; for Chatteris see M-OA: DR 2303 Nov. 1939. J. Grunfeld, *Shefford: The Story of a Jewish School Community in Evacuation* (Tiptree, 1980), p. 3 and interview with Mark Moser, 28 Nov. 1984 and J. Grunfeld, 17 July 1984 confirm the 'conversion' of the villagers to the children.

57 M-OA: DR 1206 Nov. 1939; for the Jews' Free School see M. Burkhill Imperial War Museum refugee tapes, no. 4588, and Spitalfield Books, *Where's Your Horns?* (London, 1979). pp. 22, 35; *Young Jewry*, Sept. 1944.

58 Titmuss, *op.cit.*; pp. 178–9; the Ipswich quote is in Kops, *op.cit.*; p. 97; the parrot reference in M. Allingham, *The Oaken Heart* (London, 1941), p. 96; H. Massingham, *There's No Place Like Home* (London, 1944), pp. 77–8 and Middleton in *The Adelphi*, Jan. 1940.

59 Bedford details in EBV 40, Bedfordshire County Record Office and Arnold Harris papers; *Bedfordshire Record*, 29 July and 18 Sept. 1941; Harris diary, 28 Feb. 1940. The former pupil was N. Solomon, interview with author 26 Nov. 1984. In his diary, 2 Nov. 1939 Harris referred to the boys' good behaviour. Both N. Solomon and Ansel Harris (interview with author 5 April 1984), point to the nonconformist factor.

60 Mrs. J. Wolkind, interview 2 Aug. 1984 and Spitalfield Books, *op.cit.*; p. 35 for Ely.

61 For Jews and horns see J. Grunfeld, *op.cit.*; p. 3, Spitalfield Books, *op.cit.*; p. 22; A. Hartog, *op.cit.*; p. 58; C. Bermant, *Coming Home* (London, 1976), pp. 66 and 71.

62 Spitalfield Books, *op.cit.*; pp. 35 and 58. J. Grunfeld, interview with author, 17 July 1984 refers to post-evacuation contact at such events as weddings breaking down barriers.

63 Grunfeld, *op.cit.*; pp. 36 and 59; Harris diary, 2 Dec. 1939. M. Moser, interview with author, 17 July 1984 states that extra money was paid to the hosts to cover the special religious needs; Bermant, *op.cit.*; p. 66.

64 Burkill's Imperial War Museum refugee tape (no. 4588); M-OA: DR 2303 Nov. 1939; Ruth Lesser 'Evacuation: an Impression' (unpublished ms) refers to food difficulties. For the Sunday school 'compromise', see the *JC*, 13 Feb. 1942. Spitalfield Books, *op.cit.*; p. 52 has details of Joseph, for kidnapping see Burkill's refugee tape.

65 For Egham see *JC*, 20 Oct. 1939 and confirmed by Piratin, interview with author, 8 Aug. 1985; N. Longmate, *How We Lived Then* (London, 1971), p. 55.

66 *JC*, 22 Sept. 1939; Bermant, *op.cit.*; p. 62; F. Hallgarten IWM refugee tape (no. 4494); Cigman in Johnston, *op.cit.*; p. 39 and fellow evacuee antisemitism in M-OA: FR 451.

67 This adjustment is suggested by the editor of the *Buckingham Free Press* to W. W. Simpson, 29 Aug. 1941 in BD C15/3/20 F1. Grunfeld, *op.cit.*; pp. 43–4 refers to antagonism towards parents.

68 For Brighton see the *JC*, 22 Sept. 1939; for Bournemouth M-OA: D 5080; Blackpool–J. Hodson, *Towards The Morning* (London, 1941), p. 167; North Wales, James Parkes papers, 07.006 005; Peak District BD C6/10/16 and West Country, *Western Morning News*, 21 Feb. 1944. Soutar's comments are in the same paper, 13 Nov. 1940.

69 For this distortion see comments in E. Janner, *Barnett Janner* (London,

1984), p. 74. Torquay is covered by *JC*, 10 Oct. 1941 and Blackpool in Salomon letter to Greenberg, 7 Oct. 1940 in AJA 110/5. *Hansard* HC vol. 365 col. 1971–2, 7 Nov. 1940 for Bournemouth; *Daily Worker*, 4 June 1945 for Margate.

70 Titmuss, *op.cit.*; pp. 276 and 345; Harrisson on the improvement in M-OA: FR 482.

71 13 Sept. 1940 report in HO 199/316; *JC*, 27 Sept. 1940.

72 M-OA: FR 482; INF 1/292 no. 1 (30 Sept.–7 Oct. 1940).

73 Titmuss, *op.cit.*; p. 271; M-OA: FR 412 and *JC*, 17 Oct. 1941 for Oxford.

74 Jackson, *op.cit.*; pp. 44–5; M-OA: DR 1578 Oct. 1940 for Banford, M-OA: FR 412 and letter from Hartley Aug. 1941 in BD C15/3/20 for Oxford; M-OA: FR 1669L.

75 M-OA: DR 1329, Oct. 1940; Jackson, *op.cit.*; pp. 44–5 for distortion; M-OA: DR 2489, Oct. 1940 for cultural friction and Harrisson in M-OA: FR 482 stressing the fact that this was the same with non-Jewish town evacuees. For the Home Counties experience with Jews as a whole see BD C15/3/20.

76 M-OA: FR 577.

77 The Berkhamsted reference is by Lena Barden, interview with the author, 20 Aug. 1984; renewed antisemitism in Horsham in M-OA: FR 577; FR 761 on Jewish clubs in Oxford for evacuees. The East Anglia reference is in *Young Jewry*, Sept. 1944.

78 For queues see *JC*, 10 Oct. 1941 and INF 1/292 no. 42 (16–23 July 1941) as 'hot-beds of antisemitism'. Business antagonism is covered in *Staines and Egham News*, 8 Oct. 1943 and later evacuation antisemitism in the Society of Jews and Christians minutes, 13 March 1941 and 23 June 1942 in the Parkes papers.

79 N. Longmate, *The Doodlebugs* (London, 1981), p. 211; *Mass-Observation Bulletin*, Dec. 1944–Jan. 1945; Board of Deputies report, 1944, BD E2/64.

80 INF 1/292 no. 191 (23–31 May 1944) and no. 197 (4–11 July 1944); BD E2/64 refers to regional differences.

81 For the Lakes see *Jewish Missionary Intelligence*, Feb. 1941, and BD E2/64 for Blackpool; for Brighton *Tribune*, 22 Sept. 1944 and NCCL 311/1, letter G. Myers 20 May 1943; Torquay M-OA: DR 3369 March 1943 and Miss Monkhouse letter, 16 June 1943 in NCCL 311/1, and the BUF in Brighton JDC report of 28 April 1940 in BD C6/9/1/3.

82 J. Grunfeld, *op.cit.*; p. 112 suggests the villagers were broken hearted when the children left. For long-lasting relations see *loc.cit.*; p. 100 and Spitalfield Books, *op.cit.*, p. 58.

83 1942 report in BD C6/9/1/3; B. Henriques, *Fratres* (London, 1951), p. 140 – young soldier's comments; Jackson, *op.cit.*; pp. 44–5 for Oxfordshire; report 17 Sept. 1943 in Bedfordshire County Record Office W/EV/CWL 3 for the Jewish Secondary School; BD C9/4/5 for Staines, April 1944.

84 For billet refusals see M-OA: FR 451; *JC*, 27 Oct., 22 Nov. 1940; H. Massingham, *The Harp and the Oak*, (London, 1945), pp. 195–248. For East Anglia see M. Burkill, IWM refugee tapes (no. 4588).

85 Ken Teacher quoted in I. Bald, *The Jews in Britain* (London, 1984), p. 28; S. Levin, *op.cit.*; p. 69 and C. Bermant, *Troubled Eden* (London, 1969), p. 128 for the damage to Jewish education.

86 For the impact of evacuation on Jewish residential distribution see V. D. Lipman, *Social History of the Jews in England 1850–1950* (London, 1954), p. 132; United Synagogue archive membership list 1941; LCC archive, EO/WAR/2/46 Jewish child evacuees March 1940.

Chapter 3

1 Harrisson to Laski, 6 Sept. 1939 in BD C6/10/26 and A. Brien for later comments in *New Statesman*, 13 July 1984. For early reports of war antisemitism see M-OA: TC Antisemitism Box 1 File G.

2 C. Newman (ed.), *Gentile and Jew* (London, 1945); J. J. Lynx (ed.). *The Future of the Jews* (London, 1945); *News Chronicle*, 1–5 April 1943; *Dundee Evening Telegraph*, 17 Feb. 1944; *New Statesman*, Feb.–March 1943; *The Spectator*, Jan.–Feb. 1942; Orwell in *Partisan Review*, Jan.–April 1943.

3 See introduction p. 2.

4 M-OA: D5296, 16 March 1945 and for Rothermere, S. Koss, *The Rise and Fall of the Political Press in Britain* vol. 2 (London, 1984), pp. 556–7.

5 *Daily Worker*, 14 Oct. 1940 and 22 April 1943 for an attack on *Railway Review*.

6 See L. Poliakov, *The History of Anti-Semitism* vol. IV (Oxford, 1985), pp. 196–216; K. Wilson, 'The Protocols and the Morning Post 1919–20', *Patterns of Prejudice*, XIX, 1985, p. 5.

7 *The Patriot* 27 Feb. 1941; C. Holmes, *Anti-Semitism in British Society* (London, 1979), pp. 201–2 for the NCU and BD C6/6/5 and *Empire Record*, July–Aug. 1941 for the BEU; *National Review*, Oct. 1939 and June 1941.

8 See the *Catholic Herald*, 24 Dec. 1942, 1 Jan. 1943, 14 July 1944 for doubts about atrocity stories and Oct. 1944–March 1945 on *The Protocols*; Holmes *op.cit.*; p. 212 and BD B4/CAR/11 generally. For other Catholic hostility see S. James, *A Catholic Angle on the Jewish Problem* (London, 1944).

9 W. Steed, *That Bad Man* (London, 1942), pp. 54–8; A. Keith, *The Causes of the War* (London, 1940), pp. 123; A. Bryant, *Unfinished Victory* (London, 1940); pp. 102–6 and D. Reed, *All Our Tomorrows* (London, 1942), p. 86; M-OA: FR A12, DR Oct. 1940 and March 1943.

10 H. Kopsch, 'The Approach of the Conservative Party to Social Policy During World War II' (PhD, University of London, 1970). For *Truth*'s links see *Time and Tide*, 22 Nov. 1941 and for Chesterton, intelligence report on the National Front, 20 Oct. 1945 in Ivan Greenberg papers 110/5.

11 P. Addison, *The Road to 1945* (London, 1977), p. 231; A. Calder, *The People's War* (London, 1969), p. 295; Orwell in *Partisan Review*, March–April 1942, *Tribune*, 1 Oct. 1943; Calder, *loc.cit.*; p. 499.

12 *Truth* 2 Aug. 1940 and *JC*, 22 Aug. 1941; Brooks 'Anti-Semitism and Treachery' *Truth*, 5 June 1942 and 12 Jan. 1940 for Hore-Belisha; Brooks in C. Newman, *op.cit.*; pp. 42–7.

13 H. Morris-Jones, *Doctor in the Whips' Room* (Bungay, 1955), pp. 114–15; C. Claremont, *The Innumerable Instincts of Man* (London, 1940), p. 164; M-OA: FR 1993 and M-OA: DR3257, March 1943.

14 M-OA: DR 1052, Oct. 1940.

15 *Truth*, 20 Nov. 1942; BIPO survey 1943 in Addison, *op.cit.*; p. 218 and INF 1/292 no. 114 (1–8 Dec. 1942); Benn in *Truth*, 5 Dec. 1941.

16 BD C15/3/33; Morrison note to Laski, 11 April 1942 and Salomon memo, 9 June 1942 in BD C15/3/33.

17 G. Alderman, *The Jewish Community in British Politics* (Oxford, 1983), p. 119; W. Armstrong (ed.), *Cecil King: With Malice Toward None* (London, 1970), p. 19 for *Truth* articles and S. Koss, *op.cit.*; p. 611 for Dugdale.

18 Alderman, *op.cit.*; p. 120; *Hawick Express*, 29 Sept. 1944 and BD C6/9/3/2 for Ramsay's constituents; Alderman, *loc.cit.*; pp. 120–1 and W. Rubinstein, 'Jews Among Top British Wealth Holders', *Jewish Social Studies*, XXIV, 1972, pp. 80–1 for other Conservative constituencies.

19 See Chapter 6 pp. 167–8 for the Board and fascism; Butler, 13 Sept. 1943 in BD E2/32 and letter from C. Ponsonby to Chamberlain, 21 Feb. 1940 in HO 213/44 E409.

20 *National Review*, Jan. 1945 and Addison, *op.cit.*; p. 266 for Croft. For Churchill see the *Illustrated Sunday Herald*, 8 Feb. 1920 and Addison, *loc.cit.*

21 S. Orwell and I. Angus (eds.). *The Collected Essays, Journalism and Letters of George Orwell* vol. 3 (London, 1968), pp. 375–6. For support of *Truth* see JDC report, 15 Nov. 1942 in BD C6/2/13e. Modern entryism is suggested in *The Guardian*, 10 Oct. 1983, for earlier links see the *Daily Mirror*, 28 June 1945.

22 Orwell, *op.cit.*; pp. 375–6 and S. Cohen, *That's Funny You Don't Look Anti-Semitic* (Leeds, 1984), p. 9.

23 Orwell, *op.cit.*; pp. 375–6 and in *Tribune*, 11 Feb. 1940; J. Robb, *Working Class Antisemite* (London, 1954), p. 93; M-OA: FR39 and 61. For Stokes see HO 144/22454/114–5 and Stoke, Labour Party archive Middleton papers JSM/ACP/18.

24 See Introduction p. 11.

25 *The Forward*, 3 June and 22 July 1939; R. Skidelsky, *Oswald Mosley* (London, 1975), p. 439.

26 Ibid; 5 Aug. 1939, 27 Jan. and 3 Feb. 1945.

27 *Daily Worker* 12 Jan. 1945; *The Forward*, 30 June 1945 and Skidelsky, *op.cit.*; p. 440 for the BUF link.

28 Bedford in *Peace News*, 10 Nov. 1939; for ILP support see Adams papers M-OA: Box 1 File C; Stuart Morris, chairman of PPU was a member of The Link – *Peace News*, 18 Aug. 1939; Nordic League in HO 144/22454/86 and BCCSE, PPU executive minutes, 1 March 1940, and Murry's comments in *Peace News*, 27 Nov. 1942.

29 Chapter 1 p. 24 and Domvile diaries, 13 Aug. 1943 for McGovern; *The Word*, Jan. 1942 for Ratcliffe and HO 45/25398/20–37 and 40–100 for the Anarchist Federation connection.

30 *Peace News*, 30 Oct. and 25 Dec. 1942 for Bedford and Godfrey, *Peace News*, 4 Aug. 1939 and *The Adelphi*, Jan. 1940 for Mannin and Murry; Orwell in *Partisan Review*, March–April 1942. For PPU opposition to antisemitism see *JC*, 15 March 1940 and 24 March 1944, and Spector documents 'Peace Pledge Disunion' in the Wiener Library.

31 *Daily Worker*, 19 Dec. 1939 and 21 Feb. 1940 differentiated itself from the fascist peace campaign; M. Muggeridge, *The Thirties* (London, 1940), p. 23; *Daily Worker*, 8, 11 and 13 July 1940 and F. Morton, *The Rothschilds* (London, 1962), pp. 227–9; *Daily Worker*, 13 July 1940.

32 See for example the issues of 12 Aug., 5 Oct. and 10 Nov. 1939 or 8 Jan., 29 March and 14 Oct. 1940 for attacks on antisemitism; *Daily Worker*, 15 Feb. 1934 for 'bankers', and 14 Oct. 1940 and *World News and Views*, 1 March 1941 for the qualification.

33 Z. Katin, *Clippie* (London, 1944), p. 72 refers to anti-fascist antisemitism; M-OA: DR 1235 Oct. 1940; the Belloc quote is in A. Stevens, *The Dispossessed* (London, 1975), pp. 271–2; M-OA: DR 2886, March 1943 and DR 2139, Oct. 1940.

34 D. Hyde, *I Believed* (London, 1951), p. 187; Douglas Hyde, interview with author, 17 Sept. 1983; Holmes in *Daily Worker*, 1 May 1945. For the businessmen's section see Hyde, *loc.cit.*; p. 136; B. Sokoloff, interview with author, 1 Nov. 1984 on opposition to it.

35 See N. Dale in *New Statesman*, 5 July 1985; *Socialist Appeal*, Jan. 43 and April–May 1945 and likewise *New Leader*, 19 Dec. 1942; M-OA: DR 1393 March 1943; DR 2090 for the finance justification; DR 2402, Oct. 1940.

36 A. Kershen, 'Trade Unionism Amongst the Tailoring Workers of London and Leeds, 1872–1915', (MPhil, University of Warwick, 1986) passim.

37 ULTTU records in Hackney Local History Archive.

38 S. Lerner, *Breakaway Unions* (London, 1961), p. 187; *JC*, 22, 29 Jan. 1936, Feb. 1937; BD C6/10/13p and HO 213/565 for sweating.

39 TUC General minutes, 7 Sept. 1938; *Labour Party Report of the 38th Annual Conference* (London, 1939), pp. 11–12; Citrine in *69th Trades Union Congress* (London, 1937), p. 88; *Medical World*, 1939–45.

40 MJM tape J314 for continuing hostility to refugees in munitions' works; tapes 61 and 287 report antisemitism against British Jews; Prestige, 7 Nov. 1944, in HO 213/1009 on integration.

41 N. Barou 'Notes on Anti-Jewish Economic Discrimination' Wiener Library DR 181.

42 *Daily Worker*, 14 Oct. 1940 for attacks on *Jewish* capitalists; Fred Montague MP in BD B4/Com2 and the 'Palestine' quote in JSM/210/173.

43 For Labour Party shock see the secretary, Middleton's reaction to a report of a Labour politician's support for Nazi antisemitism in 1933 JSM 210/106 and 9. The 'balance sheet' quote is from S. Cohen, *op.cit.;* p. 16. Commander Locker-Lampson MP was one of the few Tories prominent in opposing antisemitism.

44 H. Crichton-Miller in *The Spectator*, 4 Feb. 1944; Major Menzies in a British Sunday paper, 21 May 1944 quoted by *Volkischer Beobachter*, 27 May 1944.

45 Holmes, *op.cit.*; p. 104.

46 Ibid; pp. 30–1; J. Garrard, *The English and Immigration 1880–1910* (Oxford, 1971), pp. 134–6; *News Chronicle*, 20 April 1944 and Robb, *op.cit.*; p. 93 on later liberal antisemitism.

47 See Lynx, *op.cit.*; pp. 7–8 and M-OA: DR 2485 and 2090, March 1943 for this satisfaction and DR 2685, 3127, 2703, March 1943 and *News Chronicle*, 26 March 1943 for public horror; M-OA: DR 1534, March 1943 for the novelist.

48 In R. Kidd (ed.), *City, Class and Culture* (Manchester, 1985), p. 74.

49 M-OA: FR 1669L.

50 *The Fate of Homo Sapiens* (London, 1939); *All Aboard for Ararat* (London, 1940); M-OA: DR 2356, 2514, 2502 Oct. 1940 and DR 3136, 1108, 1176, 3090, March 1943 indicate popular support; Lias minute, 30 Aug. 1942 in FO 371/30917 C7839.

51 For Shaw see *JC*, 16 Oct. 1942; Orwell in *The Adelphi*; Feb. 1939; Wells in *You Can't Be Too Careful* (London, 1941), pp. 237–8.

52 Religious philosemitism is expressed in M-OA: DR 3365, 2677, 1644, March 1943; Newman, *op.cit.*; pp. 102, 304–40.

53 *The Times*, 31 July–17 Aug. 1985; *JC*, July–Nov. 1985; accusations of intolerance in *The Times*, 31 July 1985 and *JC*, 21 Sept. 1984 for fascist involvement; the distortion was evident in the claim made that there were five million Jews in Britain in a radio debate on religious slaughter – Radio 4, 3 Oct. 1985 'You the Jury'.

54 RSPCA details in BD E3/53.

55 HO 144/22454/80–90; antisemitism is evident in M. Ward, *Jewish 'Kosher'* (Ilfracombe, 1944); Ward's link to the RSPCA in BD E3/53; for her 'Protocols' language see *Jewish Kosher*, p. 10.

56 RSPCA correspondence, 1940 *op.cit*; *Northamptonshire Chronicle*, Dec. 1944–Jan. 1945; *Oxfordshire Times*, Oct. 1943–Jan. 1944 and comment 4 Jan. 1944 in BD C13/1/13.

57 See *Oxfordshire Times*, 19 Nov., 24 Dec. 1943; *Northamptonshire Chronicle*, 3 Jan. 1945.

58 Lord Horder, *The Jewish Method of Slaughtering Animals* (London, 1940) and a leaflet of the same title by E. Zeitlyn (1943); for *News Chronicle* debate see NCCL 41/7.

59 Lady Mosley in HO 144/21995/21; M-OA: FR A12: Dalton diaries, 3 Nov. 1942; the class analysis is by C. Sykes, *Nancy: The Life of Lady Astor* (London, 1972), p. 145; M. Panter-Downes, *London War Notes 1939–40* (London, 1972), p. 41; Orwell in *Partisan Review*, July–Aug. 1943; Connelly in *New Statesman*, 20 March 1943.

60 A. J. P. Taylor, *English History 1914–1945* (Oxford, 1965), p. 419; for club discrimination see NCCL 45/2 and 45/5; golf clubs – *Jewish Chronicle*, 1 June 1945 and memo 8 Nov. 1944; BD C15/3/20 for public schools; BD C6/4/2/16 and 24 for medical schools; 16 Jan. 1942 Home Intelligence report in BD B5/3/6 – small trader antisemitism; C6/9/1/3F4 – taxi-drivers; R. Broad and S. Fleming (eds.), *Nella Last's War* (Bristol, 1981), p. 83 – clerical hostility.

61 TAC report, 1942 in BD C6/10/43/2 on increasing employment discrimination, B. Kosmin in S. Wallman (ed.), *Ethnicity at Work* (London, 1977), p. 59 for economic independence and fear of antisemitism; *JC*, 20 Nov. 1942 for housing discrimination. For the 'gilded' ghettos see J. Connell in the *Bloomsbury Geographer* (1970), pp. 50–4.

62 See G. Field, 'Antisemitism with the Boots Off', *Wiener Library Bulletin* (1982), pp. 32–3 for a class analysis. The constantly antisemitic Mass-Observer was a Durham housewife see diarist no. 5296; M-OA: FR 1648, March 1943 suggests 50%; the 'liquidate' quote in M-OA: DR 3330, March 1943; the 'Freud' and similar DR 2683, 3005, 3250, March 1943. Ambivalence over European Jewry/domestic Jewry is suggested in INF 1/292 no. 198 (29 Dec. 1942–5 Jan. 1943).

63 For social mixing see M-OA: DR 3052, 2864, 3431; M. Davies (ed.), *The Diaries of Evelyn Waugh* (London, 1976), pp. 447, 486 and 523. Nicolson warned against the dangers of antisemitism in *The Spectator* 16 Jan. 1942; figures in M-OA: FR 523B; the novelist in M-OA: DR 1534, March 1943.

64 M-OA: DR 1534, March 1943; the impact of Nazi antisemitism is referred to in *JC*, 12 Jan. 1940; D. Walton, 'George Orwell and Antisemitism', *Patterns of Prejudice*, XVI, 1982, p. 24 and B. Crick, *George Orwell* (London, 1980), p. 307; 1943 report in M-OA: FR 1648.

65 M-OA: FR 1648; 'Chips' Channon's sympathy did not last the day – see R. James (ed.), *Chips: The Diary of Sir Henry Channon* (London, 1967), p. 347; B. Bergonzi, *T.S. Eliot* (New York, 1972), pp. 123–6; for Douglas, R. Croft-Cooke, *Bosie* (London, 1963), p. 293 and lastly G. Himmelfarb, 'John Buchan', *Encounter*, XV, 1960, pp. 46–53.

66 M-OA: FRA12 for Cambridge; A. Calder, *op.cit.*; p. 498.

67 Cape's files on Reed are now deposited at the University of Reading. For his success see *Now and Then*, Spring 1939 and M. Howard, *Jonathan Cape*, (London, 1971), pp. 170, 189; for *Disgrace Abounding* see G. Chapman, *A Kind of Survivor* (London, 1975); pp. 174–6 and the book itself pp. 200, 263, 278–9.

68 *Lest We Regret* (London, 1943), p. 85; *Social Crediter*, 27 March 1943; for other conspiracy plots see *All Our Tomorrows* (London, 1942), p. 336; gutter antisemitism can be found in *A Prophet at Home* (London, 1941), pp. 48, 120 and 321. For the Jewish response see *JC*, 22 Sept. 1939; *Now and Then*, 1942 and 1943.

69 *JC*, 31 Dec. 1943. For attacks on Reed see *Tribune*, 4 Sept. 1942, for praise *National Review*, Nov. 1940 and *New Statesman*, 15 Aug. 1942; Reed in *Lest We Regret*, p. 308.

70 *The Patriot*, 11 April 1940 for antisemitic praise; *Kilburn Times*, May and June 1944; M-OA: DR 2804, 2485, 3293 March 1943 for Reed's influence on the public.

71 Kemsley link – *Tribune*, 9 Feb. 1945; fascist linkages BD C6/9/3/1; hints of a conspiracy in *Daily Mail*, 30 Aug. 1943; for explicit references, *Catholic Herald*, 15 Dec. 1944 and 12 Jan. 1945.

72 *Daily Dispatch*, 6 Feb. 1943; for support see M-OA: FR 1648 and hostility *Civil Liberty*, March 1943; *Daily Dispatch*, 9 Feb. 1943 editorial; M-OA: FR 1993 suggests only 1 out of 155 wanted a ban. For Gort see N. Rose (ed.), *Baffy* (London, 1973), pp. 215–6 and similarly Lord Winterton – *JC*, 27 Nov. 1946.

73 Himmelfarb. *op.cit.*; p. 50; publishers – JDC minutes, 20 Aug. 1943 in BD C6/2/6; M. Lags and P. Furbank (eds.), *Selected Letters of E.M. Forster* vol. 2 (London, 1985), pp. 205–6; for Shylock, *The Spectator*, 20 Oct. 1942.

74 G. Field, *op.cit.*; pp. 32 and 39 lapses into talk of 'vague' expressions of antisemitism.

75 Phoney war antisemitism in HO 144/21429/39–45; I. McLaine, *Ministry of Morale* (London, 1979), pp. 8–9; the suppression of Mosley in HO 283/1/1–14; *JC*, 3 Nov. 1939.

76 For the fifth column panic see M-OA: FR 79 and FR 197; government fears were expressed in CAB 65/7 WM(40) 123, 15 May 1940; riots in M-OA: FR 184; later anti-alien feeling in M-OA: FR 486, 8 Nov. 1940; for the East End and evacuation, Chapter 2.

77 INF 1/292 no. 37 (18–25 June 1941) on the black market as 'a scapegoat for difficulties'; earlier black market antisemitism in INF 1/292 no. 42 (16–23 July 1941); for government encouragement see Lord Woolton's Diary, 4 March 1942; M-OA: FR 1781, 1943 refers to the scapegoat aspect in which 'unpatriotic' minority groups were blamed.

78 The decline in antisemitism is reported in INF 1/292 no. 151 (17–24 Aug. 1943); for the linkage of black market unpopularity and antisemitism M-OA: FR 1781 and 1648; H. Cantril, *Public Opinion 1935–46* (Princeton, 1951), p. 381.

79 *JC*, 26 Feb. and 26 March 1943; McLaine, *op.cit.*; pp. 178–80 for public concern and INF 1/292 no. 177 (15–22 Feb. 1944) for the decline in antisemitism; INF 1/292 no. 194 (2–9 March 1943) and no. 215 (7–14 Nov. 1944) for Moyne.

80 For the government see CAB 95/15 JR (43), 31 Dec. 1942; Randall, 17 Dec. 1943 in FO 371/36672 W17585 for local concern.

81 Manchester – BD B5/3/6; Leeds – BD C6/4/2/22; Glasgow – BD C6/4/2/6; *Hampstead and Highgate Express*, 12 Oct. 1945.

82 Liverpool, INF 1/292 no. 36 (3–10 June 1941); Oxford, Chapter 2 pp. 73–4; Sheffield, BD C6/2/6 and C6/4/2/52.

83 Newman, *op.cit.*; p. 328 comments on this dual pressure; for blaming the Jews for antisemitism see A. Lane of Penguin, 27 Jan. 1944 in Parkes papers, 07.006.005; Laski, 8 Jan. 1940 in Crozier papers; Rothschild in Morton, *op.cit.*; p. 20; Namier in *Conflicts* (London, 1942), p. 131.

84 For the NJC see chapter 6 and chapter 5 passim for doubts about the atrocities; M-OA: FR 1993 (1944).

Chapter 4

1 N. Cohn, *Warrant for Genocide* (London, 1967), p. 254; E. Rosenberg, *From Shylock to Svengali* (London, 1961), pp. 13–14 for 'durability'.

2 D. Sayers, *A Vote of Thanks to Cyrus* (London, 1946), p. 24; N. Rose (ed.), *Baffy: The Diaries of Blanche Dugdale 1936–1947* (London, 1973), p. xv; M. Stocks, *Eleanor Rathbone* (London, 1949), p. 323; A. Stedman, *The Growth of the Hebrew Religion* (London, 1936), pp. 1–3.

3 J. Hitchman, *Such a Strange Lady* (London, 1975), p. 172; D. Sayers, *The Man Born to be King* (London, 1969), pp. 113–21. For reactions see *JC*, 16 April 1943 and BD C6/10/7/1, 14 Aug. 1943.

4 *The Man Born*, p. 286; *Tribune*, 22 Jan. 1943. For school antisemitism see L. Heron, *Growing up Poor in London* (London, 1973), p. 10.

5 Simpson in *JC*, 17 Oct. 1941; M-OA: DR 1442, 1230, 1149, 1182 and 2118 June 1939.

6 Simpson, interview with author, 9 Sept. 1984; *JC*, 17 Oct. 1941; *Christian News Letter*, 7 May 1941 for 'well-earned' Christian explanations of antisemitism; M-OA: TC Antisemitism Box 1 File G; B. Henriques, *Fratres* (London, 1951), p. 143.

7 J. Trachtenberg, *The Devil and the Jews* (New York, 1943) on diabolic imagery; J. Westwood, *Albion* (London, 1985), pp. 197–200.

8 C. Holmes, 'The Ritual Murder Accusation in Britain', *Ethnic and Racial Studies* IV, July 1981, pp. 267, 281 and for Lamb, M. Hay, *Europe and the Jews*

(Boston, 1960), pp. 126–7; Westwood, *op.cit.*; pp. 199–200; Holmes *loc.cit.*; pp. 267–79 for later charges and C. Bermant, *Point of Arrival* (London, 1975), p. 112 for the Ripper.

9 Rev. Hutchinson to Salomon, Oct. 1940 in BD C15/3/19; 'Little Sir Hugh' by 'Steeleye Span' on their album 'Commoners Crown'. For war accusations see A. Day, *Our Friends the Jews* (London, 1943), p. 49 and Lord Rankeillour's comments in *Hansard* HL vol. 122 col. 575, 14 April 1942; Harvey is covered in chapter 1; D. Reed, *All Our Tomorrows* (London, 1942), p. 290; *The Times* 15 Oct. 1959 for Lincoln; *Punch*, 16 Oct. 1985 and *Jewish Telegraph*, 18 April 1986 for Sunday school teachers reviving the accusation.

10 *Jewish Cruelty* (Leeds, 1945); *The Times*, 12, 19, 31 May 1944 for Jews and the fur trade; F. Honigsbaum, *The Division in British Medicine* (London, 1978), p. 169 for vivisection and 'Question Master', *The Evolutionists Brain Trust* (Edinburgh, 1943), p. 71 for vaccination; *Vanguard*, Dec. 1943; M-OA: TC Antisemitism Box 1 File G; *Porth Gazette*, 19 Dec. 1942 for vaguer demonic 'Foeter judaicus' accusations.

11 Trachtenberg, *op.cit.*; pp. 50, 149–53 for sexual antisemitism and E. Bristow, *Prostitution and Prejudice* (Oxford, 1982), p. 4 for the white slave traffic; chapter 1 p. 20 for war accusations.

12 For Freud see *The Lancet*, 14 and 21 Oct. 1939; A. Stevens, *The Dispossessed* (London, 1975), pp. 166–7; S. Olson (ed.), *Harold Nicolson* (London, 1980), pp. 257–8.

13 J. Brandon, *Death in Duplicate* (London, 1945), pp. 33–4, 68, 74, 79–80; Manning Coles, *Drink to Yesterday* (London, 1984), pp. 106–7. For the beautiful Jewess see M. McKenna, *The Spy in Khaki* (London, 1941), p. 175; R. Campbell, *Broken Record* (London, 1934). For the novelist's daughter see M-OA: FR A 12.

14 J. Parkes, *The Conflict of the Church and the Synagogue* (London, 1934); Trachtenberg, *op.cit.*; p. 190; B. Glassman, *Antisemitic Stereotypes Without Jews* (Detroit, 1975) for post-expulsion imagery; Rosenberg, *op.cit.*; p. 15 for the Shylock figure; W. Tomlinson, *Bye-Ways of Manchester Life* (Manchester, 1887), pp. 29–30; C. Holmes, *Anti-Semitism in British Society*, pp. 112 and 214.

15 Ramsey in *Hansard* HC vol. 411 col. 491–2, 1 June 1945; *Truth* 25 July 1941 and *Social Crediter*, 14 Oct. 1939 for support for Edward I; M-OA: TC Antisemitism Box 1 File G.

16 T. Benson and B. Askwith, *Foreigners or the World in a Nutshell* (London, 1935), pp. 124–5; for Jewish money-lenders see J. Brandon, *Death in Duplicate*. Brandon's war books were littered with Jewish fences; Holmes, *op.cit.*; pp. 112–13 on the modernisation of Shylock; Henriques, *op.cit.*; p. 141 for the soldier.

17 G. Mitchell, 'John Buchan's Fiction', *Patterns of Prejudice*, VII, Nov.–Dec. 1973; E. Kyle, *The White Lady* (London, 1941), pp. 39, 36, 111–114; *Time and Tide*, 2 Aug. 1941; A. Parsons, 'The Case of the Missing D.F.C.', *The Sexton Blake Library*, Aug. 1944.

18 M-OA: TC Antisemitism Box 1 File G; M-OA: FR 523B, Oct. 1940.

19 For *The Protocols* see Chapter 1 passim and Chapter 3 for *Truth* and Reed.

20 J. Parkes, *Voyage of Discoveries* (London, 1969), p. 87; *Catholic Herald*, 8 Sept.–27 Oct. 1944; *The Scotsman*, 8–19 Sept. 1941; *London Teacher*, 20 Aug., 17 Sept. 1943.

21 *Medical World*, 2 Aug.–13 Sept. 1940; *Builders' Merchants' Journal*, Aug.–Sept. 1939; INF 1/292, Aug. 1941 for British Israelism.

22 H. Colquhoun, *Our Descent from Israel* (Glasgow, 1940); B. Stewart, *The Hidden Hand* (Worthing, 1940); M-OA: FR 344. Orwell in *New Statesman*, 9 Jan. 1943.

23 L. Lochner (ed.), *The Goebbels Diaries* (London, 1948), pp. 286, 296–7; M. Samuel, *The Great Hatred* (London, 1943), p. 26; M-OA: DR 5296, Oct. 1940 and FR 523 B.

24 For the press, *Truth*, 19 Jan. 1940; T. Fyvel, *George Orwell* (London, 1984), p. 140. For culture D. Reed, *A Prophet at Home* (London, 1941), p. 48 and the *Catholic Herald*, 2 Jan. 1942. Finally, the cinema – *St. Helens Reporter*, 7 May 1943.

25 Bishop of Birmingham, quoted in the *JC*, 4 April 1941; the Svengali quote in *St. Helens Reporter*, 7 May 1943; M-OA: DR 2386, Oct. 1940. See L. Lindsay, *Addled Art* (London, 1942), p. 14 for accusations over modern art; E. Betts, *The Film Business* (London, 1973), pp. 87–90.

26 M-OA: DR 1226, Oct. 1940 for the Hitler quote; *News Chronicle*, 1 April 1943 for popular estimates.

27 E. Panitz, *The Alien in Their Midst* (East Brunswick, 1981); T. Benson and B. Askwith, *op.cit.*; p. 123; W. Deeping, *The Dark House* (London, 1941), p. 2. and A. Manning, *Half-Valdez* (London, 1939), p. 35 likewise.

28 M-OA: TC Antisemitism Box 1 Files B, G; Manning, *op.cit.* For the 'Aldgate' Jew see Benson and Askwith, *op.cit.*; p. 124.

29 The lisp is still present in H. Ashton, *Tadpole Hall* (London, 1941), p. 8; the latter description in H. Massingham, *The Harp and the Oak* (London, 1945), pp. 98–9; the Hampstead quote in J. Brandon, *Yellow Gods* (London, 1940), p. 142; Massingham, *loc.cit.*; pp. 111–15, 168, 244.

30 For accusations of ostentation in London see E. Hulton in J. Lynx (ed.), *The Future of the Jews* (London, 1945), p. 56; INF 1/292 no. 78 (23–30 March 1942); for Wolfson *Daily Express*, 13 Nov. 1943, *World Press News*, 25 Nov. 1943, *JC*, 19 Nov. 1943; Crozier interview with Belisha, 20 Feb. 1942 in John Ryland's Library.

31 Frances Burdett, reviewing Anna Reiner's *The Wall* in the *Catholic Herald*, 13 Oct. 1939, George in *Tribune*, 9 Jan. and 10 April 1942 and Orwell in *Tribune*, 23 Aug. 1940.

32 P. Bottome, *The Goal* (London, 1962), p. 84 and her *Within the Cup* (London, 1943), p. 11; *Masks and Faces* (London, 1941), pp. 81–93; P. Mendelssohn, *Across the Dark River* (London, 1939), p. 136.

33 Ada Jackson in *Poetry Review*, July–Aug. 1943, p. 197; G. Johnson, 'A Young Jew', *The Fortnightly*, Dec. 1944, pp. 391–2; Bottome, *Within the Cup*, p. 281.

34 E. Baumel, 'The Jewish Refugee Children in Great Britain 1938–45' (Bar Ilan University, MA, 1981), pp. 11–12; Stocks, *op.cit.*; p. 323; Lynx, *op.cit.*; preface.

35 T. Brown, *Louis Macneice* (Dublin, 1975), p. 55; E. Dodds (ed.), *The Collected Poems of Louis Macneice* (London, 1966), pp. 180–1 and 'British Museum Reading Room', pp. 160–1 and his autobiography *The Strings are False* (London, 1965), pp. 18–19, 199.

36 M-OA: FR 523 B; E. Buckley, *Family From Vienna* (London, 1941), pp. 149, 255; S. Campion, *Makeshift* (London, 1940), pp. 105–6; J. Beresford and E. Wynne-Tyson, *Men in the Same Boat* (London, 1943), pp. 31–2; Manning Coles, *Pray Silence* (London, 1940), pp. 165, 234–5; INF 1/251 Pt. 2, memo 25 July 1941.

37 T. Harrisson, 'War Books', *Horizon*, Dec. 1941; R. Keverne, *The Black Cripple* (London, 1941), pp. 16, 66 and 204; A. Soutar, *Public Ghost Number One* (London, 1941), pp. 173–4; *Truth*, 20 Oct. 1939; Maugham in *Sunday Chronicle*, 26 Jan. 1941.

38 For the film see *Time and Tide*, 25 July 1942; and for the play see *JC*, 15 Dec. 1944 and M. McKenna, *The Spy in Khaki* (London, 1941), pp. 198–9 for claims that Jewish refugees were spies. For antisemitism as an indication of Nazism see B. Rutledge, *The Death of Lord Haw-Haw* (London, 1941), and A. Soutar, *Mr. Nobody of England* (London, 1942).

39 *Hampstead and Highgate Express*, 6 Oct. 1939, 29 Oct. 1943; D. Reed, *A Prophet at Home*, p. 23.

40 M-OA: TC Politics Box 1 File K, March 1943; sympathy is expressed in M-OA: FR 174 and *Hampstead Express* 17 May 1940; admiration in *loc.cit.*; 19 Jan. 1940 and general friendliness in M-OA: *loc.cit.*

41 Refugee rudeness in *JC*, 16 Feb. and 19 April 1940; *Tribune*, 31 May 1940 comments on the local press.

42 *Hampstead Express*, 15 March 1940 but support for internment welcomed in the same paper, 24 May 1940. For other campaigns see *JC*, 19 Feb. 1943; *Hampstead Express*, 12 Oct. 1945 for the petition.

43 INF 1/292 no. 115–124 (22 Dec. 1942–16 Feb. 1943).

44 For the black marketeer image in cartoons see M-OA: FR 1149; for the conspiracy quote INF 1/292 no. 120 (12–19 Jan. 1943); H. Cantril (ed.), *Public Opinion 1935–46* (Princeton, 1951), p. 45; *Daily Mail*, 28 Feb. 1942; *Truth*, 1 March 1942; *Justice*, 29 Oct. 1914.

45 *JC*, 22 Sept. 1939; *Action*, 23 Sept. 1939.

46 See A. Ratcliffe, *The Truth About the Jews* (Glasgow, 1943), p. 4; *Stewartry Observer*, 15 Dec. 1943 and *JC*, 16 July 1943 and M-OA: FR 1648 for Rothwell; *Daily Express*, 17 Oct. 1939.

47 For radio plays see M. Haycock's *Black Magic*, 22 May 1943 – comment in BD C6/10/7/1 pt. 2; B. Baxter in *Hansard* HC vol. 378 col. 600, 3 March 1942; B. Newman, *The Black Market* (London, 1942) for literature; *Radio Fun*, 13 Nov. 1943 and *The Dandy*, 30 May 1942 for comics and the Hospital Saving Association's *Contributer*, Nov. 1942 for the quiz.

48 INF 1/251 pt. 5, Home Planning Committee, 2 Oct. 1941; *Time and Tide*, 7 March 1942; *Daily Mirror*, 17 June 1941; *The Spectator*, 2 April 1943 and 6 Feb. 1942 for the 90% claim; May 1941 figures in the *Monthly Bulletin of the TAC*, Aug. 1941 and March 1942 information in Salomon note, 17 Sept. 1942 BD C15/3/9 F3.

49 For denials see *Newspaper World*, 11 April 1942; INF 1/292 no. 73 (16–23 Feb. 1942); Morrison in *Hansard* HC vol. 39 col. 2286–7, 8 July 1943. For sensational reporting see the *Daily Dispatch*, 18 April 1942.

50 The scapegoat mechanism is commented on in chapter 3 pp. 102–3. A. Levy, *This I Recall : 1939–45* (London, 1947) comments on the decline of press interest in the black market and E. Hargreaves and M. Gowing, *Civil Industry and Trade* (London, 1952), p. 328 suggest the black market increased.

51 For false claims see the *Catholic Herald*, 16 July 1941. The TAC report of 1943 is in BD C6/10/43/2 file 2. *Jewish Year Book 1940* (London, 1940), p. 334 has population figures; N. Barou, *The Jews in Work and Trade* (London, 1945), p. 6 for economic distribution.

52 For accusations of low business morality see 'Old Moore's Dream Book', quoted by the *Daily Worker*, 27 April 1943; Jewish economic developments in H. Pollins, *Economic History of the Jews in England* (London, 1982), pp. 150–1, 200.

53 HO 213/14; only 4% of offences were alien Jewish. For biased comments see M-OA: D 1313, March 1943; INF 1/292 no. 52 (22–9 Sept. 1941) for cases involving Jews.

54 For its centrality see B. Wasserstein, *Britain and the Jews of Europe 1939–1945* (Oxford, 1979), pp. 119–20; for an indication of singling out Jews see Greenberg to Brodetsky, 22 Feb. 1943 in AJ3 and *East End News*, 27 June 1941; for re-internment see FO 371/42786 W5555 and HO 215/126 Gen 2/4/3.

55 Board of Deputies, *Anglo-Jewry in Battle and Blitz* (London, 1943); for cowardice see M-OA: D 5375, Jan. 1943 and FR 523 B. For running away see INF 1/264 no. 33, 24 June 1940; *East London Observer*, 29 Jan. 1917 for earlier accusations; chapter 2 p. 52 for the civil defence claim; Anderson in CAB 65/7 WM 133, 22 May 1940.

56 E. Janner, *Barnett Janner* (London, 1984), p. 74; INF 1/292 no. 36 (3–10 June 1941) for fire-watching; no. 59 (10–17 Nov. 1941) for war work and no. 199 (18–25 July 1944) for Bevin boys; *The Star*, 4 June 1940 and INF 1/292 no. 86 (18–26 May 1942) for conspiracy-style reporting.

57 Figures in I. Brodie, 'British and Palestinian Jews in World War II' *American Jewish Year Book*, 1946, pp. 51–72; Manchester Jewish Museum (MJM) tape J253.

58 For the Tank officer, MJM J 7; embarrassment in L. Teeman, *Footprints in the Sand* (Leeds, 1984), pp. 665, 745–6; A. Hartog, *Born to Sing* (London, 1978), p. 52.

59 B. Henriques, *op.cit.*; p. 139; N. Bentwich, *I Understand the Risks* (London, 1950) for the refugee military experience.

60 For military comradeship see J. Ellis, *The Sharp End of War* (London, 1980), p. 350; Henriques, *op.cit.*; p. 143 and p. 139 for critical comments on differentiating Jewish friends. Name changing is referred to in MJM J 24 and 145, proving one's worth, C. Bermant, *The Cousinhood*, (London 1971), p. 390–1.

61 All quotes from Henriques, *op.cit.*; pp. 148, 151.

62 For Forces' stereotyped humour see *Blighty*, 1, 29 March 1941; BD C6/2/13 m for ENSA quips and BD 6/10/7/1 for the BBC; N. Bentwich, *My Seventy Seven Years* (London, 1962), p. 195 deals with the War Office response. For rising antisemitism in the Forces in 1943 see *New Statesman*, 20 March 1943 and D. Hopkinson 'Love in War' (Unpublished Ms), p. 151 in the IWM.

63 For religious facilities and the decline of observance I. Adelman's diaries in the IWM and D. Segre, *Memoirs of a Fortunate Jew* (London, 1987), pp. 177–8. D. Nathan, 'Let There Be Light', *JC*, 3 May 1985 on Cyril Benton's confrontation with army antisemitism. For naval hostility see Hartog, *op.cit.*; p. 42; MJM J 145 and BD C6/2/12b; for the air force M-OA: DR 2979, March 1943 and the army *New Statesman*, 20 March 1943 and C. Bermant, *op.cit.*; p. 415.

64 BEF claims were made in the *Evening News*, 28 Dec. 1939, Arnhem accusations dismissed in the *Daily Express*, 20 Oct. 1944. The BBCs Director-General's note, 17 Nov. 1943 to stress Jewish military success is in BBC, WAC, R34/277. Macneice wrote 'Zero Hour' – see the *JC*, 7 May 1943 and Priestley, *Desert Highway* (London, 1944). Also the Yiddish play 'The King of Lampedusa', based on a true story of Sergeant Pilot Cohen was a great success – see the *East London Advertiser*, 4 Feb. 1944.

65 For the press see the *JC*, 26 Feb. 1943; R. Hillary, *The Last Enemy* (London, 1942); G. Cotterell, *Then a Soldier* (London, 1944); E. Waugh, *Put Out more Flags* (London, 1942).

66 BD C6/7/3/2, 1945; for Toc H, L. James to E. Allen, 30 July 1943 in NCCL 311/2; M-OA: D 5412, 4–5 March 1943.

67 *East London Observer*, 9 Feb. 1918; Allport; *op.cit.*; p. 258 for the Boston fire in Nov. 1942.

68 For persistence see INF 1/292 no. 132 (6–13 April 1943); War Office and Foreign Office memos in FO 371/39480 C3121 and C2643 and FO 371/24481 C6231.

69 The 'Arab' quote is in BD B5/3/6 Jan. 1942. M-OA: DR 1362, March 1943.

70 Myers in the *Sunday Pictorial*, 6 Oct. 1940.

71 Myers, *op.cit.*; A. Perles, *Alien Corn* (London, 1944), p. 63; *JC*, 12 Jan. 1940 and blitz headlines in 20 Sept. 1940; Roth, 8 June 1943 in BD C6/1/4/2.

72 Myers, *op.cit.*; for other Jewish self-embarrassment see M-OA: DR 2479, Oct. 1940; *JC*, 15 Nov. 1940; R. Ullman, *The Kahn's Progress* (London, 1940), pp. 12, 78, 216. For critical comment, see the *JC*, 22 March 1940.

73 Myers, *op.cit.*; TAC in HO 213/953 report on Jewry no. 3 pt II and the *Evening Standard*, 22 July 1942; Salomon, 25 Feb. 1942 in BD C6/2/13b; *JC*, 9 Aug. 1940.

74 Myers, *op.cit.*; D. Reed, *A Prophet at Home*, p. 23; for the Vigilance Committee see BD C2/2/6. The Board's Public Relations Officer, Mrs. Petrie told the refugees to report each other – June 1940 meeting; for the Jewish community and internment, chapter 6 pp. 174–5.

75 *JC*, 11 Oct. 1940 and N. Laski in the *Sunday Pictorial*, 13 Oct. 1940.

76 B. Cheyette, 'The Jewish Stereotype and Anglo-Jewish Fiction 1880–1900', paper to JHSE 17 Jan. 1985.

77 K. Warpole, *Dockers and Detectives* (London, 1983) chapter 5; S. Blumenfeld, *They Won't Let You Live* (London, 1939), pp. 74, 228–37; B. Sheridan, *King Sol* (London, 1939), pp. 191–2.

78 W. Goldman, *East End My Cradle* (London, 1940), p. 213 and *The Spectator*, 24 May–21 June 1940 for heated debate on it; Ullman, *op.cit.*; p. 340; M. Mundlak, *Journey Into Morning* (London, 1941), pp. 24, 115–6, 202.

79 A. Calder, *The People's War* (London, 1969), p. 499. For the problem of local papers see HO 213/953 report on Jewry no. 3 pt. 11; chapter 2 pp. 59–60 for the *Hackney Gazette*; this chapter for the *Hampstead Express* and *Porth Gazette* throughout the war, particularly 16 Dec. 1939; see the *Daily Mail*, 17 June 1944 and *Daily Express*, 9 April 1943 for rare philosemitism and C. C. Salway 1 Sept. 1943 in BD C15/3/20 on *Sunday Dispatch*.

80 Sharf, *op.cit.*; p. 100. For the influence of the press over the black market issue and Jews see INF 1/292 no. 78 (23–30 March 1942) to no. 151 (17–24 Aug. 1943); for the newsworthy aspect, Waley Cohen in *Newspaper World*, 11 April 1942; *Oxford Mail* quoted by the *JC*, 25 Oct. 1940 and for the 'C.O.' HO 213/953.

81 M-OA: DR 2512, 3356, 3003, March 1943 for its influence.

82 BD C6/10/7/1 5 May 1944 BBC memo and BBC WAC R28/20. For the broadcasts see BBC WAC R34/277 and *JC*, 20 April 1945.

83 J. Richards, 'The British Board of Film Censors and Content Control in the 1930s', *Historical Journal of Film, Radio and Television*, II, 1982, pp. 39–48.

84 For Brighton see the *Daily Express*, 8 Nov. 1939; J. Robertson, 'British Film Censorship Goes to War', *Historical Journal of Film*, II, 1982, pp. 49–64. For public responses to these films see M-OA: FR 472, 764 and N. Kaizer report, 26 Oct. 1943 in NCCL 43/4. For Mr Emmanuel see K. Short, *Film and Radio Propaganda in World War II* (London, 1983), p. 147.

85 Short, *op.cit.*; pp. 156–8 for America and BD C6/10/19–1, March 1945 for the lack of progress in Britain. N. Bentwich, *Wanderer in War 1939–45* (London, 1946), p. 28 has details of 'Hold up Your Head'. Another official refugee film was abandoned in 1942 – see INF 1/199. The evacuee film was 'Living With Strangers' (1941) – INF 6/446 and the East End in 'Religion and the People' (1940) in INF 6/431.

86 Complaints in May 1942 BD C6/10/19.1 and E1/51; Comfort in D. Val Baker, *Little Review Anthology* (London, 1944), pp. 158–9; M-OA: TC Antisemitism Box 1 File G.

87 For Orwell see 'Notes on Nationalism' in S. Orwell and I. Angus (eds.), *The Collected Essays, Journalism and Letters of George Orwell* vol. III (London, 1968), pp. 375–6 and *Contemporary Jewish Record*, April 1945. For Driver's accusation see *Tribune*, 18 Feb. 1941 and note 65 for other books.

88 Orwell in *Partisan Review*, July–Aug. 1943, Harrisson in *Horizon*, Dec. 1941 and Comfort, *op.cit.*; Orwell 'Boys' Weeklies' in S. Orwell and I. Angus, *op.cit.*; vol. 1 p. 473; D. Ireland in J. M. Reilly (ed.), *Twentieth Century Crime and Mystery Writers* (London, 1980), p. 182 for the Sax Rohmer influence; Manning Coles, *Pray Silence*, pp. 165, 234–5, 248–50.

89 Orwell in *Contemporary Jewish Record*, April 1945; M-OA: Brian Ball postcard collection no. 137 and Orwell in *Horizon*, Sept. 1941.

90 M-OA: TC Jokes Box 1 File B; for Jews as cowards in jokes, Orwell comment, 21 Oct. 1940 in S. Orwell and I. Angus, *op.cit.*; vol. 2 p. 377; BD C6/10/7/1; *A Basinful of Fun* reported in the *JC*, 17 Dec. 1943; for complaints about Jewish comedians see *JC*, 1 Dec. 1939.

91 N. Longmate, *If Britain Had Fallen* (London, 1978), p. 201 on the high circulation of Jewish jokes in the war. For comics see *Radio Fun* 13 Nov. and 25 Dec. 1943 and *The Dandy*, 11 Nov. 1939, 7 Dec. 1940, 30 May 1942 and 22 July 1944; the comic executive is quoted in Allport, *op.cit.*; p. 200; *London Opinion*, June 1944 and comment in *Reynolds News*, 25 June 1944.

92 For the offence caused to Jews see *JC*, 1 Dec. 1939, 17 Dec. 1943. The impact of such jokes is dealt with by C. Davies, 'Ethnic Jokes, Moral Values and Social Boundaries' *British Journal of Sociology*, 1982, pp. 383–403 and 'Ethnic Jokes and Social Change', *Immigrants and Minorities* IV, 1985, p. 46.

93 M-OA: TC Antisemitism File C and G; E. Allen, 13 July 1943 in NCCL 311/1; for ENSA, B. Samuel to Salomon, 22 June 1944 in BD C6/2/13 m; for music hall see M-OA: *loc.cit.*; Orwell in war diary, 25 Oct. 1940 in S. Orwell and I. Angus, *op.cit.*; vol. 2, pp. 377–8; the soldier in B. Henriques, *op.cit.*; p. 140; for the influence of popular literature see R. Usborne *Clubland Heroes* (London, 1953), pp. 3–4.

94 Henriques, *op.cit.*; p. 139; A. Hartog, *op.cit.*; p. 19; for Mosley see HO 283/16/25–6; for Bedford, G. D. Phillips, *The Diehards* (Cambridge, Mass., 1979), p. 92; for the Mass-Observer see M-OA: DR 2685 March 1943.

Chapter 5

1 Maxwell to Morrison, 11 July 1941 in HO 213/298.

2 A. Walker, May 1943 in FO 371/36662 W8627. For private government concern about antisemitism see Law to Eden, 7 May 1943 in FO 371/36731 W6933 and public denials, FO371/36725 W9383, May 1943 to Sturnbeck.

3 Lias, 30 Aug. 1942 in FO 371/30917 C7839; Dixon to Martin, 16 May 1944 in PREM 4/51/8.

4 Grant, 7 Sept. 1940 in MAF 88/140; Wilkin, 4 July 1945 in MAF 88/151 and official policy in MAF 88/140 and HO 45/387 GEN 28/9 for internees.

5 R. Hammond *Food* vol. 2 (London, 1956), p. 590; *JC*, 12 Feb. 1943; MAF 99/1137, 8 June 1943; R. Henriques, *Sir Robert Waley Cohen* (London, 1966), p. 381.

6 Numbers are in MAF 99/1137, 17 Jan. 1944. See Alderman, Sept. 1942, Wheeldon, 31 March 1943, Rosevare, 3 April 1943, Greg, 15 May 1943 and for the final response, 17 Jan. 1944 memo for Woolton *loc.cit.*

7 For the Jewish section Martin memo, 1 April 1941 in INF 1/770 and BD B5/4/3, 18 July 1941; BBC WAC 910 HER, R51/488/1 and R34/789/2; film script in INF 6/431.

8 G. Alderman, *The Jewish Community in British Politics* (Oxford, 1983), p. 78; Butler in BD E2/32 and 16 Sept. 1942 Cleary memo in ED 136/240; *JC*, 23 April, 27 Aug. 1943, 14 Jan. and 27 Oct. 1944; HMSO, *Education Act 1944* (London, 1945), pp. 14 and 20.

9 See INF 1/264 for its sources; INF 1/264 no. 108 (24 Sept. 1940) but BD C6/2/6, 6 Feb. 1943, and C6/10/27 17 March 1942, 29 April and 9 Dec. 1943 for the refusal of the Ministry of Information to actively combat antisemitism. *Daily Worker*, 20 April 1943 and NCCL 41/7, 1943 conference, called for such action.

10 Carvell to Downie, 23 Feb. 1940 in FO 371/25240/1 W2812. For fears of organised antisemitism see Anderson in CAB 98/1 CRP (39) 18 (Sept. 1939); memo 7 Aug. 1944 in HO 213/1009.

11 Hammond, *op.cit.*; pp. 777–8; MAF 102/59 and MAF 99/1217 'The Rationing Week' and minutes of 16 June 1943.

12 Board memo, 16 March 1943 in BD C6/10/27 and 10 Dec. 1943 for the black market.

13 James and Elliston in *Hansard* vol. 376 col. 494, 20 Nov. 1941; Morrison minute, 3 Dec. 1941 in HO 213/14. For a summary of the report see chapter 4 p. 122; for Morrison's refusal to publish see his minute, 21 Jan. 1942.

14 *The Week*, 4 March 1943; BBC WAC R28/20 memo, 4 May 1942 and Bracken on the press, 29 April 1943 in BD C6/10/27.

15 For the brain's trust see *New Statesman*, 27 May 1944; Bracken, 10 Dec. 1943, in BD C6/10/27.

16 Newsam, June 1943 in HO 45/25398/278–9; Morrison *loc.cit.*; 28 June 1943. For the refusal to deal with antisemitism or single out Jews see Bracken's comments in *Hansard* HC vol. 397 col. 834, 23 Feb. 1944.

17 See chapter 4 p. 126; *JC*, 16 Aug. 1940 and FO 371/24481 C5143 for early complaints; R. Ainsztein, 'Polish Antisemitism in Wartime Britain', *Wiener Library Bulletin*, 1959; for evidence of distress see NCCL 310/8 and HO 213/953; for *Jestem Polakiem* see FO 371/26737 C3668; *Catholic Herald*, 16–23 Aug. 1940; *The Patriot*, 26 June 1941.

18 *Catholic Herald*, 5 May 1944 PREM 3/352/14A for Churchill; Michael Foot in the *Evening Standard*, 27 April 1944; for the left.

19 See McClaren to Roberts, 6 March 1944 in FO 371/39480 C3193; for the new recruits see Roberts *loc.cit.*; 20 Jan. 1944 C1087.

20 A. Wilkinson, 6 May 1940 suggested that Polish army antisemitism was 'justified' in FO 371/24481 C6231; FO 371/39481 C4519 for the transfer; T. Driberg, *Ruling Passions* (London, 1977), p. 203.

21 See Harrison, 23 Feb. 1944 in FO 371/39480 C2643 for the government's response. War Office response in FO 371/39480 C3231 and Home Office, 8 Jan. 1942 in HO 213/347 and *JC*, 26 March 1943 and NCCL 45/3 give an indication of Polish antisemitism spreading; Cooper, 8 Jan. 1942 in HO 213/347 indicates Home Office desires for the Jews to return.

22 B. Porter, *The Refugee Question in Mid-Victorian Politics* (Cambridge, 1979) p. 218.

23 Wasserstein in G. Hirschfeld (ed.), *Exile in Great Britain* (Highlands, 1984), p. 79; P. Hoch, 'Gaoling the Victim', *Immigrants and Minorities*, IV, 1985, pp. 78–9 on internment books.

24 J. Bird, 'Control of Enemy Alien Civilians in Great Britain, 1914–18' (London University, PhD 1981), pp. 325–6; *Hansard* HC vol. 354 col. 367, 4 Sept. 1939 and vol. 364 col. 1542–3, 22 Aug. 1940; Maxwell, 3 Jan. 1940 in HO 213/460 for the BBC.

25 HO 213/547; for a favourable refugee response see Simpson, 28 Dec. 1939 in HO 213/455; J. Wheeler-Bennett, *John Anderson* (London, 1962), p. 122; N. Bentwich, *Wanderer in the War 1939–45* (London, 1946), p. 21: F. Tennyson Jesse and H. Harrod, *London Front* (London, 1940), p. 73 for the absence of spy mania; M-OA: FR 697; *Daily Sketch*, 10 Feb. 1940 for economic opposition.

26 *New Statesman*, 6 Jan. 1940 for the BUF; *Truth* 20 Oct. 1939; *Empire Record* Feb. and March 1940; *National Review*, Feb. 1940; *Daily Mail*, 9 Oct. 1939.

27 Esther Simpson, secretary of the AAC stresses the inconsistency and caution of magistrates in IWM refugee tapes (no. 4469). For the impact of this see nos. 4497 and 4300. Guidelines from the Home Office were improved see HO 213/547 although the problem had not been solved by Jan. 1940; classification figures in HO 213/459.

28 E. Spier, *The Protecting Power* (London, 1951), pp. 15–23; for Stern, HO 283/10/3A; Kuczynsky, D. Pritt, *The Autobiography: Part One* (London, 1965), p. 231; Natan, M. Seyfert in G. Hirschfeld; *op.cit.*; p. 165. The recent release of papers relating to internment HO 215 (general questions) and HO 214 (personal files) give little indication of *why* individuals were interned.

29 Z. Szajkoswski, *Jews, Wars and Communism* vol. 21 (New York, 1974), pp. 173–6; A. Masters, *The Man Who Was M: The Life of Maxwell Knight* (Oxford, 1984), pp. 70–1, 110.

30 *Sunday Express*, 21 Jan. 1940; *Sunday Dispatch*, 7 Jan. 1940; *Sunday Pictorial*, 28 Jan. 1940; Wheeler-Bennett, *op.cit.*; p. 239; F. Allaun in the *Manchester Guardian*, 16 Feb. 1940.

31 *Sunday Dispatch*, 21 April 1940; Angell in *Picture Post*, 6 April 1940.

32 M-OA: FR84, 26 April 1940 for the lack of press impact; the percentage in *Us*, 10 May 1940 and the economic fear in M-OA: FR 79, 25 April 1940.

33 M-OA: FR 107, 14 May 1940 for the change in opinion; *Manchester Guardian*, 13 May 1940; *The Spectator*, 17 May 1940; *Daily Herald*, 17 May 1940; *JC*, 24 May 1940; 1·3% disapproved see H. Cantril (ed.), *Public Opinion 1935–1946* (Princeton, 1951), p. 12; *New Statesman* was quiet until 15 June 1940, *Tribune*, 12 July 1940.

34 C. Caroll memo, 11 May 1940 in FO 371/25244 W7848; CAB 65/7 WM (40) 137, 24 May 1940 and 161, 11 June 1940 for the changes. Figures in HO 215/153 GEN 4/2 2B.

35 CAB 65/7 WM (40) 137, 24 May 1940 and 161, 11 June 1940 for Anderson.

36 For MI5's role see Latham and Lytton minutes, 19 March and 19 April 1941 in FO 371/29176 W3503 and M. Burkill in IWM tape no. 4494 for an indication of their suspicion of 'aliens'; Morrison to Eden, Feb. 1941 in FO 371/29173 W1810.

37 V. Caventish-Bentick used the resources excuse, 29 July 1940 in FO 371/25248 W1810; critical comments from N. Stammers, 'Civil Liberties in Britain During the Second World War' (D Phil University of Sussex, 1980), p. 101; Wells in *Reynolds News*, 28 July 1940; Martin in *New Statesman*, 27 April 1940; F. Lafitte, *The Internment of Aliens* (London, 1940), p. 27; R. Stent, *A Bespattered Page?* (London, 1980), pp. 252–3.

38 Cabinet policy in C. Caroll memo, *op.cit.*; for Churchill see CAB 65/7 WM (40) 137, 24 May 1940; for Anderson, Wheeler-Bennett, *op.cit.*; p. 247 and comments to Lord Birkett, 24 July 1940 in HO 213/455.

39 For government concern with the press see HO 199/389 and INF/319; the 'red herring' claim is by Stammers, 'Civil Liberties', p. 74; for government concern to protect the aliens see Peake in *Hansard* HC vol. 364 col. 1579, 22 Aug. 1940; Anderson in CAB 67/6 WP (G) (40) 131; the Emergency Committee 4 June 1940 called for a 'sedative' talk in INF 1/254; Bland in CAB 65/7 WM (40) 123, 15 May 1940. He broadcast on 30 May 1940.

40 M-OA: FR 107, 14 May 1940.

41 Stent, *op.cit.*; p. 79 for the *Guardian; Daily Herald*, 4 July 1940; *JC*, 21 June 1940 and INF 1/264 no. 56 (23 July 1940) for the disappearance of invasion fears and no. 49 (13 July 1940) for the Arandora Star.

42 M-OA: FR 324, 10 July 1940 and H. Cantril, *op.cit.*; p. 12 for BIPO. For later figures see M-OA: FR 424 5 Aug. 1940 and FR 486 28 Sept. 1940.

43 *Hansard* HC vol. 362 col. 1210–17, 10 July 1940 and M. Stocks, *Eleanor Rathbone* (London, 1941), p. 284; release figures in FO 371/29173 W47.

44 For Warth Mills see IWM tapes no. 4300, 4343, 3771, 4483, 3941. For camp conditions report 5 March 1941 in Manchester Guardian archive, 223/5/3; *JC*, 7 March 1941 suggested that mixing in the Huyton camp had only just been cleared up. Nazi bullying of Jewish internees was reported as late 1944 – see April 1944 report, FO 371/42786 W5196; for married camps see HO 213/1053.

45 White Papers, Cmd 6217 (July 1940) and Cmd 6233 (Aug. 1940); for the unsettling effect see A. Lomnitz, *Never Mind Mr Lom* (London, 1941), p. 138; for the Pioneer Corps, PREM 3/42/2/2 Jan. 1941 and A. Perles, *Alien Corn* (London, 1944), p. 239.

46 Morrison, 20 Nov. 1940 in HO 213/565. For Churchill's more liberal stance see FO 371/29174 W1408.

47 Stent, *op.cit.*; p. 206 on the committees. See the Asquith Committee memo, Nov. 1940 in HO 213/565 for disagreement and FO 371/29174 Churchill Minute, 25 Jan. 1941 for Lytton's resignation; release figures in FO 371/29179 W9902. For later figures see B. Wasserstein, *Britain and the Jews of Europe, 1939–45* (Oxford, 1979), p. 108; FO 371/42860 WR335 and FO 371/42786 W5555, 5 April 1944 for reinternments.

48 For the impact on health see IWM refugee tape no. 4343 and HO 214/41; for the Polish Jews, J. Mallon in *The Times*, 23 July 1940; INF 1/264 no. 57 (24 July 1940) and NCCL 46/1 – case of G. Alexander, also in HO 214/54; suicides in HO 214/8, 11, 28, 75; Hoch, *op.cit.*; refers to the nostalgia factor.

49 Sir L. Guttman on refugee scientists leaving for America – IWM tape no. 4596; for Cruickshank see tape 4296 and HO 215/405; tape no. 4445 for the Manx landlady; P. and L. Gillman, *Collar the Lot!* (London, 1980), p. 253 and HO 215/263 for the Dunera, including a diary of one of its internees.

50 D. Thorneycroft, 2 Nov. 1941 of Worthing Refugee Committee in Kingsley Martin papers, Box 29 File 6; HO 213/432 indicates that some refugees preferred life as internees.

51 M-OA: FR 486, 8 Nov. 1940 indicates that the air raids revived the spy scare and 43% wanted mass internment in Oct. 1940; for later accusations see JDC report, 20 March 1944 in BD C6/7/5/1 and Lord Ailwyn in *Hansard* HL vol. 135 col. 121, 27 Feb. 1945. Economic opposition to refugees led to the formation of the Refugees Industries Committee and its work increased towards the end of the war – see Loebl in Hirschfeld, *op.cit.*; pp. 234–5.

52 For Anderson see memo 8 Feb. 1939 in HO 213/259; and his comments 13 and 23 Sept. 1939 in HO 213/262. For other medical antisemitism see *Medical World* throughout the war; memo, 'Doctors Position', 26 Oct. 1939 in HO 213/262 for the Home Office response and Maxwell note 4 Sept. 1939.

53 H. Parker, *Manpower* (London, 1957), p. 346, which suggest 90% of employable aliens were in work by 1943; the BUF revival fear – H. Prestige, 7 Aug. 1944 in HO 213/1009 and Morrison, 6 March 1942 in HO 213/1347; refugee industrialists in HO 213/1353 Feb. 1944.

54 'Employment of Aliens', 13 June 1945 in HO 213/500; liberal policy, Shackle minute, 10 April 1946 in BT 64/163, 29 Jan. 1940. For Ministry of Labour position see their 'Employment Policy in Regard to Aliens', 1944 in HO 213/1350. For refugee concern see Loebl, *op.cit.*; pp. 234–5.

55 Maxwell, 4 Sept. 1939 in HO 213/262; refugee figure, Feb. 1942 in HO 213/1347.

56 Major works are D. Wyman, *The Abandonment of the Jews, 1941–1945* (New York, 1984); Wasserstein's, *Britain and the Jews;* M. Gilbert, *Auschwitz and the Allies* (London, 1981). For a review see R. Breitman, 'The Allied War Effort and the Jews', *Journal of Contemporary History*, XX, 1985.

57 Figures are in HO 213/1009 and E. Rathbone, *Continuing Terror* (London, 1944), p. 10. E. Rathbone, *Rescue the Perishing* (London, 1943), p. 11 believes the Jewish total was small. The Anglo-American Committee of Inquiry (Cmd 6808, 1946), p. 59 gives a net increase in population of 10,000 or 20,000 gross. Wasserstein, *op.cit.*; pp. 81–2 comments on the problem of finding adequate statistics. For those who did escape to Britain in the war see C. Klein, *Escape from Berlin* (London, 1944); *The Times*, 8 Dec. 1981 for Ainsztein and *The Guardian*, 20 April 1985 for Henry Young. For Cornwall see E. Baumel, 'The Jewish Refugee Children in Great Britain' (Bar Ilan University, MA, 1981), p. 144.

58 Visa policy, Cooper to Randall, 18 Sept. 1939 in FO 371/24100 W13792; CAB 98/1 CRP (39), 25 Sept. 1939; Cooper, *loc.cit.*; for exemptions and Maxwell, 11 Dec. 1939 in HO 213/447.

59 Cooper, *op.cit.* for security concern and Maxwell *loc.cit.* for MI5 in particular; for the Colonial Office see R. Zweig, 'British Policy to Palestine: May 1939 to 1943' (PhD Cambridge, 1978), pp. 204, 243–58, 340–86; Downie, 9 May 1940 in CO 111/772/60412; 20 March 1940 in FO 371/25240/1 W2812 and 25 Jan. 1941 in CO 773/445/23.

60 Latham, 22 April 1941 in FO 371/27132 E1240; *The Patriot*, 12 Oct. 1939; for the Struma, Randall note on the Colonial Office response, 12 Feb. 1942 in FO 371/32661 W2093 and Wasserstein, *op.cit.*; pp. 143–57 and Zweig, 'British Policy', pp. 362–86. For the lack of evidence over spies see Downie to Snow, 3 Jan. 1941 in FO 371/29160 W188.

61 Maxwell, 18 Dec. 1939 in HO 213/447.

62 Latham, 4 April 1940, Burt 8 April 1940, Carvell 15 April 1940 in FO 371/25240/1 W2812.

63 Morrison, 28 Oct. 1942 in FO 371/32681 W14673 and Namier to Crozier, 30 Oct. 1942, Manchester Guardian archive, B/N8A/134 for a negative assessment of the meeting; Morrison's figures in CAB 66/29 WP(42) 427, 28 Sept. 1942 and WP (42) 444, 2 Oct. 1942.

64 CAB 95/15 JR (43), 31 Dec. 1942 and 8 Jan. 1943; for Bermuda see CAB 65/34 WN (43), 10 May 1943 and the 'token' quote by R. Law, 29 Jan. 1943 in FO 371/36694 W416.

65 The 'slander' quote is by J. Pledge, 4 March 1943 in FO 371/36654 W 3957. Foreign Office alarm over the rumour is shown in FO 371/36651 W2069. For the National Committee, see the minutes 1943–6, in the Parkes papers, 15.057, and Randall minutes in FO 371/36651 W2139 for the huge impact of Gollancz's *Let My People Go*. Its poll was published in *News Chronicle*, 26 March 1943.

66 M-OA: FR 1648 and M-OA: DR 2684, 3127, 2703, 3052 March 1943 where repugnance for Jews did not necessarily rule out sympathy for European Jewry. For Nicolson see his comments in *The Spectator*, 25 Dec. 1942. M-OA: DR 3207, 3003 March 1943 were hostile to Jews but still sent letters of protest to the government after reading Gollancz. Foreign Office papers are littered with such letters. See Cheetham minute, 4 May 1944 in FO 371/42751 W6988 for indifference to them.

67 Meeting with Ministry of Information, 19 Feb. 1942 in BD B5/3/6. The government's aim of holding back humanitarian feeling after Eden's declaration on behalf of European Jewry in the Commons, is made clear by Randall, minute 29

Jan. 1943 in FO 371/36694 W416; *New Statesman*, 2 Jan. 1943.

68 For fear of a flood see Randall, 28 Dec. 1942 in FO 371/32668 W17422; Wyman, *op.cit.*; pp. 105–23 on Bermuda; and Walker minute, 17 Sept. 1943 in FO 371/36666 after it; H. Rauschning, *Hitler Speaks* (London, 1939), p. 233.

69 For contemporary criticism of Morrison by a 'conservative' on refugee matters, see R. Law note, 16 Dec. 1942 in FO 371/32682 W17401; B. Donoughue and G. Jones, *Herbert Morrison* (London, 1973), pp. 249–58, 255; N. Laski description, Oct. 1936 in AJ 33/90.

70 Laski, *op.cit.*; Alderman, *op.cit.*; p. 116. Morrison's comments are in HO 213/14; the Zionist quote is by Namier to Crozier, 17 May 1943, B/N8A/231 in Manchester Guardian archive. For Morrison's aim to return the refugees see Randall's comments, Dec. 1943 in FO 371/36672 W17585.

71 Rathbone to Eden, 25 Feb. 1943 in FO 371/36653 W3321 on refused visas. See HO 213/615 for the continued refusal to help the Vichy Jewish children up to 1945. The policy of helping only 'useful' refugees was told to a refugee delegation, 11 Jan. 1944 in FO 371/42751 W544. For Bermuda see CAB 65/34 WM (43), 10 May 1943 and *Hansard* HC vol. 389 col. 1117–1204, 19 May 1943. For hatred of Morrison see Stocks, *op.cit.*; p. 300.

72 Such propaganda was urged by the Archbishop of Canterbury, *Hansard* HL vol. 126 col. 812, 23 March 1943.

73 Cadogan minute, 16 Sept. 1939 in FO 371/23105 C16788; *The Times*, 28 Sept. 1939. The Niemoller quote is by Roberts, 16 Oct. 1939, Goebbel's by Sargent, 29 Sept. 1939.

74 R. Kee, *The World We Left Behind* (London, 1984), p. 329. For doubt see *Truth*, 3 Nov. 1939, *Action*, 2 Nov. 1939 and *Bristol Evening News*, 30 Nov. 1939. For support see most of the national press including *The Times*, 31 Oct. 1939; government's doubts over the success of the White paper, Sargent minute, 5 Feb. 1940 in FO 371/24422 C2026. Roberts minute 8 April 1940 in FO 371/24423 C5475 indicates that Jewish suffering was not to be emphasised; Leeper minute, 21 April 1940 in FO 371/24472 C5471.

75 Loune minute, 16 April 1940 in *ibid*; the broadcast was by Lord Lytton. See Latham's objections, 22 Jan. 1941 in FO 371/29173 W821. For the Ministry of Information see INF 1/251 Pt. 4 and circular, 25 Nov. 1939 in FO 371/24548 E297, and for exceptions to this policy see the *JC*, 26 Sept. 1941 and Gilbert, *op.cit.*; pp. 39–46, and pp. 59–63 for the Bund report.

76 Downie minute, 25 Jan. 1941 in CO 733/445/23; Bennett, 7 Dec. 1942 in FO 921/10; the 'wild story' quote by Allen, 10 Sept. 1942 in FO 371/30917 C7853; Emerson memo, 14 Dec. 1942 in FO 371/32682 W17272; the standard government line by Lias to Grubb, 30 Aug. 1942 in FO 371/30917 C7839 and desire to avoid the word 'Jew', Cheetham minute, 27 Nov. 1942 in FO 371/32681 W14673.

77 Namier to Crozier, 7 Dec. 1942 in Manchester Guardian archive, 223/5/49; Eden in *Hansard* HC vol. 385 col. 2082–9, 17 Dec. 1942; R. James (ed.), *Chips; The Diary of Sir Henry Channon* (London, 1967), p. 347 and INF 1/292 no. 117 (22–29 Dec. 1942) for the popular response.

78 Foreign Office minutes in FO 371/36673 W17929 for belief that it was a mistake; Roberts minute, 11 May 1944 in FO 371/42790 W 7937 and Cranbourne in *Hansard* HL vol. 126 col. 812, 23 March 1943 for the refusal to single out Jews. Comments on the Jewish Agency, Walker, 2 July 1943 in FO 371/36663 W9659, and CAB 95/15 JR (43) 20th meeting for Bermuda. For the film see INF 1/636 and N. Ascherson in *Observer*, 8 Sept. 1985.

79 V. Caventish-Bentinck, 27 Aug. 1943 in FO 371/34551 C9705; Henderson, 15 March 1944 in FO 371/42790 W3924 and Dew, 1 Sept. 1944 for 'wailing Jews' in FO 371/42817 WR993.

80 Henderson, 11 Jan. 1945 in FO 371/51134 WR89 and FO 371/51185; Parkes, *Voyage of Discoveries* (London, 1969), p. 180.

81 Wyman, *op.cit.*; p. 79 quotes a survey in America in Jan. 1943 when 47% believed that 2 million Jews had been killed, 29% believing it was a rumour. Y. Bauer, *The Holocaust in Historical Perspective* (London, 1978), p. 83 suggests the British were better informed and M-OA: DR March 1943 confirms this analysis. For the only major propaganda coverage concentrating on the Jews see PWE directives, 10–31 Dec. 1942 in FO 898/289.

82 Wasserstein, *op.cit.*; pp. 351–7; Latham, 1 Feb. 1941 in FO 371/27132 E1240. For the bombing of Auschwitz see Gilbert, *op.cit.*; pp. 267–73, 318–22. The Home Office quote is by Prestige, 7 Aug. 1944 in HO 213/1009; Bennett reported by Rex Bloomstein in *The Listener*, 16 Sept. 1982.

83 Bennett in Dec. 1942 commented that the demand that Jews should be regarded as an allied people was 'a major fallacy'. In FO 921/10. Such blatantness was rare, but the substance of the comment summarised a wider governmental view; Breitman, *op.cit.*; p. 152.

84 Nov. 1945 memo in FO 371/45383 E8450.

85 10 Aug. 1939 memo on Jews in INF 1/770; Butler minute, 19 Feb. 1943 in FO 371/34362 C1741.

86 Thus Zionism was frowned upon – see Foreign Office minutes on the Zionist takeover of the Board of Deputies, in FO 371/36741 W12242.

Chapter 6

1 R. Lehmann, *Nova Bibliotheca Anglo-Judaica* (London, 1961), p.ix.

2 R. Routledge, *Report on the Records of the Board of Deputies of British Jews* (London, 1978), pp. i–xv; S. Salomon, *The Deputies* (London, 1937); Z. Szajkoswski, 'Conflicts in the Alliance Israelite Universelle and the Founding of the Anglo-Jewish Association . . . ', *Jewish Social Studies*, XIX, 1957, p. 32; V. Lipman, *A Century of Social Service 1859–1959: The History of the Jewish Board of Guardians* (London, 1959); *The Jewish Chronicle 1841–1941* (London, 1949).

3 S. Bayme, 'Jewish Leadership and Anti-Semitism in Britain, 1898–1918' (PhD, Columbia University, 1977), pp. 234–60 deals with the restraints on the Board. See the *JC*, 27 Oct. 1911 and BD C16/1 for its Shechita Committee; G. Alderman, *The Jewish Community in British Politics* (Oxford, 1983), p. 87 for Sunday Trading.

4 Bayme 'Jewish Leadership', pp. 43–7, 243–4 for its inaction against antisemitism and the *Eastern Post*, 20 Sept. 1902 for the Committee.

5 Alderman, *op.cit.*, p. 74; J. Buckman, *Immigrants and the Class Struggle* (Manchester, 1983) and J. White, *Rothschilds Building* (London, 1980) for class aspects; Lipman, *op.cit.*; p. 94 for the deportations.

6 B. Williams in A. Kidd and K. Roberts (ed.), *City, Class and Culture*

(Manchester, 1985), pp. 77–8 for the *Manchester Guardian*; I. Cohen, *A Jewish Pilgrimage* (London, 1956), p. 60 for *Tribune* and P. Colbenson 'British Socialism and Antisemitism, 1884–1914' (PhD, Georgia State University, 1977), pp. 449–90 for the left in general. See Chapter 4 for assimilationist thought. A. Edelstein, 'Philo-Semitism and the Survival of European Jewry' (PhD City University of New York, 1977), p. 30 fails to differentiate philosemitism from anti-antisemitism.

7 Bayme, 'Jewish Leadership', pp. 256–7, 292–316 for the war and also S. Cohen, *English Zionists and British Jews* (Princeton, 1982), p. 267. J. Bush, *Behind the Lines: East London Labour 1914–19* (London, 1984), pp. 174–5 for the FJPC and BSP and Board of Deputies, *Annual Report 1915* (London, 1916) for internment.

8 L. Wolfe, *The Jewish Bogey and the Forged Protocols of the Learned Elders of Zion* (London, 1920) and HO 45/24765/ 432156 for deportation complaints.

9 *Daily Mail*, 1 March 1926 refers to clashes between the ILP and the National Fascists; R. Waterman, *A Family of Shopkeepers* (London, 1973), pp. 169–84 and M. Levine, *Cheetham to Cordova* (Manchester, 1984), p. 14 for early Jewish CP involvement.

10 N. Branson, *History of the Communist Party of Great Britain 1927–1941* (London, 1985), pp. 110–29, 159–71; Alderman, *op.cit.*; p. 115 for the CPGB and B. Donoughue and G. Jones, *Herbert Morrison* (London, 1973), pp. 224–5 for the Labour Party.

11 G. Lebzelter, *Political Anti-Semitism in England 1918–39* (London, 1978), pp. 139–42 deals with the JPC as does P. Piratin, *The Flag Stays Red* (London, 1948), pp. 19–26 and L. Samuel in the *Jewish Quarterly* (Winter 1956), p. 35. The split with the Board is covered in a letter from N. Laski to S. Salomon, 8 Dec. 1936 in the Parkes papers, 15.053. The Board's secretary's reponse, 24 June 1937 is in the Spector documents 610, Wiener Library. See S. Rawnsley 'Fascism and Fascists in Britain in the 1930s' (PhD University of Bradford, 1981), p. 297 for the 1939 change.

12 JDC *The Problem and Meaning of Jewish Defence* (Leicester, 1944); S. Salomon 'Now it Can be Told' (London, 1950) for its contacts. C. Holmes, *Anti-Semitism in British Society 1876–1939* (London, 1979), pp. 200–2, refers to successful pressure, see BD C15/3/33 for failure with *Truth*. Yard correspondence in BD C6/10/29. For the Board, the government and refugees, Hoare in CAB 23/96 Conclusion 55 (38), 16 Nov. 1938.

13 Parkes on his own work, *Enemy of the People* in Parkes papers, 07.006, 005; L. Golding, *The Jewish Problem* (Harmondsworth, 1938), p. 11.

14 M. Lilly, *The National Council for Civil Liberties* (London, 1984); Lebzelter, *op.cit.*; pp. 165–7.

15 For co-operation see BD C6/9/1/3 F3, 3 Oct. 1939. The Board quote is by Salomon, 27 Jan. 1944 in BD C6/2/13b. For the pressure on the Ministry of Information see BD C6/9/1/3/F3 and HO 144/21429/4–5. For *JC* pressure see issues of 3 Nov. and 29 Dec. 1939 and Salomon, *loc.cit.* for the Board's change.

16 N. Laski papers, AJ 33/158 for the leaflet; *Daily Worker*, 21 Feb. 1940 and J. Attfield and S. Williams, *1939: The Communist Party and the War* (London, 1983), p. 183 for Silvertown and INF 1/139 for phoney war policy; BD 6/9/1/3 F3 for Wilmslow.

17 Salomon, 'Now It Can Be Told'; *Daily Worker*, 27 May 1940; R. Swingler, 'Antisemitism: Secret Weapon of the Ruling Class', *Daily Worker*, 14 Oct. 1940.

18 D. Hyde, *I Believed* (London, 1951), pp. 139–40.

19 *Daily Worker*, 10 April 1943 for opposition to the BNP; Hyde interview with author, 17 Sept. 1983.

20 JDC reports, 11 Dec. 1942 and 30 Nov. 1944 in BD C6/2/6; BD C15/3/9 for links with Marx House; Salomon, 30 June 1944 in BD C6/2/13m.

21 INF 1/292 no. 164 (16–23 Nov. 1943); A. Calder, *The People's War* (London, 1969), p. 551; HO 45/24894 for popular opposition to Mosley's release; Abramsky in the *JC*, 24 Dec. 1943 on the Board's inaction. See AJ/3, 1943 letter to Greenberg for *JC*/Board confrontation and the *East End Observer*, 8 May 1942 for the 'Friends'. Hyde, interview with author, 17 Sept. 1983 suggests the Board put pressure on the *JC* not to devote too much space to neo-fascist groups. See the *Daily Worker*, 6, 13 and 20 Nov. 1944 for opposition to the League and A. Hartog, *Born to Sing* (London, 1978), pp. 70–77 for the '43' group.

22 JDC note 'Future tasks', 18 Nov. 1942 in BD B5/4/3; 'A Duty to Britain' in Manchester Jewish Museum; JDC memorandum, 1940 in BD C6/2/6; JDC 'Internal Causes of Anti-Semitism' (1942) in BD C6/9/1/3 F5 and 'Defence of Aliens', 1940 in BD C2/2/6.

23 For the origins of the TAC see M. Freedman (ed.), *A Minority in Britain* (London, 1955), p. 217; memo, 6 Aug. 1945 in BD C6/2/13a for its success.

24 For the Zionist take-over see *JC*, 11 June and 2 July 1943; M. Orbach, 'Noah Barou and the TAC', in H. Infield (ed.), *Essays in Jewish Sociology, Labour and Co-operation in Memory of Dr. Noah Barou* (London, 1962), pp. 31–3. Chapter 4 pp. 127–8 outlines TAC language; *JC*, 31 July 1942 for TAC/JDC conflict.

25 *The Problem and Meaning of Jewish Defence*; S. Salomon draft on 'The Protocols', May 1944, BD C15/3/20 Fl.

26 *Civil Liberty*, March 1940 on East End fascism; *loc.cit.*; Jan. and June 1940 for attacks on non-organised antisemitism and *Daily Worker*, 5 Oct. 1939, 8 Jan., 29 March 1940 similarly. *Civil Liberty*, Oct. 1939 and R. Kidd, *British Liberty in Danger* (London, 1940), pp. 211–17, on 18B. Communist influence was denied by Kidd and E. M. Forster in *Time and Tide*, 28 June 1941. For Allen see J. Lynx (ed.), *The Future of the Jews* (London, 1945), p. 193. For the leaflet see NCCL 100/13; D. N. Pritt, *The People's Convention 1941* (London, 1941).

27 E. Allen, *It Shall Not Happen Here* (London, 1943); Allen in *Civil Liberty* July–Aug. 1942; the 1943 AGM in NCCL 41/8 and 41/7 for the campaign. Her belief in discussion is evident in Lynx, *op.cit.*; p. 98. Her attacks on all forms of hostility in *It Shall Not Happen Here*, pp. 24, 30–31.

28 *Daily Worker*, 19 April 1943; Hyde, *op.cit.*; p. 187; Holmes in the *Daily Worker*, 19 Dec. 1942; NJC minutes, 8 Dec. 1943 in Zaidman collection.

29 For NJC origins see H. Srebrnik, 'The Jewish Communist Movement in Stepney' (PhD University of Birmingham, 1983), pp. 100–101; for its anti-zionism; *Jewish Standard*, 26 May 1944; NJC, *The Jewish Question*, (London, 1944), pp. 18–19; Piratin, *op.cit.*; pp. 79–86, 201 and Srebrnik, *loc.cit.*; pp. 201–18 for the Mile End campaign.

30 W. Gallacher, *Antisemitism: What It Means to You*, (London, 1943) and I. Rennap, *Anti-Semitism and the Jewish Question* (London, 1942) stress its divisive quality; Palme Dutt, memo 10 Jan. 1943 in CUP 1262K4, British Library. For the

Workers Circle link see the Zaidman papers. William Rust, standing as the Communist in South Hackney, 1945, stated he would encourage Jewish cultural needs, also in the Zaidman collection. See Rennap, *op.cit.*; pp. 49–54, and H. Levy in the *Jewish Standard*, 16 June 1944 for opposition to assimilationist solutions.

31 Labour Party opposition from NEC member James Walker at the 1943 AGM is quoted by Poale Zion, *Labour and the Jewish People* (London 1943), p. 9. Haldane Club support in Middleton papers, 15 Dec. 1942, JSM/210/198.

32 See Barou in the TAC's *Monthly Bulletin*, Dec. 1944 and *JC*, 4 June 1943. The Board's response is in BD C4/2 and 3 and C6/7/3/2 memo on the Porter Committee, 1945; its concern with the CPGB in Law and Parliamentary Committee minutes, 4 June 1943, BD C13/1/12 and the NCCL in general minutes, 17 Oct. 1943, BD A32; G. Allport, *The Nature of Prejudice* (Reading, Mass. 1954), p. 468 on the impact of legislation in America.

33 See Chapter 6 for this issue; NCCL 45/4 for the Stoll Theatre; HO 213/347, 8 Jan. 1942 and FO 371/39480 C1087 for the Board's governmental negotiations; letter, 2 May 1944, in NCCL 45/4 for its refusal to support the public campaign. T. Driberg, *Ruling Passions* (London, 1977), p. 203 has critical comments on the Board; Z. Avital, 'The Polish Government in Exile and the Jewish Question: 1943–51', *Wiener Library Bulletin*, 1975, p. 47.

34 See Chapter 6 for the Polish Jews, Chapter 3 for evacuees.

35 R. Stent, *A Bespattered Page?* (London, 1980), p. 67; Simpson's IWM refugee tape no. 4469.

36 Winterton in *Hansard* HC vol. 364 col. 1539–41. Brodetsky wrote to Winterton, 23 Sept. 1940 asking him to recant, but he refused – BD archive, photocopies in possession of R. Stent; Gal, IWM refugee tape no. 4304. The German Aid Committee quote is in a Mepol report, 3 Feb. 1942 in HO 215/169 Gen 4/10/2. See refugee tapes nos. 4584, 4300 4479 for problems with Bloomsbury House and Sir John Lawrence in *Sunday Times*, 23 Feb. 1986.

37 *The Report of the Central Council for Jewish Refugees 1940* and Stent, *op.cit.*; p. 67 for internment policy; *East End Observer*, 27 July 1940 for the 'Committee'. See Chapter 5 p. 145–7 for *JC*'s changes over this issue; N. Bentwich, *They Found Refuge* (London, 1956), p. 121 on the 'happy' relations between the government and Bloomsbury House.

38 See Chapter 5 p. 156–7 for the public response; Harrisson in Mass-Observation, *War Begins at Home* (London, 1940), p. 183; *Time and Tide*, 13 April 1940; M-OA: DR Oct. 1940.

39 M-OA: DR 2486, 1206, 2669 Oct. 1940.

40 Opposition is referred to in W. W. Simpson's unpublished 'Autobiography' pp. 2, 17; informal Jewish-Christian links are evident in BD C15/3/17 memo, 1939. See also Bentwich, *op.cit.*; p. 121.

41 In CCJ archive and BD C15/3/21. The Society's minutes are in the Parkes papers, 15.076. Pressure for a new group by Simpson and Waley Cohen in BD C15/3/21 F2. Parkes *loc.cit.*; 16 June 1942 resigned over the 'Jewish' aims. The Christian quote is by William Temple, Archbishop of York in 'Aims of the CCJ', 20 March 1942 in CCJ archive.

42 Attacks on the black market are in Executive minutes, 7 May, 5 Nov. 1942. See Simpson's comments to Salomon, 4 Sept. 1941 in BD C15/3/20 F2 on A. Cohen's, *The Psychology of Antisemitism* (London, 1941).

43 For diplomatic work see CCJ Executive minutes, 4 March 1943. On 13 April 1942 the CCJ passed a model resolution for church groups to record their concern at Nazi antisemitism, but the CCJ appears to have taken no action until much later that year.

44 For the Law delegation see FO 371/32682 W17401 and CCJ Executive minutes, 3 Dec. 1942 and 7 Jan. 1943; Brodetsky to Greenberg, 8 Dec. 1942 in AJA 110/4.

45 Law, 16 Dec. 1942 in FO 371/32682 W17401. The Foreign Office description is by Randall, 22 Dec. 1942 in *loc.cit.*; W17521. Law, 18 Dec. 1942, *loc.cit.*; referred to the 'new situation' and his recommendation, 29 Dec. 1942 is in FO 371/36651 W2069; Law, 29 Jan. 1943 in FO 371/36694 W416.

46 Law was aware of the CCJ's distrust of Morrison – see comments of 16 Dec. 1942 in FO 371/32682 W17401. Eleanor Rathbone, whilst critical of Morrison, absolved the Refugee Department of the Foreign Office – see her comments, 9 Aug. 1943 in FO 371/36665. The delegation to Law, 29 Jan. 1943 is in FO 371/36694 W416, Law's response, 7 May 1943 in FO 371/36731 W6933.

47 For the Bermuda Conference see Chapter 5; Roberts comments, 24 April 1943 in FO 371/36658 W5550 and 12 Oct. 1944 in FO 371/39454 C14201; N. Bentwich, *Wanderer in War 1939–45* (London, 1946), pp. 102–3; S. Brodetsky, *Memoirs* (London, 1960), p. 208 and M. Sompolinsky, 'The Anglo-Jewish Leadership, the British Government and the Holocaust' (PhD, Bar Ilan University, 1977).

48 See the minutes of the National Committee, 1943–5 in the Parkes papers 15.057; V. Gollancz, *Let My People Go* (London, 1942) and E. Rathbone, *Rescue the Perishing* (London, 1943). For letters see *The Times*, 22 Dec. 1942, 9 and 16 Feb. 1943; and resolutions in FO 371/36655 W4400 and FO 371/42751 W6988. For its later struggle, minutes 21 July 1943 and H. Nicolson in *The Spectator*, 17 Dec. 1943.

49 The suggestion is by B. Litvinoff, *A Peculiar People* (London, 1969), pp. 152–3. M. Gilbert. *Auschwitz and the Allies* (London, 1981), pp. 135–6 has details of Zygielbojm, the unidentified minute is in FO 371/26172 quoted by B. Wasserstein, *Britain and the Jews of Europe 1939–45* (Oxford, 1979), p. 37. The Jewish dilemma was recognised by Brotman and Brodetsky in a meeting with Law, 29 Jan. 1943 in FO 371/36694 W416.

50 Executive minutes, CCJ 4 March 1943 and for attention on domestic antisemitism, 6 May 1943. Chapter 5 deals with the Board's meetings with the Home Office and Ministry of Information on antisemitism. Holmes, *op.cit.*; pp. 107–8 on the Board varying on the issue of antisemitism. Litvinoff, *op.cit.*; pp. 152–3 on its fear of appearing disloyal.

51 See HO 45/24894 for the government reaction to the outcry against Mosley's release. Morrison stressed antisemitic sentiment rather than the reverse to a deputation, 28 Oct. 1942, in FO 371/32681 W1463. In April 1943 a meeting of Bloomsbury House delegates followed the government line, not referring to Jews but to refugees. See Namier to Crozier, 15 April 1943 in Manchester Guardian archive, B/N8A/209. The demand for respectability was strong within the CCJ. See its Executive minutes, 8 April 1943 and 16 May 1944.

52 For a cross-section of the leaflets see BD C15/2/4. A JDC report, 18 Nov. 1942 in BD B5/4/3 acknowledged its weakness; N. Bentwich, *op.cit.*; pp. 178–9.

53 For criticisms see the *Jewish Standard*, 31 Dec. 1943 and self-awareness of weaknesses by the Board, Brodetsky in preliminary CCJ meeting, 19 Nov. 1941 and similarly *JC*, 15 Dec. 1944; *Truth*, 8 Dec. 1944 and 5 Jan. 1945; *The Patriot*, 27 Feb. 1941.

54 F. Weiss, *Insanity . . . abounding* (London, 1942), and Salomon review, *JC*, 5 Feb. 1943.

55 For the black market see Chapter 5 and Bracken, 10 Dec. 1943 in BD C6/10/27: M-OA: DR 1313, March 1943 was not convinced about Jewish involvement despite hearing a BBC denial; Hill in *Hansard* HC vol. 389 col. 1182–9, 19 May 1943 and also letter to Simpson, 8 June 1943 in BD C15/3/21 F2. For attacks on black market antisemitism see *Evening Standard*, 25 July 1942; *Manchester Guardian*, 14 Jan. 1942 – used in defence of Jews by Home Office official – AM note, 16 Jan. 1942 in HO 213/14.

56 JDC report, 23 June 1942 in BD executive minutes, and BD C6/2/13a for the impact of defence literature; *New Statesman*, 24 April 1943; *Kilburn Times*, May–June 1944 for debate on a public meeting in Willesden; NCCL 45/1 for press discussions.

57 M-OA: DR 2512, 3003, 3356 March 1943 suggest a negative impact with a recent *New Statesman* debate; NCCL 4/8 concentrated on the idea that antisemitism was organised. The National Council of Labour Colleges told Salomon, 17 July 1944 that organised talks on the dangers of antisemitism did 'much good'-BD C15/3/19.

58 Anon, *Britain's Fifth Column* (Tiptree, 1940), p. 8; J. Lunn, *Treachery and Antisemitism*, (London, 1942); I. Cohen, 'Antisemitism and Treachery' *New Statesman*, 30 May 1942 and *Truth*, 5 June 1942 in response.

59 H. Pelling, *The British Communist Party* (London, 1975), pp. 139 and 192; Marx House, *Anti-Semitism: A Nazi Weapon* (London, 1944), p. 1; J. Gollan, 'Antisemitism' *Labour Monthly*, June 1943, p. 177; Gallacher, *op.cit.*; pp. 3–12 reads like a Board defence pamphlet; *JC*, 18 Feb. 1944 suggested that JDC work was at last bearing fruit as non-Jews were using it.

60 *Lancashire News*, Feb. 1943 indicates the widespread nature of the CPGB campaign; Low in the *Evening Standard*, 18 June 1943; S. Goldberg, *What of the Jews?* (London, 1944); *Daily Express*, 7 Jan. 1943.

61 Details of the Defence Fund are in BD C6/7/5/1. For its failure see *JC*, 31 Dec. 1943 and 7 Jan. 1944 and Board Executive minutes, 18 June 1944 for recognition of public disagreements. For left-wing Jewish success in fund raising see H. Srebrnik, 'The Jewish Communist Movement', p. 187. The Board's own defence is in *The Problem and Meaning of Jewish Defence*, p. 3; Gollancz's in 22 May 1944 in BD C15/3/17 and C6/10/22.

62 Bayme, 'Jewish Leadership', p. 319 on its limited options; *JC*, 22 Dec. 1944; critique by Alderman, *op.cit.*; p. 116.

63 Salomon, 25 Feb. 1942 in BD C6/2/13b for business behaviour, *JC*, 9 Aug. 1940 for economic diversity; Board of Deputies, *Annual Report 1943*, (London, 1944), p. 28 on social ostentation; JDC, *While You are in England* (London, 1939) warned the refugees. The 'disease' comment is in JDC 18 Nov. 1942 in BD B5/4/3 and the psychological analysis in Cohen, *op.cit.*.

64 For Bell see Calder, *op.cit.*; pp. 484, 92 and R. Jasper, *George Bell*, (London, 1967); Chief Rabbi to Brodetsky, 26 May 1942 in BD C15/3/21;

W. Simpson interview with author, 6 April 1984.

65 Parkes to Brotman, 15 June 1942 in BD C15/3/21 F2 and his *Voyage of Discoveries* (London, 1969), pp. 149, 174–5. Simpson, interview with author, 6 April 1984 regarded the CCJ as 'a little ahead of public opinion'.

66 R. Crossman, *Palestine Mission* (London, 1947), p. 27; G. Sacks, *The Jewish Question* (London, 1937), p. 87.

67 The CPGB Leaflet 'Antisemitism: Plain Speaking' attacked all forms of antisemitism and *Daily Worker*, 17 April 1943 castigated *Railway Review* on this ground; Gollan, *op.cit.*; p. 181; W. Holmes in *Daily Worker*, 30 June 1944.

68 *New Statesman*, 9 Dec. 1939, 27 April 1940, 13 Feb., 20 March, 24 April 1943; *Tribune*, 31 May 1940, 6 March 1942, 29 Jan. 1943, 21 July 1944; *Time and Tide*, 28 Oct. 1939, 24 April 1943; *Reynolds News*, 14 March 1943; *News Chronicle*, 1 April 1943; Driberg in *Daily Express*, 7 Jan. 1943; Nicolson in *The Spectator*, 27 Oct. 1939, 16 Jan. 1942; Deedes in *The Highway*, Dec. 1944.

69 For Priestley and Macneice chapter 5; Calder, *op.cit.*; p. 498; M-OA: FR 1993, Jan. 1944.

70 M-OA: DR 2281, 1578 Oct. 1940.

71 Simpson, interview with author, 9 Sept. 1984; *JC*, 30 April, 9 July, 6 Aug., 3 Sept. 1943 and NCCL 45/2 for 'Unity'.

72 M-OA: FR A12; R. Breitman, 'The Allied War Effort and the Jews, 1942–3' *Journal of Contemporary History*, 1985, p. 152.

Conclusion

1 L. Dawidowicz, *The War Against the Jews, 1933–45* (Harmondsworth, 1983), p. 479.

2 I. Cohen, *Contemporary Jewry* (London, 1950), pp. 221–3; *Jewish Echo*, 6 Oct. 1944 for violence against ex-servicemen; *Time*, 10 June 1943 for the U.S.A.

3 M. Marrus and R. Paxton, *Vichy France and the Jews* (New York, 1983), pp. 356–9; Y. Bauer, *The Holocaust in Historical Perspective* (London, 1978), pp. 52–62 for Poland; L. Yahil, *The Rescue of Danish Jewry*, (Philadelphia, 1969); J. Presser, *Ashes in the Wind; The Destruction of Dutch Jewry*, (London, 1968).

4 R. Maugham, *Jersey under the Jackboot* (London, 1946), p. 38; N. Longmate, *If Britain Had Fallen* (London, 1972), p. 201.

5 C. Sykes, *Two Studies in Virtue* (London, 1953), p. 135; J. Vincent in *The Times Higher Education Supplement*, 16 Nov. 1979; P. Howard in *The Times*, 19 Oct. 1984 refers to the golf-club variety; *JC*, 7 Feb. 1936.

6 R. Kee, *The World We Left Behind: A Chronicle of 1939* (London, 1984), p. 248; B. Halpern, 'America is Different' in M. Sklare (ed.), *The Jew in American Society* (New York, 1974), p. 72; *New English Weekly*, 25 June 1942.

7 L. Baker, *Days of Sorrow and Pain: Leo Baeck and the Berlin Jews*, (New York, 1978), p. 221; Marrus and Paxton, *op.cit.*; pp. 25–6.

8 Marrus and Paxton, *op.cit.*; pp. 58–71, 121–76; see Chapter 5 for deportations and rescue policy; N. Nicolson (ed.), *Harold Nicolson: Diaries and Letters, 1930–1939* (London, 1966), pp. 52–3 for the Foreign Office; M. Box, *Odd Woman Out* (London, 1974), pp. 155–6 for the Air Ministry; Namier to Crozier, 28 Feb. 1940 for Palestine Land discrimination in Manchester Guardian archive B/N8A/5.

9 S. Gordon, *Hitler, Germans and the 'Jewish Question'* (Princeton, 1984), p. 207; Marrus and Paxton, *op.cit.*; pp. 137–188; D. Wyman, *The Abandonment of the Jews: America and the Holocaust 1941–1945* (New York, 1984), pp. 9–10; G. Saron and L. Hotz, *The Jews in South Africa: A History* (London, 1955), p. 383.

10 S. Gordon, *op.cit.*; pp. 207–8; Bauer, *op.cit.*; p. 73 and Marrus and Paxton, *op.cit.*; pp. 209–13.

11 M-OA: DR 2535, 1145, 2402 Oct. 1940 and DR 2265, 2829, 2485 March 1943 – roughly 1% – advocated extermination; M-OA: D 5296, 19 April 1945, although a profound antisemite, was horrified to hear the news from the concentration camps; M-OA: DR 1145 Oct. 1940 for support for Hitlerite antisemitism; Marrus and Paxton, *op.cit.*; p. 213; R. Burnett, *These My Brethren* (London, 1946), pp. 33–4 for the cyanide capsules.

12 I. McLaine, *Ministry of Morale* (London, 1979), pp. 116–17; Introduction pp. 3–5 for Belisha.

13 Chapter 4 for army dodging/black marketeering; Chapter 2 passim for blitz co-operation.

14 For public opposition to the fascists chapter 1 p. 22 and chapter 5 p. 150–1 for government concern.

15 L. Golding, *The Jewish Problem* (Harmondsworth, 1938), p. 148; *Time and Tide*, 29 Nov. 1941; M-OA: TC Antisemitism File G and BBC WAC R9/13/5/1 for Joyce's impact. For Polish antisemitism see chapter 5 p. 140 Marrus and Paxton, *op.cit.*; p. 189–90 for French, Presser *op.cit.*; p. 327 for Dutch; Allen, *op.cit.*; p. 20 for American.

16 Mosley, 22 July 1940 in HO 283/16/25.

17 See chapter 4 pp. 119–22.

18 Wedgwood in *Hansard* HL vol. 124 col. 344, 10 Sept. 1942. For the Italians see INF 1/264 no. 19 (8 June 1940) and no. 21 (11 June 1940).

19 J. Parkes to Salomon, Aug. 1943 in BD C15/3/19 and Captain James MP to *The Times*, 10 April 1943 for the identification of refugee with Jew; INF 1/292 no. 168 (14–21 Dec. 1943) for anti-Americanism linked to the black market and M-OA: FR 523B for the American image.

20 Harrisson in *New Statesman*, 28 Sept. 1940 for Jewish racism and Henriques in the *Bulletin of the Society of Jews and Christians*, Nov. 1941 for the reverse. For Liverpool see INF 1/292 no. 36 (3–10 June 1941); for Glasgow HO 45/25398/286–7; for Belfast, *JC*, 16 July 1943.

21 Prestige, 7 Nov. 1944 in HO 213/1009; J. Jackson, *The Irish in Britain* (London, 1963), pp. 102–4; A. Richmond, *Colour Prejudice in Britain* (London, 1954), pp. 35–50.

22 Richmond, *op.cit.*, pp. 59, 70–8; Jackson, *op.cit.*; p. 157. M-OA: FR 523B for the Italians.

23 *JC*, 22 Dec. 1944; M-OA: FR 1669L 'Means of overcoming antisemitism'.

24 H. Pollins, *Economic History of the Jews in England* (London, 1982), pp. 209–17.

25 Chapter 3 p. 96–7 for discrimination; B. Litvinoff, *A Peculiar People* (London, 1969), p. 70; M. Freedman (ed.), *A Minority in Britain* (London, 1955), pp. 209, 219, 220, 239 for the dual pressure on Anglo-Jewry.

26 *Jewish Bulletin*, June 1942; N. Mosley, *Beyond the Pale; Sir Oswald Mosley 1933–1980* (London, 1983), p. 290 onwards is useful on Mosley post-1945; M.

Walker, *The National Front* (Glasgow, 1977), pp. 43–6 on neo-nazi influence and *The Guardian*, 10 Oct. 1983 and the *JC*, 19 April, 10 and 17 May 1985 for right-wing entryism.

27 Chapter 5 p. 160 for a summary of Revisionism in the war; G. Seidel, *The Holocaust Denial* (Leeds, 1986) for later developments; O. Mosley, *My Life* (London, 1968); R. Skidelsky, *Oswald Mosley* (London, 1975) and J. Guinness, *The Mitfords* (London, 1984) for Mosley revisionism.

28 Chapter 3 pp. 99–101 for Reed; Chapter 1 pp. 44–6 for Harvey, and Chapter 3 pp. 101, 221 (note 72) for Winterton and Gort. For Eden see B. Wasserstein, *Britain and the Jews of Europe, 1939–1945*, (Oxford, 1979), p. 34.

29 J. Rae, *The Custard Boys* (Bath, 1975), p. 55; M-OA: FR 2515 and *JC*, 8–15 Aug. 1947 for the riots.

30 D. Leitch in M. Sissons and P. French (eds.) *Age of Austerity 1945–1951* (London, 1963), p. 60; for Weinstock see S. Aris, *The Jews in Business* (London, 1970), p. 75.

31 D. Rosenberg, 'Racism and Antisemitism in Contemporary Britain', *Jewish Quarterly*, 1985, pp. 23–4; for Brittan see A. Watkins in *The Observer*, 26 Jan. 1986 and *JC*, 31 Jan. 1986.

32 JACOB, *With a Strong Hand* (London, 1966), pp. 10–15 for 1960s violence; *JC*, 12 July 1985 for more recent attacks; *JC*, 11 April 1986 for increased fascist antisemitism. For attacks on Jewish and Muslim education see *The Guardian*, 25 March 1987.

33 *Sunday Express* quoted by Rosenberg, *op.cit.*; pp. 23–4. There were similar comments in the Brittan affair – *JC*, 31 Jan. 1986.

34 For post-war imagery see M-OA: FR 2463 and H. Eysenck, *Uses and Abuses of Psychology* (Harmondsworth, 1953), pp. 261–2. For 'Spivs' see the *Daily Express*, 24 June 1947 and John Gross in Sissons and French, *op.cit.*; pp. 272–3 for antisemitism and the Lynskey case; *Morecambe and Heysham Visitor*, 6 Aug. 1947.

35 See Chapter 5 passim for government fear of antisemitism.

36 Ben Lewins's Channel 4 docu-drama, 'The Dunera Boys', which only hinted at British antisemitism, brought a heated response from viewers on Channel 4's Right to Reply, 18 Oct. 1985, who denied that the British could possibly be hostile to Jews. See Chapter 5 passim for Britain's refugee policy in the war; Diana Geddes in *The Times*, 2 Dec. 1985 for the difficulty of dealing with Britain's 'hidden' racism.

Select bibliography

The research necessary for the 'total' approach adopted in this work has involved examining a vast range of sources, from comics such as the *Dandy* to Cabinet minutes and MI5 reports. As the book is annotated at length, I list here, for economy of space, only primary sources. Those who wish to pursue the research further are advised to consult my doctoral thesis – 'British Antisemitism in the Second World War' (Sheffield University, 1986) – where there is a full listing of secondary works used and also much additional source material in the footnotes.

(A) Unpublished material

1 *Governmental* (Public Record Office, Kew)

AIR 8; BT 64; CAB 65, 66, 67, 68, 95, 98; CO 733; ED 136; FO 371, 898, 921; HO 45, 144, 199, 206, 213, 214, 215, 283; INF 1, 6; MAF 88, 99, 100, 102; MEPOL 2; P COM 9; PREM 4.

2 *Papers of individuals and organisations in public archives*

Anglo-Jewish Archive, University College, London
Selig Brodetsky papers.
Ivan Greenberg papers.
Neville Laski papers.

BBC Written Archives Centre, Caversham, Reading.
R 28, 34, 41, 51; T 58, 511.

Board of Deputies of British Jews, Woburn House, London.
A 30–2; B 4, 5; C2, 6, 8, 9, 13, 15; E 1, 2, 3; G 4.

Bodleian Library, Oxford.
Diaries and papers of Lord Woolton.

British Library, London.
Palme Dutt Papers.

British Library of Political and Economic Science, London.
Hugh Dalton diaries.

Greater London Council Archive, London.
Evacuation records.

Hackney Local History Archive, London.
United Ladies Tailors Trade Union records.

House of Lords Record Office, London.
Lord Beaverbrook papers.
Percy Harris diaries.
Bruce Lockhart diaries.

Hull University Library, Hull.
National Council for Civil Liberties papers: 3, 41, 43, 44, 45, 46, 76, 100, 310, 311.

Imperial War Museum, London.
Oral history recordings: 'Britain and the Refugee Crisis 1933–1947'.
Thames Television recorded interviews: 'The World at War'.

Labour Party Archive, London.
Executive Minutes.
J. S. Middleton papers.

Manchester Central Reference Library, Manchester.
Manchester Information Committee Minutes.
Barash papers.

Manchester Jewish Museum
Harris House diary.
Manchester Studies Oral History collection.

Manchester University, Manchester.
W. P. Crozier papers.

Manchester Guardian archive.
Lewis Namier papers.

National Maritime Museum, London.
Admiral Sir Barry Domvile papers and diaries.

Reading University Library, Reading.
Jonathan Cape archive.

Sheffield City Library, Sheffield.
Sheffield Information Committee.

Southampton University Library, Southampton.
James Parkes papers.

Sussex University Library, Falmer, Sussex.
Mass-Observation archive.
Kingsley Martin diaries and papers.

Swiss Cottage Library, London.
Hampstead Borough Council Minutes.

Tower Hamlets Local History Library, London.
D. L. Munby papers.
Stepney Borough Council Minutes.

Trades Union Congress
Refugee and International Committee papers.

Wiener Library, London.
Spector papers.

3 *Papers of individuals and organisations in private collections*

Association of Jewish Youth, London.
Executive Minutes and papers.

Council of Christians and Jews, London.
Executive and Council Minutes (now at Southampton University).

Ansel Harris, London.
Diaries of Arnold Harris and papers relating to the Bedford Refugee Centre.

Manchester Jewish Representative Council, Manchester.
Executive Minutes and papers of the Council of Manchester and Salford Jews.

Peace Pledge Union, London.
Executive Minutes and papers.

Toynbee Hall, London.
Papers relating to the East End in the Second World War.

United Synagogue, Woburn House, London.
Evacuation records.

Ray Zaidman, London.
Lazar Zaidman papers (now at Sheffield University).

4 *Interviews with the author*

Lena Barden, 1 August 1984, London.
Ann Baron, 6 September 1984, London.
Louis Behr, 12 September 1983, London.
Miss A. Cohn, 17 July 1984, London.
Hans and Kate Freyhan, 10 May 1984, Bedford.
Morris Goldsmith, 9 April 1984, London.
Dr Judith Grunfeld, 17 July 1984, London.
Naomi Grunfeld, 17 July 1984, London.
Ansel Harris, 5 April 1984, London.
Douglas Hyde, 17 September 1983, London.
Abby Levy, 6 September 1984, London.
Jane Levy, 8 August 1985, London.
Jack Miller, 15 September 1983, London.
Mick Mindel, 6 August 1985, London.
Mark Moser, 28 November 1984, London.
Phil Piratin, 18 July 1984, London.
Mr. I. Pushkin, 23 February 1983, London.
Monty Richardson, 8 August 1983, London.
Celia Rose, 13 September 1983, London.
W. W. Simpson, 6 April and 9 September 1984, London.
Mr. N. Solomon, 26 November 1984, London.
Bertha Sokoloff, 1 November 1984, Sheffield.

Mr. K. J. Spector, 7 April 1984, London.
Arthur Super, 10 May 1984, London.
Mr. and Mrs Jack Wolkind, 2 August 1984, London.

5 *Unpublished theses*

E. J. Baumel, 'The Jewish Refugee Children in Great Britain 1938–1945' (MA, Bar-Ilan University Israel, 1981).
H. Kopsch, 'The Approach of the Conservative Party to Social Policy During World War II' (PhD, University of London, 1970).
H. Loebl, 'Government Financed factories and the Establishment of Industries by Refugees in the Special Areas of the North of England 1937–61' (M.Phil., University of Durham, 1978).
M. Sompolinsky, 'The Anglo-Jewish Leadership, the British Government and the Holocaust' (PhD, Bar-Ilan University Israel, 1977).
H. F. Srebrnik, 'The Jewish Communist Movement in Stepney: Ideological Mobilization and Political Victories in an East London Borough, 1935–1945' (PhD, University of Birmingham, 1983).
N. Stammers, 'Civil Liberties in Britain During the Second World War' (DPhil, University of Sussex, 1980).
R. W. Zweig, 'British Policy To Palestine: May 1939 to 1943: The Fate of the White Paper' (PhD, Cambridge University, 1978).

6 *Unpublished papers*

B. Cheyette, 'The Jewish Stereotype and Anglo-Jewish Fiction 1880–1900' (delivered to the Jewish Historical Society of England, 17 January 1985).
Jewish Central Information Office, 'Organized Antisemitism in Great Britain, 1942–46'.
Trevelyan Scholarship Project 1960 'The British Union of Fascists in Yorkshire 1934–40'.

7 *Unpublished memoirs and biographies*

R. Bellamy, 'We Marched With Mosley' (in the possession of Dr. S. Rawnsley, Bradford and Ilkley Community College).
Nellie Driver, 'From the Shadows of Exile' (Nelson Public Library).
Ruth Lesser, 'Evacuation: An Impression' (in my possession).
Edith Ramsay, 'Life in Stepney: 1920–1945' (Tower Hamlets Local History Library).
W. W. Simpson, 'Autobiography' (in the possession of the author, London).
H. W. Snow, 'In Wartime London' (Imperial War Museum, Department of Manuscripts).

(B) Printed sources

1 *Governmental*

Hansard (5th Series); House of Commons Debates, 1939–1945.
House of Lords Debates, 1939–1945.

2 *Newspapers and journals* (1939–45 unless stated)

(a) *Cutting collections* at the:
Wiener Library (London)
NCCL archive (Hull)
Council of Christians and Jews (Southampton)
Tower Hamlets Local History Library (London)
Board of Deputies of British Jews (London)

(b) *National*

Daily Worker; The Economist; New Statesman; The Spectator; Time and Tide; The Times; Tribune; Truth.

(c) *Local*

East End News; East End Observer; East London Advertiser; Hackney Gazette; Hampstead and Highgate Express; Kilburn Times; Oxford Times; Porth Gazette.

(d) *Jewish*

The Bradian, 1944-45; *Jewish Bulletin*, 1941–44; *Jewish Chronicle; Jewish Echo*, 1943; *Jewish Gazette*, 1943; *Jewish News*, 1942–45; *Jewish Standard*, 1940–44; *Jewish Telegraphic Agency Bulletin; Monthly Bulletin of the TAC*, 1940–45; *On Guard*, 1947–48; *Young Jewry*, 1943–44.

(e) *Fascist and antisemitic journals*

Action, 1939–40; *The British Lion*, 1939–40; *British National News*, 1942; *The British Trader*, 1939; *British Union Quarterly*, 1939–40; *The Fascist*, 1938–39; *Free Press*, 1939–40; *Gothic Ripples*, 1946–7; *Information and Policy*, 1939–40; *New Order*, 1943; *New Pioneer*, 1939–40; *Parliament Christian*, 1940–45; *The Patriot; Peoples Post*, 1939–40 and 1945; *Reality; The Recorder's Quarterly Gazette*, 1941 and 1944; *The Right Review; Social Crediter; The Talking Picture News; The Vanguard; Weekly Angles*, 1939–40; *Weekly Review*.

(f) *Miscellaneous*

The Adelphi; The Aeroplane, 1939–40; *The Beano*, 1944; *Blighty*, 1941; *Builders' Merchants' Journal*, 1939–40; *Bulletin of the Society of Jews and Christians*, 1940–41; *Catholic Herald; Christians and Jews*, 1943–45; *Civil Liberty; The Dandy; Empire Record; The Ex-Serviceman*, 1944–46; *The Forward; Jewish Missionary Intelligence; London Opinion*, 1940–44; *Medical World; M-O Bulletin*, 1941–5; *National Review; New English Weekly; New Leader*, 1942; *Now*, 1940–44; *Now and Then*, 1939–43; *Peace News; Radio Fun*, 1943; *Sefton Review*, 1940–41; *Socialist Appeal*, 1943–45; *Swiss Cottager*, 1940; *The Tablet*, 1939–40; *Tomorrow*, 1940–45; *US*, 1940; *The Word*, 1942–45; *World News and Views*, 1941.

Index

Action 4, 16–17, 19, 21, 25, 30
Acworth, Captain Bernard 32
Adelphi, The 86
Aims of Industry 81
air raids 53–8, 77
Aldred, Guy 86
Aliens Act (1905) 11, 141, 164–5
'aliens', Jews as 9–11, 81–2, 91, 102, 114–15; *see also* assimilation of Jews
Allen, Elizabeth 171, 173
Allen, Mary 21
Allen, Sydney 21
ambivalence *see* Jews
Americans 195–6
Anderson, Dr G. C. 150
Anderson, Sir John 15, 26, 46, 53, 142, 144–6
Angell, Sir Norman 144
Anglo-Jewish Association 163
'anti-Christs' 108–9
antisemitism 1–13, 188–202
  before World War II 8–13
  and class 4–5, 79, 88, 96–7
  definition 2–5
  development during the war 101–4
  East End 48–65
  impact of 191–4
  international 1–2, 188–90, 194
  Jewish evacuees 65–77
  Jewish image in the UK 106–33
  Jewish question in the UK 78–105
  literature 44–7, 99–101, 108–15, *passim*, 131
  and morale 17, 53, 103–4, 138, 191–2
  organisations 14–47
  and psychology 7, 180–1
  and respectability 14, 45–6, 83–4, 92, 98–101, 147, 189, 195, 199, 202
  response to 163–87
  UK 1–13, 189–95
  UK government and the Jews 134–62
Armed Forces, Jews in 122–6
Asquith Committee on aliens 89, 149
assimilation of Jews 92–6, 183–4, 197–8
atrocity stories 157–60

Banister, Joseph 164
Barou, Noah 170
Beaverbrook, Lord 12, 24, 84, 129, 143, 147
Beckett, John 16, 23, 31, 86
Bedford, Duke of 23, 32, 35, 45, 86, 133; *see also* Tavistock, Lord
Bedfordshire 67–70, 76
Bell, George, Bishop of Chichester 184
Belloc, Hilaire 9, 79, 81, 87, 194
Benn, Sir Ernest 81–2
Bennett, J. 158, 160
Bentwich, Norman 142, 178
Berger, Elizabeth 29
Bermant, Chaim 69–71
Bermuda Conference 155, 178, 180
Bethnal Green 50, 59–61, 125–6, 195
Beveridge Report 40, 46, 82

Bible, and Jewish image 106–8
Birkett, Norman 24
black market 62–3, 102–3, 119–22, 127–8, 138–9, 194, 201
Bland, Sir Nevile 146
blitz, the 53–8, 77
blood libel *see* ritual, murder
Bloomsbury House 174, 176
Blumenfeld, Simon 128
Board of Deputies of British Jews 135, 138–9, 163–70, 173–4, 179–84
  Jewish Defence Committee (JDC) 12, 34, 54, 166, 169–70, 180–1, 183–4
  Trades Advisory Council (TAC) 127–8, 170
Bolshevism and Jews 79–80
Bottome, Phyliss 115–16
Bowman, Frederick 45, 47
Bracken, Brendan 139
Brandon, John G. 110, 131
British Broadcasting Corporation (BBC) 130, 137
British Brothers' League 11, 164
British Council for Christian Settlement in Europe (BCCSE) 23, 31
British Empire Union (BEU) 80, 143
British Institute of Public Opinion (BIPO) 103, 147, 154
British Israelites 113
British Medical Association (BMA) 150
British National Party (BNP) 31–2
British People's Party (BPP) 12, 15, 23, 35–6
British Union of Fascists (BUF) 79
  antisemitism 18–19, 120
  appeal of 44
  British Traders' Bureau 22, 44
  by-elections 20–1, 22, 44
  and the East End 21–2, 30, 50
  ideology 42–3
  and ILP 86
  and internment 22–3, 30
  and Jewish evacuation 65
  membership 15
  and the war 15, 16–19, 29
  and women 21
British Union of Freemen 30
Britons, The 14, 31, 38, 41, 47
Brittan, Leon 200
Brodetsky, Selig 83, 173, 177–8
Brogan, D. W. 100–1
Brooks, Collin 35, 81
Brotman, A. 178
Bryant, Arthur 80
Buchan, John 98, 111–12
Buckley, Eunice 117
Budd, Zola 200
Bulman, Rev. 100
Burgess, Victor 34–5
Butler, R. A. 83, 137, 161

Cadogan, Sir Alexander 3, 157
Cambridgeshire 67–8
Campion, Sarah 117
Cape, Jonathan 99–100, 199
Catholic Church
  antisemitism 80, 140
  East End 49, 56–7
Catholic Herald 80, 113, 129, 140, 198
Cavendish-Bentinck, V. 159
Chamberlain, Neville 3–4
Channon, Sir Henry 4, 159
Chaucer, Geoffrey 108–9
Chesterton, A. K. 16, 35–6, 43, 81
Christianity
  Biblical image of Jews 106–8
  Catholic Church 49, 56–7, 80
  response to antisemitism 163–87 *passim*, 199
Churchill, Sir Winston 28, 84, 140, 146, 149
cinema 113–14, 130–1, 137
Citrine, Walter 90
civil defence 51–2, 60, 122
Claremont, Claude 81
Clarke, 'Mick' 17
class *see* antisemitism
Coles, Manning 110, 117, 131
Colonial Office, and Palestine 152–3, 160
Comfort, Alex 130–1
Communist Party 163, 166
  antisemitism 87, 96
  and fascism 168–9, 185

Jewish People's Council (JPC) 166–7
National Jewish Committee (NJC) 105, 171–2
response to antisemitism 87–8, 163–173 *passim*, 179, 185
Stepney 49, 55–6
see also Bolshevism; *Daily Worker*
Connolly, Cyril 96
Conservative Party 80–3, 139
conspiracy theory 12, 37–40, 43, 46, 112–14
Cotterell, Geoffrey 125, 131
Council of Christians and Jews (CCJ) 107, 163, 176–7, 179, 184, 186, 199
Council on Aliens 149
Croft, Lord 84
Crossman, Richard 184–5
crucifixion of Jesus 107
Cruickshank, Dame Joanna 149
Cuthbert, Inspector 149

Daily Express 115, 183
Daily Mail 143
Daily Mirror 120
Daily Worker 49, 87, 168, 182
Dalton, Hugh 96
Day, Alfred 47
Deedes, Wyndham 185
Deeping, Warwick 114
Defence Regulation 18B 22, 29, 40
Dell, James 38, 41
discrimination against Jews 10, 76, 83, 92, 197–8, 200
Domvile, Admiral Barry 15, 23–4, 31
Donegall, Marquess of 57
Donovan, B. D. 19, 27
Douglas, Lord Alfred 98
Douglas, Major C. H. 37, 43
Downie, H. F. 152, 158
Driberg, Tom (William Hickey) 141, 173, 183, 185
Driver, Cedric 131
Duff Cooper, Alfred 3
Dugdale, Blanche 55, 101, 106
Dugdale, Sir Thomas 83
Dunlop, George 34–5

East Anglia 67–9, 74, 76–7
East End 48–65
before World War II 9, 51
Bethnal Green disaster 60–1, 125–6, 195
blitz 53–8, 77
BUF and 20–2, 30, 50
Catholic Church 49, 56–7
civil defence 51–2, 60
clubs and associations 63–4
effects of war 50–3
fascist revival 58–60
industry 63
M-O antisemitism surveys 48–50, 53, 55
Eden, Anthony 158–9, 177, 199
education 10, 67–8, 96, 137
Edward I, King of England 19, 45, 111
18-B groups 30, 33–6
elections contested by fascists 20–1, 22, 32, 44
Eliot, T. S. 98
emancipation of Jews 1–2, 91, 135
Emerson, Sir Herbert 153, 158
English National Association (ENA) 32
Entertainments National Service Association (ENSA) 132
evacuation of Jews 50, 65–77
reactions to 66–9
and religious observance 70, 74
seaside resorts 71–2, 75
exclusivity, Jewish 92–6, 183–4, 197–8
extermination of the Jews, advocation 42, 191

fascism
antisemitic ideology 36–43
and antisemitism 168–9, 182–3, 185–7, 198–9
see also organisations, antisemitic and fascist
Federal Union project 39, 46
'Fenwick' 132
financiers, Jewish 12, 18, 43, 85, 87
Food, Ministry of 135–6, 138
Foreign Jews' Protection Committee 165

Foreign Office
  and British antisemitism 135
  and Jews of Europe 152–67
foreigners in the UK 195–6; *see also* aliens; refugees
Forster, E. M. 101
Forward, The 85, 91
Freud, Sigmund 97, 109
Fuller, J. F. C. 35
Fuller, Roy 131
furniture trade 89
Fyfe, Hamilton

Gal, Hans 174
Game, Sir Philip 18
garment trade 89
George, Daniel 115
Glasgow, 46–7, 103–4, 197
Godfrey, Edward 31–3, 47, 86
Goebbels, Josef 113
Golding, Louis 64, 130, 167, 186, 193
Goldman, Willy 129
Gollan, John 185
Gollancz, Victor 81, 154, 178, 183
Gort, Lord 3, 101, 199
government, UK
  and aid for European Jews 2, 151–7, 175–80
  and fascist groups 22, 29, 36, 40
  Hore-Belisha case 3–5, 138
  and the Jews 10–11, 134–62
    and antisemitism 137–9, 161
    attitudes towards German persecution 157–61, 177–9
    education 137
    European Jews, policy on 135, 151–5
    internment of aliens 143–50
    Jewish food 135–6
    refugees 141–3
    religious observance 135–7
    see also Colonial Office and Palestine; Food, Ministry of; Foreign Office; Home Office; Information, Ministry of; MI5; War Office
Green, G. F. 35
Greene, Ben 31, 35
Groser, Father 57

Hackney 59–60
Hackney Gazette 59–60, 129
Halifax, Lord 3, 24
Hallgarten family 71
Hamm, Jeffrey 34–5
Hampstead 104, 118–19; *see also* North-West London
Harrisson, Tom 48, 56, 72–3, 78, 117, 131, 175
Hart, E. D. 43
Hartog, Alexander 64, 123
Harvey, John Hooper 29, 44–7, 100, 108–9, 199
Haslam, F. 22
Henriques, Basil 124
Hey, Norman 31
Hickey, William *see* Driberg, Tom
Hill, Prof. A. V. 181
Hillary, Richard 125, 131
Hitler, Adolf 7, 38, 155, 187
Hodson, James 44
Holmes, Walter 88, 171
'Holocaust', the 1, 92, 101, 144, 188–90
  denial of 41, 88, 158–60, 198–9
  UK government reactions to 157–61, 177–9
  UK public opinion of 154–5, 175, 186, 199
Home Counties 63, 66, 68–9
Home Office
  and antisemitism 139–40
  and Polish Jews 141
  and refugees 150–1
see also Morrison, Herbert
Hore-Belisha, Leslie 3–5, 81–2, 102, 104, 115, 138, 191–22
Houston, 'Jock' 17–20
Hugh of Lincoln 108–9
Huxley-Williams, Rev. 100
Hyde, Douglas 36, 47, 88, 168, 171

ideology, antisemitic 36–43, 79
Imperial Fascist League (IFL) 12, 14–15, 17, 23–31 *passim*, 35, 44
Independent Labour Party (ILP) 85–6

Information, Ministry of 3, 102, 136–9, 146, 191
internment
of aliens 143–50, 173–4
of fascist leaders 22–3, 29–31
in World War I 11, 174
Isle of Man 148–9

Jackson, Ada 5, 116–17
Janner, Barnett 96
Janner, Elsie 123
Jewish Agency 159
Jewish Board of Guardians 163–4
Jewish Chronicle 51, 66, 120, 127, 145, 164, 167, 169, 196–7
Jewish Defence Committee (JDC) *see* Board of Deputies of British Jews
Jewish image in the UK 106–33, 194
aliens 114–15
'anti-Christs' 108–9
Armed Forces 122–6
Bible and 106–8
black market 119–22, 127–8
conspiracy theory 112–14
finance 110–14
refugees 115–19, 128
self-image 126–7
sexuality 20, 51, 56, 109–10
Jewish People's Council (JPC) 166–7
Jewish question in the UK 78–105
Communist Party 87–8, 96
Conservative Party 80–3
development of antisemitism 101–4
Jewish exclusivity 92–6
Labour Party 83–4, 85, 96
liberalism 91–2
and politics 78–92
social attitudes 96–101
socialism and antisemitism 79, 85, 90–1
Jews
as 'aliens' 9–11, 81–2, 91, 102, 114–15
ambivalence of attitudes towards 2–5, 7, 97–8
and Bolshevism 79–80
East End 48–65
evacuation of 65–77
exclusivity 92–6, 183–4, 197–8
Nazi persecution *see* Nazi persecution of Jews and other minorities 44, 48, 55, 57, 129, 195–6, 200
as power in society 11–12
pressure to conform 10, 92–3
religious observance 70, 74, 93–5, 135–7
Jews' War accusation 12, 15–22, 57, 87, 101–2, 113, 191–2
job discrimination 63, 97, 150–1
Johnson, Geoffrey 116
jokes, antisemitic 20, 131–2, 193
Joyce, William ('Lord Haw-Haw') 16–17, 27, 35

Kaufman, Gerald 200
Kaye, Clarence 53
Keith, Arthur 80
Kell, Sir Vernon 16
Kemsley newspapers 84, 100, 129, 143, 147
Kent, Herman 138
Kent, Tyler 26–7, 29
Kidd, Ronald 171
Kisch, Major 125
Knight, Maxwell 27, 143
Kops, Bernard 57, 61
kosher food 70, 74, 93–5, 135–6
Kuczynsky, Jurgen 143
Kyle, Elizabeth 111–12

Labour Party 83–4, 85, 96,
Lafitte, F. 145
Lake District 65–6, 75
Lamb, Charles 108
Laski, Harold 41, 81, 83–4, 86
Laski, Nathan 104
Laski, Neville 128, 155
Latham, R. T. 152–3, 160
Law, Richard 177–8
League of Empire Loyalists 36
League of Ex-Servicemen 21, 32, 34–5
Leeds 8, 21, 85, 97, 103–4, 167
Lees, A. T. O. 24–5, 27, 35
Leese Arnold 7, 29, 31, 38, 42, 45, 108, 194

Lewey, Frank 53
liberalism 91–2, 141
Limehouse 53
Link, The 12, 15–16, 23, 28
Lipson, Daniel 83
literature
  anti-antisemitism 180–1, 183
  antisemitism in 44–7, 99–101, 108–15 *passim*, 131
  Jewish 128–9
  philosemitism in 116–17
Liverman, Gordon 12–13
Liverpool 37, 44, 104
London *see* East End; North West London
Longmate, Norman 71
Low, David 183, 186
Lymington, Lord 43
Lytton, Lord 149

McGill, Donald 131
McGovern, John 24, 86
Macniece, Louis 116–17, 125, 186
Mallon, J. J. 54
Manchester, 15, 22, 97, 103–4, 110, 125–6, 197
Manchester Guardian 145, 147, 165
Mannin, Ethel 86
Marconi scandal 8, 12
Marlowe, Christopher 110
Marr, Wilhelm 2
Martin, Kingsley 145
Mass-Observation (M-O) surveys
  antisemitism 48–50, 53, 55, 78, 80–2, 87–8, 96–8, 100, 107–9, 132
  BUF 20–1, 34
  by-elections 20-1, 32, 84–5
  evacuations 65–7, 73–5
  internment 147
  Nazi persecution of Jews 154–5, 175, 186, 199
Massingham, Hugh 68, 76, 115
Maugham, W. Somerset 118
Maxse, Leo 12
Maxwell, Sir Alexander 134, 150
Medical Policy Association (MPA) 40
Medical Practitioners' Union 90
medical profession 40, 90, 113, 150
Mendelssohn, Peter 116
MI5
  and aliens 143, 145, 149
  and fascism 16, 23, 26–7
Middleton by-election 22
Militant Christian Patriots (MCP) 37, 85
Miller, Joan 26
Mills, H. T. 24, 29, 35
Mitford, Unity 16
money-lending 110–11
morale *see* antisemitism
Moran, Tommy 20–1
Morning Post 12, 79–80
Morrison, Herbert
  and the black market 121, 139
  and fascist organisations 31–3
  fear of domestic antisemitism 103, 139–40
  and internment of fascists 29, 169, 180
  and Jews, 155–6
  and refugee aliens 145, 148–9, 151, 153–6, 160
  and *Truth* 82
Mosley, Lady Cynthia 96
Mosley, Sir Oswald
  antisemitism 5, 22, 42–3, 133, 187, 194, 199
  and the East End 9
  and Federal Union 39
  and Hitler 24–5, 27–8
  internment 22–4, 28–30, 33–4, 169
  and the war 15–18
Moyne, Lord 103
Muggeridge, Malcolm 12, 87
Mundlak, Max 129
Murry, John Middleton 68, 86
Myers, Denis 127–8

Namier, Lewis 104, 158
Natan, Alec 143
National Citizens Union (NCU) 80
National Committee for Rescue from Nazi Terror 154, 178–9
National Council for Civil Liberties (NCCL) 132, 163, 167, 170–1, 179–82, 186

National Front 36, 84, 198
National Front After Victory 35–6
National Jewish Committee (NJC) *see* Communist Party
National Review 12, 84, 143
National Socialist League 12, 15, 17
Nationalist Association 17–18, 19–20, 23
Nazi persecution of Jews 1, 92, 101, 144, 188–90
  UK government reactions 157–61, 177–9
  UK public opinion 154–5, 175, 186, 199
New Pioneer 15
New Statesman 145, 181–2, 185
Newman, Chaim 93
News Chronicle 49, 78, 95, 185
Newsam, Frank 139
Nicolson, Harold 2, 98, 109–10, 154, 185
Nordic League 12, 15, 17, 23–5
Norfolk 68
North West London 35, 114–15, 118–19

Orbach, Maurice 170
organisations
  anti-antisemitism 168–74
  antisemitic and fascist 14–47
    after internment 29–36
    cooperation between 23–5
    18-B groups 30, 33–6
    ideology 36–43
    impact of 44–7
    Kent-Wolkoff-Ramsay affair 26–9
    membership 15, 44
    and the war 14–29
  refugee 174–5
Orwell, George
  and antisemitism 78, 96, 113, 131
  attitudes towards Jews 7–8, 98
  class 96
  and conservatism 81, 84
  and Jewish exclusivity 93
  and Jewish persecution 115
Oxford 73, 98–9, 104
Oxfordshire 72–4, 76, 104

pacifism 23, 86–7, 198
Pakenham-Walsh, Major-Gen. 3
Palestine 42, 91, 103, 152–3, 161, 199, 202
Palme-Dutt, R. 172
Panter-Downes, Mollie 96
Parkes, James 112, 159–60, 184
Parsons, Anthony 112
Patriot, The 12, 14, 32–3, 37–40, 47, 80
Peace News 86
Peace Pledge Union (PPU) 23, 86–7
People's Common Law Parliament (PCLP) 32–3
Perles, Alfred 127
philosemitism 4–5, 98, 106–8, 115–17, 165, 185
Piratin, Phil 49, 64, 172
police
  and antisemitism 20
  and fascists 16–18, 166
Polish Army, antisemitism in 125, 140–1, 173–4
Political and Economic Planning (PEP) 38–40, 46, 82
politicians, Jewish 3–5, 115, 200
politics, and antisemitism 78–92
Pollitt, Harry 155
Poplar 49
Portsmouth, Lord 35
Potocki, Count 32, 45–7
power in society, Jews as 11–12; *see also* conspiracy theory
prejudice *see* antisemitism
press and antisemitism 84, 127
  black market 100, 120–1
  espionage 79
  internment 143–7
  Jewish wealth 115
  local 59–60, 73, 118, 129
  refugees 118, 129–30
Priestley, J. B. 125, 186
Pritchard, Councillor, Mayor of Stepney 62–3
Protocols of the Elders of Zion, The 8, 12, 18–19, 37–40, 47, 80, 99, 112–13; *see also* conspiracy theory

radio 130, 137

Ramsay, Captain 3–4, 23–8, 31, 83, 85, 111
Randall, A. G. 177
Ratcliffe, Alexander 32, 38, 46–7, 86, 109, 139, 198
Rathbone, Eleanor 106–7, 116, 147, 154, 178–9
rationing 135–6
Raven Thomson, A. 18, 22
Reavely, Cuthbert 35
Reed, Douglas 14, 38, 46, 80, 99–101, 108, 118, 199
refugees in UK 195
  in army 123–4, 148
  child refugees 67, 68, 71, 75
  and fascists 19
  government policy on 151–7
  image of 115–19, 128
  and trade unions 89–90
  and work 150–1
response to antisemitism 163–87
  before World War II 163–7
  and fascism 168–9, 182–3, 185–7
  and internment 174–5
  and Jewish exclusivity 183–4
  literature 180–1, 183
  organisations 168–75
  pressure to aid European Jews 175–80
  see also philosemitism
Ridout, P. J. 20
Right Club 12, 15, 23–7
riots, antisemitic 6, 8–9, 164–5, 188
ritual
  Jewish religious observance 70, 74, 93–5, 135–7
  murder 45, 94, 108–9, 133
  slaughter of animals 94–5, 109
Roberts, Frank 178
Roth, Cecil 127
Rothermere, Lord 79, 84, 129, 143, 147
Rothschild, Barons Edouard and Maurice de 87
Rothschild, Lord 104
Rothwell, J. B. 100, 120
Royal Society for the Prevention of Cruelty to Animals (RSPCA) 94–5
Sacks, George 185
Salomon, Sidney 128, 170, 181
Samuel, Maurice 113
Sayers, Dorothy 106–7
'scapegoat' model 5–7, 155–6, 194
Scottish Protestant League 38
Scrutton, R. J. 32–3
sexuality, Jewish image 109–10
Shakespeare, William 110–11
Shaw, George Bernard 93
shechita 94–5, 109
Sheffield 104
shelters, air-raid 52, 54–8, 61
Sheridan, Barnett 129
Shinwell, Emmanuel 86
Sieff, Israel Moses 38–40
Sikorski, General 93
Silvertown 20–1, 53, 84–5
Simpson, Esther 174
Simpson, W. W. 107, 176, 186
Sitwell, Osbert 33
slaughter of animals, ritual 94–5, 109
social attitudes towards Jews 96–101
Social Credit movement 31, 37–9, 43, 46, 113
socialism and antisemitism 79, 85, 90–1; *see also* Communist Party
Society of Individualists 81
Society of Jews and Christians 166, 176
Solomon, Charles 198
Soutar, Andrew 71–2, 117
Spectator, The 12, 79–80, 100, 120, 145
Spender, Stephen 4–5
Spier, Eugen 143
spies, Jews portrayed as 117–18, 143–4, 150
Stanley, Oliver 101
Stanley, Sidney 201
Steed, Wickham 80
Stencl, A. N. 58
Stepney 48–51, 54–8, 62–3
Stepney Communist Party 49, 55–6
Stepney Tenants' Defence League 49, 52, 55
stereotypes, Jewish *see* Jewish image in the UK
Stern, Ewald 143

Stewart, Basil 113
Stokes, Richard 24, 85
Strauss, George 81
Suffolk 68
Sunday Dispatch 129, 144
Sunday trading 138
'sweated labour' 89

Tavistock, Lord 24
Tilbury shelter 54–5, 58
Time and Tide 120, 145, 175, 185
Times, The 12, 79–80
Tottenham Liberal and Radical Working Men's Club 92
Toynbee Hall 54–5, 58, 63–4
trade union movement 88–90
Trades Advisory Council (TAC) *see* Board of Deputies of British Jews
Tribune 115, 145
Tripoli 135
Truth 3–4, 14, 32, 46–7, 81–3

Ullmann, Richard 127, 129
United Socialist Movement 86
universities, and antisemitism 98–9
usury 110–11

Vansittart, Lord 35
violence against Jews in Britain 1–2, 6, 8, 10, 18, 54, 64, 71, 188, 199–200

Wales, 20, 65, 71
  riots against Jews in 6, 8, 164
Waley Cohen, Sir Robert 136
War Office
  and antisemitism 124
  and Hore-Belisha 3–5
  and internment 145–7
  and Polish–Jewish soldiers 140–1, 174
Ward, M. Dudley 94
Ward Price, G. 143
Waugh, Evelyn 98, 131
Webster, John 20
Webster, Nesta 37–8
Wedgwood, Col. (Lord) 3, 195
Weekly Review 14, 38
Weinstock, Arnold 200
Welfare State plans 40
Wells, H. G. 93, 145
White, Arnold 11, 194
white slave traffic 20, 51
Wigram, Major 125
Williamson, Henry 33, 35
Williamson, Hugh Ross 33
Winterton, Edward, Lord 174, 199
Wolfson, Isaac 115
Wolkoff, Anna 26–9
women
  antisemitism 49
  and the BUF 21
Woolton, Lord 136, 161
Word, The 86
World War I, antisemitism in 8–9, 51, 119–20, 122–3, 165

xenophobia 195–6; *see also* aliens

Yeats-Brown, Francis 33, 41
Yiddish 55, 58, 76–7, 172

Zak, William 89
Zionism 42, 64, 136, 152–3, 155, 165, 199
Zygielbojm, Samuel 179